Study Guide

for use with

Psychology
The Science of Mind and Behavior

Fourth Edition

Michael W. Passer
Ronald E. Smith

Prepared by

Dianne Leader
Georgia Institute of Technology

Boston   Burr Ridge, IL   Dubuque, IA   Madison, WI   New York   San Francisco   St. Louis
Bangkok   Bogotá   Caracas   Kuala Lumpur   Lisbon   London   Madrid   Mexico City
Milan   Montreal   New Delhi   Santiago   Seoul   Singapore   Sydney   Taipei   Toronto

The McGraw·Hill Companies

McGraw-Hill Higher Education

Study Guide for use with
PSYCHOLOGY: THE SCIENCE OF MIND AND BEHAVIOR
Michael W. Passer and Ronald E. Smith

Published by McGraw-Hill, an imprint of The McGraw-Hill Companies, Inc., 1221 Avenue of the Americas, New York, NY 10020. Copyright © 2008, 2007, 2004, 2001 by The McGraw-Hill Companies, Inc. All rights reserved.

No part of this publication may be reproduced or distributed in any form or by any means, or stored in a database or retrieval system, without the prior written consent of The McGraw-Hill Companies, Inc., including, but not limited to, in any network or other electronic storage or transmission, or broadcast for distance learning.

2 3 4 5 6 7 8 9 0 QPD/QPD 0 9 8

ISBN: 978-0-07-721500-2
MHID: 0-07-721500-1

www.mhhe.com

Chapter 1
THE SCIENCE OF PSYCHOLOGY   1

Chapter 2
STUDYING BEHAVIOR SCIENTIFICALLY   29

Chapter 3
GENES, ENVIRONMENT AND BEHAVIOR   61

Chapter 4
THE BRAIN AND BEHAVIOR   85

Chapter 5
SENSATION AND PERCEPTION   119

Chapter 6
STATES OF CONSCIOUSNESS   154

Chapter 7
LEARNING: THE ROLE OF EXPERIENCE   184

Chapter 8
MEMORY   219

Chapter 9
LANGUAGE AND THINKING   249

Chapter 10
INTELLIGENCE   280

Chapter 11
MOTIVATION AND EMOTION   309

Chapter 12
DEVELOPMENT OVER THE LIFE SPAN   342

Chapter 13
PERSONALITY   377

Chapter 14
ADJUSTING TO LIFE: STRESS, COPING, AND HEALTH   411

Chapter 15
PSYCHOLOGICAL DISORDERS   439

Chapter 16
TREATMENT OF PSYCHOLOGICAL DISORDERS   472

Chapter 17
SOCIAL THINKING AND BEHAVIOR   501

Chapter 1
THE SCIENCE OF PSYCHOLOGY

A. Learning Objectives: *These objectives are expanded from the Focus Questions found in the margins of your textbook. When you have mastered the material in this chapter, you will be able to:*

1.1   Define psychology, and indicate what types of behaviors it incorporates.

1.2   Differentiate between basic and applied research, and describe studies illustrating the relationship between them.

1.3   List and describe the central goals of psychology.

1.4   Discuss psychology's philosophical and scientific roots.

1.5   Describe the psychodynamic perspective, highlighting Freud's psychoanalytic theory.

1.6   Describe the behavioral perspective, highlighting the work of Pavlov, Thorndike, Watson, and Skinner.

1.7   Describe the humanistic perspective, highlighting the work of Maslow and Rogers.

1.8   Describe the cognitive perspective, including Gestalt psychology, cognitive neuroscience, and social constructivism.

1.9   Describe the sociocultural perspective, and define culture, norms, and socialization.

1.10 Explain the importance of cultural psychology in today's world.

1.11 Describe the biological perspective, highlighting research in behavioral neurosciences, behavioral genetics, and evolutionary psychology.

1.12 Contrast evolutionary and sociocultural perspectives in explaining behavioral phenomena.

1.13 Explain how the levels-of-analysis framework integrates the six perspectives of psychology.

1.14 Using the three levels of analysis, outline possible causal factors in depression.

1.15 List and describe the major professional associations of psychologists.

1.16   Explain how psychology helps to shape public policy.

1.17   Describe research-based strategies to improve academic performance, including effective time management, improving study habits, and preparing for and taking tests.

B. Chapter Overview

This chapter introduces some of the basic aspects of psychology, which is defined as the scientific study of behavior (observable actions) and the mind (internal thoughts and feelings). Critical thinking is an important component of scientific study. Rather than passively accepting facts and conclusions presented by others, the critical thinker actively investigates and considers alternate possibilities and implications of the evidence. Psychology is both a basic and an applied science, meaning that psychologists both search for knowledge for its own sake and also use that knowledge to solve practical problems. As a science, psychology has five central goals: to describe, understand, predict, and influence behavior, as well as to apply psychological knowledge in ways that enhance human welfare in personal lives, education, business, law, health, medicine, and many other areas.

We can use a simple, three-part framework to help us understand the complex ways that people behave, think, and feel. Events occur simultaneously at the biological, the psychological, and the environmental levels of analyzing human behavior. The three-levels-of-analysis approach focuses our attention on important factors at each level of analysis, as well as on how these factors interact and influence one another across levels. For example, eating involves biological activity in the brain and endocrine system, in mutual interaction with psychological responses and the environmental stimuli that influence them. Psychologists have long debated whether behavior is primarily determined by "nature" (innate factors) or "nurture" (environmental factors). The three-levels-of-analysis framework helps us to see that both nature and nurture, as well as their ongoing interaction, all influence who we are, and why we behave as we do.

Early psychologists used scientific methods to study the mind-body relationship being debated by philosophers. Structuralists tried to identify the basic building blocks of the mind, whereas functionalists took a more holistic approach. Over time, a variety of viewpoints developed that psychologists now use to understand human behavior and experience. These include the psychodynamic, behavioral, humanistic, cognitive, sociocultural, and biological perspectives.

Adherents of the psychodynamic perspective concentrate on internal factors, believing that unconscious conflicts of which we are unaware are the most powerful influences that determine our behavior and personalities. Modern psychodynamic theorists focus more on social factors and less on hidden sexual and aggressive motives than did Freud, the founder of the psychodynamic approach.

The behavioral perspective, in contrast, focuses attention on external factors. According to this approach, the environment is the primary factor that molds our observable behavior through the process of learning. Unobservable internal factors such as unconscious conflicts, thoughts, and personality are not studied by radical behaviorists. Cognitive behaviorism is a more recent development that proposes that people develop beliefs and expectations through interacting with the environment, and that these internal cognitions in turn influence the individual's behavior.

Humanists focus on the unique experience of each individual who strives to find meaning in life. The emphasis of this approach is on freedom and choice as people move toward their full potential or self-actualization. The modern positive psychology movement highlights the study of human strengths, fulfillment, and optimal living.

The cognitive perspective grew out of the structuralists' and functionalists' interest in using scientific methods to study the mind. Inspired by the metaphor of the computer, cognitive psychologists view humans as information processors and problem solvers. Cognitive neuroscientists use sophisticated equipment to examine brain activity as people engage in cognitive tasks. Social constructivists believe that we each create our own "reality" from our cognitive perceptions.

The sociocultural perspective suggests that cultural norms, or rules for behavior, shape our actions and experiences. Today's growing field of cross-cultural psychology explores the similarities and differences among different cultures in shaping people's behavior, thoughts, and feelings.

The biological perspective suggests that behavior is best explained by studying how the brain, biochemical processes, and genetic factors influence behavior. Behavioral neuroscientists examine the brain processes and other physiological functions underlying our actions, experiences, and thoughts. Behavioral geneticists explore the role of heredity in studying people's behavioral tendencies. A modern-day movement in psychology focuses on how evolutionary processes, such as natural selection, may have shaped the development of the human brain as well as our behavior.

Each perspective contributes to our understanding of psychology, but none provides a full account. Many psychologists emphasize the need to integrate the perspectives to provide a more complete explanation of human behavior. The three-levels-of-analysis framework offers one way of integrating the different perspectives in psychology.

Psychology is a vast field with many different specialty areas including clinical, counseling, educational, experimental, industrial/organizational, developmental, social, personality, physiological, and quantitative psychologies.

Basic and applied research in psychology provide an evidence-based foundation for public policies on important social issues such as education, violence prevention, and access to mental health.

Psychological findings can enhance your own life as well. Perhaps the most advantageous way in which you, the student, can use psychology is to apply it to the way you study and learn. Research has suggested that students can improve their academic performance by implementing certain time-management techniques, effective study habits, use of focus questions to spark active learning, and strategies for test preparation and test taking.

C. Chapter Outline

THE NATURE OF PSYCHOLOGY
    Psychology as a Basic and Applied Science
        Robber's Cave and the Jigsaw Classroom
    The Goals of Psychology
    Psychology's Broad Scope: A Levels-of-Analysis Framework
        Mind-Body and Nature-Nurture Interactions
    In Review
PERSPECTIVES ON BEHAVIOR
    Psychology's Intellectual Roots
    Early Schools: Structuralism and Functionalism
    The Psychodynamic Perspective: The Forces Within
        Psychoanalysis: Freud's Great Challenge
        Modern Psychodynamic Theory
    The Behavioral Perspective: The Power of the Environment
        Origins of the Behavioral Perspective
        Behaviorism
        Cognitive Behaviorism
        What Do You Think? Are the Students Lazy?
    The Humanistic Perspective: Self-Actualization and Positive Psychology
    The Cognitive Perspective: The Thinking Human
        Origins of the Cognitive Perspective
            Renewed Interest in the Mind
        The Modern Cognitive Perspective
    The Sociocultural Perspective: The Embedded Human
        Cultural Learning and Diversity
    Research Close-Up: Love and Marriage in Eleven Cultures
    The Biological Perspective: The Brain, Genes, and Evolution
        Behavioral Neuroscience
        Behavior Genetics
        Evolutionary Psychology
    In Review
USING LEVELS OF ANALYSIS TO INTEGRATE THE PERSPECTIVES

An Example: Understanding Depression
Summary of Major Themes
Beneath the Surface: What Did You Expect?
In Review
PSYCHOLOGY TODAY
A Global Science and Profession
Psychology and Public Policy
Psychology and Your Life
Applying Psychological Science: How to Enhance Your Academic Performance
In Review

D. Review at a Glance: *Write the term that best fits the blank to review what you learned in this chapter.*

The Nature of Psychology

Psychology is the scientific study of (1) _____ and the (2) _____. An important part of scientific study is (3) _____ thinking, which involves (4) _____ four important (5) _____.

Psychologists have a quest for knowledge for its own sake, which is called (6) _____ _____, and to also pursue knowledge that is designed to solve specific practical problems, a type of research known as (7) _____ _____.

The Robber's Cave study by Sherif et al. (1961) showed that hostility between groups could be reduced by having children work together in (8) _____ _____. This basic research was later used by Aronson et al. (1978) in the (9) _____ _____, which required children to cooperate in order to achieve a goal that none of them could achieve alone.

As scientists, psychologists have five central goals: to (10) _____, (11) _____, (12) _____, and (13) _____ behavior and also to (14) _____ psychological knowledge.

The three main levels of analysis that can be used to understand behavior are the (15) _____, (16) _____, and (17) _____ levels. These levels are usually combined to explain behavior. Indeed, the presence of one factor can influence the effects of other factors, a process called (18) _____.

Perspectives on Behavior

(19) _____ are vantage points for analyzing behavior. The work of most psychologists can be categorized into the (20) _____, (21) _____, (22)

_____, (23) _____, (24) _____, and (25) _____ perspectives.

The ancient Greek belief that the mind is a spiritual entity not subject to the physical laws that govern the body is called (26) _____-_____ _____. The alternative view that mind and body are one is called (27) _____.

The perspective emphasizing the role of unconscious processes and unresolved past conflicts is known as the (28) _____ perspective and is most associated with (29) _____ _____.

The behavioral perspective developed from (30) _____ _____, which held that all ideas and knowledge are gained empirically. Today, behaviorists emphasize the (31) _____ determinants of behavior. An attempt to bridge the gap between the behavioral and cognitive perspectives is called (32) _____ _____.

Humanistic psychologists emphasize the importance of conscious motives and free will and believe that we are motivated to reach our full potentials, a state called (33) _____-_____. The cognitive perspective views people as problem solvers and (34) _____ _____. Today's cognitive perspective has roots in the debate between the structuralist, functionalist, and Gestalt camps. The structuralists, who believed that sensations are the basic elements of consciousness, attempted to study consciousness through the technique of (35) _____. In contrast, the approach that held that psychology should study the "whys" of consciousness, or (36) _____, was influenced by evolutionary theory. The study of how elements of experience are organized into wholes, or (37) _____ _____, suggested that the whole was greater than the sum of its parts. Modern cognitive psychologists study cognitive processes involved in activities such as decision making and problem solving.

(38) _____ _____ was one of the most prominent theorists in the study of childhood cognitive development. Theorists who maintain that "reality" is in large part our own mental creation are known as (39) _____ _____.

The body of enduring beliefs, values, behaviors, and traditions shared by a large group of people, known as (40) _____, also influences our behavior. The rules that society establishes to indicate what behavior is acceptable are known as (41) _____.

The biological perspective emphasizes the roles of the brain, biochemical processes, and (42) _____ _____. According to Darwin's evolutionary theory, a species will maintain any inheritable characteristic that increases the likelihood of survival because individuals having the characteristic will be likely to survive and reproduce. This process is known as (43) _____ _____. Psychologists in the field of (44) _____ _____ emphasize the idea that behaviors are products of evolution, as an organism's evolved biology determines its behavioral capacities, and its behavior determines whether it will survive. Similarly, (45) _____ _____ study the ways in which genetic factors influence behavioral tendencies. Another area within the biological perspective is (46) _____ _____, which explores which regions of the brain—which neural circuits and brain chemicals—influence our behavior, sensory experiences, emotions, and thoughts.

Psychology Today

There are a number of specialty fields within the larger field of psychology. For instance, (47)_____ psychologists are involved with the diagnosis and treatment of psychological disorders, whereas (48)_____ psychologists study behavior in work settings—for example, factors related to employee satisfaction and performance. The (49) _____ _____ _____, founded in 1892, is the largest psychological association in the world.

How to Enhance Your Academic Performance

An important habit for success in college is to manage your (50) _____ effectively. To do this, write out your daily (51) _____ and set (52) _____. The Focus Questions in the margins of your textbook are designed to encourage (53) _____ _____. (54)_____ is not an effective test preparation strategy because it is fatiguing, taxes your memory, and often increases test anxiety which, in turn, interferes with learning and actual test performance.

E. Concept Cards

Truly learning a concept means integrating it into the way *you* think about things. To integrate concepts successfully, you must translate the words and examples your text or instructor provides into words and examples that are meaningful to you.

For this exercise, obtain some note cards (3" × 5" or 4" × 6") to make a deck of concept cards. On one side of each card, write the *concept* from the list following (e.g., "basic research") at the top. Read the textbook definition provided, and then write the definition *in your own words* on the concept card (e.g. for "basic research," you might write "when you do a study just because you're interested in the question, not for some practical reason such as solving a specific problem.") Simply imagine that a friend has asked you what the concept means, and write down what you would answer. Writing the definition in your own words requires you to think deeply about its meaning. When next you see your own version of the definition, it will make intuitive sense to you—no translation required.

On the second side of the card, write your own example of the concept. Again, coming up with your own example requires you to think deeply about the application of the concept, and you will more easily understand and remember the example when you study for a test. If you use an example from the text, or from class, make it your own by writing it in your own words. You can always check with your instructor to ensure that your example is indeed a good example of the concept.

CONCEPT	Example of the concept in my own words, preferably drawn from my own experience
Definition in my own words	
(side 1 of card)	(side 2 of card)

The following is a list of all of the boldface concepts from your textbook, with the author's definition. Write the definition in your own words, together with your own example of the concept, to create a concept card as described above, or write in the space provided.

Psychology: The scientific study of behavior and the mind

Basic research: Research that reflects the quest for knowledge purely for its own sake

Applied research: Research that is designed to solve specific, practical problems

Mind-body dualism: The belief that the mind is a spiritual entity not subject to physical laws that govern the body

Monism: The idea that the mind and body are one, and the mind is not a separate spiritual entity

British empiricism: The concept that all ideas and knowledge are gained empirically—that is, through the senses

Structuralism: The analysis of the mind in terms of its basic elements

Functionalism: A school of thought that holds that psychology should study the functions of consciousness rather than its structure

Psychodynamic perspective: A perspective that searches for the causes of behavior within the inner workings of our personality; and emphasizes the role of unconscious processes

Psychoanalysis: The analysis of internal and primarily unconscious psychological forces

Defense mechanism: Psychological techniques that help us cope with anxiety and the pain of traumatic experiences

Object relations theories: Theories that focus on how early experiences with caregivers shape the views that people form of themselves and others

Behavioral perspective: A perspective that focuses on the role of the external environment in governing our actions

Behaviorism: A school of thought that emphasizes environmental control of behavior through learning

Cognitive behaviorism: An idea that proposes that learning experiences and the environment influence our expectations and other thoughts, and that, in turn, our thoughts influence how we behave

Humanistic perspective (humanism): Viewpoint that emphasizes free will, personal growth, and the attempt to find meaning in one's existence

Positive psychology movement: Movement that emphasizes the study of human strengths, fulfillment, and optimal living

Cognitive perspective: Perspective that examines the nature of the mind, and how mental processes influence behavior

Gestalt psychology: A school of thought that examines how elements of experience are organized into wholes

Cognitive psychology: A school of thought that focuses on the study of mental processes

Cognitive neuroscience: An area of psychology that uses sophisticated electrical recording and brain-imaging techniques to examine brain activity as people engage in cognitive tasks

Social constructivism: A viewpoint that maintains that what we consider "reality" is largely our own mental creation

Sociocultural perspective: Perspective that examines how social environment and cultural learning influence our behavior, thoughts, and feelings

Culture: The enduring values, beliefs, behaviors, and traditions that are shared by a large group of people and passed from one generation to the next

Norms: Rules that specify what behavior is acceptable and expected for members of a group

Socialization: The process by which culture is transmitted to new members and internalized by them

Cultural psychology (cross-cultural psychology): Psychology that explores how culture is transmitted to its members and examines psychological similarities and differences that occur among people from diverse cultures

Individualism: An emphasis on personal goals and self-identity based primarily on one's own attributes and achievements

Collectivism: Idea in which individual goals are subordinated to those of the group, and personal identity is defined largely by the ties that bind one to the extended family and other social groups

Biological perspective: Perspective that examines how brain processes and other bodily functions regulate behavior

Behavioral neuroscience (physiological psychology): Psychology that examines brain processes and other physiological functions that underlie our behavior, sensory experiences, emotions, and thoughts

Neurotransmitters: Chemicals released by nerve cells that allow them to communicate with one another

Behavior genetics: The study of how behavioral tendencies are influenced by genetic factors

Natural selection: Darwin's thought process specifying that if an inherited trait gives certain members an advantage over others, these members will be more likely than other members to survive and pass these characteristics on to their offspring

Evolutionary psychology: Psychology that seeks to explain how evolution shaped modern human behavior

Interaction: The way in which one factor influences behavior depends on the presence of another factor

F. What's the Difference? A Concept Card Exercise

An important skill in learning concepts is being able to differentiate among concepts that are similar or related in some way. This skill is particularly relevant for multiple-choice tests, especially if you often find yourself wavering between two answers.

Once you have created your own deck of concept cards, select them two by two, each time answering the question "What's the difference between these two concepts?" You can use the word definitions of the concepts or the examples of the concepts to enhance your mastery of the material. In each case, choose pairs of concepts to compare those that are related or similar or that sound the same or that could in some way be confused. It's much easier to spot the difference between two concepts when you are studying, with the textbook available, rather than when you are considering the question for the first time in a testing situation.

G. Apply What You Know

1. Explain the focus of study of each of the six psychological perspectives.

Perspective/Focus of Study

Behavioral

Biological

Cognitive

Humanistic

Psychodynamic

Sociocultural

2. Think of a self-help book that you've read recently. Which psychological perspective(s) does the book use? Give some specifics.

3. Choose a topic such as workplace violence, alcohol abuse, smoking, or obesity, and analyze the possible causes of the behavior by using each of the three levels of analysis (biological, psychological, and environmental). You might also choose a current event in the news and analyze the behavior of someone involved in terms of each of the three levels of analysis—for example, a current scandal, court case, or natural disaster.

Biological explanation

Psychological explanation

Environmental explanation

H. On the Web: *As with any online research, it is important to consider how legitimate a given source is before you rely on the information it presents. Your instructor or Internet adviser may give you some specific guidelines for distinguishing which kinds of Web sites tend to be reputable.*

A. Your text mentions a number of individuals who have made notable contributions to the field of psychology. Search the Web for more information about some of those listed. Learning more about these pioneers will add to your understanding of their work and its significance.

Eliot Aronson

Walter Cannon

René Descartes

Charles Darwin

Sigmund Freud

William James

John Locke

Wilhelm Wundt

Edward Titchener

Ivan Pavlov

Edward Thorndike

John B. Watson

B. F. Skinner

Abraham Maslow

Carl Rogers

Noam Chomsky

Jean Piaget

Robert Guthrie

Karl Lashley

Donald Hebb

B. Take a look at the concept cards you have created for this chapter, or the key concepts listed in section E. In the space provided,, make a list of any whose definitions or associations you are not yet confident of, and any you'd like to learn more about. Try entering the terms on your list into your search engine. Make notes of any helpful information you find.

Key Term/Information Found

C. Search the Web for answers to the following questions, or any others stimulated by the material in your text. In your answers, include any additional pieces of information you find that are of interest.

1. Who was the first woman to be elected president of the American Psychological Association?

2. In what year was she elected?

3. What percentage of doctorates in psychology are currently awarded to women?

4. What percentage of doctorates in psychology are currently awarded to African Americans

5. What percentage of doctorates in psychology are currently awarded to Hispanics?

6. What percentage of doctorates in psychology are currently awarded to Asian Americans?

7. What percentage of doctorates in psychology are currently awarded to Native Americans?

8. Who was the first American woman to be awarded a doctorate in psychology?

9. Who was the first African American male to be awarded a doctorate in psychology?

10. Who became the American Psychological Association's first African American president?

I. Analyze This: *Chapter 1 of your textbook begins by presenting these four basic steps in the critical thinking process:*
- *"What exactly are you asking me to believe?"*
- *"How do you know? What is the evidence?"*
- *"Are there other possible explanations?"*
- *"What is the most reasonable conclusion?"*

You might picture this as a four-step analysis to help you decide whether to accept a given theory or assertion. Now it's your turn to put your textbook to this test.

Review the sections in Chapter 1 of your textbook under the headings "Psychology's Intellectual Roots" and "Early Schools: Structuralism and Functionalism." There you will find a discussion of the early techniques of reason and introspection. If someone told you that empirical observation is a better way to gather scientific information than reason or introspection, would you agree? Analyze that assertion in the space provided. When you have finished, consider using this four-step analysis to evaluate other assertions you encounter.

"What exactly are you asking me to believe?"

"How do you know? What is the evidence?"

"Are there other possible explanations?"

"What is the most reasonable conclusion?"

J. Practice Test

Multiple-Choice Items: *Write the letter corresponding to your answer in the space to the left of each item.*

_____ 1. According to your textbook, *psychology* is best defined as the ____.
   a. study of people's subjective mental lives
   b. scientific study of behavior and the mind
   c. examination of unconscious factors
   d. study of personality

_____ 2. Dr. Antonini is a psychologist who studies language development in children. Her research explores questions such as the mechanisms of language development and the relationship between language development and cognitive skills. Dr. Antonini's research is best categorized as ____ research.
   a. applied
   b. basic
   c. psychodynamic
   d. interaction

_____ 3. The jigsaw program (Aronson et al., 1978) reduced intergroup conflict because ____.
   a. working together on jigsaw puzzles created more cooperation
   b. cooperative experiences only increase intergroup conflict
   c. the groups of children were required to cooperate to reach a goal that a single group could not reach alone
   d. groups almost always prefer to cooperate rather than to fight each other

_____ 4. Dr. Schmidt is a psychologist who is interested in studying aggression in sports. For his research, he attends high school basketball games and records the number of aggressive acts he observes. Dr. Schmidt's research is best viewed as meeting the ____ goal of psychology.
   a. description
   b. understanding

c. prediction
d. influence

_____ 5. The modern _____ psychology movement highlights the study of human strengths, fulfillment, and optimal living.
a. evolutionary
b. structuralist
c. neuroscience
d. positive

_____ 6. To explain Ray's extreme shyness around women, a psychologist oriented to the _____ perspective might explore whether Ray is unconsciously afraid of his sexual impulses and therefore avoids putting himself into dating situations in which he would have to confront those hidden impulses.
a. structural
b. psychodynamic
c. evolutionary
d. biological

_____ 7. Monists believed that _____.
a. the mind is a spiritual entity not subject to physical laws
b. the biological perspective was wrong
c. mental events are a product of physical events in the brain
d. the love of money is the root of all evil

_____ 8. Researchers in the area of behavioral neuroscience might investigate which of the following questions?
a. Are neurotic people more likely than other people to commit suicide?
b. Which areas of the brain are involved in learning and memory?
c. Is it more effective to toilet-train a child using rewards or using punishment?
d. Are twins more alike in personality than non-twin siblings?

_____ 9. Chemicals released by nerve cells that allow them to communicate with one another are known as _____.
a. behavior genetics
b. gestalts
c. neurotransmitters
d. natural selection

_____ 10. The idea that any inheritable characteristic that increases the likelihood of survival will be maintained in the species because individuals having the characteristic will be more likely than those without it to survive and reproduce is known as _____.
a. evolution
b. sociobiology

c. natural selection
d. behavior genetics

_____ 11. In extreme circumstances, parents will sometimes sacrifice their lives to ensure the survival of their children. A sociobiologist would argue that these instances ____.
   a. are due to innate altruistic drives within every human being
   b. occur because genetic survival (of members of the species who share the parent's genes) is more important than individual survival
   c. are due to the conflict between unconscious psychological forces and psychological defenses
   d. occur because of the reinforcement of altruistic behavior by culture and society

_____ 12. The study of both identical and fraternal twins in an attempt to understand behavior is used primarily in the field of ____.
   a. behavior genetics
   b. evolutionary psychology
   c. sociobiology
   d. cognitive psychology

_____ 13. Inspired by the metaphor of the ____, cognitive psychologists view humans as information processors and problem solvers.
   a. pressure cooker
   b. computer
   c. cell phone
   d. microwave oven

_____ 14. Gestalt psychology is concerned with ____.
   a. biological influences on behavior
   b. environmental determinants of behavior
   c. how elements of experience are organized into meaningful wholes
   d. behavior genetics

_____ 15. Freud speculated that because sexual desires and needs in childhood are punished, we learn to fear them and become anxious when we are aware of their presence. This leads us to develop ____, psychological techniques that help us cope with anxiety and the pain of traumatic experiences.
   a. denials
   b. defense mechanisms
   c. phobias
   d. neurotransmitters

_____ 16. Skinner's behaviorist theory ____.
   a. has had no effect on contemporary psychological theory
   b. continues to influence both basic and applied psychology

c. continues to influence basic but not applied psychology
d. is still considered infallible by nearly all of today's psychologists

_____ 17. In a study of the importance of being in love with a potential marriage partner, students from economically disadvantaged countries with _____ cultures were less likely than others to view love as a prerequisite to marriage.
a. Communist
b. individualistic
c. Buddhist
d. collectivistic

_____ 18. People associated with the philosophical perspective of British empiricism _____.
a. view observation as a more valid approach to knowledge than reasoning
b. view reasoning as a more valid approach to knowledge than observation
c. believe that internal factors are the major determinants of human behavior
d. assume that most human behavior is motivated by unconscious forces

_____ 19. A psychologist, Dr. Washington, is being interviewed on a local television news program regarding recent problems with school violence. Dr. Washington proposes that we need to change the school and home environments in which our children are being raised by rewarding the children more frequently for the prosocial behavior we want them to exhibit. Dr. Washington is most likely associated with the _____ psychological perspective.
a. humanistic
b. psychodynamic
c. cognitive
d. behavioral

_____ 20. Modern psychodynamic theory _____.
a. no longer regards the unconscious as an important influence on behavior
b. downplays the role of hidden sexual and aggressive motives
c. pays little attention to social factors such as family relationships
d. emphasizes the influence of conscious thoughts on people's actions

_____ 21. Sara is having trouble with anxiety and is working with a psychotherapist to address this problem. The therapist teaches Sara (1) how to change her anxiety-provoking thoughts and (2) how to change her environment so that it reinforces the new behaviors she wants to learn. Sara's therapist is *most likely* associated with the _____ area of psychology.
a. humanistic
b. psychodynamic
c. sociocultural
d. cognitive-behavioral

_____ 22. A cognitive psychologist approaches the long-standing conflict between the Catholics and Protestants in Northern Ireland by focusing on the idea that what members of each group consider "reality" is largely their own mental creation. This psychologist *most likely* adheres to the _____ cognitive viewpoint.
   a. evolutionary
   b. cognitive neuroscience
   c. introspection
   d. social constructivism

_____ 23. The _____ perspective tends to ignore mental processes because they are not directly observable. In contrast, the _____ perspective acknowledges the importance of both the environment and internal mental processes in determining behavior.
   a. cognitive-behavioral; behavioral
   b. humanistic; cognitive
   c. behavioral; cognitive
   d. behavioral; cognitive-behavioral

_____ 24. Nguyen is working with a psychotherapist who pays a great deal of attention to how he finds personal meaning in his life. The therapist also focuses on the power of choice and free will. This therapist *most likely* adheres to the _____ psychological perspective.
   a. behavioral
   b. psychodynamic
   c. humanistic
   d. biological

_____ 25. Humanistic theorists believe that people are motivated to reach their full potential, a state called _____.
   a. self-actualization
   b. self-potentiation
   c. existential anxiety
   d. existential bliss

_____ 26. Gabriella was raised in a family where individual achievement and accomplishment were rewarded. Both of her parents consistently encouraged her to set personal goals for herself and to strive to achieve them. The values emphasized by Gabriella's family are *most consistent* with _____.
   a. collectivism
   b. structuralism
   c. individualism
   d. functionalism

_____ 27. On most U.S. campuses, a student who arrived for class dressed in a swimsuit would be violating _____.

a. culture
b. the law
c. the principles of collectivism
d. cultural norms

_____ 28. Which of the following questions is part of the method of critical thinking about a claim that someone asserts?
a. What are qualifications of the person making the claim?
b. What is the evidence for the claim?
c. Why is the person making the claim?
d. How many people agree with the claim?

_____ 29. The three-levels-of-analysis approach for understanding behavior refers to _____.
a. the conscious, the unconscious, the preconscious
b. the behavioral, the sociocultural, the cognitive-behavioral
c. the evolutionary, the humanistic, the behavior genetic
d. the biological, the psychological, the environmental

_____ 30. What is the "nature-nurture question" in psychology?
a. "Are the primary influences on people's behavior their innate dispositions or environmental factors?"
b. "Why does it seem to be people's nature to nurture their children?"
c. "Which influences on people's behavior are more powerful, biological factors or early childhood experiences?"
d. "Are conscious or unconscious influences more important in determining people's behavior?"

True/False Items: *Write T or F in the space provided to the left of each item.*

_____ 1. The goal of basic research is to solve practical problems.

_____ 2. Psychologists are interested in predicting behavior.

_____ 3. Natural selection is a process that selects behaviors that have survival value according to evolutionary psychology.

_____ 4. According to the biological perspective, evolution has not played a role in the development of modern human behavior.

_____ 5. Gestalt psychology is concerned with how elements of experience are organized into wholes.

_____ 6. According to the social constructivist view, reality is objective and applies to everyone.

_____ 7. The perspective that puts most emphasis on unconscious processes is the psychodynamic perspective.

_____ 8. An attempt to bridge the gap between the behavioral and cognitive perspectives is called cognitive behaviorism.

_____ 9. Individual goals are subordinated to those of the group in individualistic cultures.

_____ 10. In an interaction, the presence or strength of one factor can influence the effects of other factors.

Short-Answer Questions

1. How do monism and dualism differ?

2. What are the basic principles of evolutionary psychology?

3. What kinds of factors do biological psychologists use to explain human behavior?

4. What kinds of factors do humanistic psychologists use to explain human behavior?

5. How do sociocultural factors affect behavior?

Essay Questions

1. Why did you enroll in this introductory psychology course, and what do you hope to learn from it? Note: If you are taking introductory psychology merely to fulfill a requirement, you might as well make the best of it. There is no sense fulfilling a requirement and doing poorly in the course. Think of some good reasons for taking introductory psychology, even if you personally don't buy into them 100%, and outline some things one might hope to gain from the course.

2. If we believe that behavior is affected by environmental factors, does that mean that people don't have personal control over their behavior? Explain your answer and cite some specifics from your own experience to support your position.

3. Although *both* biological and environmental factors are likely to affect behavior, would one set of factors be more important than the other? Why or why not? If so, which would be the more important factor?

Answer Keys

Answer Key for Review at a Glance

1. behavior
2. mind
3. critical
4. asking
5. questions
6. basic research
7. applied research
8. cooperative experiences
19. Perspectives
20. psychodynamic
21. behavioral
22. humanistic
23. cognitive
24. sociocultural
25. biological
26. mind-body dualism
37. Gestalt psychology
38. Jean Piaget
39. social constructivists
40. culture
41. norms
42. genetic factors
43. natural selection
44. evolutionary psychology

9. jigsaw program
10. describe
11. understand
12. predict
13. influence
14. apply
15. biological
16. psychological
17. environmental
18. interaction
27. monism
28. psychodynamic
29. Sigmund Freud
30. British empiricism
31. environmental
32. cognitive behaviorism
33. self-actualization
34. information processors
35. introspection
36. functionalism
45. behavior geneticists
46. behavioral neuroscience
47. clinical
48. industrial/organizational
49. American Psychological Association
50. time
51. schedule
52. priorities
53. critical thinking
54. Cramming

Answer Key for Practice Test Multiple-Choice Items

1. b
2. b
3. c
4. a
5. d
6. b
7. c
8. b
9. c
10. c
11. b
12. a
13. b
14. c
15. b
16. b
17. d
18. a
19. d
20. b
21. d
22. d
23. d
24. c
25. a
26. c
27. d
28. b
29. d
30. a

Answer Key for Practice Test True/False Items

1. F
2. T
3. T
4. F
5. T
6. F
7. T
8. T
9. F
10. T

Answer Key for Practice Test Short-Answer Questions

1. Monists believed that the mind is not separate spiritual entity from the body and thus is subject to the same physical forces as the body is. Mind-body dualists, on the

other hand, believed that the mind is a separate spiritual entity from the body and thus is not governed by physical laws. Most modern biological psychologists would agree with the monist position.

2. Evolutionary psychologists believe that evolution has played an important role in the development of human behavior. Behaviors that enhanced the abilities of individuals to adapt to their environment, in turn, increased the likelihood of survival of these individuals and their ability to reproduce. These behaviors were then selected through natural selection.

3. Psychologists using the biological perspective rely on several factors in explaining human behavior. They study the structures and processes of the brain, a field known as behavioral neuroscience. They study genetic factors through twin and adoption studies in the field of behavior genetics; biochemical factors also play a role. In addition, they study the influence of evolution on the development of modern human behaviors.

4. Humanistic psychologists emphasize a number of tendencies in their explanations of human behavior. They believe that people have free will, have innate tendencies toward growth and self-actualization, and attempt to find meaning from their existence. This is a positive view of human nature, as it suggests that people will grow to their full potential if the environment is nurturing.

5. The sociocultural perspective emphasizes the roles of culture (enduring values, beliefs, behaviors, and traditions shared by a group of people) and norms. Norms are rules that specify proper behavior for a particular culture or society.

Answer Key for Practice Test Essay Questions

As you may have guessed, there are no right or wrong answers to the essay questions in this practice test. That does not mean, however, that all essays are equally good. To get maximum learning benefit from the essay questions, do the following:

- Review each essay a day or two after you wrote it, noting any necessary corrections and any additional support for your points that you can think of.
- Review the section in your textbook that pertains to the topic of each essay. Annotate your essay with any corrections or additional support for your points that you find in the text.
- Spend a few minutes researching the topic of each essay on the Internet. Annotate your essay further with any additional (reliable) information you find.
- Finally, reread each essay with the annotations you have added.

Chapter 2
STUDYING BEHAVIOR SCIENTIFICALLY

A. Learning Objectives: *These objectives are expanded from the Focus Questions found in the margins of your textbook. When you have mastered the material in this chapter, you will be able to:*

2.1 Describe the three primary attitudes associated with scientific inquiry

2.2 Using Darley and Latané's research, illustrate the five steps of the scientific inquiry.

2.3 Explain the major drawbacks of hindsight understanding.

2.4 List the characteristics of a good theory.

2.5 Describe the importance of operational definitions and recognize examples of them.

2.6 Identify the major ethical issues in human and animal research.

2.7 Discuss the advantages and disadvantages of descriptive research.

2.8 Explain the importance of random sampling when conducting survey research.

2.9 Describe the purpose and methods of correlational research.

2.10 Explain why scientists are unable to draw causal conclusions from correlational research.

2.11 Describe and interpret correlation coefficients and scatterplots, and explain how correlational research can be used to predict behavior.

2.12 Describe the characteristics of an experiment, and explain how experiments can be used to investigate causal relations among variables.

2.13 Define and differentiate between independent and dependent variables.

2.14 Describe how random assignment and counterbalancing are used in designing an experiment.

2.15 Explain the process of using two independent variables in the same experiment.

2.16 Define internal validity, and explain how it is threatened by confounding variables, demand characteristics, placebo effects, and experimenter expectancy.

2.17 Explain how placebo effects and experimenter expectancy effects can be minimized.

2.18 Define external validity, and explain why replication is important.

2.19 Indicate three things done by critical consumers of statistics.

2.20 List three methods of central tendency and two measures of variability.

2.21 Explain the purpose of inferential statistics, and describe statistical significance.

2.22 Explain the purpose of meta-analysis.

2.23 Explain how critical-thinking skills can be used to evaluate claims made in everyday life.

B. Chapter Overview

This chapter will help you understand how to evaluate psychological research. It begins by defining science as an approach to asking and answering questions that is based on evidence and critical thinking. We then outline some basic steps in the scientific process which apply to all scientific research, not just that in psychology.

As a scientist, you start by identifying a question of interest. Then you review any relevant information about the topic, form a tentative explanation, and develop a hypothesis which is a testable prediction about the phenomenon of interest. To test the hypothesis, you conduct research and analyze the data obtained in order to determine if your hypothesis may be correct or whether it must be rejected. At this point, scientists communicate their findings to the scientific community, usually in professional journals or at conferences, so that others can participate in critical thinking and conducting their own studies on the topic. Further research on the phenomenon helps to build a theory, which is a set of formal statements about how and why certain events are related, and hence specific new hypotheses to be tested.

People use two major approaches to understanding behavior: hindsight understanding (after-the-fact explanations) and understanding through prediction, control, and theory building (the scientific approach). While hindsight understanding is typical of everyday "common sense," psychologists use the scientific method to study and measure variables, operationally defining them in terms of the procedures used to measure them. Psychologists gather data related to a variable from self-reports, reports by others, measures of overt behavior, psychological tests, and physiological measures.

Ethical standards are very important to safeguard the rights of participants in psychological research. The American Psychological Association (APA) has a detailed ethics code for all psychologists based on the principles of beneficence, responsibility, integrity, justice, and respect. The APA's guideline of informed consent states that research participants should be given a full description of the procedures to be followed, notified of any potential risks that might be involved, told that they have the right to withdraw from the study without penalty, and informed whether and how confidentiality of responses will be maintained. Psychologists sometimes use deception studies in which participants are misled about the nature of the research. These experiments are controversial but may be necessary to obtain natural, spontaneous responses from people, and the researchers must reveal the true purpose of the study to participants after it is over. Ethical standards also apply for the humane treatment of research animals. Although research with animals is controversial, most research psychologists would argue that it is a valuable way to further knowledge of both animal and human behavior.

Psychologists act as detectives, using several different research methods to learn more about their topics of interest. Descriptive research identifies how humans and animals behave and are often a good source of hypotheses for further study. Case studies are a type of descriptive research involving in-depth analyses of individuals, groups, or events. Studies of animals or humans in natural settings are examples of naturalistic observation. In survey research, psychologists administer questionnaires or interview people. Regardless of the descriptive method used, it is important for the sample of research subjects to represent the characteristics of the population being studied. A representative sample allows the researchers to make accurate conclusions about the population; this is often accomplished through random sampling.

Naturally occurring associations between variables are measured through correlational research. If two variables are correlated, that does not necessarily mean that one variable *causes* the other variable, but it does help us to predict the value of either variable from the other, with greater accuracy as the strength of the correlation increases. The correlation coefficient is a statistic that measures the strength of the relationship between the variables. A positive correlation occurs when higher scores on one variable are associated with higher scores on another variable, whereas a negative correlation occurs when higher scores on one variable are associated with *lower* scores on another variable. The plus or minus sign of a correlation coefficient tells you the *direction* of the relationship, whereas the absolute value of the statistic tells you the *strength* of the relationship. Naturalistic observation and surveys are methods that may be used for correlational as well as for descriptive research, when the data are analyzed in terms of relationships among variables rather than simply presented as descriptions.

To determine cause-and-effect relationships, researchers must use experiments. In designing an experiment, a researcher intentionally *manipulates* one or more variables (the independent variable[s], or hypothesized cause[s]) and measures whether this manipulation produces changes in a second variable or variables (the dependent variable[s], or hypothesized effect[s]). The researcher attempts to control for other factors that might influence the outcome. In many experiments, participants are randomly assigned to either an experimental group (receives the treatment) or a control group (does not receive the treatment). To reach conclusions, the researcher compares the experimental and control groups statistically to see if there is any difference between them. Another way to design an experiment is to expose each participant to all conditions of the experiment.

Psychologists are particularly interested in the validity of their research. Internal validity represents the degree to which an experiment supports clear causal conclusions. It is important to try to rule out other factors that may have influenced the results so that the researcher can conclude that it was the manipulation of the independent variable, rather than some other factor, that produced changes in the dependent variable. If the researcher cannot do that, he or she has a problem with the confounding of variables. Some problems that researchers try to control are placebo effects, in which participants' expectancies affect their behavior; and experimenter expectancy effects, by which researchers subtly and unintentionally influence the behavior of their participants through their actions. The double-blind procedure, in which both the participant and the experimenter are kept blind as to which experimental condition the participant is in, simultaneously minimizes participant placebo effects and experimenter expectancy effects.

External validity refers to the extent to which the results of a particular study can be generalized to other people, settings, and conditions. Researchers rely on replication to determine the external validity of the findings. A study has high external validity if the results are the same when the study is repeated using various samples of people, settings, and conditions.

Descriptive statistics are used to summarize and describe the characteristics of a set of data. The mode, median, and mean are different ways of describing the central tendency, or "middle," of a set of scores. The mode is the score that occurs most frequently, the median is the point that divides the scores such that half are above and half are below the median, and the mean is the arithmetic average of the scores. The mean takes into account the size of each score but is also distorted by extreme scores. Measures of variability tell us how much the scores in our set cluster together or are spread out. The range describes the difference between the highest and lowest scores in the set of data. The standard deviation takes into account how much each score differs from the mean.

Inferential statistics tell us how confident we can be in making inferences about a population based on findings obtained from a sample. If a finding is statistically significant, it is very unlikely to be due to chance alone, but statistical significance does not tell us whether the finding is important or trivial from a practical point of view. Meta-analysis is a statistical procedure for combining the results of different studies on a given topic, effectively summarizing the results of a body of research evidence related to a particular phenomenon.

In today's world, we frequently encounter oversimplifications, overgeneralizations, and pseudoscientific misinformation. You can avoid being misled by claims such as those in newspapers, advertisements, and solicitations by applying the critical-thinking skills you are learning in this course. Critical thinkers balance open-mindedness with healthy skepticism and evaluate evidence before deciding what to believe.

C. Chapter Outline

SCIENTIFIC PRINCIPLES IN PSYCHOLOGY
    Scientific Attitudes
    Gathering Evidence: Steps in the Scientific Process
    Two Approaches to Understanding Behavior
        Hindsight (After-the-Fact Understanding)
        Understanding through Prediction, Control, and Theory Building
    Defining and Measuring Variables
        Self-Reports and Reports by Others
        Measures of Overt Behavior
        Psychological Tests
        Physiological Measures
    In Review
ETHICAL PRINCIPLES IN RESEARCH
    Ethical Standards in Human Research
    Ethical Standards in Animal Research
    In Review
METHODS OF RESEARCH
    Descriptive Research: Recording Events
        Case Studies: The Hmong Sudden Death Syndrome
        Naturalistic Observation: Bullies in the Schoolyard
        Survey Research: Adolescents' Exposure to Abuse and Violence
            What Do You Think? Should You Trust Internet and Pop Media Surveys?
    Correlational Research: Measuring Associations between Events
        Research Close-Up: Very Happy People
        Correlation Does Not Establish Causation
            What Do You Think? Does Eating Ice Cream Cause People to Drown?
        The Correlation Coefficient
        Correlation as a Basis for Prediction
    Experiments: Examining Cause and Effect
        Independent and Dependent Variables
        Experimental and Control Groups
        Two Basic Ways to Design an Experiment
        Manipulating Two Independent Variables: Effects of Cell Phone Use and Traffic
            Density on Driving Performance
    In Review
THREATS TO THE VALIDITY OF RESEARCH
    Confounding of Variables

Placebo Effects
   Experimenter Expectancy Effects
   Replicating and Generalizing the Findings
   Beneath the Surface: Science, Psychics, and the Paranormal
   In Review
ANALYZING AND INTERPRETING DATA
   Being a Smart Consumer of Statistics
   Using Statistics to Describe Data
      Measures of Central Tendency
      Measures of Variability
   Using Statistics to Make Inferences
   Meta-Analysis: Combining the Results of Many Studies
   In Review
CRITICAL THINKING IN SCIENCE AND EVERYDAY LIFE
   Applying Psychological Science: Evaluating Claims in Research and Everyday Life
      Some Interesting Claims
      Critical Analyses of the Claims
   In Review

D. Review at a Glance: *Write the term that best fits the blank to review what you learned in this chapter.*

Scientific Principles in Psychology

Doing scientific research involves using the scientific process, an approach based on (1) _____ and (2) _____ _____. After a researcher identifies a question of interest and forms a tentative explanation, the next step is to formulate a (3) _____, or tentative prediction. The researcher then tests the idea, analyzes the data, and determines if the hypothesis may be correct, or is false and must be rejected. As additional evidence comes in, researchers attempt to build (4) _____, which are sets of formal statements that explain how and why events are related. Science is a public process, whereby researchers also (5) _____ their findings to their professional colleagues.

There are two main approaches to understanding behavior. After-the-fact understanding, also known as (6) _____ _____, is often used in everyday life to explain a behavior or other phenomenon. Psychologists, though, typically try to understand a behavior through (7) _____, (8) _____, and (9) _____ _____. Psychologists study (10) _____, which are characteristics that vary. A(n) (11)_____ definition defines a variable in terms of the specific procedures used to measure or produce it. Psychologists measure behavior in a number of different ways. Measures that ask people to report on their own knowledge, beliefs, or feelings are called (12) _____-_____ _____. Sometimes psychologists ask for reports from (13) _____ _____. Another method is to observe and record people's (14) _____ behavior. Psychologists also develop and use specialized (15) _____ to measure many types of characteristics, such as personality and intelligence. Measures of heart rate, blood pressure, and the like, known as (16) _____ _____ are also used in psychological research. Preexisting records that are used for research are known as (17) _____ _____.

Ethical Principles in Research

The ethics code of the (18) _____ _____ _____ regulates the conduct of psychologists who do research. In order to give (19) _____ _____, research participants must be given a full description of the research, informed of risks, and told that they are free to (20) _____ _____ the study without penalty. When studies involve (21) _____ to obtain natural, spontaneous responses from participants, the researchers are obligated to explain the (22) _____ of the study after it is over. The ethical standards of the APA also require (23) _____ treatment of animals used in research.

Methods of Research

Psychologists use several different research methods. (24) _____ research identifies how humans and animals behave and are often a good source of hypotheses for further study. An in-depth analysis of an individual, group, or event is called a (25) _____ _____. Sometimes researchers are interested in recording behavior that occurs in its natural setting, a type of research called (26) _____ _____. (27) _____ _____ involves obtaining information about a topic by administering questionnaires or interviews to many people.

Because it is often impractical to study the entire set of individuals we are interested in making conclusions about, called the (28) _____, researchers typically study a subset of that population called a (29) _____. To draw valid conclusions about the population, the sample must accurately reflect the characteristics of the population. Such a sample is known as a (30) _____ _____. When every member of the population has an equal probability of being chosen for the sample, the researcher has created a (31) _____ _____.

When researchers are interested in measuring the associations between events, they conduct (32) _____ research. Although such studies do not indicate (33) _____, they are helpful for (34) _____ one variable from another. A statistic that measures the direction and strength of the relationship between two variables is called a (35) _____ _____. When higher scores on one variable are associated with lower scores on a second variable, the researcher has discovered a (36) _____ correlation. When higher scores on one variable are associated with higher scores on a second variable, the researcher has discovered a (37) _____ correlation.

(38)_____ research methods are used to determine cause-and-effect relationships. The variable that is the hypothesized "cause" is manipulated by the experimenter and known as the (39) _____ variable, whereas the variable that is measured by the experimenter and hypothesized to be the "effect" is known as the (40) _____ variable. Participants in an experiment are often assigned, through a process of (41) _____ _____, to either the (42) _____ group, which receives the treatment, or a (43) _____ group, which does not. To reach conclusions, the researcher compares the experimental and control groups (44) _____ to see if there is any difference between them. Another way to design an experiment is to expose each participant to (45) _____ _____ of the experiment.

Threats to the Validity of Research

It is important for researchers to establish that their research is valid. (46)_____ _____ represents the degree to which an experiment supports clear causal conclusions. When two variables are intertwined in such a way that we cannot determine which one has influenced a dependent variable, there is a threat to internal validity known as (47)_____ _____ _____. Researchers also try to control (48) _____ _____, in which participants' expectancies affect their behavior, and (49) _____ _____ effects, by which researchers subtly and unintentionally influence the behavior of their participants through their actions. Researchers can minimize participant placebo effects and experimenter expectancy effects by using a (50) _____-_____ study design.

Researchers are interested in establishing not only internal validity but also (51) _____ validity, which is the degree to which the results of a study can be generalized to other people, settings, and conditions. To determine whether a tentative conclusion reached in one study is valid for other people, settings, and conditions, the results of the study must be (52) _____.

Analyzing and Interpreting Data

Descriptive statistics are used to (53) _____ and (54) _____ the characteristics of a data set. The mode, median, and (55) _____ are different ways of describing the (56)_____ _____ of a set of scores. Measures of variability, or how much the scores in our set cluster together, include the (57) _____ and (58) _____ _____.
(59)_____ statistics tell us how confident we can be in making inferences about a population based on findings obtained from a (60) _____. When a finding is statistically (61) _____, this means that the results are very unlikely to be due to chance, but it does not necessarily mean that the results are important from a practical point of view. Research designed to combine the results of many studies involves a statistical procedure known as (62) _____-_____.

Chapter 2 37

Critical Thinking in Science and Everyday Life

In today's world, we encounter many oversimplifications, overgeneralizations, and pieces of (63) _____ _____. You can avoid being misled by claims such as those in advertisements by applying the (64) _____-_____ skills you are learning in this course. Critical thinkers need to balance open-mindedness with healthy (65) _____ and evaluate (66) _____ before deciding what to believe.

E. Concept Cards

Truly learning a concept means integrating it into the way *you* think about things. To integrate concepts successfully, you must translate the words and examples your text or instructor provides into words and examples that are meaningful to you.

For this exercise, obtain some note cards (3" × 5" or 4" × 6") to make a deck of concept cards. On one side of each card, write the *concept* from the list following (e.g., "operational definition") at the top. Read the textbook definition provided, and then write the definition *in your own words* on the concept card (e.g. for "operational definition," you might write "exactly what you do to measure the variable, or to set up different levels of the variable in an experiment.") Simply imagine that a friend has asked you what the concept means, and write down what you would answer. Writing the definition in your own words requires you to think deeply about its meaning. When next you see your own version of the definition, it will make intuitive sense to you—no translation required.

On the second side of the card, write your own example of the concept. Again, coming up with your own example requires you to think deeply about the application of the concept, and you will more easily understand and remember the example when you study for a test. If you use an example from the text, or from class, make it your own by writing it in your own words. You can always check with your instructor that your example is indeed a good example of the concept.

CONCEPT	Example of the concept in my own words, preferably drawn from my own experience
Definition in my own words	
(side 1 of card)	(side 2 of card)

The following is a list of all the boldface concepts from your textbook with the author's definition. Write the definition in your own words, together with your own example of the concept, to create a concept card as described earlier, or write in the space provided.

Hypothesis: A specific prediction about some phenomenon

Theory: A set of formal statements that explains how and why certain events are related to one another

Variable: Any characteristic or factor that can vary

Operational definition: Definition of a variable in terms of the specific procedures used to produce or measure it

Unobtrusive measures: Measures that record behavior in a way that keeps participants unaware that they are being observed

Archival measures: Records or documents that already exist

Informed consent: The APA guideline saying that when people agree to participate in research, they should be given a full description of the procedures, informed about any risks involved, and told they are free to withdraw from the study at any time without penalty

Descriptive research: Research seeking to identify how humans and other animals behave, particularly in natural settings

Case study: An in-depth analysis of an individual, group, or event

Naturalistic observation: Observation of behavior as it occurs in a natural setting

Survey research: Research based on obtaining information about a topic by administering questionnaires or interviews to many people

Population: All the individuals that we are interested in drawing conclusions about

Sample: A subset of individuals drawn from a larger population

Representative sample: A sample that reflects the important characteristics of the population

Random sampling: A method of sampling whereby every member of a population has an equal probability of being chosen to participate in the survey

Correlational research: Research based on measuring one variable (X) and another variable (Y), and then statistically determining whether X and Y are related

Correlation coefficient: A statistic that indicates the direction and strength of the relation between two variables

Positive correlation: A relationship in which higher scores on one variable are associated with higher scores on a second variable

Negative correlation: A relationship in which higher scores on one variable are associated with lower scores on a second variable

Scatterplot: A graph on which the correlation between two variables can be depicted

Experiment: A research method based on a researcher manipulating one or more variables and measuring whether this manipulation influences other variables, while attempting to control extraneous factors that might influence the outcome of the experiment

Independent variable: The factor that is manipulated by the experimenter

Dependent variable: The factor that is measured by the experimenter and may be influenced by the independent variable

Experimental group: The group that receives a treatment or an "active" level of the independent variable

Control group: The group that is not exposed to the treatment or receives a zero level of the independent variable

Random assignment: A procedure in which each participant has an equal likelihood of being assigned to any one group within an experiment

Counterbalancing: A procedure in which the order of conditions is varied so that no condition has an overall advantage relative to others

Internal validity: The degree to which an experiment supports clear, causal conclusions

Confounding of variables: Research in which two variables are intertwined in such a way that we cannot determine which one has influenced a dependent variable

Placebo: A substance that has no pharmacological effect

Placebo effect: A research outcome in which people receiving treatment show a change in behavior because of their expectations, not because the treatment itself had any specific benefit

Experimenter expectancy effects: The subtle and unintentional ways researchers influence their participants to respond in a manner that is consistent with the researcher's hypothesis

Double-blind procedure: A research procedure wherein both the participant and experimenter are kept blind as to which experimental condition the participant is in

External validity: The degree to which the results of a study can be generalized to other people, settings, and conditions

Replication: The process of repeating a study to determine whether the original findings can be duplicated

Descriptive statistics: Statistics that allow us to summarize and describe the characteristics of a "set" (also called a "distribution") of data

Mode: The most frequently occurring score in a distribution

Median: The point that divides a distribution of scores in half, when those scores are arranged in order from lowest to highest

Mean: The arithmetic average of a set of scores

Range: The difference between the highest and lowest score in a distribution

Standard deviation: A measure of variability that takes into account how much each score in a distribution differs from the mean

Inferential statistics: Statistics that tell us how confident we can be in making inferences about a population based on findings obtained from a sample.

Statistical significance: The conclusion that it is very unlikely that a particular finding occurred by chance alone

Meta-analysis: A statistical procedure for combining the results of different studies that examine the same topic

F. What's the Difference? A Concept Card Exercise

An important skill in learning concepts is being able to differentiate among concepts that are similar or related in some way. This skill is particularly relevant for multiple-choice tests, especially if you often find yourself wavering between two answers.

Once you have created your own deck of concept cards, select them two by two, each time answering the question "What's the difference between these two concepts?" You can use the word definitions of the concepts or the examples of the concepts to enhance your mastery of the material. In each case, choose pairs of concepts to compare that are related or similar or that sound the same or that could in some way be confused. It's much easier to spot the difference between two concepts when you are studying, with the textbook available, rather than considering the question for the first time in a testing situation.

G. Apply What You Know

1. Remember that an operational definition defines a variable in terms of the specific procedures used to produce or measure it. Write operational definitions for each of the following concepts: *academic performance*, *success*, *stress*, *aggression*, *love*, and *happiness*.

Term	Operational Definition
academic performance	

success

stress

aggression

love

happiness

2. Famed psychologist Dr. Lena Onmee hypothesizes that stress and anger cause depression. However, having been out of school too long, Dr. Onmee has forgotten the basics of experimentation, so she turns to you, ace psychology student, for help in designing her experiment. Describe how you would advise her to set up the experiment.

Designing an Experiment

Hypothesis: Stress and anger cause depression

Chapter 2   45

Independent variables:

Dependent variable:

Operational definitions of independent variables:

Operational definition of dependent variable:

Diagram the experimental design (experimental and control groups, random assignment, etc.):

3. Evaluate the following study, and identify seven problems with it:

Space psychologist Spiff lands on the dreaded planet Zorg. Nothing much is known of the Zorgian people, but they are rumored to be vicious and dangerous to humans. To determine whether this is the case, Spiff decides to do an experiment. He hypothesizes that the Zorgians are likely to be vicious and dangerous only when they are angered, so he defines anger as his dependent variable. A group of southern Zorgians, who are known to be quite different from the northern Zorgians, volunteer to participate in Spiff's study. He lets the angry Zorgians be in his control group and the nonangry Zorgians be in his experimental group and tells them the hypothesis of the study before it begins. He then measures the viciousness and dangerousness of both groups and compares them by using meta-analysis.

Problems with the Design

1.

2.

3.

4.

5.

6.

7.

H. On the Web: *As with any online research, it is important to consider how legitimate a given source is before you rely on the information it presents. Your instructor or Internet adviser may give you some specific guidelines for distinguishing which kinds of Web sites tend to be reputable.*

A. Take a look at the concept cards you have created for this chapter, or at the key concepts listed in section E. In the space below, make a list of any whose definitions or associations you are not yet confident of and any you'd like to learn more about. Try entering the terms on your list into your search engine. Make notes of any helpful information you find.

Key Term/Information Found

B. Access the U.S. Census Bureau website (http://www.census.gov). Determine the percentages of males and females, racial groups, and age groups in the county where your school is located in the most recent census. Describe how a researcher would draw a representative sample from that population.

County:

Percentage of males and females:

Percentage of racial groups:

Percentage of age groups:

How to draw a representative sample:

C. Review the section in your textbook entitled "Manipulating Two Independent Variables: Effects of Cell Phone Use and Traffic Density on Driving Performance." Search the Internet for Web sites related to the subject of cell phone usage and driving performance. To what extent does driving performance seem to be affected by drivers using cell phones? For what reasons? If you were going to design an experiment to study under what conditions cell phone usage affects driving performance, how would you do it? Based on the research you have read on the topic, do you have any suggestions to minimize adverse effects on driving from the use of cell phones? How would you design a study to test each of your suggestions for effectiveness?

I. Analyze This: *Chapter 1 of your textbook begins by presenting these four basic steps in the critical thinking process:*
- *"What exactly are you asking me to believe?"*
- *"How do you know? What is the evidence?"*
- *"Are there other possible explanations?"*
- *"What is the most reasonable conclusion?"*

You might picture this as a four-step analysis to help you decide whether to accept a given theory or assertion. Now it's your turn to put your textbook to this test.

Review the section in Chapter 2 of your textbook under the heading "Correlation as a Basis for Prediction." If someone told you that correlational research lacks scientific validity, would you agree? Analyze that assertion in the space below. When you have finished, consider using this four-step analysis to evaluate other assertions you encounter.

Chapter 2										49

"What exactly are you asking me to believe?"

"How do you know? What is the evidence?"

"Are there other possible explanations?"

"What is the most reasonable conclusion?"

J. Practice Test

Multiple-Choice Items: *Write the letter corresponding to your answer in the space to the left of each item.*

_____ 1. "Subjects who learn to type using the "Sight & Sound" method will type faster and more accurately than subjects who learn to type using the "Hunt & Peck" method." This statement is best described as a(n) _____.
   a. behavioral observation
   b. operational definition
   c. hypothesis
   d. variable

_____ 2. Theories are _____.
   a. tentative predictions about some phenomenon
   b. formal statements that explain how and why events are related
   c. characteristics that vary
   d. definitions of variables in measurable terms

_____ 3. One of the problems with after-the-fact or "hindsight" explanations is that _____.

   a. there are many ways of explaining past events, and there is usually no way to know which of these ways is correct
   b. they fail to provide a foundation on which further scientific study can occur
   c. they are usually too theoretically complex and sophisticated

d. they overemphasize the importance of external validity

_____ 4. A researcher is interested in studying factors that influence interpersonal attraction. In a study designed to explore this variable, the researcher uses a very attractive person as an assistant. Interpersonal attraction is then assessed by whether or not the people participating in the study call up the attractive assistant to ask the person on a date. In this example, calling up the attractive assistant represents a(n) _____ of interpersonal attraction.
   a. correlational study
   b. hypothesis
   c. case study
   d. operational definition

_____ 5. A social psychologist is interested in studying aggression in sports fans. He goes to various sporting events and keeps track of the number of aggressive acts that occur between fans using a well-defined coding system. This psychologist is using _____ to measure behavior.
   a. self-report measures
   b. physiological measures
   c. behavioral observations
   d. reports by others

_____ 6. Josh volunteers for a psychology experiment as part of his course requirement in Psychology 101. Before he can participate, the researcher follows informed consent procedures by giving him a full description of the procedures to be followed, _____ and telling him that he is free to withdraw from the study at any time without penalty.
   a. informing him of any risks that might be involved
   b. obtaining his roommate's permission
   c. assessing his psychological risk
   d. assessing his external validity

_____ 7. Trying to determine why young women are motivated to excel in athletics, a research psychologist studies in depth the young woman who won five gold medals in track-and-field events in the last Olympics. This psychologist is using the _____ method of study.
   a. correlational
   b. experimental
   c. archival
   d. case study

_____ 8. To learn about the social behavior of children, a developmental psychologist goes to an elementary school, finds a seat near one of the windows in a classroom, and watches the children playing on the playground outside during recess. This psychologist is engaged in _____.
   a. naturalistic observation

Chapter 2
51

        b. correlational research
        c. a case study
        d. experimental research

_____ 9. Dr. Smith decides to study freshman attitudes toward religion by recruiting students from three different universities in the United States to answer questions about their attitudes toward religion. Dr. Smith plans to apply his conclusions to all freshmen at universities in the United States. In this case, Dr. Smith is defining "all freshmen at universities in the United States" as his ____ for the study.
        a. sample
        b. random sample
        c. representative sample
        d. population

_____ 10. Dr. Smith decides to study freshmen attitudes toward religion by recruiting students from three different universities in the United States. Dr. Smith plans to apply his conclusions to all freshmen at universities in the United States. In this case Dr. Smith is defining his ____ as the students he has recruited from the three different universities.
        a. sample
        b. random sample
        c. representative sample
        d. population

_____ 11. The use of a ____ sample best establishes ____ validity.
        a. nonrandom; internal
        b. representative; external
        c. representative; internal
        d. nonrandom; external

_____ 12. Dr. Patel has heard that people tend to become more politically conservative as they get older and decides to conduct a study to see if this is true. She conducts a telephone survey in which she asks participants how old they are and their political identification. She then uses statistics to see if there is a relationship between age and political identification. The design that best describes Dr. Patel's investigation is ____.
        a. experimental research
        b. correlational research
        c. naturalistic observation
        d. descriptive research

_____ 13. Dr. Gonzalez has just completed a correlational study where he found a strong association between parental expectations and child academic achievement. In other words, children who perform well in school tend to have

parents who have high expectations for their children. On the basis of these research findings, Dr. Gonzalez can conclude that _____.
   a. parents' high expectations cause children to perform better in school
   b. children who perform better in school cause their parents to have higher expectations
   c. some unknown factor (e.g., being rich) leads both to parents having high expectations for their children and to the children doing well in school
   d. we don't know why, but there is a relationship between parental expectations and how children do in school

_____ 14. Which of the following correlation coefficients represents the strongest relationship between two variables?
   a. +.80
   b. +.01
   c. −.04
   d. −.92

_____ 15. After a few semesters playing video games in his dorm room, Paul realized that the more time he spent playing video games, the lower his GPA for the semester seemed to be. In other words, Paul noticed a _____ relationship between his game playing and his academic success.
   a. negative correlational
   b. positive correlational
   c. zero correlational
   d. statistically significant

_____ 16. For psychologists, _____ provide the most direct method for testing cause-and-effect relationships.
   a. correlational studies
   b. archival studies
   c. surveys
   d. experiments

_____ 17. A defining characteristic of an experiment, as compared to other research methods, is _____.
   a. the experimental manipulation of an independent variable
   b. the experimental manipulation of a dependent variable
   c. the use of random sampling of subjects
   d. the use of operational definitions of variables

_____ 18. Dr. Weiss wants to look at the impact of failure on self-esteem. Dr. Weiss designs an experiment in which half of the participants are led to believe they have failed on an ambiguous task and the other half of the participants are told they have succeeded. Dr. Weiss then has all participants complete a questionnaire measuring self-esteem, and looks to see if there are any

differences between the success and failure groups. In this example, self-esteem would be considered the ____ variable.
a. dependent
b. independent
c. placebo
d. confounding

_____ 19. A clinical psychologist has developed a new form of psychotherapy to treat a particular personality disorder. To test its effectiveness, a group of people with the personality disorder is selected to receive the therapy for 8 weeks. A second group of people with the disorder is also created but receives no therapy at all. At the end of the 8 weeks, the mental health of the people in both groups is assessed to evaluate the new psychotherapy. In this study, the people who did not receive any therapy would be in the ____ group.
a. experimental
b. control
c. random
d. sample

_____ 20. In survey research, ____ is typically used to ensure that a sample is representative.
a. random sampling
b. random assignment
c. counterbalancing
d. confounding of variables

_____ 21. In experiments, random ____, in which each participant has an equal chance of being in a given experimental (or control) group, is used to balance differences between participants across groups.
a. sampling
b. constancy
c. assignment
d. correlation

_____ 22. Dr. McGovern is interested in interpersonal attraction and the factors that affect it. He designs a study where he looks at the effect of similarity and social warmth on interpersonal attraction. Participants in his study meet a target person who either is or is not similar to the participant (the similarity variable), and who is either friendly or aloof (the social warmth variable). After interacting with the target person under these conditions, participants are then asked to rate how attractive they think the target person is. In this study, similarity and social warmth are the ____ variables and interpersonal attraction is the ____ variable.
a. independent; dependent
b. dependent; independent
c. confounding; dependent

d. independent; confounding

_____ 23. Sally has had depression for a while and finally decides to seek help from a clinical psychologist. After a couple of months of therapy, Sally's depression starts to lift. However, her improvement really isn't due to any of the therapy she has received from her therapist but instead is a product of Sally's expectation that psychotherapy is supposed to be effective and therefore she should be getting better. This example is best considered an example of _____.
a. experimenter expectancy effects
b. the double-blind effect
c. the placebo effect
d. a study with high external validity

_____ 24. Dr. Halb has developed a new cognitive therapy for depression that she believes will be a great improvement on the standard cognitive therapy. To evaluate her program, she conducts therapy with two groups of depressed patients—one group receiving the new and the other the standard type of cognitive therapy. She evaluates all study subjects on the same depression questionnaire at the end of their therapy. The group given Dr. Halb's new type of therapy is much less depressed on the final evaluation than the group receiving the standard therapy, suggesting that Dr. Halb's new treatment is more effective than the old standard. However, an alternative explanation for the results obtained might be confounding due to _____.
a. social desirability
b. experimenter expectancy effects
c. the placebo effect
d. random sampling

_____ 25. Researchers can minimize participant placebo effects and experimenter expectancy effects by using a(n) _____ study design.
a. correlational
b. experimental
c. double-blind
d. operational

_____ 26. To determine whether a conclusion reached in one study is valid for other people, settings, and conditions, the results of the study must be _____.
a. varied
b. confounded
c. replicated
d. randomized

_____ 27. Measures of central tendency and variability are _____.
a. descriptive statistics
b. measures of internal validity

c. inferential statistics
d. measures of external validity

_____ 28. ____ statistics tell us how likely it is that our research findings are due merely to ____.
a. Descriptive; a distribution
b. Inferential; chance
c. Experimental; random sampling
d. Correlational; random assignment

_____ 29. Researchers use ____ to statistically combine the results of different studies on a given topic, effectively summarizing the results of a body of research evidence.
a. meta-analysis
b. internal validity
c. external validity
d. central tendency

_____ 30. To avoid being misled by bogus claims, people need to evaluate ____ before deciding what to believe.
the independent and dependent variables
a. their critical thinking skills
b. the evidence
c. the credentials of the person making the claim

True/False Items: *Write T or F in the space provided to the left of each item.*

_____ 1. A hypothesis is a specific prediction about some phenomenon.

_____ 2. An operational definition is defined as any characteristic that can vary.

_____ 3. The tendency to respond in a socially acceptable manner rather than according to how one truly feels or wants to behave is called informed consent.

_____ 4. Already-existing records or documents used to study some behavioral phenomenon are called archival measures.

_____ 5. When every member of the population has an equal probability of being chosen for the sample, the sample is called a representative sample.

_____ 6. If I predict that the more questions from this study guide you get correct, the higher the score you will get on your next exam, I am predicting a positive correlation between the variables.

_____ 7. The variable that is manipulated by an experimenter is called the independent variable.

_____ 8. The degree to which an experiment supports a clear causal conclusion is known as the study's external validity.

_____ 9. Placebo effects occur when both the participant and the experimenter are kept blind as to which experimental condition the participant is in.

_____ 10. The process of repeating a study to determine whether the original findings can be duplicated is known as meta-analysis.

Short-Answer Questions

1. What types of physiological measures are used by psychologists to study behavior, and why are they subject to interpretive problems?

2. Describe the basic purpose of correlational research; explain what correlation coefficients are, and what they mean.

3. How are independent and dependent variables and experimental and control groups used in experiments?

4. Distinguish between random sampling and random assignment.

5. What are some of the basic ethical standards used in human research?

Essay Questions

1. Compare the reporting of scientific research that you encounter in the popular media (TV news, consumer magazines, etc.) against the style of reporting in articles from scientific journals such as those published by the APA. Why do the media usually announce research results in more direct terms than do scientists, who generally use qualifiers such as *this suggests* and *this tends to indicate*? Name some advantages and some disadvantages of the media's directness.

2. Think of a hypothesis you would like to test or a phenomenon you would like to investigate. Using the basic sequence of prediction, control, and theory building that is outlined in this chapter, state your prediction, and propose at least two experimental ways to control a variable that relates to your prediction. If your proposed experiments were to support your prediction, what theories might result? Explain also how you would be able to tell, on the basis of your proposed experiments, if your hypothesis was false.

3. Write a case study of a person, group, or event that relates to an issue you are interested in. Your goal is to discover principles of behavior that may hold true for other people or situations. As your textbook mentions, case study data may be gathered in a variety of ways; for purposes of this essay, use observation as your data source.

Answer Keys

Answer Key for Review at a Glance

1. evidence
2. critical thinking
3. hypothesis
4. theories
5. communicate
6. hindsight understanding
7. prediction
8. control
9. theory building
10. variables
11. operational
12. self-report measures
13. other people
14. overt
15. tests
16. physiological measures
17. archival measures
18. American Psychological Association
19. informed consent
20. withdraw from
21. deception
22. purpose
23. humane
24. Descriptive
25. case study
26. naturalistic observation
27. Survey research
28. population
29. sample
30. representative sample
31. random sample
32. correlational
33. causation
34. predicting
35. correlation coefficient
36. negative
37. positive
38. Experimental
39. independent
40. dependent
41. random assignment
42. experimental
43. control
44. statistically
45. all conditions
46. internal validity
47. confounding of variables
48. placebo effects
49. experimenter expectancy
50. double-blind
51. external
52. replicated
53. summarize
54. describe
55. mean
56. central tendency
57. range
58. standard deviation
59. Inferential
60. sample
61. significant
62. meta-analysis
63. pseudoscientific misinformation
64. critical-thinking
65. skepticism
66. evidence

Answer Key for Practice Test Multiple-Choice Items

1. c
2. b
3. a
4. d
5. c
6. a
7. d
8. a
9. d
10. a
11. b
16. d
17. a
18. a
19. b
20. a
21. c
22. a
23. c
24. b
25. c
26. c

12. b
13. d
14. d
15. a

27. a
28. b
29. a
30. c

Answer Key for Practice Test True/False Items

1. T
2. F
3. F
4. T
5. F

6. T
7. T
8. F
9. F
10. F

Answer Key for Practice Test Short-Answer Questions

1. Psychologists use several different types of physiological measurements of behavior. Heart rate, blood pressure, respiration rate, and hormonal secretions are often studied. Electrical and biochemical processes in the brain are also studied. The problem in interpreting these measures is that it is often unclear how these physiological measures are linked to specific patterns of behavior.

2. Correlational research is used to study the relationships between variables. Two variables (X and Y) are measured and then are statistically analyzed to determine whether they are related. The statistic that is used to measure the association is called a correlation coefficient. The sign of the coefficient (+ or –) indicates whether the variables are positively or negative correlated. A positive correlation means that as one variable increases, the other also increases, whereas a negative correlation means that as one variable increases, the other decreases. The absolute value of the correlation coefficient indicates the strength of the relationship.

3. In the simplest kind of experiment, participants are first randomly assigned to either an experimental group or a control group. The experimental group receives the treatment or active level of the independent variable; the control group does not. The independent variable is manipulated by the experimenter. The dependent variable is then measured by the experimenter for each group, and the groups are statistically compared to determine if there is a difference between them.

4. In random sampling, every member of the population has an equal probability of being included in the sample. Random samples are used to try to make the sample representative of the population and to increase the study's external validity. Random assignment is used in experiments to assign people to the various conditions of the experiment. Random assignment helps to increase the internal validity of the experiment.

5. According to the APA's guidelines regarding informed consent, research participants should be given a full description of the procedures to be followed, informed about any possible risks of the research, and told that they are free to withdraw from the study at any time without penalty. Researchers are also concerned with a participant's right to privacy, the psychological risk (e.g., emotional stress) to the participant, and the social risk (e.g., whether information about the individual might become known by others and have detrimental effects) to the participant.

Answer Key for Practice Test Essay Questions

As you may have guessed, there is no right or wrong answer to the essay questions in this practice test. That does not mean, however, that all essays are equally good. To get maximum learning benefit from the essay questions, do the following:

- Review each essay a day or two after you wrote it, noting any necessary corrections and any additional support for your points that you can think of.
- Review the section in your textbook that pertains to the topic of each essay. Annotate your essay with any corrections or additional support for your points that you find in the text.
- Spend a few minutes researching the topic of each essay on the Internet. Annotate your essay further with any additional (reliable) information you find.
- Finally, reread each essay with the annotations you have added.

Chapter 3
GENES, ENVIRONMENT AND BEHAVIOR

A. Learning Objectives: *These objectives are expanded from the Focus Questions found in the margins of your textbook. When you have mastered the material in this chapter, you will be able to*:

3.1 Differentiate between genotype and phenotype.

3.2 Describe dominant, recessive, and polygenic influences on phenotype.

3.3 Explain how family, adoption, and twin studies are used to estimate genetic and environmental determinants of behavior.

3.4 Define heritability.

3.5 Contrast the behaviorist and ethological assumptions regarding the development of behavior.

3.6 Discuss the relationship of evolution and culture to learning.

3.7 Explain the impact of heritability on individual differences in intelligence.

3.8 Describe the shared and unshared environmental influences on intelligence.

3.9 Describe the heritability of personality.

3.10 Explain the hypothesized effects of reaction range on the genetic expression of intelligence.

3.11 Describe the ways that genotype can affect environmental influence of behavior.

3.12 Describe how gene modification methods are used to study the causes of behavior.

3.13 Describe the ethical and societal issues that are involved in genetic screening.

3.14 Explain how natural selection produces adaptations.

3.15 Explain the way that brain evolution illustrates the natural selection of biological mechanisms.

3.16 Describe how evolutionary principles have been used to account for diverse cultures.

3.17 Explain how genetically based diseases provide an argument against natural selection.

3.18 Describe how human behavior suggests innate evolved mechanisms.

3.19 Contrast sexual strategies and social structure explanations for mate preferences.

3.20 Explain how evolutionary theory accounts for the universal nature of the Big Five personality traits.

3.21 Describe the fallacies that can arise from misinterpreting evolutionary theory.

B. Chapter Overview

This chapter explores the influence of genes and the environment in shaping the similarities and differences in human behavior. The field of genetics highlights how the particular genes we are born with influence our actions. A distinction is made between a person's genotype, or the specific genetic makeup of the individual, and the phenotype, or the individual's observable characteristics. Genotype is present from conception, but phenotype can be affected both by other genes and by the environment.

The physical material of heredity is the chromosome, which is a molecule of deoxyribonucleic acid (DNA) within the cell, or basic unit of life in the human body. The information of heredity is coded within the genes which are combinations of four chemical bases (referred to as A, T, G, and C) that occur throughout the chromosome. Each gene carries the ATGC codes for manufacturing specific proteins, as well as when and where in the body they will be made. Genetic commands trigger the production of proteins that control body structures and processes.

Genotype (an individual's genetic structure) and phenotype (an individual's outward appearance) are not identical, in part because some genes are dominant and others are recessive. Many characteristics are polygenic, that is, influenced by the interactions of multiple genes. The Human Genome Project has mapped the genetic structure in each of the 23 chromosome pairs in the human body, allowing scientists to explore which genes and combinations of genes underlie various conditions, and how and under what circumstances genes are expressed or remain dormant.

Behavior geneticists study the contributions of genetic and environmental factors to psychological traits and behaviors. Family, adoption, and twin studies are the major research methods used in an attempt to disentangle hereditary and environmental factors. Especially useful is the study of identical (monozygotic) and fraternal (dizygotic) twins who were separated early in life and raised in different environments. These studies suggest that many psychological characteristics have appreciable genetic contributions. Behavior geneticists calculate a heritability coefficient to estimate how much the variation in a particular characteristic *in a group* can be attributed to genetic rather than environmental factors, with the understanding that genetic and environmental factors interact significantly. Behavior geneticists also make an important distinction between shared and unshared environmental influences in their research.

Historically, behaviorists and ethologists have approached the influence of environmental factors in different ways. Behaviorists emphasize the impact of environmental factors in shaping behavior, and they minimize the importance of innate biological differences among species, whereas ethologists focus on the adaptive significance of behavior, that is, how innate behavior patterns influence an organism's chances of survival and reproduction in its natural environment. The perspectives converge in understanding that we come into the world with biologically based abilities to adapt to the environment, and that the environment influences behavior in two fundamental ways. Personal adaptation occurs as we interact with our immediate environment, which shapes our behavior according to the principles of behaviorism. Species adaptation occurs according to the principle of natural selection, whereby biologically based qualities that contribute to survival and reproductive success increase in the population over long periods of time.

Research suggests that intelligence has a strong genetic basis with shared family environment and educational experiences playing an important role. Personality traits also have a genetic component, albeit weaker than that for intelligence, with unshared individual experiences rather than shared family environment as an important determinant of personality. The environment can influence gene expression by affecting where in the genetically determined reaction range an attribute, such as intelligence or personality, is expressed. Genetically based characteristics may also shape a person's environment, or evoke responses from people in the environment, or influence the self-selection of environments.

Gene manipulation allows scientists to duplicate and modify genetic material or, potentially, to repair dysfunctional genes. Techniques include the knockout procedure, whereby a particular function of a gene is eliminated and the effects on behavior are observed, and the knock-in procedure, whereby a new gene is inserted into an animal during the embryonic stage. These procedures promise groundbreaking advances in the treatment of diseases, including psychological disorders, but they also raise momentous ethical and moral issues.

Evolutionary psychologists suggest that human nature reflects the adaptations that have evolved through natural selection to solve problems specific to the human environment. The idea that multiple—even contradictory—behavioral strategies might be adaptive in certain environments is called strategic pluralism. Evolution, as per Darwin's theory, is a change over time in the frequency with which particular genes occur within an interbreeding population according to the principle of natural selection. Such important characteristics include development of the brain as well as genetically based behavioral tendencies. Evolutionary accounts of cultural diversity, gender differences in sexuality and mate preferences, and the universal nature of the Big Five personality traits are among those vigorously debated with proponents of other approaches. Evolutionary psychologists are cautioned to avoid circular reasoning about evolutionary causes and effects, to emphasize that people can override genetically based behavioral tendencies, and to take into account current situational influences in explaining human behavior.

C. Chapter Outline

GENETIC INFLUENCES ON BEHAVIOR
    Chromosomes and Genes
        Dominant, Recessive, and Polygenic Effects
        The Human Genome
        A Genetic Map of the Brain
    Behavior Genetics
        Family, Adoption, and Twin Studies
        Heritability: Estimating Genetic Influence
    In Review
ADAPTING TO THE ENVIRONMENT: THE ROLE OF LEARNING
    How Do We Learn? The Search for Mechanisms
    Why Do We Learn? The Search for Functions
    Learning, Culture, and Evolution
        Shared and Unshared Environments
    In Review
BEHAVIOR GENETICS, INTELLIGENCE, AND PERSONALITY
    Genes, Environment, and Intelligence
        Heritability of Intelligence
        Environmental Determinants
            Shared family environment
            Environmental enrichment and deprivation
            Educational experiences
    Personality Development
        Heritability of Personality
        Environment and Personality Development
    In Review
GENE-ENVIRONMENT INTERACTIONS
    How the Environment Can Influence Gene Expression
    How Genes Can Influence the Environment
    In Review
GENETIC MANIPULATION AND CONTROL
    Applying Psychological Science: Thinking Critically About Genetic Screening
    In Review
EVOLUTION AND BEHAVIOR: INFLUENCES FROM THE DISTANT PAST
    Evolution of Adaptive Mechanisms
        Natural Selection

Chapter 3

        Evolutionary adaptations
        Brain evolution
        Evoked culture
What Do You Think? Natural Selection and Genetic Diseases
Evolution and Human Nature
    Sexuality and Mate Preferences
Research Close Up: Sex Differences in the Ideal Mate: Evolution or Social Roles?
    Evolutionary Approaches to Personality
Beneath the Surface: How *Not* to Think About Evolutionary Theory
In Review

D. Review at a Glance: *Write the term that best fits the blank to review what you learned in this chapter.*

Genetic Influences on Behavior

The field of (1) _____ highlights how the particular genes we are born with influence our actions. A distinction is made between the specific genetic makeup of the individual, known as the (2) _____, and the observable characteristics produced by that genetic endowment, or the person's (3) _____. One's (4) _____ is present from conception, but phenotype can be affected both by (5) _____ _____ and by the (6) _____.

The physical material of heredity is the (7) _____, which is a molecule of deoxyribonucleic acid (DNA) within the human cell. The information of heredity is coded within the (8) _____, which are combinations of four chemical bases (referred to as A, T, G, and C) that occur throughout the chromosome. Each gene carries the ATGC codes for manufacturing specific (9) _____, as well as when and where in the body they will be made.

Some genes are dominant and others are (10) _____. Many characteristics are (11) _____, that is, influenced by the interactions of multiple genes. The Human (12) _____ Project has mapped the genetic structure in each of the (13) _____ pairs of chromosomes in the human body, allowing scientists to explore which genes and combinations of genes underlie various conditions, and how and under what circumstances genes are (14) _____ or remain dormant.

(15) _____ _____ study the contributions of genetic and environmental factors to psychological traits and behaviors. Family, (16) _____, and twin studies are the major research methods used in an attempt to disentangle hereditary and environmental factors. Especially useful is the study of (17) _____ (monozygotic) and fraternal (18) _____) twins who were separated early in life and raised in different environments. These studies suggest that many (19) _____ characteristics have appreciable genetic contributions. Behavior geneticists calculate a (20) _____ coefficient to estimate how much the variation in a particular characteristic *in a* (21) _____ can be attributed to genetic rather than

environmental factors, with the understanding that genetic and environmental factors (22) _____ significantly. Behavior geneticists also make an important distinction between shared and (23) _____ environmental influences in their research.

Adapting to the Environment: The Role of Learning

Historically, behaviorists and ethologists have approached the influence of environmental factors in different ways. (24)_____ emphasize the impact of environmental factors in shaping behavior, and they minimize the importance of innate (25) _____ differences among species, whereas (26) _____ focus on the adaptive significance of behavior, that is, how innate behavior patterns influence an organism's chances of (27) _____ and reproduction in its natural environment. The perspectives converge in understanding that we come into the world with (28) _____ based abilities to (29) _____ to the environment, and that the environment influences behavior in two fundamental ways. (30)_____ adaptation occurs as we interact with our immediate environment, which shapes our behavior according to the principles of (31)_____. Species adaptation occurs according to the principle of (32) _____ _____, whereby biologically based qualities that contribute to survival and (33) _____ success (34) _____ in the population over long periods of time.

Behavior Genetics, Intelligence, and Personality

Research suggests that intelligence has a strong (35) _____ basis, with (36) _____ family environment and educational experiences playing an important role. Personality traits also have a genetic component, albeit (37) _____ than that for intelligence, with (38) _____ individual experiences rather than shared family environment as an important determinant of personality.

Gene-Environment Interactions

The environment can influence gene expression by affecting where in the genetically determined (39) _____ range an attribute such as intelligence or personality is expressed. Genetically based characteristics may also shape a person's environment, or evoke (40) _____ from people in the environment, or influence the self-(41) _____ of environments.

Genetic Manipulation and Control

Gene manipulation allows scientists to duplicate and (42) _____ genetic material or, potentially, to repair dysfunctional genes. Techniques include the (43) _____ procedure, whereby a particular function of a gene is eliminated and the effects on behavior are observed, and the (44) _____-_____ procedure, whereby a new gene is inserted into an animal during the embryonic stage. These procedures promise groundbreaking advances in the treatment of (45) _____, including psychological disorders, but they also raise momentous (46) _____ issues.

Evolution and Behavior: Influences from the Distant Past

Evolutionary psychologists suggest that human nature reflects the (47) _____ that have evolved through natural selection to solve problems specific to the human environment. The idea that multiple—even contradictory—behavioral strategies might be adaptive in certain environments is called (48)_____ pluralism. Evolutionary accounts of cultural diversity, gender differences in (49) _____ preferences, and the universal nature of the (50) _____ _____ personality traits are among those vigorously debated with proponents of other approaches. Evolutionary psychologists are cautioned to avoid (51) _____ reasoning about evolutionary causes and effects, to shun the concept of genetic (52) _____ (the idea that genes have invariant and unavoidable effects that can't be altered), and to take into account current (53) _____ influences in explaining human behavior.

E. Concept Cards

Truly learning a concept means integrating it into the way *you* think about things. To integrate concepts successfully, you must translate the words and examples your text or instructor provides into words and examples that are meaningful to you.

For this exercise, obtain some note cards (3" × 5" or 4" × 6") to make a deck of concept cards. On one side of each card, write the *concept* from the list following (e.g., "adaptations") at the top. Read the textbook definition provided, and then write the definition *in your own words* on the concept card (e.g. for "adaptations," you might write "physical or behavior changes that help people survive in their environment.") Simply imagine that a friend has asked you what the concept means, and write down what you would answer. Writing the definition in your own words requires you to think deeply about its meaning. When next you see your own version of the definition, it will make intuitive sense to you—no translation required.

On the second side of the card, write your own example of the concept. Again, coming up with your own example requires you to think deeply about the application of the concept, and you will more easily understand and remember the example when you study for a test. If you use an example from the text, or from class, make it your own by writing it in your own words. You can always check with your instructor that your example is indeed a good example of the concept.

CONCEPT	Example of the concept in my own words, preferably drawn from my own experience
Definition in my own words	
(side 1 of card)	(side 2 of card)

The following is a list of all the boldface concepts from your textbook, with the author's definition. Write the definition in your own words, together with your own example of the concept, to create a concept card as described above, or write in the space provided.

Genotype: The specific genetic makeup of an individual

Phenotype: The individual's observable characteristics

Chromosome: A double-stranded and tightly coiled molecule of DNA

Genes: The biological units of heredity

Alleles: Alternative forms of genes that produce different characteristics

Dominant gene: A gene which is received from both the mother and father and is most displayed

Recessive gene: A gene which will not show up unless the partner gene inherited from the partner is also recessive

Polygenic transmission: A process whereby a number of gene pairs combine their influences to create a single phenotypic trait

Behavior genetics: A study of how heredity and environment interact to influence psychological characteristics

Family study: A study in which researchers compare relatives to determine if genetic similarity is related to similarity on a particular trait

Adoption study: A study in which people who were adopted early in life are compared on some characteristic with both their biological parents with whom they share genetic endowment, and with their adoptive parents with whom they share no genes

Twin studies: Studies that compare trait similarities in identical and fraternal twins

Heritability statistic: A statistic that estimates the extent to which the differences, or variation, in a specific characteristic within a group of people can be attributed to their differing genes

Adaptive significance: The extent to which a behavior influences an organism's chances of survival and reproduction in its natural environment

Fixed action pattern: An unlearned response automatically triggered by a particular stimulus

Shared environment: An environment or living space shared with others who share and experience many common features

Unshared environment: Environments, living spaces, or experiences which are unique to the individual

Reaction range: The range of possibilities for a genetically influenced trait; the upper and lower limits that a genetic code allows

Knockout procedure: A procedure whereby a particular function of a gene is knocked out or eliminated

Knock-in procedure: A procedure whereby a new gene is inserted into an animal during the embryonic stage, and its impact on behavior is studied

Biologically based mechanisms: Mechanisms that enable us to take in, process, and respond to information, predisposing us to behave, to feel, and even to think in certain ways

Evolution: A change over time in the frequency with which particular genes—and the characteristics they produce—occur within an interbreeding population

Mutations: Random events and accidents in gene reproduction during the division of cells

Natural selection: A process whereby characteristics that increase the likelihood of survival and reproduction within a particular environment will be more likely preserved in the population and therefore will become more common in the species over time

Adaptations: Physical or behavioral changes that allow organisms to meet recurring environmental challenges to their survival thereby increasing their reproductive ability

Evoked culture: A concept in which cultures themselves may be the product of biological mechanisms that evolved to meet specific adaptation challenges faced by specific groups of people in specific places at specific times

Sexual strategies/Parental investment theory: An evolutionary viewpoint which states that mating strategies and preferences reflect inherited tendencies shaped over the ages in response to different types of adaptive problems that men and women faced

Social structure theory: Theory that maintains that men and women display different mating preferences not because nature impels them to do so, but because society guides them into different social roles

Evolutionary personality theory: An approach which looks for the origin of presumably universal personality traits in the adaptive demands of our species' evolutionary history

Strategic pluralism: The idea that multiple—even contradictory—behavioral strategies might be adaptive in certain environments and would therefore be maintained through natural selection

Genetic determinism: The idea that genes have invariant and unavoidable effects that can't be altered

F. What's the Difference? A Concept Card Exercise

An important skill in learning concepts is being able to differentiate among concepts that are similar or related in some way. This skill is particularly relevant for multiple-choice tests, especially if you often find yourself wavering between two answers.

Once you have created your own deck of concept cards, select them two by two, each time answering the question "What's the difference between these two concepts?" You can use the word definitions of the concepts or the examples of the concepts to enhance your mastery of the material. In each case, choose pairs of concepts to compare those that are related or similar or that sound the same or that could in some way be confused. It's much easier to spot the difference between two concepts when you are studying, with the textbook available, rather than considering the question for the first time in a testing situation.

G. Apply What You Know

Describe two scenarios that illustrate ethical/moral dilemmas that may be generated by the process of gene manipulation in humans. How would you handle each dilemma?

Scenario 1:

Ethical/moral dilemma and my approach:

Scenario 2:

Ethical/moral dilemma and my approach:

H. On the Web: *As with any online research, it is important to consider how legitimate a given source is before you rely on the information it presents. Your instructor or Internet adviser may give you some specific guidelines for distinguishing which kinds of Web sites tend to be reputable.*

A. A number of individuals have made notable contributions to the fields of evolution and genetics. Search the Web for more information about some of those listed below to enhance your understanding of the biological foundations of behavior.

Charles Darwin

Gregor Mendel

James Watson and Francis Crick

Rosalind Franklin

Francis Collins

Craig Venter

B. Take a look at the concept cards you have created for this chapter, or the key concepts listed in section E. In the space provided, make a list of any whose definitions or associations you are not yet confident of, and any you'd like to learn more about. Try entering the terms on your list into your search engine. Make notes of any helpful information you find.

Key Concept/Information Found

C. Search the internet for information on the Human Genome Project. Learn the story of the race to sequence the human genome. Find out the current state of our knowledge about the human genome, and the related scientific and public-policy controversies that have ensued. List the controversies you have uncovered.

I. Analyze This: *Chapter 1 of your textbook begins by presenting these four basic steps in the critical thinking process:*
- *"What exactly are you asking me to believe?"*
- *"How do you know? What is the evidence?"*
- *"Are there other possible explanations?"*
- *"What is the most reasonable conclusion?"*

You might picture this as a four-step analysis to help you decide whether to accept a given theory or assertion. Now it's your turn to put your textbook to this test.

Review the section in Chapter 3 of your textbook under the heading "Family, Adoption, and Twin Studies." There you will find a discussion of the ways in which these studies are useful in behavior genetics. If someone told you that adoption studies of nontwins are more conclusive than studies of twins raised together, would you agree? Analyze and write that assertion in the area provided. When you have finished, consider using this four-step analysis to evaluate other assertions you encounter.

"What exactly are you asking me to believe?"

"How do you know? What is the evidence?"

"Are there other possible explanations?"

"What is the most reasonable conclusion?"

J. Practice Test

Multiple-Choice Items: *Write the letter corresponding to your answer in the space to the left of each item.*

_____ 1. The principle stating that a biologically based characteristic that contributes to survival will increase in a population over time because those who lack the characteristic are less likely to pass on their genes is known as _____.

a. a genetically based disease
   b. behavior genetics
   c. inheritance
   d. natural selection

_____ 2. Evolutionary psychologists must use critical thinking to avoid _____ reasoning
   a. genetic
   b. behavioral
   c. circular
   d. environmental

_____ 3. Hereditary potential is carried within the _____ portion of the 23 pairs of _____.
   a. dominant; twins
   b. evolutionary; chromosomes
   c. DNA; genes
   d. DNA; chromosomes

_____ 4. Both of Perry's parents have blue eyes, and Perry himself also has the gene for blue eyes, yet Perry's eyes are brown. This indicates that the gene for blue eyes is _____.
   a. polygenic
   b. phenotypic
   c. recessive
   d. dominant

_____ 5. Behavior geneticists focus on the potential role of _____ factors in accounting for _____ among people.
   a. environmental; similarities
   b. environmental; differences
   c. genetic; similarities
   d. genetic; differences

_____ 6. The probability of a child sharing any particular gene with his or her parents is _____.
   a. .05
   b. .25
   c. .50
   d. 1.0

_____ 7. Identical twins are known as _____.
   a. Dizygotic, because they developed from two zygotes
   b. Monozygotic, because they developed from a single zygote
   c. Monozygotic, because each twin has only one zygote
   d. genotypic

_____ 8. A person's genotype refers to _____.

Chapter 3   77

        a. an individual's observable characteristics
        b. an individual's genetic makeup
        c. the proteins that an individual's DNA manufactures
        d. the heritability of an individual's observable characteristics

_____ 9. An individual's phenotype ____.
        a. is present from conception
        b. can be affected by the environment
        c. will be inherited by the person's children
        d. is a molecule of DNA within the cell

_____ 10. Genetic commands trigger the production of ____ that control(s) body structures and processes.
        a. cells
        b. ATCG codes
        c. DNA
        d. proteins

_____ 11. If a characteristic or disorder is polygenic, ____.
        a. it results from the action of a specific gene
        b. it results from the influence of a specific environmental factor
        c. it is influenced by the interactions of multiple genes
        d. it is impossible to say whether it results from genetic or environmental influences

_____ 12. Adoption studies compare adopted people on a particular characteristic with ____ on that characteristic.
        a. their adoptive parents and adoptive siblings
        b. their biological parents and biological siblings
        c. their adoptive parents and their biological parents
        d. their adoptive siblings and unrelated people of the same age as themselves

_____ 13. Behavior geneticists calculate ____ to estimate how much a particular characteristic in a group can be attributed to genetic rather than environmental factors.
        a. a heritability coefficient
        b. the recessive potential
        c. the reaction range
        d. the dominant potential

_____ 14. The heritability coefficient refers to the relative contribution of genetic and environmental factors to variability within ____.
        a. a particular group of people
        b. a particular individual
        c. a particular family

d. human beings in general

_____ 15. Ethologists focus on the importance of _____
   a. personal adaptation to the specific conditions of an individual's life
   b. shared environment in determining human behavior
   c. unshared environmental factors in shaping animal behavior
   d. innate biological differences among species that influence their behavior

_____ 16. Research suggests that intelligence has a _____ genetic basis, with _____ family environment and educational experiences also playing an important role.
   a. strong: shared
   b. weak; shared
   c. strong; unshared
   d. weak; unshared

_____ 17. The environment can influence gene expression by_____.
   a. evoking responses from people in the environment
   b. influencing the self-selection of environments
   c. affecting where in the reaction range an attribute is expressed
   d. shaping a person's environment

_____ 18. Personality traits have a genetic component that is _____.
   a. produced by the shared environment of the individual
   b. due primarily to recessive rather than dominant genes
   c. weaker than that of intelligence
   d. equivalent to that of intelligence

_____ 19. The knockout procedure is _____.
   a. a statistical procedure to evaluate the heritability coefficient
   b. a technique of genetic modification
   c. a behavioral strategy of natural selection
   d. a characteristic of inbreeding populations

_____ 20. A new gene is inserted into an animal during the embryonic stage. This is known as _____.
   a. the reaction range
   b. genetic expression
   c. the knock-in procedure
   d. species adaptation

_____ 21. Strategic pluralism is the idea that _____.
   a. multiple behaviors may be adaptive in certain environments
   b. the interaction of multiple genes is required to influence a person's phenotype
   c. scientists may be able to repair dysfunctional genes in the future

d. people often self-select their environments

_____ 22. The concept of _____ suggests that cultures themselves may be the product of biological mechanisms that evolved to meet specific adaptation challenges faced by specific groups of people in specific places at specific times
   a. evoked culture
   b. strategic pluralism
   c. the reaction range
   d. shared environment

_____ 23. Maria believes that she is doomed to develop depression because of the genes she has inherited from her mother, since genes have invariant effects that can't be altered. Maria apparently believes in _____.
   a. genetic determinism
   b. circular reasoning
   c. ethology
   d. evolutionary personality theory

_____ 24. Social structure theory maintains that men and women display different mating preferences _____.
   a. because nature impels them to do so
   b. because society guides them into different social roles
   c. because men and women face different adaptive challenges to survival
   d. because promiscuous women help men ensure that their genes will be passed on

_____ 25. Accidents in gene reproduction during the division of cells create _____.
   a. dominant genes
   b. polygenic transmission
   c. mutations
   d. adaptations

_____ 26. A dominant gene is received from _____ and is most displayed.
   a. both the mother and father
   b. the parent of the same gender as the child
   c. the parent of the opposite gender of the child
   d. the father alone

_____ 27. Genetically based diseases provide an argument against natural selection because _____.
   a. the genes of those with genetically based diseases should have died out in the population according to the principle of natural selection
   b. the genes of those with genetically based diseases should have increased in the population according to the principle of natural selection
   c. the majority of diseases today are genetically based
   d. the majority of diseases today are environmentally based

_____ 28. Evolutionary psychologists tend to underemphasize ___ in explaining human behavior.
   a. behavioral adaptations
   b. heritability coefficients
   c. genetic mutations
   d. current situational influences

_____ 29. An important determinant of personality, aside from the genetic component, is ____.
   a. shared family environment
   b. unshared individual experiences
   c. general level of intelligence in the family
   d. shared individual experiences

_____ 30. Ethologists refer to an unlearned response that is automatically triggered by a particular environmental stimulus as a ____.
   a. tabula rasa
   b. fixed action pattern
   c. knock-in process
   d. reaction range

True/False Items: *Write T or F in the space provided to the left of each item.*

_____ 1. According to Darwin's theory of evolution, a trait persists in a species when individuals possessing that trait kill off individuals who lack it thereby dominating the gene pool.

_____ 2. The knock-in procedure involves inserting a new gene into an animal during the embryonic stage.

_____ 3. Genetic commands trigger the production of chromosomes that control body structures and processes.

_____ 4. A characteristic that is polygenic is influenced by the interactions of multiple genes.

_____ 5. An individual's genetic structure is called their phenotype.

_____ 6. Behavior geneticists study the circumstances under which behavior is monozygotic or dizygotic.

_____ 7. A person's heritability coefficient estimates the relative influence of genetic and environmental factors on the individual's behavior.

_____ 8. Behaviorists minimize the importance of innate biological differences among species.

_____ 9. Research suggests that intelligence has a strong genetic basis.

_____ 10. The idea that multiple behavioral strategies might be adaptive in certain environments is called strategic pluralism.

Short-Answer Questions

1. Explain what psychology has to do with evolution.

2. Describe some ways in which a person's genetic inheritance and the environment in which they live can interact and mutually influence each other.

3. What do we mean by gene manipulation? Describe two specific techniques of gene manipulation.

Essay Questions

1. Describe the behavioral tendencies of two people you know who are closely related to each other. (One of the people may be you, if you wish.) Do these two people have any striking behavioral similarities? Any striking behavioral differences? Now choose two people who are *not* related to each other, and describe *their* behavioral tendencies. What, if anything, do your observations of their behavioral tendencies suggest about genetic influences on behavior?

2. If you knew that you or your spouse carried a genetically linked disease, how might that knowledge influence your decisions about having children? (If you are already sure, regardless of any hereditary conditions, that you do not intend to have any children, then write this essay about a hypothetical couple who may be considering starting a family.)

Answer Keys

Answer Key for Review at a Glance

1. genetics
2. genotype
3. phenotype
4. genotype
5. other genes
6. environment
7. chromosome
8. genes
9. proteins
10. recessive
11. polygenic
12. Genome
13. 23
14. expressed
15. Behavioral geneticists
16. adoption
17. identical
18. dizygotic
19. psychological
20. heritability
21. group
22. interact
23. unshared
24. Behaviorists
25. biological
26. ethologists
27. survival
28. biologically
29. adapt
30. Personal
31. behaviorism
32. natural selection
33. reproductive
34. increase
35. genetic
36. shared
37. weaker
38. unshared
39. reaction
40. responses
41. selection
42. modify
43. knockout
44. knock-in
45. diseases
46. ethical
47. adaptations
48. strategic
49. mate
50. Big Five
51. circular
52. determinism
53. situational

Answer Key for Practice Test Multiple-Choice Items

1. d
2. c
3. d
4. c

16. a
17. c
18. c
19. b

5. d	20. c
6. c	21. a
7. b	22. a
8. b	23. a
9. b	24. b
10. d	25. c
11. c	26. a
12. c	27. a
13. a	28. d
14. a	29. b
15. d	30. b

Answer Key for Practice Test True/False Items

1. F	6. F
2. T	7. F
3. F	8. T
4. T	9. T
5. F	10. T

Answer Key for Practice Test Short-Answer Questions

1. Psychology is the study of thinking and behavior, and genetic factors influence many of the ways in which we think and behave. According to the principle of natural selection, biologically based characteristics that contribute to survival and reproductive success increase in the population over long periods of time because those who lack these characteristics are less likely to reproduce successfully and hence to pass on their genes. Such important characteristics include genetically based behavioral tendencies. An understanding of how various traits may have evolved can help psychologists to understand how the brain and the rest of the nervous system function and influence our thinking and behavior.

2. The environment can influence how genes express themselves, even prenatally, such as when the mother's drug use or malnutrition retards gene-directed brain development. Enriched or impoverished environments can affect the unfolding development of the individual, for example, by influencing where in the genetically determined reaction range an attribute such as intelligence or personality is expressed. Genetically based characteristics may also shape a person's environment, such as when highly intelligent parents provide a stimulating environment for their children. Genetically based characteristics may evoke responses from people in the environment, such as social attention for an exceptionally attractive individual, and they may influence the self-selection of environments, for example, when an introverted individual shuns social situations.

3. Gene manipulation occurs when scientists duplicate and modify genetic material, in some cases even transplanting genes from one species to another. Techniques include the knockout procedure, whereby a particular function of a gene is eliminated and the effects on behavior are observed, and the knock-in procedure, whereby a new gene is inserted into an animal during the embryonic stage.

Answer Key for Practice Test Essay Questions

As you may have guessed, there is no right or wrong answer to the essay questions in this practice test. That does not mean, however, that all essays are equally good. To get maximum learning benefit from the essay questions, do the following:

- Review each essay a day or two after you wrote it, noting any necessary corrections and any additional support for your points that you can think of.
- Review the section in your textbook that pertains to the topic of each essay. Annotate your essay with any corrections or additional support for your points that you find in the text.
- Spend a few minutes researching the topic of each essay on the Internet. Annotate your essay further with any additional (reliable) information you find.
- Finally, reread each essay with the annotations you have added.

Chapter 4
THE BRAIN AND BEHAVIOR

A. Learning Objectives: *These objectives are expanded from the Focus Questions found in the margins of your textbook. When you have mastered the material in this chapter, you will be able to:*

4.1 Describe the functions of the three main parts of the neuron.

4.2 Discuss the chemical actions created by the neuron's resting and action potential.

4.3 Explain the importance of the myelin sheath.

4.4 Describe five important steps in neurotransmitter function.

4.5 Describe the roles played by acetylcholine and the consequences that occur when its functioning is disrupted.

4.6 Explain the agonist and antagonist functions that underlie the neural and behavioral effects of psychoactive drugs.

4.7 Discuss the three major types of neurons and their functions.

4.8 Explain the primary functions of the two divisions of the peripheral nervous system.

4.9 Describe the two main structures in the central nervous system.

4.10 Describe four methods used to study brain-behavior relations.

4.11 Contrast the different uses for CAT scans, PET scans and MRI procedures.

4.12 Explain the functions of the medulla, the pons, and the cerebellum.

4.13 Describe the roles played by the ascending and descending reticular formation.

4.14 Describe the structural characteristics of the thalamus and the hypothalamus.

4.15 Discuss the role of the hippocampus and amygdala in psychological function.

4.16 Describe the location and function of the four lobes of the brain.

4.17 Explain how the Wernicke's and Broca areas are involved in speech.

4.18 Describe the role of the frontal cortex in higher mental functions.

4.19 Define hemispheric lateralization, and discuss what functions are located in the left versus right hemispheres.

4.20 Describe the results of Sperry's split brain research.

4.21 Explain how age, environment, and behavior play a role in neural plasticity.

B. Chapter Overview

This chapter explores how the functioning of our neural, endocrine, and immune systems form the biological foundations of our behavior.

The brain is our most important physical organ from a psychological point of view. Specialized cells called neurons are the building blocks of our brain and nervous system. Each neuron has three main parts: dendrites, which collect information from neighboring neurons and send it on to the cell body; the cell body, which contains the biochemical structures that keep the neuron alive; and the axon, which conducts electrical impulses away from the cell body to other neurons, muscles, and glands. Glial cells support neurons by holding them in place, manufacturing nutrient chemicals, and absorbing toxins and waste materials. Glial cells also guide newly formed neurons to their place in the brain during prenatal development.

Neurons are like tiny batteries at rest. When stimulated, they generate electricity to create a nerve impulse and also release chemicals that allow them to communicate with other neurons and with muscles and glands. The nerve impulse, or action potential, begins when positively charged sodium ions flood into the cell creating a sudden reversal of charge in the neuron's membrane called depolarization. A smaller shift in the cell membrane's electrical potential is called a graded potential. If the graded potential is large enough to reach the action-potential threshold, an action potential occurs. Either an action potential occurs or it does not according to the all-or-none law. Immediately after an impulse passes any point on the axon, an interlude called a refractory period occurs during which another action potential cannot occur. Some axons in the brain and spinal cord are covered by the tube-like myelin sheath, a fatty insulating substance that enhances neural transmission.

Neurons communicate with one another through chemical transmission at the synapse. The synapse is a tiny gap between the axon terminal of one neuron and a dendrite of another neuron. Chemical substances called neurotransmitters, which are stored in synaptic vesicles at the end of the axon, carry messages across the synapse and bind to receptor sites on the receiving neuron. Receptor sites are customized for specific neurotransmitters in a lock-and-key fashion. Once a neurotransmitter molecule binds to its receptor, it may have an excitatory or an inhibitory effect on the receiving neuron which may also receive messages from many other neurons. If, in aggregate, the excitatory threshold for an action potential is reached in the receiving neuron, then the nerve impulse is transmitted, but if the graded potential is not great enough, then the neural impulse is inhibited. The nervous system is characterized by a delicate balance of neural excitation and inhibition.

Neurotransmitters are deactivated after binding to a receptor site. One method of deactivation is reuptake in which the transmitter molecules are taken back into the presynaptic neuron. Neurotransmitters may also be broken down by other chemicals in the synapse. There are many types of neurotransmitters, including acetylcholine (Ach), which is involved in muscle activity and memory and is an important factor in Alzheimer's disease. Most neurotransmitters affect only specific neurons that have special receptors for them, but some neurotransmitters, called neuromodulators, have a more widespread and general influence on the sensitivity of large numbers of neurons.

Psychoactive drugs produce alterations in consciousness, emotion, and behavior by influencing the activity of neurotransmitters. Various drugs function as agonists (increasing the activity of a neurotransmitter) or antagonists (decreasing neurotransmitter activity).

There are three major types of neurons in the nervous system. Sensory neurons input messages from the sense organs to the spinal cord and brain, motor neurons carry impulses from the brain and spinal cord to the muscles and organs, and interneurons perform connective or associative functions within the nervous system. The brain and spinal cord comprise the central nervous system (CNS). The peripheral nervous system (PNS) contains all of the neural structures that lie outside of the brain and spinal cord.

The PNS is divided into two systems. The somatic nervous system consists of sensory and motor neurons, whereas the autonomic nervous system regulates the body's glands and involuntary functions such as breathing, circulation, and digestion. The autonomic nervous system, in turn, is subdivided into the sympathetic and parasympathetic branches. The sympathetic branch activates or arouses bodily organs, and the parasympathetic branch slows down bodily processes. The sympathetic and parasympathetic systems work together to maintain homeostasis, a carefully balanced or constant internal state. Most nerves enter and leave the CNS via the spinal cord. Some simple stimulus-response sequences, such as pulling away from a hot stove, can be triggered at the level of the spinal cord, typically don't involve the brain, and are known as spinal reflexes.

Psychologists use a number of methods to study the brain. Neuropsychological tests measure verbal and nonverbal behaviors that are known to be affected by brain damage. Researchers may destroy neurons under controlled conditions or stimulate them with electrical current or with chemicals. The activity of large groups of neurons is often studied via an electroencephalogram (EEG). The newest tools of discovery involve brain imaging. Computerized axial tomography (CT or CAT) scans use X-ray technology to study brain structures. Pictures of brain *activity* involve the use of positron emission tomography (PET) scans. A technique to measure both brain structures and functions is called magnetic resonance imaging (MRI); functional MRI (fMRI) yields snapshots of brain activity taken less than a second apart.

The brain historically has been divided into three main divisions: the hindbrain, the midbrain, and the forebrain. The hindbrain, the most primitive area, consists of the brain stem and cerebellum. The brain stem, containing the medulla and the pons, is involved in life support. The medulla plays a major role in vital body functions such as heart rate and respiration. The pons is a bridge carrying nerve impulses between higher and lower levels of the nervous system. The cerebellum is concerned primarily with muscular coordination. The midbrain, lying just above the hindbrain, is an important relay center for the visual and auditory systems. Within the midbrain is the reticular formation which is involved in brain arousal, sleep, and attention.

The forebrain's size and complexity distinguish humans from lower animals. An important sensory relay station in the forebrain is the thalamus, and the hypothalamus plays a major role in motivational and emotional behavior. The limbic system helps to coordinate memory, emotion, and motivational urges. Within the limbic system are the hippocampus, which is involved in the formation and storage of memories, and the amygdala, which is linked to aggression and fear.

The outermost layer of the brain, constituting 80 percent of human brain tissue, is the cerebral cortex. Each hemisphere of the cortex is divided into the frontal, parietal, occipital, and temporal lobes, each of which is associated with particular sensory and motor functions. Lying at the rear of the frontal lobe and adjacent to the central fissure is the motor cortex which is involved in controlling muscles. The somatic sensory cortex receives sensory input related to touch, balance, and body movements. Two specific speech areas are also located in the cortex: Wernicke's area, which is involved in understanding speech, and Broca's area, which is involved in producing speech. The association cortex is involved in the highest levels of mental functions. People who suffer from agnosia, the inability to identify familiar objects, often have suffered damage to their association cortex. The frontal lobe is far more developed in humans than in other animals. This area is involved in emotional experience and also appears to be the site of distinctively human qualities such as self-awareness, planning, initiative, and responsibility. The prefrontal cortex may be the seat of executive functions such as goal setting, judgment, and planning that allow people to direct their behavior in an adaptive fashion..

The brain is also divided into two hemispheres: the left and the right. The location of a function primarily in a single hemisphere is known as lateralization. Some differences in cognitive and emotional functions have been found. The left hemisphere is relatively more active when positive emotions are being experienced, whereas the right hemisphere tends to be more active during the experience of negative emotions such as sadness and anger. The corpus callosum is a neural bridge that helps the two hemispheres communicate and work together. Split-brain research explores the relative functions of the hemispheres when the corpus callosum, and hence communication between the two hemispheres, is cut. Split-brain research suggests that the left hemisphere tends to be more involved with language and mathematical abilities, and the right hemisphere is relatively more specialized for spatial abilities.

The ability of neurons to change in structure and function is known as neural plasticity. Brain development is genetically programmed but can be powerfully affected by the environment in which we develop particularly early in life and even including while in the womb. Each individual's brain changes and adapts as it is molded by the person's life experiences. There are often sensitive periods during which environmental factors have their greatest (or only) effects on plasticity.

A person's ability to recover from brain damage depends on several factors but is generally greatest early in life and declines with age. When neurons die, surviving neurons can sprout enlarged dendritic networks and extend axons to form new synapses. Neurons can also increase the amount of neurotransmitter substance they release and the number of receptors on postsynaptic neurons so that they are more sensitive to stimulation. Recent findings suggest that the brains of mature primates and humans are capable of producing new neurons (neurogenesis). Current advances in the treatment of neurological disorders include experiments on neuron regeneration and the injection of neural stem cells into the brain, where they find and replace diseased or dead neurons.

The endocrine system consists of numerous glands distributed throughout the body. The system conveys information via hormones, which are chemical messengers secreted by the glands into the bloodstream. The adrenal glands secrete a variety of hormones including stress hormones, which mobilize the body's immune system. When foreign substances, known as antigens, invade the body, the immune system produces antibodies to destroy them. Recent research suggests that the brain, the immune system, and the endocrine system all communicate with and influence one another. These studies have stimulated further investigation of the interaction of biological, psychological, and environmental influences on the immune system.

C. Chapter Outline

NEURONS
    The Electrical Activity of Neurons
        Nerve Impulses: The Action Potential
            It's All or Nothing
            The Myelin Sheath
HOW NEURONS COMMUNICATE: SYNAPTIC TRANSMISSION
    Neurotransmitters
    Specialized Neurotransmitter Systems
    Applying Psychological Science: Understanding How Drugs Affect Your Brain
    In Review
THE NERVOUS SYSTEM
    The Peripheral Nervous System

　　　　The Somatic Nervous System
　　　　The Autonomic Nervous System
　　The Central Nervous System
　　　　The Spinal Cord
　　　　The Brain
　　　　Unlocking the Secrets of the Brain
　　　　　　Neuropsychological Tests
　　　　　　Destruction and Stimulation Techniques
　　　　　　Electrical Recording
　　　　　　Brain Imaging
　In Review
THE HIERARCHICAL BRAIN: STRUCTURES AND BEHAVIORAL FUNCTIONS
　　The Hindbrain
　　　　The Brain Stem: Life-Support Systems
　　　　The Cerebellum: Motor-Coordination Center
　　The Midbrain
　　　　The Reticular Formation: The Brain's Gatekeeper
　　The Forebrain
　　　　The Thalamus: The Brain's Sensory Switchboard
　　　　The Hypothalamus: Motivation and Emotion
　　　　The Limbic System: Memory, Emotion, and Goal-Directed Behavior
　　　　The Cerebral Cortex: Crown of the Brain
　　　　　　The Motor Cortex
　　　　　　The Sensory Cortex
　　　　　　Speech Comprehension and Production
　　　　　　Association Cortex
　　　　　　The Frontal Lobes: The Human Difference
　Research Close-Up: Inside the Brain of a Killer
HEMISPHERIC LATERALIZATION: THE LEFT AND RIGHT BRAINS
　　The Split Brain: Dividing the Hemispheres
　　What Do You Think? Two Minds in One Brain?
　　In Review
PLASTICITY IN THE BRAIN: THE ROLE OF EXPERIENCE AND THE RECOVERY OF FUNCTION
　　How Experience Influences Brain Development
　　Healing the Nervous System
　　Beneath The Surface: Do We Really Use Only Ten Percent of Our Brain Capacity?
　　In Review
INTERACTIONS WITH THE ENDOCRINE AND IMMUNE SYSTEMS
　　Interactions with the Endocrine System
　　Interactions Involving the Immune System
　　In Review

D. Review at a Glance: *Write the term that best fits the blank to review what you learned in this chapter.*

Neurons

Specialized cells called (1) _____ are the building blocks of the nervous system. Each neuron has three main parts. The (2) _____ _____ contains the biochemical structures that keep the neuron alive, and the genetic information that controls cell development and function is in its nucleus. (3)_____ collect information from neighboring neurons and send it on to the cell body. The part of the neuron that conducts electrical impulses away from the cell body to other neurons, muscles, and glands is called the (4)_____. Cells known as (5) _____ _____ support neurons by guiding their development, holding them in place, manufacturing nutrient chemicals, and absorbing toxins and waste materials.

How Neurons Communicate: Synaptic Transmission

Neurons are like tiny (6) _____ at rest. When stimulated they generate electricity to create a nerve impulse and also release chemicals that allow them to communicate with other neurons and with muscles and glands. The nerve impulse, or (7) _____ _____, begins when positively charged (8) _____ ions flood into the cell, creating a sudden reversal of charge in the neuron's membrane, called (9) _____. A smaller shift in the cell membrane's electrical potential is called a (10) _____ potential. If the graded potential is large enough to reach the (11) _____-_____ threshold, an action potential occurs. Either an action potential occurs or it does not, according to the (12) _____-_____-_____ _____law. Immediately after an impulse passes any point on the axon, an interlude called a (13) _____ period occurs, during which another action potential cannot occur. A tube-like fatty substance covering some axons in the brain and spinal cord is the (14) _____ _____, which (15) _____ neural transmission. Neurons communicate with one another through (16) _____ transmission at the synapse. The synapse is a tiny (17) _____ between the axon terminal of one neuron and a (18) _____ of another neuron. Chemical substances called (19) _____ carry messages across the synapse and bind to (20) _____ _____. Once a neurotransmitter molecule binds to its receptor, it continues to activate or inhibit the neuron until deactivation occurs. One method of deactivation is (21) _____, in which the transmitter molecules are taken back into the presynaptic neuron. There are many types of neurotransmitters. One involved in memory and muscle activity, which also has some significance for Alzheimer's disease, is (22) _____. Psychoactive drugs produce alterations in consciousness, emotion, and behavior by influencing the activity of (23) _____. A substance that increases the activity of a neurotransmitter is known as a(n) (24)_____, whereas one that decreases neurotransmitter activity is a(n) (25)_____.

The Nervous System

There are three major types of neurons in the nervous system. (26)_____ neurons input messages from the sense organs to the spinal cord and brain, (27)_____ neurons carry impulses from the brain and spinal cord to the muscles and organs, and (28)_____ perform connective or associative functions within the nervous system. The division of the nervous system containing the brain and spinal cord is called the (29) _____ nervous system. The (30) _____ nervous system contains all the neural structures that lie outside of the brain and spinal cord. The PNS is divided into two systems. The (31) _____ nervous system consists of sensory and motor neurons, whereas the (32) _____ nervous system regulates the body's glands and involuntary functions such as breathing, circulation, and digestion. The autonomic nervous system consists of two branches. The (33) _____ branch activates or arouses bodily organs; conversely, the (34) _____ branch slows down body processes. Most nerves enter and leave the CNS via the spinal cord. Some simple stimulus-response sequences, such as pulling away from a hot stove, typically don't involve the brain and are known as (35)_____ _____.

Psychologists use a variety of methods to study the brain. (36)_____ tests measure verbal and nonverbal behaviors that are known to be affected by brain damage. Sometimes researchers destroy neurons under controlled conditions or stimulate them with electrical (37) _____ or with chemicals. The newest tools of discovery involve brain imaging. A(n) (38)_____ facilitates studying the activity of large groups of neurons. An X-ray technology used to study brain structures is called (39) _____ _____ _____. Pictures of brain *activity* involve the use of (40) _____ _____ _____. A technique to measure both brain structures and function is called (41) _____ _____ _____. This technique has been expanded to allow sequences of images taken less than a second apart, known as (42) _____ MRI.

The Hierarchical Brain: Structures and Behavioral Functions

The brain's three main divisions begin with the hindbrain, consisting of the brain stem and cerebellum. The brain stem is involved in (43) _____ _____. A structure in it that plays a major role in vital body functions, such as heart rate and respiration, is the (44)_____. The (45) _____ is a bridge carrying nerve impulses between higher and lower levels of the nervous system. The cerebellum is concerned primarily with (46) _____ _____. An important relay center for the visual and auditory systems is contained in the (47) _____. Within the midbrain is the (48) _____ _____, involved in brain arousal, sleep, and attention.

The size and complexity of the (49) _____ separates humans from lower animals. An important sensory relay station in the forebrain is the (50) _____; located beneath it, the (51) _____ plays a major role in motivational and emotional behavior. The (52) _____ system helps to coordinate behaviors needed to satisfy emotional and motivational urges. Within the limbic system are the (53) _____, which is involved in the formation and storage of memories, and the (54) _____, which is linked to aggression and fear.

The outermost layer of the brain is called the (55) _____. Each hemisphere of the cortex is divided into four lobes: the frontal, (56) _____, (57) _____, and (58) _____ lobes, each of which is associated with particular sensory and motor functions. Lying at the rear of the frontal lobe is the (59) _____ cortex, which is involved in controlling muscles. The (60) _____ sensory cortex receives sensory input related to touch, balance, and body movements. Two specific speech areas are also located in the cortex. (61)_____ area is involved in understanding speech, whereas (62)_____ area is involved in producing speech. People who have (63) _____, the inability to identify familiar objects, often have suffered damage to their association cortex. The (64) _____ lobe is far more developed in humans than other animals, and appears to be the site of distinctively human qualities, such as self-awareness, planning, initiative, and responsibility. The (65) _____ cortex may be the seat of (66) _____ functions, such as goal setting, judgment, and planning.

Hemispheric Lateralization: The Left and Right Brains

The brain is also divided into two hemispheres: the left and the right. The location of a function primarily in one hemisphere is known as (67) _____. The left hemisphere is relatively more active when (68) _____ emotions are being experienced, whereas the (69) _____ hemisphere tends to be more active during the experience of (70) _____ emotions, such as sadness and anger. The (71) _____ is a neural bridge that helps the two hemispheres communicate and work together. Split-brain research explores the relative functions of the hemispheres when the corpus callosum, and hence communication between the two hemispheres, is cut. Split-brain research suggests that the (72) _____ hemisphere tends to be more involved with language and mathematical abilities, and the (73) _____ hemisphere is relatively more specialized for (74) _____ abilities.

Plasticity in the Brain: The Role of Experience and the Recovery of Function

The ability of neurons to change in structure and function is known as (75) _____. Brain development is (76) _____ programmed, but each individual's brain changes and adapts as it is molded by the person's life experiences, particularly (77)_____ in life. When neurons die, surviving neurons can sprout enlarged (78) _____ networks and extend axons to form new (79) _____. Neurons can also increase the amount of (80) _____ substance they release, as well as the number of receptors on post-synaptic neurons, so they are more (81) _____ to stimulation. Recent findings suggest that the human brain is capable of producing new neurons, a process called (82) _____. Current advances in the treatment of neurological disorders include experiments on neuron regeneration and the injection of neural (83) _____ into the brain, where they find and replace diseased or dead neurons.

Interactions with the Endocrine and Immune Systems

The (84) _____ system consists of numerous glands distributed throughout the body. The system conveys information via (85) _____, which are chemical messengers secreted by the glands into the bloodstream. The (86) _____ glands secrete stress hormones, which mobilize the body's immune system. When foreign substances known as (87) _____ invade the body, the immune system produces antibodies to destroy them. Recent research suggests that the (88) _____, the immune system, and the (89) _____ system all communicate with and influence one another.

E. Concept Cards

Truly learning a concept means integrating it into the way *you* think about things. To integrate concepts successfully, you must translate the words and examples your text or instructor provides into words and examples that are meaningful to you.

For this exercise, obtain some note cards (3" × 5" or 4" × 6") to make a deck of concept cards. On one side of each card, write the *concept* from the list provided (e.g., "adaptations") at the top. Read the textbook definition provided, and then write the definition *in your own words* on the concept card (e.g. for "adaptations," you might write "physical or behavior changes that help people survive in their environment.") Simply imagine that a friend has asked you what the concept means, and write down what you would answer. Writing the definition in your own words requires you to think deeply about its meaning. When next you see your own version of the definition, it will make intuitive sense to you—no translation required.

On the second side of the card, write your own example of the concept. Again, coming up with your own example requires you to think deeply about the application of the concept, and you will more easily understand and remember the example when you study for a test. If you use an example from the text, or from class, make it your own by writing it in your own words. You can always check with your instructor that your example is indeed a good example of the concept.

CONCEPT	Example of the concept in my own words, preferably drawn from my own experience
Definition in my own words	
(side 1 of card)	(side 2 of card)

The following is a list of all the boldface concepts from your textbook with the author's definition. Write the definition in your own words, together with your own example of the concept, to create a concept card as described earlier, or write in the space provided.

Neurons: The basic building blocks of the nervous system

Dendrites: Specialized receiving units, like antennae, that collect messages from neighboring neurons and send them on to the cell body

Axon: A part of the neuron that conducts electrical impulses away from the cell body to other neurons, glands, or muscles

Resting potential: The voltage differential between the inside and outside of a neuron (about −70 mV) when the neuron is at rest; the interior is negatively charged compared to the exterior of the cell and is said to be polarized

Action potential: A nerve impulse resulting from an electrical shift from −70 mV to +40 mV in the voltage differential between the inside and outside of a neuron or depolarization of an axon's cell membrane

Absolute refractory period: A period of time when the membrane is not excitable and cannot discharge another impulse

All-or-none law: The law stating that action potentials occur at a uniform and maximum intensity, or they do not occur at all

Graded potentials: Changes in the negative resting potential that do not reach the −50 mV action-potential threshold

Myelin sheath: A whitish, fatty insulation layer derived from glial cells during development

Synaptic space: A tiny gap between the axon terminal and the next neuron

Neurotransmitters: Chemical substances that carry messages across the synaptic gap to other neurons, muscles, or glands

Synaptic vesicles: Chambers within the axon terminals

Receptor sites: Large protein molecules embedded in the receiving neuron's cell membrane

Reuptake: A deactivation mechanism in which the transmitter molecules are taken back into the presynaptic axon terminal

Acetylcholine (ACh): A neurotransmitter involved in muscle activity and memory

Neuromodulators: Neurotransmitters that have a more widespread and generalized influence on synaptic transmission

Psychoactive drugs: Chemicals that produce alterations in consciousness, emotion, and behavior

Agonist: A drug that increases the activity of a neurotransmitter

Antagonist: A drug that inhibits or decreases the action of a neurotransmitter

Sensory neurons: Neurons that carry input messages from the sense organs to the spinal cord and brain

Motor neurons: Neurons that transmit output impulses from the brain and spinal cord to the body's muscles and organs

Interneurons: Neurons that perform connective or associative functions within the nervous system

Peripheral nervous system: All the neural structures that lie outside of the brain and spinal cord

Somatic nervous system: Sensory neurons that are specialized to transmit messages from the eyes, ears, and other sensory receptors, and motor neurons that send messages from the brain and spinal cord to the muscles that control our voluntary movement

Autonomic nervous system: Neurons that are specialized to sense the body's internal functions and control the glands and the smooth (involuntary) muscles that form the heart, the blood vessels, and the lining of the stomach and intestines

Sympathetic nervous system: A system that has an activation or arousal function and tends to act as a total unit

Parasympathetic nervous system: A system that slows down body processes and maintains a state of tranquility, generally affecting one or a few organs at a time

Homeostasis: A delicately balanced or constant internal state

Central nervous system: A system that contains the brain and the spinal cord, which connects most parts of the peripheral nervous system with the brain

Electroencephalograph (EEG): A machine that measures the activity of large groups of neurons through a series of large electrodes placed on the scalp
Computerized axial tomography (CT, or CAT) scan: A process that uses X-ray technology to study brain structures

Magnetic resonance imaging (MRI): A technology that creates images based on how atoms in living tissue respond to a magnetic pulse delivered by the device

Position-emission tomography (PET) scan: A scan that measures brain activity, including metabolism, blood flow, and neurotransmitter activity

Functional MRI (fMRI): A scan that can produce pictures of blood flow in the brain taken less than a second apart

Hindbrain: The lowest and most primitive level of the brain

Brain stem: A part of the brain that support vital life functions

Medulla: A part of the brain that plays an important role in vital body functions such as heart rate and respiration

Pons: A part of the brain that lies just above the medulla and serves as a bridge carrying nerve impulses between the higher and lower parts of the nervous system

Cerebellum: A part of the brain that is concerned primarily with muscular movement coordination but that also plays a role in learning and memory

Midbrain: A part of the brain that contains clusters of sensory and motor neurons

Reticular formation: A structure that acts as a kind of sentry, both alerting higher centers of the brain that messages are coming and then either blocking messages or allowing them to go forward

Forebrain: The brain's most advanced portion from an evolutionary standpoint

Cerebrum: Outer part of the brain containing two large hemispheres, a left side and a right side

Thalamus: Referred to as the brain's "switchboard," a part of the brain that organizes input that sense organs and routes them to appropriate areas of the brain

Hypothalamus: A part of the brain that plays a major role in many aspects of motivation and emotion, including sexual behavior, temperature regulation, sleeping, eating, drinking, and aggression

Limbic system: A system that helps coordinate behaviors needed to satisfy emotional and motivational urges that arise in the hypothalamus and is also involved in memory

Hippocampus: A structure in the limbic system involved in forming and retrieving memory

Amygdala: A structure in the limbic system that organizes motivational and emotional response patterns, particularly those linked to aggression and fear

Cerebral cortex: A quarter-inch thick sheet of gray cells that form the outermost layer of the human brain

Motor cortex: A section of cerebral cortex that controls the 600 or more muscles involved in the voluntary body movements

Somatic sensory cortex: A section of cerebral cortex that receives sensory input that gives rise to our sensations of heat, touch, and cold and to our senses of balance and body movement (kinesthesis)

Wernicke's area: An area in the temporal lobe that is involved in speech comprehension

Broca's area: An area in the frontal lobe that is involved in the production of speech through its connections with the motor cortex region that controls the muscles used in speech

Association cortex: An area of cortex that is involved in many important mental functions, including perception, language, and thought

Prefrontal cortex: An area of cortex located just behind the forehead, the seat of the so-called executive functions

Corpus callosum: A neural bridge consisting of white myelinated fibers that acts as a major communication link between the two hemispheres and allows them to function as a single unit

Lateralization: The relatively greater localization of a function in one hemisphere rather than in the other

Aphasia: The partial or total loss of the ability to communicate

Neural plasticity: The ability of neurons to change in structure and function

Neurogenesis: The production of new neurons in a nervous system

Neural stem cells: Immature cells that can mature into any type of neuron or glial cell needed by the brain

Endocrine system: A system consisting of numerous hormone-secreting glands distributed throughout the body

Hormones: Chemical messengers that are secreted from the endocrine system's glands into the bloodstream

Adrenal glands: Twin structures perched atop the kidneys that serve, quite literally, as hormone factories, producing and secreting about 50 different hormones that regulate many metabolic processes within the brain and other parts of the body

Antigens: Foreign substances that trigger a biochemical response from the immune system

F. What's the Difference? A Concept Card Exercise

An important skill in learning concepts is being able to differentiate among concepts that are similar or related in some way. This skill is particularly relevant for multiple-choice tests, especially if you often find yourself wavering between two answers.

Once you have created your own deck of concept cards, select them two by two, each time answering the question "What's the difference between these two concepts?" You can use the word definitions of the concepts or the examples of the concepts to enhance your mastery of the material. In each case, choose pairs of concepts to compare those that are related or similar or that sound the same or that could in some way be confused. It's much easier to spot the difference between two concepts when you are studying, with the textbook available, rather than considering the question for the first time in a testing situation.

G. Apply What You Know

1. Describe what is occurring in the diagram below.

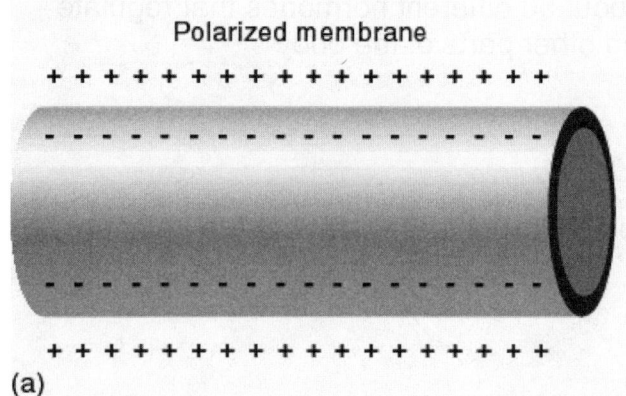

(a) Polarized membrane

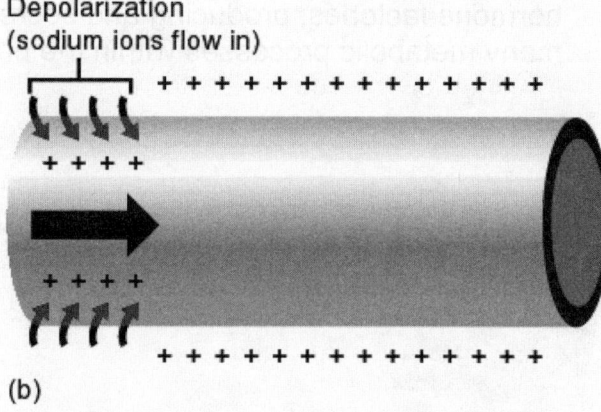

(b) Depolarization (sodium ions flow in)

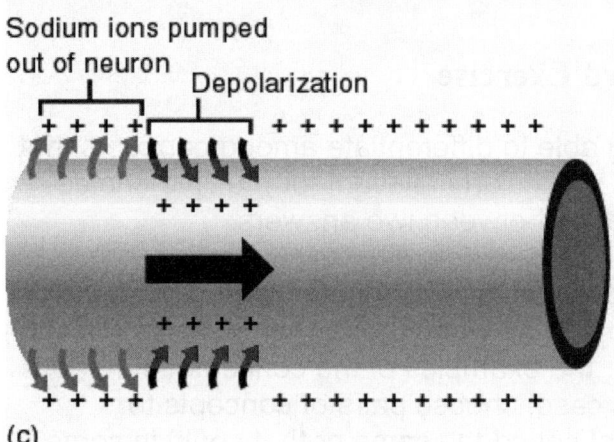

(c) Sodium ions pumped out of neuron / Depolarization

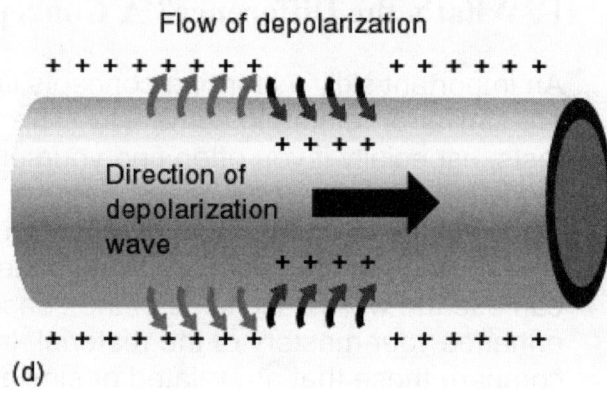

(d) Flow of depolarization / Direction of depolarization wave

2. Label the parts of the neuron shown below. (The myelin sheath and axon are already labeled for you.)

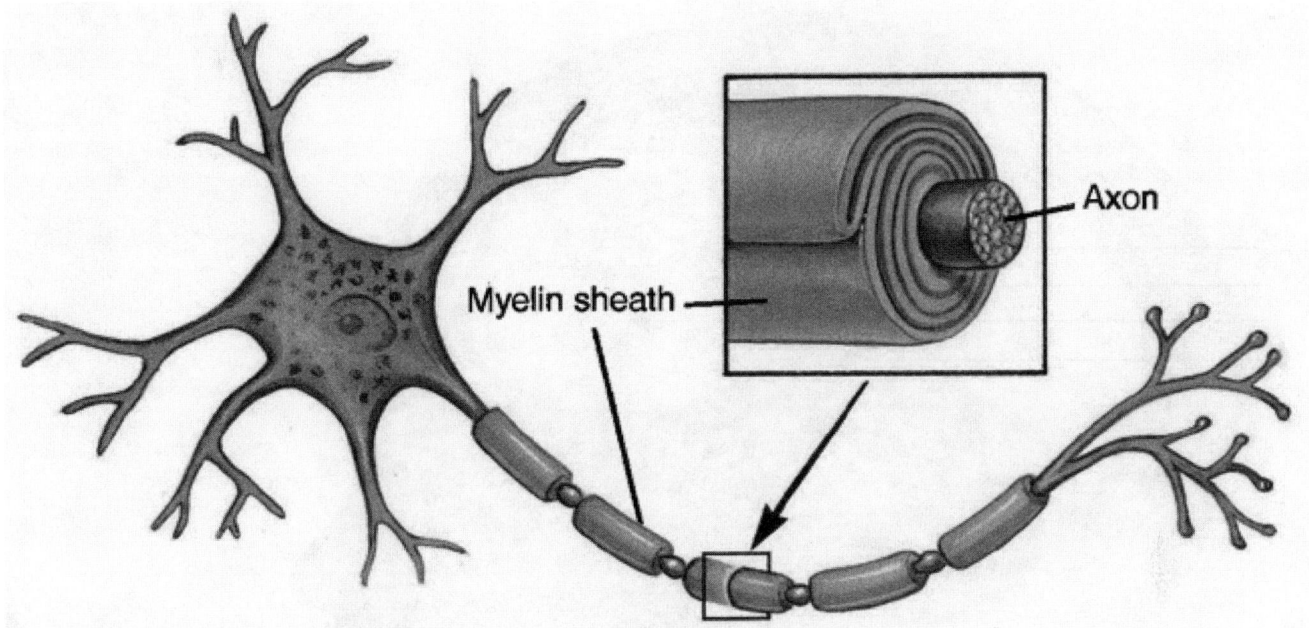

3. Label the parts of the brain shown below.

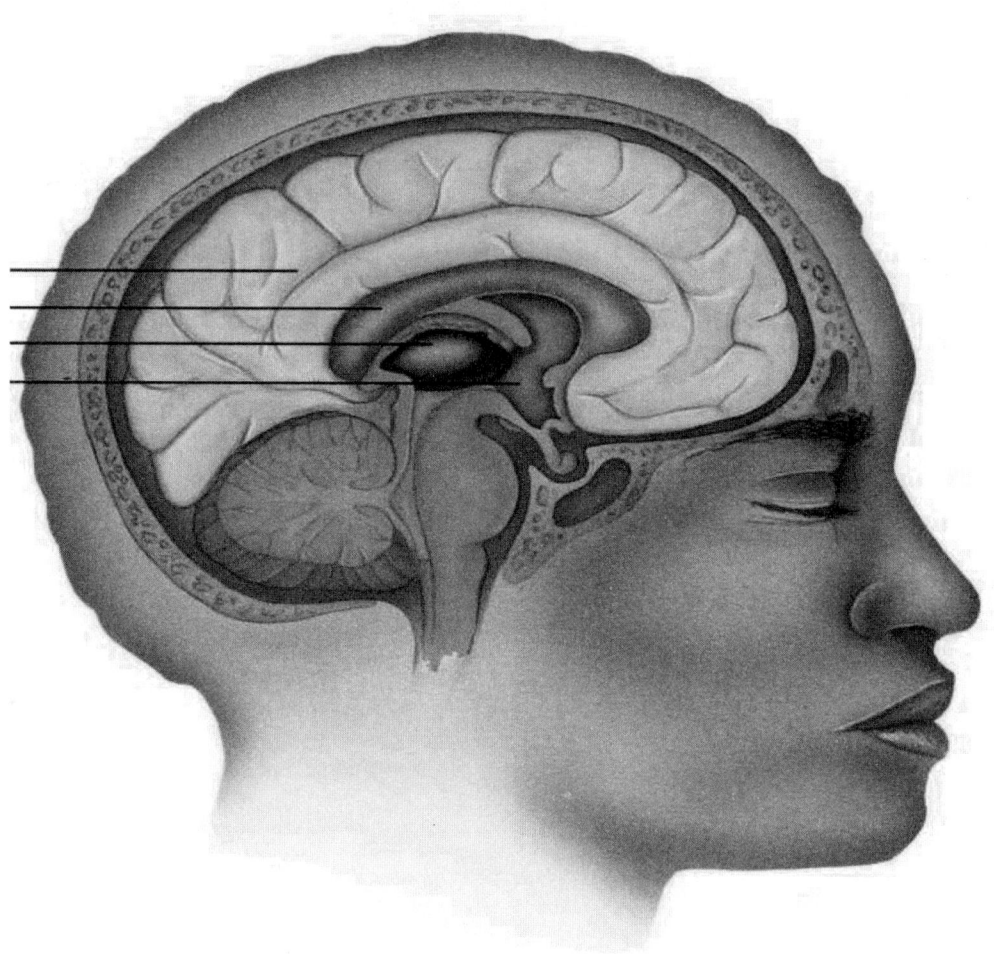

H. On the Web: *As with any online research, it is important to consider how legitimate a given source is before you rely on the information it presents. Your instructor or Internet adviser may give you some specific guidelines for distinguishing which kinds of Web sites tend to be reputable.*

A. Your text mentions a number of individuals who have made notable contributions to our understanding of the brain. Search the Web for more information about some of those listed below to enhance your understanding of the biological foundations of behavior.

Allan Cormack and Godfrey Hounsfield

Phineas Gage

Michael Gazzaniga

Alan Hodgkin and Andrew Huxley

Karl Lashley

James Olds

Oliver Sacks

Roger Sperry

Jacqueline Stoddard

B. Take a look at the concept cards you have created for this chapter, or the key concepts listed in section E. In the space provided, make a list of any whose definitions or associations you are not yet confident of and any you'd like to learn more about. Try entering the terms on your list into your search engine. Make notes of any helpful information you find.

Key Concept/Information Found

C. What can you find on the Web about the latest advances in neural plasticity research? In addition to running *neural plasticity* through your search engine, examine the online Psychological Abstracts (available in most college libraries) and visit additional sites such as Medscape and those for the journals *The Lancet* and *The Scientist*. Summarize your findings, citing any articles, books, or other publications that would particularly useful for further research.

I. Analyze This: *Chapter 1 of your textbook begins by presenting these four basic steps in the critical thinking process:*
- "What exactly are you asking me to believe?"
- "How do you know? What is the evidence?"

- *"Are there other possible explanations?"*
- *"What is the most reasonable conclusion?"*

You might picture this as a four-step analysis to help you decide whether to accept a given theory or assertion. Now it's your turn to put your textbook to this test.

Review the section in Chapter 4 of your textbook under the heading "Plasticity in the Brain: The Role of Experience and the Recovery of Function." There you will find a discussion of the ways in which experience influences brain development. If someone told you that the brains of children who are raised in environments that expose them to high levels of violence are different from those of children who are raised in more benign environments, would you agree? Analyze that assertion in the space provided. When you have finished, consider using this four-step analysis to evaluate other assertions you encounter.

"What exactly are you asking me to believe?"

"How do you know? What is the evidence?"

"Are there other possible explanations?"

"What is the most reasonable conclusion?"

J. Practice Test

Multiple-Choice Items: *Write the letter corresponding to your answer in the space to the left of each item.*

_____ 1. The specialized cells that make up the basic building blocks of the nervous system are called ____.
   a. axons
   b. dendrites
   c. neurons
   d. glial cells

_____ 2. A sudden reversal in the cell membrane's voltage, during which the membrane voltage moves from –70 mV to +40 mV, is called ____.
   a. the action potential threshold
   b. the all-or-none law
   c. a graded potential
   d. an action potential

_____ 3. The changes in the electrical potential of a neuron that are proportional to the amount of incoming stimulation from other neurons are called ____ potentials.
   a. resting
   b. action
   c. graded
   d. polarized

_____ 4. A tiny gap between the axon terminal and the next neuron through which the neurotransmitters pass is called the ____.
   a. synapse
   b. synaptic vesicle
   c. myelin sheath
   d. brain stem

_____ 5. The postsynaptic neuron's receptor sites are located in the ____ of the receiving neuron.
   a. dendrites
   b. cell body
   c. axon
   d. synaptic vesicles

_____ 6. Neurotransmitters that depolarize the postsynaptic neuron are called ____.
   a. excitatory transmitters
   b. inhibitory transmitters
   c. receptor sites
   d. synaptic vesicles

_____ 7. The refractory period is ____.
   a. the time it takes for a neural signal to reach the synapse
   b. a time period during which another action potential cannot occur
   c. a period during which
   d. a resting potential

_____ 8. The ____ nervous system consists of all the neurons of the brain and spinal cord.
   a. sympathetic
   b. parasympathetic
   c. peripheral
   d. central

_____ 9. The sympathetic and parasympathetic nervous systems play complementary roles in maintaining ____, which refers to a balanced or constant internal state.
   a. homeosynthesis
   b. homeostasis
   c. neural plasticity
   d. a resting potential

_____ 10. Andrea accidentally touched a very hot stove. Reflexively, she immediately and automatically withdrew her hand from the stove. This reflexive response depended primarily on her ____.
   a. brain
   b. spinal cord
   c. sympathetic nervous system
   d. reticular formation

_____ 11. CAT scans, PET scans, MRIs, and fMRIs are all examples of ____.
   a. electrical recording
   b. destruction and stimulation techniques
   c. brain imaging
   d. neuropsychological tests

_____ 12. A newborn baby is having such trouble regulating his breathing and heart rate that doctors are forced to place him on life support. If we assume that his symptoms are due to some abnormalities in or damage to his nervous system, the most likely area to investigate is the infant's ____.
   a. thalamus
   b. hypothalamus
   c. amygdala
   d. medulla

_____ 13. Researchers destroy a particular area of a male rat's brain, and the rat subsequently loses its sex drive (i.e., he no longer shows interest in sexual opportunities). It is most likely that the rat's ____ was the site of the damage.
   a. hippocampus
   b. thalamus
   c. amygdala
   d. hypothalamus

_____ 14. The ____ system helps to coordinate behaviors needed to satisfy motivational and emotional urges produced by the ____.
   a. parasympathetic; thalamus
   b. sympathetic; thalamus
   c. limbic; hypothalamus
   d. hippocampal; hypothalamus

_____ 15. Drugs affect behavior and _____ by influencing the activity of _____.
   a. thoughts; the myelin sheath
   b. consciousness; neurons
   c. body movements; the association cortex
   d. consciousness; Broca's area

_____ 16. As a result of a head trauma, Tom loses his ability to create speech but can still understand what people say to him. He has most likely suffered damage to _____.
   a. Broca's area
   b. the amygdala
   c. the cerebellum
   d. Wernicke's area

_____ 17. Scientists have suggested that the entire period of human evolution could be labeled "the age of the _____ lobe."
   a. occipital
   b. temporal
   c. parietal
   d. frontal

_____ 18. The neural link between the two hemispheres that allows them to act as a single unit is called _____.
   a. Wernicke's area
   b. the corpus callosum
   c. aphasia
   d. agnosia

_____ 19. Research demonstrating that rat pups raised in stimulating environments had larger neurons with more dendritic branches than did rat pups raised in standard cages is an example of _____.
   a. neural plasticity
   b. split-brain research
   c. what happens when the corpus callosum is cut
   d. functions influenced by Wernicke's area

_____ 20. Immature, "uncommitted" cells that can mature into any type of neuron or glial cell needed by the brain are called _____.
   a. neural plastic cells
   b. neural stem cells
   c. interneurons
   d. motor neurons

_____ 21. The _____ system consists of numerous glands distributed throughout the body.

a. endocrine
b. immune
c. central nervous
d. parasympathetic nervous

_____ 22. Hormones are the primary method of communication for the ___.
a. nervous system
b. endocrine system
c. immune system
d. central nervous system

_____ 23. Functional MRI (fMRI) is an imaging technique that shows ___.
a. brain structure only
b. brain function only
c. both brain structure and brain function
d. neither brain structure nor brain function

_____ 24. Split-brain research suggests that the left hemisphere tends to be more involved with ___, and that the right hemisphere is relatively more specialized for ___.
a. language abilities; spatial abilities
b. consciousness; mathematical abilities
c. spatial abilities; language abilities
d. mathematical abilities; consciousness

_____ 25. The brain structure which is most involved in brain arousal, sleep, and attention is the ___.
a. reticular formation
b. limbic system
c. motor cortex
d. association cortex

_____ 26. Research suggests that the ___ is relatively more active when positive rather than negative emotions are being experienced.
a. midbrain
b. hindbrain
c. left hemisphere of the brain
d. right hemisphere of the brain

_____ 27. A person's ability to recover from brain damage is generally greatest ___.
a. once they have reached adolescence
b. when the damage occurs during a sensitive period
c. early in life
d. when the damage is caused by mechanical rather than chemical means

_____ 28. A mechanism by which the brain attempts to recover from brain damage is by _____.
   a. sprouting new axons
   b. reducing its dendritic networks
   c. extending axons to form new synapses
   d. inhibiting the release of excitatory neurotransmitters

_____ 29. Neurogenesis refers to _____.
   a. the process of producing new neurons
   b. the all-or-none nature of the action potential
   c. the process of glial cells absorbing toxins and waste materials from the neurons
   d. the excitatory function of neurotransmitters

_____ 30. The neural, endocrine, and _____ systems _____ one another.
   a. immune; function independently of
   b. limbic; function independently of
   c. immune; interact and influence
   d. limbic; interact and influence

True/False Items: *Write T or F in the space provided to the left of each item.*

_____ 1. The thalamus is the seat of executive functions such as goal setting, judgment, and planning.

_____ 2. The ability of neurons to change in structure and function is known as neural plasticity.

_____ 3. Hormones are secreted by glands in the endocrine system.

_____ 4. Psychoactive drugs produce alterations in consciousness, emotion, and behavior by electrically destroying the myelin sheath surrounding the glial cells.

_____ 5. The basic building blocks of the nervous system are dendrites.

_____ 6. A person's ability to recover from brain damage generally declines with age.

_____ 7. The two divisions of the central nervous system are the parasympathetic and sympathetic.

_____ 8. PET scans measure brain structure.

_____ 9. The cerebellum is concerned primarily with muscular movement coordination, but it also plays a role in learning and memory.

_____ 10. The association cortex is involved in the highest levels of mental functions, including perception, language, and thought.

Short-Answer Questions

1. Describe the functions of the different parts of neurons.

2. Describe the divisions of the peripheral nervous system and their functions.

3. Describe four types of procedures, or methods, that researchers use to study the brain's structures and activities, or "unlock the secrets of the brain."

Essay Questions

1. Have you or anyone you know undergone a medical imaging procedure such as an EEG, CAT scan, or MRI? (If not, use your need to gather information on this topic as a way to meet new people.) What symptoms or other indications did the patient present that made the imaging procedure appropriate? What was the experience of having the procedure like for the patient? How might the patient's diagnosis and course of treatment have been different if medical imaging did not exist?

2. For each part of the nervous system that you have studied (e.g., occipital lobe of the cerebral cortex), what symptoms would result if that part were damaged (e.g. the person would have trouble seeing).

Answer Keys

Answer Key for Review at a Glance

1. neurons
2. cell body
3. Dendrites
4. axon
5. glial cells
6. batteries
7. action potential
8. sodium
9. depolarization
10. graded
11. action potential
12. all-or-none law
13. refractory
14. myelin sheath
15. enhances
16. chemical
17. gap
18. dendrite
19. neurotransmitters
20. receptor sites
21. reuptake
22. acetylcholine
23. neurotransmitters
24. agonist
25. antagonist
26. sensory
27. motor
28. interneurons
29. central
30. peripheral
31. somatic
32. autonomic
33. sympathetic
34. parasympathetic
35. spinal reflexes
36. Neuropsychological
37. current
38. electroencephalogram (EEG)
39. computerized axial tomography (CAT)
40. positron emission tomography (PET)
41. magnetic resonance imaging (MRI)
42. functional
43. life support
44. medulla
45. pons
46. motor coordination
47. midbrain
48. reticular formation
49. forebrain
50. thalamus
51. hypothalamus
52. limbic
53. hippocampus
54. amygdale
55. cerebral cortex
56. parietal
57. occipital
58. temporal
59. motor
60. somatic
61. Wernicke's
62. Broca's
63. agnosia
64. frontal
65. prefrontal
66. executive
67. lateralization
68. positive
69. right
70. negative
71. corpus callosum
72. left
73. right
74. spatial
75. neural plasticity
76. genetically
77. early
78. dendritic
79. synapses
80. neurotransmitter
81. sensitive
82. neurogenesis
83. stem cells
84. endocrine
85. hormones
86. adrenal
87. antigens
88. brain
89. immune

Answer Key for Practice Test Multiple-Choice Items

1. c
2. d
3. c
4. a
16. a
17. d
18. b
19. a

5. a
6. a
7. b
8. d
9. b
10. b
11. c
12. d
13. d
14. c
15. b
20. b
21. a
22. b
23. c
24. a
25. a
26. c
27. c
28. c
29. a
30. c

Answer Key for Practice Test True/False Items

1. F
2. T
3. T
4. F
5. F
6. T
7. F
8. F
9. T
10. T

Answer Key for Practice Test Short-Answer Questions

1. The neuron has three main parts: the axon, dendrites, and a cell body. The cell body contains the biochemical structures needed to keep the neuron alive. Its nucleus contains the genetic information that determines how the cell develops. The dendrites collect messages from neighboring neurons and send the messages to the cell body. The axon conducts electrical impulses away from the cell body to other neurons, muscles, and glands.

2. The main divisions of the peripheral nervous system are the somatic and autonomic nervous systems. The somatic nervous system consists of the sensory neurons that are specialized to transmit messages from the body's sense organs and the motor neurons that send messages from the brain and spinal cord to the muscles. The autonomic nervous system controls the glands and smooth involuntary muscles of the heart and other organs and controls involuntary functions such as respiration and digestion. The autonomic nervous system is divided into two branches: the sympathetic and parasympathetic. The sympathetic activates or arouses behavior, while the parasympathetic branch slows down body processes. The interaction between the two branches generally creates a state of homeostasis, a balanced internal state.

3. Neuropsychological tests measure verbal and nonverbal behaviors that are known to be affected by brain damage. Destruction and stimulation techniques are used to destroy brain structures and stimulate them via electrical or chemical measures,

respectively, to determine the functions of the structures. Electrical recordings, such as EEGs, are used to measure the activity of large groups of neurons. Brain imaging techniques such as CT and PET scans, as well as MRIs and fMRIs, are used to study both the structure and activities of the brain.

Answer Key for Practice Test Essay Questions

As you may have guessed, there are no right or wrong answers to the essay questions in this practice test. That does not mean, however, that all essays are equally good. To get maximum learning benefit from the essay questions, do the following:

- Review each essay a day or two after you wrote it, noting any necessary corrections and any additional support for your points that you can think of.
- Review the section in your textbook that pertains to the topic of each essay. Annotate your essay with any corrections or additional support for your points that you find in the text.
- Spend a few minutes researching the topic of each essay on the Internet. Annotate your essay further with any additional (reliable) information you find.
- Finally, reread each essay with the annotations you have added.

Chapter 5
SENSATION AND PERCEPTION

A. Learning Objectives: *These objectives are expanded from the Focus Questions found in the margins of your textbook. When you have mastered the material in this chapter, you will be able to:*

5.1 Differentiate between sensation and perception.

5.2 Describe the absolute threshold and signal detection methods of detecting stimuli.

5.3 Describe research findings on how subliminal stimuli affect attitudes and behavior.

5.4 Differentiate between absolute and difference thresholds.

5.5 Discuss the dysfunctions of myopia and hyperopia.

5.6 Identify and describe how the structures of the human eye are involved in the sense of vision.

5.7 Explain the transduction process that occurs in the photoreceptors of the eye.

5.8 Describe visual transduction and how it explains brightness vision and dark adaptation.

5.9 Explain color vision and color-deficient vision using the trichromatic, opponent-process, and dual-process theories.

5.10 Describe the process of perception in the visual cortex, including a description of feature detectors.

5.11 Describe the components of energy that are involved in the sense of audition.

5.12 Identify and describe how the structures of the ear are involved in the sense of hearing.

5.13 Explain audition using the frequency and place theories of pitch perception.

5.14 Identify the different types of deafness, and explain how they occur.

5.15 Identify the structures involved in gustation, and describe important functions of the sense of taste.

5.16   Identify the structures involved in olfaction, and describe how olfaction regulates social and sexual behaviors.

5.17   Identify and describe the structures involved in the tactile and body senses.

5.18   Describe recent innovations in sensory prosthetics for patients with damage to specific sense systems.

5.19   Contrast bottom-up and top-down processing of sensory information.

5.20   Describe the two complementary processes that occur in attention.

5.21   Provide examples of Gestalt principles of perceptual organization.

5.22   Describe the roles of perceptual schemas, perceptual sets, and perceptual constancies in stimulus detection.

5.23   Describe the factors that account for shape, brightness, and size constancy in vision.

5.24   Describe and recognize monocular and binocular depth cues and cues for movement.

5.25   Define illusion, and describe how constancies and context are involved in visual illusions.

5.26   Describe the biological development of perceptual skills, and explain how they are affected by cross-cultural factors, critical periods, and experience.

5.27   Describe how studies of restricted stimulation and restored vision illustrate the role of critical periods in perceptual development.

B. Chapter Overview

This chapter covers the basic processes of sensation and perception and is divided into sections on sensory processes, the sensory systems, perception, illusions, and perceptual development.

The scientific area that studies relations between the physical characteristics of stimuli and sensory capabilities is called psychophysics. Psychophysicists are interested in studying both the absolute limits of sensitivity and the sensitivity to distinguish between different stimuli. The lowest intensity at which a stimulus can be detected fifty percent of the time is called the absolute threshold of the stimulus. Signal-detection theorists study the factors that influence such sensory judgments. There has been a lot of study of subliminal stimuli, stimuli so weak or brief that it cannot be perceived consciously, since the 1950s. Such studies have indicated that behavior cannot be controlled subliminally, but subliminal stimuli can affect perception and attitudes, at least in the laboratory.

The difference threshold (also known as the just noticeable difference, or jnd) is defined as the smallest difference between two stimuli that can be perceived 50 percent of the time. Weber's law states that the jnd is directly proportional to the magnitude of the stimulus with which the comparison is being made. For instance, the jnd for weight is 1/50, so if one object weighs 50 grams, then a second object would have to have a weight of at least 51 grams for you to notice a difference in weight (or if one object weighs 100 grams, then a second object would have to weigh 102 grams for you to notice it). Sensory adaptation is the phenomenon of diminishing sensitivity to an unchanging stimulus, and it occurs in all sensory modalities. Changes in stimulation may signal a threat, hence there is survival value in having our sensory systems being finely attuned to environmental change.

Psychologists study a number of sensory systems, including vision, audition, gustation, olfaction, and the tactile senses. The eye consists of several important structures such as the lens and retina. Nearsightedness, or myopia, occurs when the lens focuses the visual image in front of the retina; farsightedness, or hyperopia, occurs when the image is focused behind the retina. Rods are black-and-white brightness receptors in the eye. Cones are color receptors. Bipolar cells have synaptic connections with rods and cones and also connect to ganglion cells, whose axons bundle to form the optic nerve. Transduction is the process by which the characteristics of a stimulus are converted into nerve impulses. People must adapt to both bright and dark conditions. The progressive improvement in brightness sensitivity that occurs over time under conditions of low illumination (as when you step into a movie theater) is called dark adaptation. Cones adapt to the dark more quickly than do rods, but dark-adapted rods are more sensitive to light than cones are.

There are several theories of color vision. The trichromatic theory developed by Young and Helmholtz suggests that there are three types of color receptors in the retina that are differentially sensitive to blue, green, or red. The opponent-process theory suggests that each of the three different receptor types responds to *two* different wavelengths: one to red or green, a second to blue or yellow, and a third to black or white. Dual-process theory combines both theories. Trichromatic theory describes how color vision functions at the level of the cones, whereas opponent-process theory describes the subsequent processing of color vision later in the visual process. About 7 percent of males and 1 percent of females have some form of color deficiency which is caused by an absence of hue-sensitive photopigment in certain types of cones. Dichromats are color deficient in only one of the systems. A few people are monochromats, sensitive only to black and white.

The optic nerve sends visual information to the thalamus, which acts as a relay station, forwarding information to the primary visual cortex in the occipital lobe at the rear of the brain. Groups of neurons within the primary visual cortex, called feature detectors, are organized to receive and translate nerve impulses coming from the retina. Different feature detectors fire selectively in response to specific features of a visual stimulus, such as line orientation, color, or movement, thereby helping to analyze and reconstruct visual scenes. Many aspects of the visual stimulus are processed simultaneously, integrated, and interpreted in light of our memories and knowledge in the visual association cortex where the final processes of constructing a visual representation occur.

The stimuli for hearing are sound waves which have two characteristics: frequency (measured in hertz [Hz]), which relates to the pitch of a sound, and amplitude (measured in decibels [db]), which reflects loudness. Sound waves are collected by the outer ear and funneled into the auditory canal leading to the eardrum, a membrane which vibrates in response to the sound waves. This vibration is amplified by three small bones in the middle ear, which in turn transmit the sound waves to the fluid-filled cochlea in the inner ear. It is here that auditory transduction takes place. The fluid waves vibrate the basilar membrane causing a bending of thousands of tiny hair cells in the organ of Corti. This bending triggers a release of neurotransmitters into the synapse between the hair cells and neurons of the auditory nerve, and nerve impulses are then sent to the brain.

To use sound, we must code both pitch and loudness. Loudness is coded by a greater bend by the hair cells resulting in the release of more neurotransmitters and a higher rate of firing in the auditory nerve. The frequency theory of pitch suggests that nerve impulses sent to the brain match the frequency of the sound wave. The place theory of pitch suggests that the specific point in the cochlea where the fluid wave peaks and most strongly bends the hair cells serves as a frequency coding cue. Rather than being contradictory, both theories are applicable. Frequency theory holds true at lower frequencies, and place theory provides the mechanism for coding pitch at higher frequencies.

We can localize sounds because we have two ears, which give us binaural ability. Sounds arrive first and loudest at the ear closest to the sound, and a little later and more softly at the ear further from the sound, allowing us to figure out where it is coming from. More than 20 million people in the United States have hearing loss. Conduction deafness occurs when there is a problem in the system that sends sound waves to the cochlea, for example, if the small bones in the middle ear are fused. Nerve deafness is caused by damage to the receptors in the inner ear or to the auditory nerve.

Gustation, our chemical sense of taste, depends on taste receptors concentrated on the tongue. Through neural activity we combine the four taste qualities (sweet, sour, salty, and bitter) in complex ways to create a distinctive "taste" for a given substance. Olfaction refers to our chemical sense of smell. Humans have about 40 million olfactory receptors. Pheromones, chemical signals found in natural body scents, may affect human behavior. For instance, some studies show that women who live together or are close friends develop similar menstrual cycles, a phenomenon called menstrual synchrony. The human tactile senses perceive at least four sensations: touch, pain, warmth, and cold. The sense of kinesthesis provides us with feedback about the positions of our muscles and joints, allowing us to coordinate body movements. Our vestibular sense is the sense of body orientation or equilibrium with receptors located in the fluid-filled semicircular canals in the inner ear.

Perception is an active, creative process that can cause different people to experience exactly the same stimulus in very different ways. To create perceptions, the brain uses both bottom-up and top-down processing. In bottom-up processing, the constituent parts of a stimulus are combined and then interpreted as a unified perception. In top-down processing, expectations and existing knowledge are used to interpret new information.

Because there are so many stimuli impinging on our senses, we can only pay attention to a small fraction of them. Experiments with a technique called shadowing suggest that we are incapable of attending to more than one stimulus at a time, but we can shift attention rapidly from one stimulus to another. Unattended stimuli register in the nervous system, but they do not enter into immediate experience. We can look right at something and not see it if attending to something else, which is called inattentional blindness. Attention is affected by both the nature of the stimulus and by personal factors. People are especially attentive to stimuli that might represent a threat to their well-being.

People tend to organize the world to make it simpler to understand. Gestalt theorists suggested that people use top-down processing to organize their worlds. For instance, we tend to organize stimuli into both a foreground and a background, a process called figure-ground relations. People group and interpret stimuli according to the four Gestalt laws of perceptual organization: similarity, proximity, closure, and continuity. Recognizing an image requires that we have a perceptual schema (a representation of the image in memory) to compare it with. We make interpretations of stimulus input and sensory information based on our knowledge and experience. For instance, you can recognize what you're sitting on right now as a chair or sofa on the basis of your experience with such objects in the past. Perceptual sets are sets of expectations that affect our perceptions. Perceptual constancies allow us to recognize familiar stimuli under varying conditions, allowing us to enter into different environments and be able to function. Without perceptual constancies, we would have to relearn what stimuli are in each environment we enter.

We perceive depth through both monocular (one-eye) and binocular (two-eye) cues. For instance, light and shadow (a monocular cue) helps us to see "depth" in paintings. Each eye sees a slightly different image (binocular disparity), and the resulting disparity is analyzed by feature detectors in the brain, which allow us to see depth. The perception of movement requires the brain to perceive various movement cues. Illusions are incorrect perceptions that often result from the inaccurate perception of both monocular and binocular depth cues.

Finally, some kinds of perception depend on cultural learning or other environmental factors. Critical periods are intervals during which certain kinds of experiences must occur if perceptual abilities and the brain mechanisms that underlie them are to develop. For example, congenitally blind people, whose vision is restored in adulthood, are unable to learn certain visual tasks that people with normal sight often take for granted.

C. Chapter Outline

SENSORY PROCESSES
    Stimulus Detection: The Absolute Threshold
    Signal Detection Theory
    Subliminal Stimuli: Can They Affect Behavior?
    Beneath the Surface; Are Subliminal Self-Help Products Effective?
    The Difference Threshold
    Sensory Adaptation
    In Review
THE SENSORY SYSTEMS
    Vision
        The Human Eye
        Photoreceptors: The Rods and Cones
        Visual Transduction: From Light Waves to Nerve Impulses
        Brightness Vision and Dark Adaptation
        Color Vision
             The trichromatic theory
             Opponent process theory
             Dual processes in color transduction
             Color-deficient vision
        Analysis and Reconstruction of Visual Scenes
        In Review
    Audition
        Auditory Transduction: From Pressure Waves to Nerve Impulses
        Coding of Pitch and Loudness
        Sound Localization
        WHAT DO YOU THINK? Navigating in Fog: Professor Mayer's Topophone
        Hearing Loss
    Taste and Smell: The Chemical Senses
        Gustation: The Sense of Taste
        Olfaction: The Sense of Smell
    The Skin and Body Senses
        The Tactile Senses
        The Body Senses
        Applying Psychological Science Sensory Prosthetics: "Eyes" for the Blind, "Ears" for the Hearing Impaired
        In Review
PERCEPTION: THE CREATION OF EXPERIENCE
    Perception Is Selective: The Role of Attention
        Inattentional Blindness

Chapter 5

      Environmental and Personal Factors in Attention
  Perceptions Have Organization and Structure
      Gestalt Principles of Perceptual Organization
  Perception Involves Hypothesis Testing
  Perception Is Influenced by Expectations: Perceptual Sets
  Stimuli Are Recognizable Under Changing Conditions: Perceptual Constancies
     What Do You Think? Why Does That Rising Moon Look So Big?
  In Review
PERCEPTION OF DEPTH, DISTANCE, AND MOVEMENT
  Depth and Distance Perception
    Monocular Depth Cues
    Binocular Depth Cues
  Perception of Movement
ILLUSIONS: FALSE PERCEPTUAL HYPOTHESES
    What Do You Think? Explain This Striking Illusion
    Research Close-Up Stalking a Deadly Illusion
  In Review
EXPERIENCE, CRITICAL PERIODS, AND PERCEPTUAL DEVELOPMENT
  Cross-Cultural Research on Perception
  Critical Periods: The Role of Early Experience
  Restored Sensory Capacity
  In Review
  Some Final Reflections

D. Review at a Glance: *Write the term that best fits the blank to review what you learned in this chapter.*

Sensory Processes

We experience the world through our senses. Sensations are the raw input from our sensory receptors to the brain; perception is our integrated experience of what is happening in the world. Most people experience sensory inputs in a fairly similar way, but people with a condition called (1) _____ experience sounds as colors or tastes as touch. The study of the relationships between physical characteristics of stimuli and sensory capabilities is called (2) _____. One thing that psychophysicists study is the intensity needed to detect a stimulus. The minimum intensity required for a stimulus to be detectable 50% of the time is called the (3) _____ _____.

People are sometimes uncertain about whether they have detected a stimulus and set their own (4) _____ _____ to decide whether they have detected it or not. The theory that is concerned with the factors that influence sensory judgment is called (5) _____-_____ theory. A stimulus so weak or brief that it cannot be perceived consciously is called a (6) _____ stimulus. People must also be able to distinguish between stimuli. The smallest difference between two stimuli that people can perceive 50 percent of the time is called the (7) _____ threshold or the (8) _____ _____ difference. (9) _____ _____ states that the jnd is directly proportional to the magnitude of the stimulus with which the comparison is made. Sensory systems are attuned to changes in stimulation. The diminishing of sensitivity to an unchanging stimulus over time is called (10) _____ _____.

The Sensory Systems

Nearsightedness, or (11) _____, is caused by the (12) _____ focusing images in front of the (13) _____. The opposite condition, (14) _____, occurs when the lens focuses the image behind the retina. The cells in the eye that detect color are called (15) _____, whereas the cells that detect black and white and brightness are called (16) _____. Rods and cones translate light waves into nerve impulses with the action of protein molecules called (17) _____ in the process of (18) _____. Rods and cones have synaptic connections with (19) _____ _____, which in turn have synaptic connections with ganglion cells, the axons of which form the (20) _____ _____. A small area of the retina containing only cones is called the (21) _____, where the cones have individual connections to bipolar cells. Our ability to see fine detail, or our (22) _____ _____, is greatest when the visual image projects directly onto the fovea. Our environment provides us with different levels of illumination to which we must adapt. The progressive improvement in brightness sensitivity that occurs when we enter, for example, a movie theater is called (23) _____ _____, a process that involves both the rods and the cones.

Several theories suggest how we sense color. According to the (24) _____ theory, there are three types of color receptors, each of which responds maximally to red, to green, or to (25) _____ wavelengths of light. The (26) _____-_____ theory also has three types of color receptors but suggests that each is sensitive to a pair of different wavelengths: either red-green, (27) _____-_____, or black-white. A modern approach, called the (28) _____-_____ theory of color vision, combines both theories into a two-stage process. First, a trichromatic process takes place in the (29) _____, then opponent-process coding of color occurs at the level of the (30) _____ cells and farther along in the visual system.

Visual information is analyzed and integrated in the brain to help us perceive a visual stimulus. Specialized cells in the primary visual cortex, called (31) _____ _____, respond selectively to specific characteristics of a visual stimulus, such as the orientation of a line, movement, depth, or color. Many aspects of the visual stimulus are processed simultaneously, integrated and interpreted in light of our memories and knowledge in the (32) _____ _____ _____.

Psychologists also study how we detect sound. Sound waves are measured both in the number of sound waves per second, or frequency, which we experience as the (33)

_____ of the sound, and in their vertical size, or (34) _____, which determines loudness. Sound waves travel into the auditory canal of the ear and stimulate the three tiny bones of the middle ear, which (35) _____ the sound wave. The pressure created sets the fluid in the (36) _____ into motion. The resulting fluid waves vibrate the (37) _____ membrane and set the (38) _____ cells into motion. Neurotransmitters are then released and nerve impulses are sent to the brain. There are two theories of how we perceive the pitch of a tone. The (39) _____ theory suggests that nerve impulses sent to the brain match the frequency of the sound wave, whereas the (40) _____ theory suggests that the specific point in the cochlea where the fluid wave peaks and most strongly bends the hair cells serves as a frequency-coding cue. A type of hearing loss called (41) _____ deafness occurs when the system sending sound waves to the cochlea is damaged. (42) _____ deafness occurs when there is damage to inner ear receptors or to the auditory nerve.

(43) _____ is the sense of taste, and (44) _____ refers to our sense of smell. Receptors called (45) _____ _____ concentrated on the tongue allow us to experience the taste sensations of sweet, (46) _____, salty, and (47) _____. Some researchers believe that (48) _____, chemical signals found in natural body scents, may affect human and animal behavior. Humans are sensitive to at least four tactile senses: touch, pain, warmth, and cold. The body senses include (49) _____, which provides us with feedback about the positions of our muscles and joints and the (50) _____ sense, which is the sense of body orientation or equilibrium.

Perception: The Creation of Experience

Perception is an active, creative process. To create perceptions, the brain uses both (51) _____-_____ processing, which involves taking in individual elements of a stimulus and then combining them into a unified perception, and (52) _____-_____ processing, which is when the brain uses existing knowledge and expectations to perceive a stimulus. We focus on only some of the many stimuli in our environment and (53) _____ out the rest. For example, one can look right at something without seeing it if attending to something else, which is called (54) _____ _____. Attentional processes are affected by the nature of the stimulus and by personal factors such as (55) _____ and (56) _____. The perceptual system appears to be especially vigilant to stimuli that denote (57) _____.

Perceptions have organization and structure. (58) _____ theorists discovered many of the basic principles of organization. For example, we tend to organize stimuli into foreground figures and backgrounds, a process called (59) _____-_____ relations. The four Gestalt principles of organization are (60) _____, (61) _____, (62) _____, and (63) _____. Perception involves hypothesis testing. A representation of an image in memory that allows us to recognize it is a (64) _____ _____. We are able to recognize familiar stimuli under different environmental conditions because of perceptual (65)_____.

Perception of Depth, Distance, and Movement

To judge depth, the brain relies on (66) _____ cues, which require one eye, and (67) _____ cues, which require two eyes. Important stimulus cues to depth include (68) _____ perspective, patterns of (69) _____ and (70) _____, and relative (71) _____, all of which require (72) _____ eye(s) for inferring depth. Binocular cues include (73) _____ _____, which is based on the fact that each eye sees a slightly different image, and (74)_____ which depends on feedback from the muscles that turn our eyes inward to view a near object. The brain integrates information from several different senses, including our internal bodily senses, to perceive (75) _____, which is inferred from relative changes in the position of the (76) _____ _____ of a stimulus over time.

Illusions: False Perceptual Hypotheses

Incorrect perceptions, known as (77) _____, are often caused by inaccurate perception of cues to (78) _____, distance, and apparent (79) _____. For example, most visual illusions can be attributed to perceptual (80) _____ that ordinarily help us perceive more accurately.

Experience, Critical Periods, and Perceptual Development

Culture and early experience can both influence our perceptual abilities. For some aspects of perception, there are (81) _____ _____, during which certain kinds of experiences must occur if perceptual abilities and the (82) _____ _____ that underlie them are to develop. If an individual does not have any experiences stimulating the development during this time, then it is too late to undo the deficit.

E. Concept Cards

Truly learning a concept means integrating it into the way *you* think about things. To integrate concepts successfully, you must translate the words and examples your text or instructor provides into words and examples that are meaningful to you.

For this exercise, obtain some note cards (3" × 5" or 4" × 6") to make a deck of concept cards. On one side of each card, write the *concept* from the list below (e.g., "sensation") at the top. Read the textbook definition provided, and then write the definition *in your own words* on the concept card (e.g., for "sensation," you might write "a message from your sense organs to your brain about the environment"). Simply imagine that a friend has asked you what the concept means, and write down what you would answer.

Writing the definition in your own words requires you to think deeply about its meaning. When next you see your own version of the definition, it will make intuitive sense to you—no translation required.

On the second side of the card, write your own example of the concept. Again, coming up with your own example requires you to think deeply about the application of the concept, and you will more easily understand and remember the example when you study for a test. If you use an example from the text, or from class, make it your own by writing it in your own words. You can always check with your instructor that your example is indeed a good example of the concept.

CONCEPT Definition in my own words (side 1 of card)	Example of the concept in my own words, preferably drawn from my own experience (side 2 of card)

The following is a list of all the boldface concepts from your textbook with the author's definition. Write the definition in your own words, together with your own example of the concept, to create a concept card as described earlier, or write in the space provided.

Synesthesia: Literally, "mixing of senses," meaning individuals experience sounds as colors, or taste as touch sensations of different shapes

Sensation: The stimulus-detection process by which our sense organs respond to and translate environmental stimuli into nerve impulses that are sent to the brain

Perception: The active process of organizing the stimulus input and giving it meaning

Psychophysics: The study of relations between the physical characteristics of stimuli and sensory capabilities

Absolute threshold: The lowest intensity at which a stimulus can be detected 50 percent of the time

Decision criterion: A standard of how certain people must be that a stimulus is present before they will say they detect it

Signal detection theory: Theory that is concerned with the factors that influence sensory judgments

Subliminal stimulus: A stimulus that is so weak or brief that although it is perceived by the senses, it cannot be perceived consciously

Difference threshold: The smallest difference between two stimuli that people can perceive 50 percent of the time

Weber's law: The difference threshold, or jnd, is directly proportional to the magnitude of the stimulus with which the comparison is being made

Sensory adaptation: The diminishing sensitivity to an unchanging stimulus

Transduction: The process whereby the characteristics of a stimulus are converted into nerve impulses

Lens: An elastic structure that becomes thinner to focus on distant objects and thicker to focus on nearby objects

Retina: A multilayered light-sensitive tissue at the rear of the fluid-filled eyeball

Rods: Black and white brightness receptors that function best in dim light

Cones: Color receptors

Fovea: A small area in the center of the retina that contains no rods but many densely packed cones

Optic nerve: Ganglion cells whose axons are collected into a bundle

Visual acuity: The ability to see fine detail

Photopigments: Pigments that absorb light

Dark adaptation: The progressive improvement in sensitivity that occurs over time under conditions of low illumination

Young-Helmholtz trichromatic theory: Theory that states there are three types of color receptors in the retina

Hering's opponent-process theory: Proposes that each of three cone types responds to two different wavelengths

Dual-process theory: Theory that combines the trichromatic and opponent-process theories to account for the color transduction process

Feature detectors: Cells that fire selectively in response to visual stimuli that have specific characteristics

Frequency: The number of sound waves, or cycles, per second

Hertz (Hz): The technical measure of number of sound waves, or cycles, per second

Amplitude: The vertical size of sound waves, or the amount of compression and expansion of the molecules

Decibels (dB): A measure of physical pressures that occurs at the eardrum

Cochlea: A coiled, snail-shaped tube in the ear that is filled with fluid and contains the basilar membrane

Basilar membrane: A sheet of tissue that runs the length of the cochlea

Organ of Corti: Organ that rests on the basilar membrane and contains thousands of tiny hair cells that are the actual sound receptors

Frequency theory of pitch perception: Theory that suggests that nerve impulses sent to the brain match the frequency of the sound waves

Place theory of pitch perception: Theory that suggests that the specific point in the cochlea where the fluid wave peaks and most strongly bends the hair cells serves as a frequent coding cue

Conduction deafness: Deafness caused by problems involving the mechanical system that transmits sound waves to the cochlea

Nerve deafness: Deafness caused by damaged receptors within the inner ear or damage to the auditory nerve itself

Gustation: The sense of taste

Olfaction: The sense of smell

Taste buds: Chemical receptors concentrated along the edges and back surface of the tongue

Olfactory bulb: A forebrain structure immediately above the nasal cavity

Pheromones: Chemical signals found in natural body scents

Menstrual synchrony: The tendency of women who live together or are close friends to become more similar in their menstrual cycles

Kinesthesis: A sense that provides us with feedback about our muscles' and joints' positions and movements

Vestibular sense: The sense of body orientation or equilibrium
Sensory prosthetic devices: Devices that provide sensory input that can, to some extent, substitute for what cannot be supplied by the person's sensory receptors

Bottom-up processing: A process whereby the sensory system takes in individual elements of the stimulus and then combines them into a unified perception

Top-down processing: A process whereby sensory information is interpreted in light of existing knowledge, concepts, ideas, and expectations

Inattentional blindness: The failure of unattended stimuli to register in consciousness

Figure-ground relations: The tendency to organize stimuli into a central, or foreground, figure and a background

Gestalt laws of perceptual organization: Factors that make it likely for stimuli to be perceived as a unified whole; the four factors that define this are similarity, proximity, closure, and continuity

Perceptual schema: A mental representation or image containing the critical and distinctive features of people, objects, events, and other perceptual phenomena

Perceptual set: A readiness to perceive stimuli in a particular way

Perceptual constancies: The ability to recognize familiar stimuli under varying conditions

Monocular depth cues: Cues that require only one eye

Binocular depth cues: Cues that require both eyes

Binocular disparity: The principle in which each eye sees a slightly different image

Convergence: A binocular distance cue that is produced by feedback from muscles that turn the eyes inward to view a near object

Stroboscopic movement: An illusory movement produced when a light is briefly flashed in darkness and then, a few milliseconds later, another light is flashed nearby

Illusions: Compelling but incorrect perceptions

Critical periods: Periods during which certain kinds of experiences must occur if perceptual abilities and the brain mechanisms that underlie them are to develop normally

F. What's the Difference? A Concept Card Exercise

An important skill in learning concepts is being able to differentiate among concepts that are similar or related in some way. This skill is particularly relevant for multiple-choice tests, especially if you often find yourself wavering between two answers.

Once you have created your own deck of concept cards, select them two by two, each time answering the question "What's the difference between these two concepts?" You can use the word definitions of the concepts or the examples of the concepts to enhance your mastery of the material. In each case, choose pairs of concepts to compare those that are related or similar or that sound the same or that could in some way be confused. It's much easier to spot the difference between two concepts when you are studying, with the textbook available, rather than when considering the question for the first time in a testing situation.

G. Apply What You Know

1. Describe how visual stimuli are projected to the two hemispheres by referring to the diagram below.

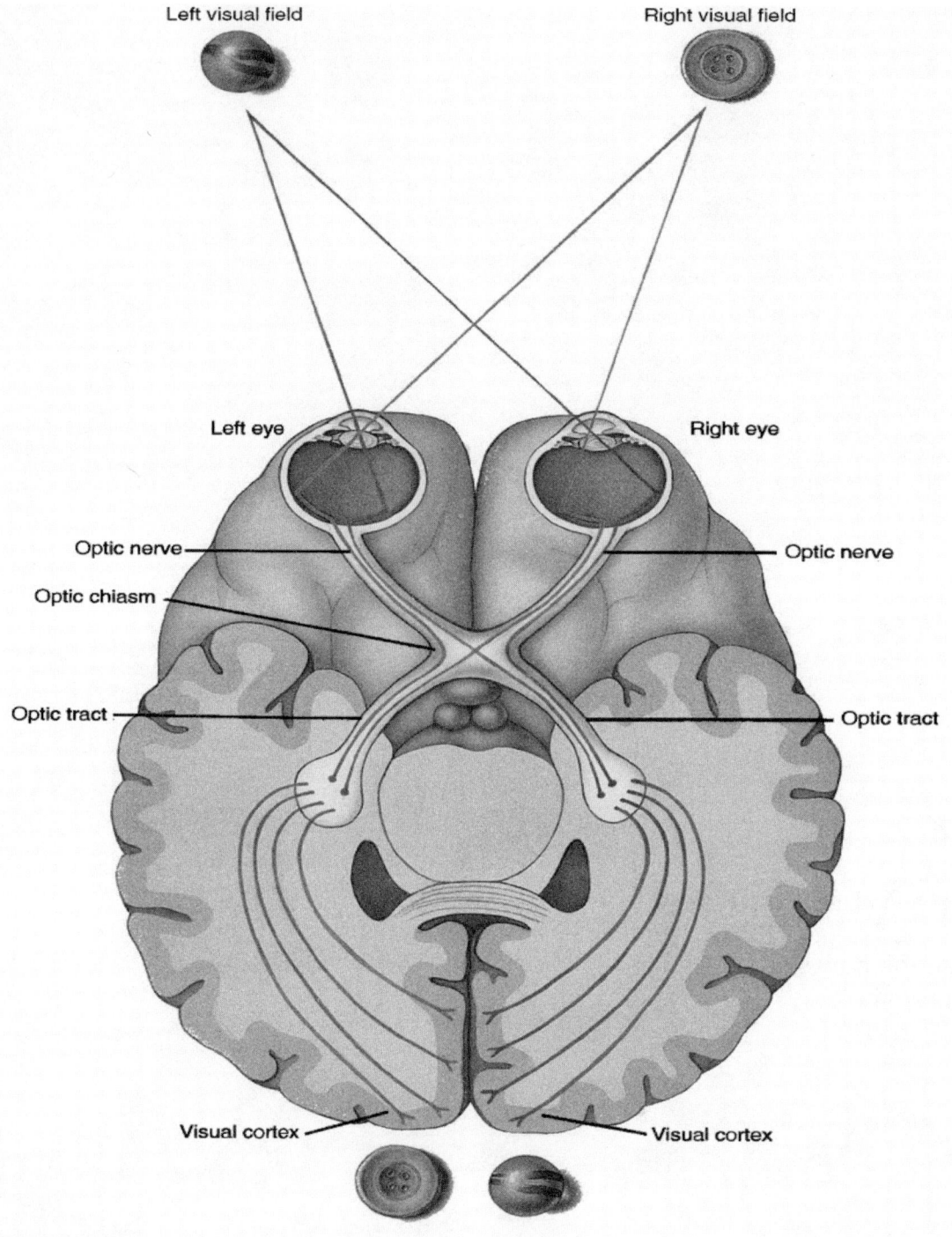

Chapter 5

2. Describe the process shown in the diagram below.

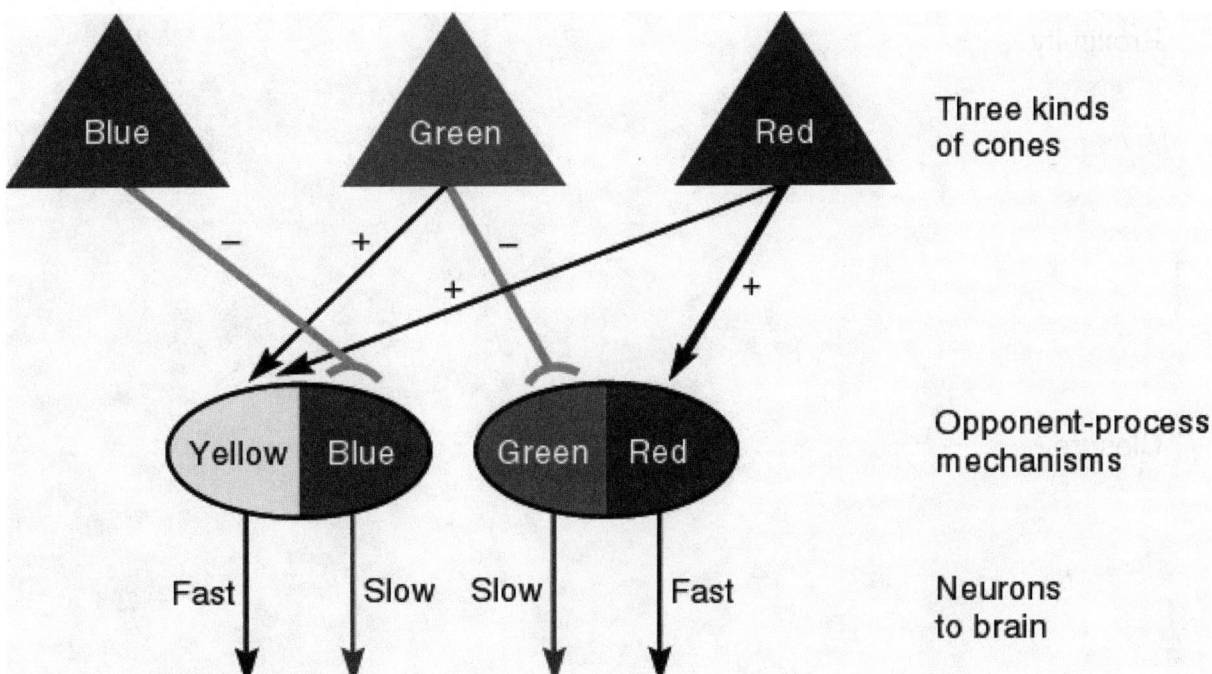

3. Draw a figure using each of the four Gestalt principles of perceptual organization.

Similarity

Proximity

Closure

Continuity

H. On the Web: *As with any online research, it is important to consider how legitimate a given source is before you rely on the information it presents. Your instructor or Internet adviser may give you some specific guidelines for distinguishing which kinds of Web sites tend to be reputable.*

A. Your text mentions a number of individuals who have made notable contributions to the study of sensation and perception. Search the Web for more information about some of those listed to enhance your understanding of how we come to experience our world.

Georg von Bekesy

Colin Blakemore and Grahame Cooper

Anthony Greenwald

Ewald Hering

Conrad L. Kraft

George Stratton

James Vicary

Thomas Young and Hermann von Helmholtz

B. Take a look at the concept cards you have created for this chapter, or the key concepts listed in section E previously. In the space provided, make a list of any whose definitions or associations you are not yet confident of and any you'd like to learn more about. Try entering the terms on your list into your search engine. Make notes of any helpful information you find.

Key Concept/Information Found

C. If perception is a subjective phenomenon, we would expect that people of different cultures would perceive the same objects or events in quite different ways. Using the online PsycINFO database or Psychological Abstracts (available in your college library), find two studies that examine such cultural differences, and report their findings.

Study 1:

Study 2:

I. Analyze This: *Chapter 1 of your textbook begins by presenting these four basic steps in the critical-thinking process:*
- *"What exactly are you asking me to believe?"*
- *"How do you know? What is the evidence?"*
- *"Are there other possible explanations?"*
- *"What is the most reasonable conclusion?"*

You might picture this as a four-step analysis to help you decide whether to accept a given theory or assertion. Now it's your turn to put your textbook to this test.

Review the section in Chapter 5 of your textbook under the heading "Illusions: False Perceptual Hypotheses." There you will find a research close-up on a study of pilot error during night landings. If someone told you that it is always safer for pilots to land an airplane by relying on the cockpit instruments rather than by relying on their own visual perceptions, would you agree? Analyze that assertion in the space provided. When you have finished, consider using this four-step analysis to evaluate other assertions you encounter.

"What exactly are you asking me to believe?"

"How do you know? What is the evidence?"

"Are there other possible explanations?"

"What is the most reasonable conclusion?"

J. Practice Test

Multiple-Choice Items: *Write the letter corresponding to your answer in the space to the left of each item.*

_____ 1. The lowest intensity at which a stimulus can be detected 50 percent of the time is known as the ____.
   a. difference threshold
   b. absolute threshold
   c. signal detection
   d. just noticeable difference

_____ 2. Tom is a security screener at Kennedy International Airport. His job is to view X-rays of passengers' hand luggage to detect any hidden weapons a passenger might be hiding in the hand luggage. Yesterday a plane was blown up in midair by a hijacker who had managed to smuggle a bomb onboard the plane. Tom is now more likely to perceive an ambiguous spot on a luggage X-ray as a potential weapon than he was before the recent hijacking, indicating that his ____ has changed.
   a. difference threshold
   b. decision criterion
   c. just noticeable difference
   d. signal detector

_____ 3. Regarding the impact of subliminal messages on attitudes and behavior, experimental research has suggested that subliminal messages have ____.
   a. no impact on attitudes and behaviors
   b. an equal impact on attitudes and behaviors
   c. a stronger impact on behaviors than on attitudes
   d. a stronger impact on attitudes than on behaviors

_____ 4. The ____ threshold is defined as the smallest difference between two stimuli that can be perceived 50 percent of the time.
   a. absolute
   b. sensation
   c. difference
   d. perceptual

_____ 5. According to a Weber fraction, the jnd for weight is 1/50. Therefore, if an object weighed 1 kilogram (1,000 grams), a second object would have to weigh at least ____ for you to notice a difference between the two objects.

a. 2 kilograms
b. 1,020 grams
c. 1,050 grams
d. 50 grams

_____ 6. You have just prepared a bath for yourself. As you are getting into the tub, you find that the water feels very hot, almost too hot. However, you continue to ease yourself into the tub, and pretty soon, even though it has remained the same temperature, the water no longer feels so hot. The characteristic of sensory neurons that is responsible for this phenomenon is known as ____.
a. sensory adaptation
b. the refractory period
c. the all-or-none law
d. signal detection

_____ 7. The receptors for black and white and brightness are called ____, whereas the receptors for color are called ____.
a. rods; cones
b. cones; rods
c. ganglion cells; bipolar cells
d. bipolar cells; ganglion cells

_____ 8. The department of transportation contacts you and asks what color they should make their road signs so that they will be most visible at night. Given what you have learned in this chapter about the sensitivity of rods under conditions of low illumination, which color would be best to recommend?
a. red
b. blue-red
c. yellow-red
d. yellow-green

_____ 9. The progressive improvement in brightness sensitivity that occurs over time under conditions of low illumination is called ____ and involves ____.
a. light adaptation; rods
b. dark adaptation; rods and cones
c. visual acuity; cones
d. dark adaptation; rods

_____ 10. The current theory of color sensation uses the ____ theory to explain the behavior of the cones in color vision. A modified version of the ____ theory that emphasizes the role of ganglion cells explains the presence of afterimages and certain types of color blindness.
a. trichromatic; additive color mixture
b. dual-process; trichromatic
c. opponent-process; dual-process
d. trichromatic; opponent-process

_____ 11. Groups of neurons within the primary visual cortex that respond to specific characteristics of a visual stimulus, such as line orientation or movement, are called _____.
   a. ganglion cells
   b. bipolar cells
   c. feature detectors
   d. opponent processors

_____ 12. People who talk on cell phones while they drive may not notice important driving hazards, such as pedestrians crossing the road, according to research on _____.
   a. parallel processing
   b. bottom-up processing
   c. transduction
   d. inattentional blindness

_____ 13. Fluid waves from inside the _____ vibrate the basilar membrane causing a bending in the _____ in the organ of Corti.
   a. semicircular canals; eardrum
   b. middle ear; cochlea
   c. cochlea; hair cells
   d. middle ear; hair cells

_____ 14. The place theory of pitch perception states that pitch is determined by _____.
   a. neurons that fire at the same frequency as the incoming stimulus
   b. neurons that fire at the same amplitude as the incoming stimulus
   c. the specific place in the cochlea where the fluid wave peaks most
   d. the way that the eardrum resonates in response to different frequencies

_____ 15. While cleaning his ear a little too vigorously, Steve accidentally punctures the eardrum in his right ear and is unable to hear out of this ear. Steve's injury would be classified as an example of _____ deafness.
   a. conduction
   b. temporal lobe
   c. nerve
   d. localized

_____ 16. The chemical sense of taste is called _____; the chemical sense of smell is called _____.
   a. the vestibular sense; olfaction
   b. gustation; olfaction
   c. olfaction; the vestibular sense
   d. olfaction; kinesthesis

_____ 17. The four qualities that our sense of taste responds to are ____.
   a. sweet, sour, salty, bitter
   b. sweet, sour, salty, tart
   c. sour, salty, biting, tart
   d. sweet, sour, salty, sugary

_____ 18. Chemical signals found in natural body scents that may affect human behavior are called ____.
   a. olfactors
   b. olfactory bulbs
   c. gustators
   d. pheromones

_____ 19. Humans are sensitive to at least four tactile sensations: ____.
   a. tickle, warmth, pain, itch
   b. touch, heat, itch, pain
   c. warmth, pain, pressure, touch
   d. pressure, pain, warmth, cold

_____ 20. Maria had a bad cold; her ears, nose, and sinuses were very congested, and she felt dizzy when she stood up. The dizziness was probably caused by poor functioning of Maria's ____ sense, which provides information about body orientation and equilibrium.
   a. kinesthetic
   b. vestibular
   c. olfactory
   d. tactile

_____ 21. As you are reading this question, feature detectors in your visual system are analyzing the various stimulus components and recombining them into your perception of letters and words. This is an example of ____ processing.
   a. figure-ground
   b. top-down
   c. parallel
   d. bottom-up

_____ 22. Perceptual set is an example of ____ processing.
   a. figure-ground
   b. top-down
   c. parallel
   d. bottom-up

_____ 23. A new commercial presents its product in a rather novel and intense way, making use of a lot of movement and special effects. If this ad were to capture your attention, it would best be viewed as an example of how ____ can affect attention.

a. personal motives
b. sensory adaptation
c. internal factors
d. environmental factors

_____ 24. You would likely recognize the following stimulus as crossed lines rather than as two touching arrowheads due to the Gestalt principle of _____.

a. similarity
b. figure-ground
c. proximity
d. continuity

_____ 25. Many political cartoonists have an uncanny ability to capture the most noteworthy facial features of famous people, so that we can easily recognize the person represented by even the simplest line sketch. This is an example of the way we use _____.
a. closure
b. bottom-up processing
c. perceptual schemas
d. sensory habituation

_____ 26. A binocular distance cue produced by feedback from the muscles that turn your eyes inward to view a near object is called _____.
a. stroboscopic movement
b. convergence
c. monocularism
d. perceptual constancy

_____ 27. Stroboscopic movement is _____.
a. the movement of a visual image to an area outside the fovea
b. the principle behind motion pictures
c. an illusory movement caused by inaccurate binocular depth cues
d. a subliminal technique that has been outlawed

Chapter 5   149

_____ 28. Compelling but incorrect perceptions of stimuli are called ____.
   a. illusions
   b. perceptual schemas
   c. perceptual sets
   d. stroboscopic movements

_____ 29. Artists use light and dark areas of paint to represent depth in three-dimensional objects portrayed on canvas. This representation relies on ____.
   a. binocular cues
   b. deception
   c. monocular cues
   d. sensory adaptation

_____ 30. Bill had been blind from birth, but when he was 30, he underwent surgery that enabled him to see. Unfortunately, however, he was never able to recognize faces other than those of people he knew well. This is most likely because the ____.
   a. schema for facial recognition was inaccurate
   b. critical period for facial recognition was already past
   c. sensory adaptation had already taken place
   d. surgeon was incompetent

True/False Items: *Write T or F in the space provided to the left of each item.*

_____ 1. People who experience sounds as colors or tastes have synesthesia.

_____ 2. A standard of how certain people must be when a stimulus is present before they will say they detect it is called the absolute threshold of the stimulus.

_____ 3. In people who have myopia, the lens focuses the visual image behind the retina.

_____ 4. Transduction is the process whereby the characteristics of a stimulus are converted into nerve impulses.

_____ 5. Opponent-process theory proposed that each of three types of visual sensory receptors responds to two different wavelengths of light.

_____ 6. It is possible to look right at something and not see it when attending to some other stimulus.

_____ 7. There is no evidence for the hypothesis of menstrual synchrony.

_____ 8. Perceptual constancies allow us to recognize familiar objects under varying conditions.

_____ 9. People of all cultures perceive distance cues in the same way.

_____ 10. If certain patterns of perception do not develop during critical periods, it will not be possible to make up the deficit later.

Short-Answer Questions

1. What is sensory adaptation?

2. Describe the differences between the Young-Helmholtz trichromatic theory and Hering's opponent-process theory.

3. What is the difference between frequency and amplitude of a sound wave?

4. What is the difference between bottom-up and top-down processing?

5. How do perceptual schemas and perceptual set affect perception?

Essay Questions

1. Do you have a sensory deficit such as myopia or hyperopia, color blindness, or impaired hearing? If you do not, surely you know someone who does. How does this condition affect the person's life? If (as in the case of mild to moderate visual impairment) the condition is easily corrected with a device such as prescription lenses, how would it affect the person's life if such a device did not exist?

2. Think of a time when you and someone else both experienced a sensory stimulus (i.e., a sight, sound, taste, odor, or haptic sensation), but the other person perceived it quite differently from the way you did. Describe the situation, and recount what happened as a result of your differing perceptions. Was the outcome humorous, disastrous, or inconsequential?

3. Considering what you have learned in this chapter about critical periods, explain why it is important for infants and toddlers to receive frequent medical checkups that include evaluation of their sensory and perceptual development.

Answer Keys

Answer Key for Review at a Glance

1. synesthesia
2. psychophysics
3. absolute threshold
4. decision criterion

29. cones
30. ganglion
31. feature detectors
32. visual association cortex

57. threat
58. Gestalt
59. figure-ground
60. similarity

5. signal-detection
6. subliminal
7. difference
8. just noticeable
9. Weber's law
10. sensory adaptation
11. myopia
12. lens
13. retina
14. hyperopia
15. cones
16. rods
17. photopigments
18. transduction
19. bipolar cells
20. optic nerve
21. fovea
22. visual acuity
23. dark adaptation
24. trichromatic
25. blue
26. opponent-process
27. yellow-blue
28. dual-process
33. pitch
34. amplitude
35. amplify
36. cochlea
37. basilar
38. hair
39. frequency
40. place
41. conduction
42. Nerve
43. Gustation
44. olfaction
45. taste buds
46. sour
47. bitter
48. pheromones
49. kinesthesis
50. vestibular
51. bottom-up
52. top-down
53. filter
54. inattentional blindness
55. motives
56. interests
61. proximity
62. closure
63. continuity
64. perceptual schema
65. constancies
66. monocular
67. binocular
68. linear
69. light
70. shadow
71. size
72. one
73. binocular disparity
74. convergence
75. movement
76. retinal image
77. illusions
78. size
79. movement
80. processes
81. critical periods
82. brain mechanisms

Answer Key for Practice Test Multiple-Choice Items

1. b
2. b
3. d
4. c
5. b
6. a
7. a
8. d
9. b
10. d
11. c
12. d
13. c
14. c
15. a
16. b
17. a
18. d
19. d
20. b
21. d
22. b
23. d
24. d
25. c
26. b
27. b
28. a
29. c
30. b

Answer Key for Practice Test True/False Items

1. T
6. T

2. F	7. F
3. F	8. T
4. T	9. F
5. T	10. T

Answer Key for Practice Test Short-Answer Questions

1. Sensory adaptation refers to the diminishing sensitivity to an unchanging stimulus. This type of adaptation is sometimes called habituation. Sensory adaptation helps us to get used to stimuli that pose no threat to us.

2. Trichromatic theory argued that there are three types of cones, one sensitive to wavelengths that correspond to blue, another to green, and the third to red. Opponent-process theory argued that each of the three color receptors corresponds to two wavelengths: the first type to red or green, the second type to blue or yellow, and the third type to black or white.

3. Frequency is the number of sound waves, or cycles, per second and is measured in hertz (Hz). Frequency is a measure of the sound's pitch. Amplitude refers to the vertical size of the sound wave and is measured in decibels (db). Amplitude is a measure of the sound's loudness.

4. In bottom-up processing, feature detectors break down stimuli into their constituent parts, and the system then combines the parts into a unified perception. In top-down processing, existing knowledge and expectations guide the process of perceiving a stimulus.

5. Perceptual schemas are mental representations to which we compare new stimuli in order to recognize them. Perceptual sets are sets of expectancies that influence our perceptions of new stimuli.

Answer Key for Practice Test Essay Questions

As you may have guessed, there are no right or wrong answers to the essay questions in this practice test. That does not mean, however, that all essays are equally good. To get maximum learning benefit from the essay questions, do the following:

- Review each essay a day or two after you wrote it, noting any necessary corrections and any additional support for your points that you can think of.
- Review the section in your textbook that pertains to the topic of each essay. Annotate your essay with any corrections or additional support for your points that you find in the text.
- Spend a few minutes researching the topic of each essay on the Internet. Annotate your essay further with any additional (reliable) information you find.
- Finally, reread each essay with the annotations you have added.

Chapter 6
STATES OF CONSCIOUSNESS

A. Learning Objectives: *These objectives are expanded from the Focus Questions found in the margins of your textbook. When you have mastered the material in this chapter, you will be able to:*

6.1   Define the characteristics of consciousness.

6.2   Contrast the psychodynamic and cognitive views of the mind, and contrast controlled and automatic processing.

6.3   Describe how visual agnosia, blindsight, and priming illustrate unconscious processing.

6.4   Describe how consciousness enhances the ability to adapt to the environment.

6.5   Describe how scientists identify brain pathways involved in conscious versus unconscious processing.

6.6   Identify and describe the brain structures involved in maintaining circadian rhythms.

6.7   Describe conditions associated with disrupted circadian rhythms and interventions used to treat associated problems.

6.8   Describe how environmental and cultural factors affect sleep.

6.9   Discuss the differences in brain wake patterns of waking states and stages of sleep.

6.10 Describe the types of sleep deprivation and their effects on functioning.

6.11 Explain how different types of sleep deprivation affect mood and behavior.

6.12 Describe the theories regarding the purposes of sleep, including the restoration model, the evolutionary/circadian model, and the memory consolidation model.

6.13 Describe the symptoms, causes and treatment of major sleep disorders.

6.14 Outline research findings on the content of dreams.

6.15 Describe theories regarding the purposes of dreaming, including wish fulfillment, activation-synthesis theory, problem-solving models, and cognitive-process

Chapter 6 155

theories.

6.16   Contrast daydreams with nighttime dreams.

6.17   Describe how agonist and antagonist drugs affect neurotransmitters.

6.18   Define tolerance and withdrawal, explain how they are influenced by classical conditioning, and explain how they are involved in the diagnosis of substance dependence.

6.19   Describe the effects of the major drug classes—including depressants, stimulants, opiates, hallucinogens, and marijuana—on the nervous system and behavior.

6.20   Outline the ways that amphetamines, cocaine, and Ecstasy affect the brain.

6.21   Describe the effects of opiates, hallucinogens, and marijuana.

6.22   Use the three levels of analysis to describe how the interaction of genetic, psychological, and environmental factors explains drug use and dependence.

6.23   Describe research findings on hypnosis with regard to involuntary behaviors, pain tolerance, hypnotic amnesia, and memory enhancement.

6.24   Contrast dissociation and social cognitive theories of hypnosis, and explain how proponents of each theory understand brain activity during hypnosis.

B. Chapter Overview

This chapter covers various aspects of consciousness, including what consciousness is thought to be, circadian rhythms, and states of altered consciousness that include sleep and dreaming, drugs, and hypnosis.

Consciousness is defined as our moment-to-moment awareness of ourselves and our environment. It is subjective, meaning that everyone's sense of reality is different. It is also private: Other people don't have direct access to your consciousness. It is dynamic or changing in that we go through different states of awareness at different times. Consciousness is also self-reflective, in that the mind is aware of itself, and hence central to how we define our "selves." Through a process called selective attention, we focus our awareness on some stimuli to the exclusion of others, and are not fully conscious of every stimulus at all times. Scientists use self-report methods, behavioral techniques, and physiological assessments as operational definitions of private inner states of consciousness.

Freud proposed that we have a conscious mind, containing what we are currently aware of; a preconscious mind, containing things that can be brought into consciousness; and an unconscious mind, containing things that ordinarily cannot be brought into conscious awareness. Modern psychodynamic views suggest that emotional and motivational processes may operate unconsciously. Current cognitive psychologists view conscious and unconscious processes as complementary forms of information processing. People use both voluntary conscious effort, or controlled processing, and little or no conscious effort, or automatic processing, to perform various tasks. Automatic processing facilitates divided attention, enabling us to do several things at the same time.

Research has demonstrated that information perceived unconsciously can influence people's behavior and feelings. For example, people with brain damage who have visual agnosia cannot consciously perceive some stimuli but nevertheless act in ways that indicate that their brain is processing the information. Those who have blindsight are blind in part of their visual field, yet they respond appropriately to stimuli that they report not being able to see. People's verbal and emotional responses and evaluations of ambiguous stimuli can be influenced by prior exposure to stimuli that were presented too briefly to be consciously perceived, a process known as priming using subliminal stimuli.

Consciousness enhances our ability to adapt to our environment. It makes information available to brain regions involved in planning and decision making, aids in impulse control, and helps us cope with new situations. Brain-imaging studies of healthy people and of brain-damaged people have discovered separate neural circuits for conscious versus unconscious information processing. Many theorists propose that the mind consists of many information-processing modules that work separately but also communicate with one another. Global-workspace models propose that consciousness arises from the unified, coordinated activity of multiple modules located in different brain areas.

Circadian rhythms are our daily biological clocks and are controlled by the suprachiasmatic nuclei of the hypothalamus. These rhythmic changes in body temperature, certain hormonal secretions, and other bodily functions such as sleep and waking states are on an approximately 24-hour cycle. Environmental changes such as seasons, jet lag, and night-shift work can alter circadian rhythms. For example, seasonal affective disorder (SAD) is a cyclic tendency to become psychologically depressed during certain months of the year (usually fall or winter).

Psychologists have been very interested in the nature of the sleep cycle. Electroencephalographic (EEG) recordings of brain waves show that beta waves, which have high frequency and low amplitude, occur during active waking states; alpha waves occur during feelings of relaxation or drowsiness. We go through five stages of sleep. Stage 1 is a stage of light sleep from which we can easily be awakened. As sleep becomes deeper in stage 2, sleep spindles, periodic bursts of brain wave activity, occur in the EEG patterns. Very slow and large delta waves occur in stage 3 and in stage 4 sleep, and then the EEG pattern changes as we go back into stage 3 and 2 patterns. At this point in the sleep cycle, people enter rapid-eye-movement (REM) sleep. During REM sleep, dreaming occurs frequently (although dreaming can also occur in non-REM stages) and physiological arousal increases to daytime levels for many people. Paradoxically, although the body is aroused during REM sleep, the muscles lose tone, become relaxed, and are effectively paralyzed during this stage.

The brain has no one "sleep center," but certain areas in the brain stem regulate falling asleep and REM sleep. Limbic system structures such as the amygdala are intensely active during REM sleep. Environmental factors and cultural norms also influence sleep. As we age, we sleep less and spend less time in stages 3 and 4. REM sleep declines during infancy and early childhood and then remains fairly stable. The number of hours of sleep we need is affected by both genetic and environmental factors. Cross-cultural differences in normal sleep patterns have been found. Studies of sleep deprivation have shown deficits in mood and in cognitive and physical performance.

Why do we sleep? The restoration model argues that sleep recharges our rundown bodies. Evolutionary/circadian sleep models suggest that sleep developed through evolutionary processes. Early humans may have performed tasks like hunting and food gathering during the day and stayed in shelter at night to avoid predators. Thus, the typical modern human sleeps at night. Both models contribute to a two-factor model of why we sleep. Although many theorists believe that REM sleep enhances memory consolidation, others argue for a purely biological function of keeping the brain healthy; the issue remains controversial.

There are several types of sleep disorders. Insomnia refers to chronic difficulty in falling or staying asleep. Narcoleptics have extreme daytime sleepiness and sudden, uncontrollable sleep attacks. People with REM-sleep behavior disorder (REM-BD) don't experience normal REM sleep paralysis and may kick violently or throw punches while asleep. Sleepwalkers typically walk during stage 3 or 4 sleep; though they seem vaguely aware of their environment, they are typically unresponsive to other people. Most people have nightmares, and some, typically children, have night terrors. People with sleep apnea repeatedly stop and restart breathing during sleep.

When and why do we dream? We tend to dream during REM states and during the last few hours of sleep. We typically dream about familiar people and places. Our cultural backgrounds, life experiences, and current concerns influence the content of our dreams. Freud's psychoanalytic theory argued that dreams serve "wish fulfillment." According to activation-synthesis theory, dreams occur because the cortex is trying to make sense of random neural activity. Problem-solving models suggest that dreams help us find creative solutions to problems. Cognitive-process dream theories argue that both dreaming and waking thought are produced via the same neural processes.

Psychologists study the effects of various drugs on the brain and on behavior. Agonists are drugs that increase neurotransmitter activity, whereas antagonists are drugs that decrease it. When a drug is used repeatedly, people may develop a tolerance to it and have compensatory responses, which are opposite to the drug effects. Stopping the use of a drug produces withdrawal symptoms, during which more compensatory processes occur. Substance dependence is a maladaptive pattern of drug use (commonly called drug addiction) that significantly impairs the user's life. Depressants such as alcohol, barbiturates, and tranquilizers depress nervous system activity. Stimulants such as amphetamines, cocaine, and Ecstasy (MDMA) increase neural firing. Opiates such as heroin produce pain relief and a sense of euphoria. Hallucinogens such as LSD produce hallucinations. Marijuana contains THC which binds to receptors throughout the brain. Marijuana smoke is carcinogenic, and the drug impairs reaction time, thinking, and other skills while users are "high." Many factors, from genetic and biological ones to environmental and cultural ones, seem to determine how a given drug affects a given individual.

Hypnosis is a state of heightened suggestibility. Hypnotized people subjectively experience their actions to be involuntary, but hypnosis does not seem to involve any unique power that would get people to act against their wills. People under hypnosis sometimes perform what seem to be fantastic physical feats, but the effects may simply be placebo effects. On the other hand, hypnosis seems to increase pain tolerance. Researchers seem to agree that hypnosis can affect amnesia, but they dispute the causes. Whether hypnosis can *improve* memory is highly debatable, and hypnotized study subjects have been shown to remember things that did not happen (pseudomemories). Dissociation theories of memory suggest that hypnosis literally involves a dissociation of consciousness such that a person simultaneously experiences two streams of consciousness. Social cognitive theories suggest that people are acting out the *role* of being hypnotized when under a hypnotic trance and thus act in ways that conform to the role of what they believe a hypnotized person can do.

C. Chapter Outline

THE PUZZLE OF CONSCIOUSNESS
    Characteristics of Consciousness
    Measuring States of Consciousness
    Levels of Consciousness
        The Freudian Viewpoint
        The Cognitive Viewpoint
    Unconscious Perception and Influence
        Visual Agnosia
        Blindsight
        Priming
        The Emotional Unconsciousness
    Why Do We Have Consciousness?
    The Neural Basis of Consciousness
        Windows to the Brain
        Consciousness as a Global Workspace
    In Review
CIRCADIAN RHYTHMS: OUR DAILY BIOLOGICAL CLOCKS
    Keeping Time: Brain and Environment
        Early Birds and Night Owls

What Do You Think? Early Birds, Climate, and Culture
Environmental Disruptions of Circadian Rhythms
Applying Psychological Science Outsmarting Jet Lag, Night-Work Disruptions, and Winter Depression
Melatonin Treatment: Uses and Cautions
Regulating Activity Schedules
In Review

SLEEP AND DREAMING
Stages of Sleep
Stage 1 through Stage 4
REM Sleep
Getting a Night's Sleep: From Brain to Culture
How Much Do We Sleep?
Do We Need Eight Hours of Nightly Sleep?
Sleep Deprivation
Why Do We Sleep?
Sleep and Bodily Restoration
Sleep as an Evolved Adaptation
Sleep and Memory Consolidation
Sleep Disorders
Insomnia
Narcolepsy
REM - Sleep Behavior Disorder
Sleepwalking
Nightmares and Night Terrors
Sleep Apnea
The Nature of Dreams
When Do We Dream?
What Do We Dream About?
Beneath the Surface When Dreams Come True
Why Do We Dream?
Activation-synthesis theory
Cognitive theories
Toward integration
Daydreams and Waking Fantasies
In Review

DRUG-INDUCED STATES
Drugs and the Brain
How Drugs Facilitate Synaptic Transmission
How Drugs Inhibit Synaptic Transmission
Drug Tolerance and Dependence
Learning, Drug Tolerance, and Overdose
Drug Addiction and Dependence
Misconceptions about substance dependence
Depressants
Alcohol

  Research Close-Up Drinking and Driving: Decision Making in Altered States
  Barbiturates and Tranquilizers
 Stimulants
  Amphetamines
  Cocaine
  Ecstasy (MDMA)
 Opiates
 Hallucinogens
 Marijuana
  Misconceptions about Marijuana
 From Genes to Culture: Determinants of Drug Effects
  Biological Factors
  Psychological Factors
  Environmental Factors
 In Review
HYPNOSIS
 The Scientific Study of Hypnosis
 Hypnotic Behaviors and Experiences
  Involuntary Control and Behaving Against One's Will
  Amazing Feats
  What Do You Think? Hypnosis and Amazing Feats
  Pain Tolerance
  Hypnotic Amnesia
  Hypnosis, Memory Enhancement, and Eyewitness Testimony
 Theories of Hypnosis
  Dissociation Theories
  Social-Cognitive Theories
 The Hypnotized Brain
 In Review

D. Review at a Glance: *Write the term that best fits the blank to review what you learned in this chapter.*

The Puzzle of Consciousness

(1)_____ is defined as our moment-to-moment awareness of ourselves and our environment. It is subjective, private, dynamic, and central to our sense of (2) _____. One of the earliest theorists about consciousness was (3) _____, who believed that the mind contains three levels of awareness: the conscious mind, the preconscious mind, and the (4) _____. Today, cognitive psychologists believe that both conscious and unconscious thought are complementary forms of (5) _____ _____. People use both voluntary attention and conscious effort, or (6) _____ processing, and (7) _____ processing, which is performed with little or no conscious effort. Automatic processing facilitates (8) _____ _____, which allows us to do more than one thing simultaneously.

Research has demonstrated that information perceived unconsciously can influence people's (9) _____ and (10) _____. People who have (11) _____ _____ and (12) _____ cannot consciously perceive some stimuli but nevertheless act in ways that indicate that their brain is processing the information.

Consciousness enhances our ability to (13) _____ to our environment. Brain-imaging studies have discovered separate neural circuits for (14) _____ versus (15) _____ information processing. (16) _____-_____ models propose that consciousness arises from the unified, coordinated activity of multiple modules located in different brain areas.

Circadian Rhythms: Our Daily Biological Clocks

The daily biological cycles that we are all subject to are called (17) _____ rhythms. These daily cycles are regulated by the (18) _____ _____ of the hypothalamus. Environmental disruptions such as jet lag, night-shift work, and changes of season can affect circadian rhythms. A disorder called (19) _____ _____ _____ (SAD) is a cyclic tendency to become psychologically depressed during certain months, which may result from a circadian rhythm disruption.

Sleep and Dreaming

When we are awake and alert, our brains show an EEG pattern of (20) _____ waves; (21) _____ waves typically occur when we are relaxed or drowsy. We cycle through different stages of sleep approximately every 90 minutes. Stage 1 is a stage of light sleep. Stage 2 is characterized by (22) _____ _____ in the EEG pattern. Stages 3 and 4 are characterized by (23) _____ waves in the EEG pattern; together they are called (24) _____-_____ sleep. Rapid eye movements and relaxation of the muscles due to lost muscle tone occur during (25) _____ sleep. It is not exactly clear *why* we sleep. The (26) _____ model argues that we sleep to recover from physical and mental fatigue. (27) _____/_____ models argue that the main purpose of sleep is to increase a species' chances of survival.

Many people have sleep disorders. A chronic difficulty in falling or remaining asleep is called (28) _____. Extreme daytime sleepiness and sudden, uncontrollable sleep attacks are characteristic of (29) _____. When the loss of muscle tone that causes normal REM sleep "paralysis" fails to occur, a person experiences (30) _____-_____ _____ _____. (31) _____ _____ is a condition in which people repeatedly stop and restart breathing during sleep.

Dreams more intense than nightmares often experienced by children are called (32) _____ _____. Freud believed that main function of dreaming is (33) _____ _____, and he distinguished between a dream's manifest content (the surface story) and the (34) _____ content, the disguised psychological meaning of the dream. A more modern theory argues that dreams are the result of the action of the cortex as it tries to make sense of random (35)_____ _____. This theory is called (36) _____-_____ theory. According to (37) _____-_____ models, dreams can help us find creative solutions to problems. Theories that focus on the process of how we dream and argue that dreams and waking states are governed by the same mental systems in the brain are called (38) _____-_____ dream theories. People who daydream so much that they virtually live in a vivid fantasy world that they control are said to have a (39) _____-_____ personality.

Drug-Induced States

The (40) _____-_____ barrier screens out many foreign substances from the brain but admits vital nutrients and many drugs. When a drug is used repeatedly, the intensity of its effects tends to decrease over time, a process called (41) _____. Because drugs affect homeostasis, the brain tries to adjust for the imbalance by producing (42) _____ responses. The occurrence of compensatory responses after discontinued drug use is called (43) _____. Drug addiction, technically called (44) _____ _____, is a maladaptive pattern of substance use that causes significant distress or impairment to the person. Drugs that decrease nervous system activity are called (45) _____, whereas drugs that increase neural firing are called (46) _____. Excessive use of alcohol, a depressant, may cause people not to monitor their actions or think about the long-term consequences of their behavior, a phenomenon called (47) _____ _____. Ecstasy (MDMA) has a chemical structure that partly resembles both the (48) _____ methamphetamine and the hallucinogen (49) _____. Other examples of (50) _____ are LSD and psilocybin. Drugs derived from the opium poppy, which relieve pain and are often strongly addictive, are called (51)_____ . Marijuana works by binding to receptors throughout the (52) _____. A drug's effects depends on its chemical actions, the physical and (53) _____ setting, cultural (54) _____ and learning, as well as the user's (55) _____ predispositions, expectations, and personality.

Hypnosis

Hypnosis is a state of heightened (56) _____ in which some people are able to experience imagined suggestions as if they were real. A standard series of pass-fail questions to determine the degree to which a person is subject to hypnotic induction is called a (57) _____ _____ scale. (58)_____ theories proposes that hypnosis involves a division of awareness such that a person simultaneously experiences two streams of (59)_____. A second set of theories of hypnosis called (60) _____-_____ theories suggest that people under hypnosis are simply acting out social roles. Brain-imaging studies reveal that hypnotized people show brain activity that is (61) _____ with their subjectively reported experiences.

E. Concept Cards

Truly learning a concept means integrating it into the way *you* think about things. To integrate concepts successfully, you must translate the words and examples your text or instructor provides into words and examples that are meaningful to you.

For this exercise, obtain some note cards (3" × 5" or 4" × 6") to make a deck of concept cards. On one side of each card, write the *concept* from the list provided (e.g., "selective attention") at the top. Read the textbook definition provided, and then write the definition *in your own words* on the concept card (e.g. for "selective attention," you might write "we pay attention to only some of the many things that surround us") Simply imagine that a friend has asked you what the concept means, and write down what you would answer. Writing the definition in your own words requires you to think deeply about its meaning. When next you see your own version of the definition, it will make intuitive sense to you—no translation required.

On the second side of the card, write your own example of the concept. Again, coming up with your own example requires you to think deeply about the application of the concept, and you will more easily understand and remember the example when you study for a test. If you use an example from the text, or from class, make it your own by writing it in your own words. You can always check with your instructor that your example is indeed a good example of the concept.

CONCEPT Definition in my own words (side 1 of card)	Example of the concept in my own words, preferably drawn from my own experience (side 2 of card)

The following is a list of all the boldface concepts from your textbook with the author's definition. Write the definition in your own words, together with your own example of the concept, to create a concept card as described previously, or write in the space provided.

Visual agnosia: An inability to visually recognize objects; however, it is not blindness

Consciousness: Our moment-to-moment awareness of ourselves and our environment

Selective attention: The process that focuses awareness on some stimuli to the exclusion of others

Controlled (conscious) processing: The conscious use of attention and effort to process information

Automatic (unconscious) processing: Information processing that does not require conscious awareness or effort

Divided attention: The capacity to attend to and perform more than one activity at the same time

Blindsight: Having blindness in part of one's visual field, yet being able to respond correctly to stimuli in that field despite reporting an inability to see those stimuli

Priming: Exposure to a stimulus influences (i.e., "primes") how a person subsequently responds to that same or another stimulus
Circadian rhythms: Daily biological cycles

Suprachiasmatic nuclei (SCN): Brain structures in the hypothalamus that regulate most circadian rhythms

Melatonin: A hormone that has a relaxing effect on the body

Chapter 6

Seasonal affective disorder (SAD): A cyclic tendency to become psychologically depressed during certain months of the year

Beta waves: The brain's electrical activity when a person is awake and alert

Alpha waves: The brain's electrical activity when a person is relaxed and drowsy; slower than beta waves

Delta waves: The brain's electrical activity when a person is in deep sleep; the waves are very slow and large

Slow-wave sleep: A state during which a person is in a deep slumber, the body is relaxed, activity in various parts of the brain has decreased, the person is hard to awaken, and the person may dream

REM sleep: A unique sleep stage characterized by rapid eye movements (REM), high arousal, muscular paralysis, and frequent dreaming

Restoration model: A theory proposing that sleep recharges our run-down bodies and allows us to recover from physical and mental fatigue

Evolutionary/circadian sleep models: Theories emphasizing that sleep's main purpose is to increase a species' chances of survival in relation to its environmental demands

Memory consolidation: The strengthening of neural circuits involved in remembering important information or experiences that we encountered during the day

Insomnia: Chronic difficulty in falling asleep, staying asleep, or experiencing restful sleep

Narcolepsy: Extreme daytime sleepiness and sudden, uncontrollable sleep attacks that may last from less than a minute to an hour

REM-sleep behavior disorder (RBD): A sleep disorder that occurs when the loss of muscle tone that causes normal REM-sleep paralysis is absent

Night terrors: Frightening dreams that arouse the sleeper to a near-panic state

Sleep apnea: The repeated stopping and restarting of breathing during sleep

Wish fulfillment: The gratification of our unconscious desires and needs

Activation-synthesis theory: The theory that dreams do not serve any particular function—they are merely a by-product of REM neural activity

Chapter 6

Problem-solving dream models: Theories suggesting that because dreams are not constrained by reality, they can help us find creative solutions to our problems and ongoing concerns

Cognitive-process dream theories: Theories that focus on the process of how we dream

Fantasy-prone personality: Person who often lives in a vivid, rich fantasy world that he or she controls

Blood-brain barrier: A special lining of tightly packed cells that lets vital nutrients pass through so that neurons can function

Agonist: A drug that increases the activity of a neurotransmitter

Antagonist: A drug that inhibits or decreases the action of a neurotransmitter

Tolerance: The decreasing responsivity to a drug

Compensatory responses: Reactions opposite to that of a drug

Withdrawal: An occurrence of compensatory responses after discontinued drug use

Substance dependence: A maladaptive pattern of substance use that causes a person significant distress or substantially impairs that person's life

Depressants: Drugs that decrease nervous system activity

Alcohol myopia: A "shortsightedness" in thinking caused by the inability to pay attention to as much information as sober people do

Stimulants: Drugs that increase neural firing and arouse the nervous system

Opiates: Opium and drugs derived from it, such as morphine, codeine, and heroin

Hallucinogens: Powerful mind-altering drugs that produce hallucinations

THC (Tetrahydrocannabinol): Marijuana's major active ingredient

Hypnosis: A state of heightened suggestibility in which some people are able to experience imagined situations as if they were real

Hypnotic susceptibility scales: A test containing a standard series of pass-fail suggestions that are read to a study subject after a hypnotic induction

Dissociation theories: Theories that view hypnosis as an altered state involving a division (dissociation) of consciousness

Social cognitive theories: Theories that propose that hypnotic experiences result from the expectations of people who are motivated to take on the role of being hypnotized

F. What's the Difference? A Concept Card Exercise

An important skill in learning concepts is being able to differentiate among concepts that are similar or related in some way. This skill is particularly relevant for multiple-choice tests, especially if you often find yourself wavering between two answers.

Once you have created your own deck of concept cards, select them two by two, each time answering the question "What's the difference between these two concepts?" You can use the word definitions of the concepts or the examples of the concepts to enhance your mastery of the material. In each case, choose pairs of concepts to compare those that are related, or similar, or that sound the same, or that could in some way be confused. It's much easier to spot the difference between two concepts when you are studying, with the textbook available, rather than when considering the question for the first time in a testing situation.

G. Apply What You Know

1. Keep track of your dreams for one week. The best way to do this is to write down whatever you can remember about your dreams immediately after you wake up. Then, at the end of the week, look back at the content of your dreams, and indicate whether you think that the content of your dreams best supports activation-synthesis theory or problem-solving theories.

Sunday:

Monday:

Tuesday:

Wednesday:

Thursday:

Friday:

Saturday:

Which theory (or theories) do the content of your dreams support? Explain why.

2. Not everyone sleeps 8 hours per night. Design a survey to examine the mean numbers of hours people sleep per night, and administer it to several of your fellow students. Graph your results. What do they show about the average sleeping habits of students at your school?

N (sample size):

Mean number of hours of sleep:

Graph of Results (Don't forget to label your axes!)

H. On the Web: *As with any online research, it is important to consider how legitimate a given source is before you rely on the information it presents. Your instructor or Internet adviser may give you some specific guidelines for distinguishing which kinds of Web sites tend to be reputable.*

A. Your text mentions a number of individuals who have made notable contributions to various topics in the study of consciousness. Search the Web for more information about some of those listed.

James Braid

Tanya Chartrand

Edouard Claparède

James Esdaile

Sigmund Freud

Calvin Hall and Robert Van de Castle

Stephen Kosslyn

Anton Mesmer

Martin Orne and Frederick Evans

B. Take a look at the concept cards you have created for this chapter, or the key concepts listed in section E. In the space provided, make a list of any whose definitions or associations you are not yet confident of and any you'd like to learn more about. Try entering the terms on your list into your search engine. Make notes of any helpful information you find.

Key Concept/Information Found

C. Investigate the latest research on sleep disorders, their causes, prevalence, and treatment. In addition to entering "sleep disorder" into your search engine, visit sites such as SleepNet, the National Center on Sleep Disorders Research, the American Academy of Sleep Medicine, and Medlineplus: Sleep Disorders. Summarize what you find.

I. Analyze This: *Chapter 1 of your textbook begins by presenting these four basic steps in the critical thinking process:*
- *"What exactly are you asking me to believe?"*
- *"How do you know? What is the evidence?"*
- *"Are there other possible explanations?"*
- *"What is the most reasonable conclusion?"*

You might picture this as a four-step analysis to help you decide whether to accept a given theory or assertion. Now it's your turn to put your textbook to this test.

Review the section in Chapter 6 of your textbook under the heading "Drug-Induced States." There you will find a discussion of various ways of studying how drugs affect people, including specific descriptions of individual drugs. If someone told you that alcohol is a more dangerous drug than marijuana, would you agree? Analyze that assertion in the space provided. When you have finished, consider using this four-step analysis to evaluate other assertions you encounter.

"What exactly are you asking me to believe?"

"How do you know? What is the evidence?"

"Are there other possible explanations?"

"What is the most reasonable conclusion?"

J. Practice Test

Multiple-Choice Items: *Write the letter corresponding to your answer in the space to the left of each item.*

_____ 1. Consciousness _____.
   a. is subjective in that everyone's sense of reality is different
   b. is public in that people can directly access others' conscious experience
   c. is static and unchanging for the individual

d. is not central to our sense of self

_____ 2. Selective attention _____.
   a. is a self-report measure of consciousness
   b. means we are fully conscious of all the many stimuli around us
   c. is a physiological measure of consciousness
   d. means we are fully conscious of only some of the many stimuli around us

_____ 3. When a person is learning how to type, their behavior usually involves _____ processing, but someone who can type quickly, efficiently, and accurately is probably using more _____ processing.
   a. automatic; controlled
   b. controlled; automatic
   c. automatic; effortful
   d. effortful; controlled

_____ 4. Most circadian rhythms are regulated by the brain's _____.
   a. thalamus
   b. suprachiasmatic nuclei
   c. biological clock
   d. sleep waves

_____ 5. Information-processing perspectives from cognitive psychology support some modern psychodynamic views that suggest that _____.
   a. the mind is made up of visual agnosia
   b. unconscious emotional and motivational urges influence our behavior
   c. divided attention is the source of all of our abilities
   d. the manifest content of dreams is the source of unconscious desires

_____ 6. _____ models propose that consciousness arises from the unified, coordinated activity of multiple modules located in different brain areas.
   a. Activation-synthesis
   b. Emotional-unconscious
   c. Circadian-rhythm
   d. Global-workspace

_____ 7. Olaf is a normal, happy person during the summer months in his home near the North Pole, but he becomes psychologically depressed every year during the dreary winter months and does not want to participate in any fun activities. Olaf's wife knows that he will probably feel better once springtime begins, as has happened before, but she wants them to have some enjoyable winter activities together and convinces Olaf to see his doctor. On the basis of this description, the doctor is most likely to suspect that Olaf has _____.
   a. priming
   b. sleep apnea
   c. SAD

       d. REM-sleep behavior disorder

_____ 8. Studies of people who have blindsight show that ____.
       a. they respond appropriately to stimuli that they report not being able to see
       b. they do not feel any pain even when painful stimuli are administered to them
       c. they often get too much sleep
       d. they are conscious of what other people are thinking

_____ 9. EEG recordings of the brain's electrical activity show ____ waves during alert waking states, ____ waves during relaxation and drowsy states, and ____ waves during deep sleep states.
       a. alpha; beta; delta
       b. alpha; delta; beta
       c. beta; alpha; delta
       d. delta; alpha; beta

_____ 10. REM is a period of sleep when ____.
       a. dreaming does not occur
       b. physiological arousal can increase to daytime levels
       c. dreams are shorter than in non-REM sleep
       d. legs and arms typically flail away

_____ 11. Studies examining the sleep habits of identical and fraternal twins have revealed that ____.
       a. genetic factors are significant, but environmental factors also account for important sleep differences
       b. twins have insomnia more than other people do
       c. genetic factors account for essentially all of the sleep differences
       d. environmental factors account for essentially all of the sleep differences

_____ 12. Patients who have ____ are often misdiagnosed as having a mental disorder rather than a sleep disorder, and may be mistakenly viewed as lazy at work, because they become drowsy or fall asleep uncontrollably. They report a lowered quality of life and are prone to accidents.
       a. sleep walking
       b. night terrors
       c. narcolepsy
       d. visual agnosia

_____ 13. You awaken in the middle of the night to find your roommate standing in the corner of your room with an aggressive look on his face, punching a pillow, and running in place. Despite this strange behavior, you realize that your roommate is still asleep. When you wake him, he tells you he was having a bizarre dream about being in a fight while running on a treadmill. Given what

you have learned in introductory psychology, it is *most likely* that your roommate _____.
a. may have narcolepsy
b. was having a night terror
c. may have sleep apnea
d. may have REM behavior disorder

14. A wife is disturbed many times during the night by her husband's apparent difficulty breathing, although he doesn't have a cold or allergies. Every few minutes, her husband's breathing seems to stop until he gasps or snorts and then starts breathing again. It is *most likely* that the husband has _____.
a. sleep apnea
b. night terrors
c. side effects from REM sleep
d. nightmares related to drowning

15. Stage 2 sleep is characterized by _____.
a. paralysis of the limbs
b. rapid eye movements
c. sleep spindles
d. delta waves

16. Because of censorship codes in the early years of motion pictures, directors could not show sexual activity on-screen. Instead, they sometimes used metaphors for sex such as picturing a train going into a tunnel. If such content appeared in a dream, Freud would consider the content as a symptom of _____.
a. problem-solving
b. activation-synthesis
c. the brain's attempt to understand random neural content
d. wish fulfillment

17. Criticism of the activation-synthesis theory of dreaming has suggested that it overestimates the_____ of dreams and fails to consider the fact that dreams also occur _____.
a. wish fulfillment; during REM sleep
b. problem-solving ability; during REM sleep
c. bizarreness; during non-REM sleep
d. interpretive capacity; in the daytime

18. The theories that suggest that dreaming and waking thought are produced by the same mental systems in the brain are called _____ theories.
a. problem-solving
b. activation-synthesis
c. wish fulfillment
d. cognitive-process

_____ 19. Beth has a very vivid imagination. Though she has an ordinary job, she often imagines she is working on top-secret projects with national security implications. When at home by herself, she is easily able to visualize herself in many exciting and exotic places that she has in fact never actually visited. According to the text, Beth would *best* be classified as having ____.
   a. high hypnotic susceptibility
   b. a fantasy-prone personality
   c. divided attention
   d. a hallucinatory personality

_____ 20. Drugs that inhibit or decrease the actions of a neurotransmitter ____.
   a. are called stimulants
   b. are called antagonists
   c. are called agonists
   d. breach the blood-brain barrier

_____ 21. Opiates such as morphine and codeine both contain molecules that are similar to endorphins, the body's natural painkillers. Opiates like these bind to receptor sites that are keyed to endorphins and trigger similar pain reducing responses. Given these characteristics, both morphine and codeine would be classified as ____.
   a. antagonists
   b. hallucinogens
   c. antigens
   d. agonists

_____ 22. In order to stay up late to study for exams, Sara starts drinking beverages containing caffeine. After continuing this practice for several months, Sara notices that she needs to consume more caffeine to stave off drowsiness. This decrease in her response to caffeine is *best viewed* as an example of ____.
   a. drug withdrawal
   b. drug tolerance
   c. the placebo effect
   d. drug dependence

_____ 23. If a drug is introduced into the nervous system, the body attempts to maintain its state of optimal physiological balance, called ____, by adjusting for this imbalance by producing ____, which are reactions opposite to the effect of the drug.
   a. tolerance; compensatory responses
   b. withdrawal symptoms; homeostasis
   c. homeostasis; compensatory responses
   d. compensatory responses; withdrawal symptoms

_____ 24. Alcohol is a(n) _____.
   a. depressant
   b. stimulant
   c. hallucinogen
   d. agonist

_____ 25. Drugs such as LSD and mescaline are called _____. They tend to distort or intensify sensory experience and can blur the boundary between reality and fantasy.
   a. depressants
   b. hallucinogens
   c. opiates
   d. stimulants

_____ 26. Marijuana contains THC, which binds to receptors _____.
   a. for cancer
   b. that make the person more susceptible to hypnosis
   c. on the brain stem in particular
   d. throughout the brain

_____ 27. Research in the area of forensic psychology has found that hypnosis _____ a reliable way to enhance memory, and that hypnotized participants typically remember information _____ than nonhypnotized participants who are asked to use imagery or other memory tricks to facilitate recall.
   a. is not; no better
   b. is; no better
   c. is not; better
   d. is; better

_____ 28. Hypnosis is a state of _____.
   a. stage 3 asleep
   b. unusual strength
   c. heightened suggestibility
   d. activation-synthesis

_____ 29. Studies of hypnosis have shown that _____.
   a. hypnosis can increase pain tolerance
   b. hypnosis usually improves one's memory
   c. people under hypnotic induction are much stronger than nonhypnotized people
   d. hypnotized people subjectively experience their actions to be entirely voluntary

_____ 30. Which theory argues that hypnotic effects occur, because people are acting out a social role?
   a. dissociation theory

b. divided-consciousness theory
c. social cognitive theory
d. selective-attention theory

True/False Items: *Write T or F in the space provided to the left of each item.*

_____ 1. The voluntary use of attention and conscious effort in the performance of tasks is called automatic processing.

_____ 2. Most circadian rhythms are regulated by the brain's suprachiasmatic nuclei.

_____ 3. A pattern of beta waves occurs in stage 1 sleep.

_____ 4. Dreams occur only in REM sleep.

_____ 5. Almost all adults need at least 8 hours of sleep per night.

_____ 6. People who have narcolepsy have sudden, uncontrollable sleep attacks.

_____ 7. Decreasing responsivity to a drug is called withdrawal.

_____ 8. Alcohol is a stimulant, which explains why partygoers become livelier when they drink.

_____ 9. Marijuana has no proven ill effects.

_____ 10. Hypnosis can increase one's pain tolerance.

Short-Answer Questions

1. Distinguish between controlled and automatic processing.

2. What are circadian rhythms, and how are they controlled by the brain?

3. Describe three different sleep disorders.

4. What is the relationship between drug tolerance, compensatory responses, and withdrawal symptoms?

5. Describe the difference between the dissociation and social cognition theories of hypnosis.

Essay Questions

1. In view of what you learned about circadian rhythms in this chapter, what measures do you think workers and employers should take to reduce the effects of circadian rhythm disruption caused by work schedules?

2. How can a person tell if he or she is developing a substance dependence? What is the relationship between substance dependence and drug tolerance/withdrawal?

3. Do you support the legalization of marijuana for medical use? If so, under what circumstances and conditions? Defend your position for or against legalization, citing information in this chapter.

Answer Keys

Answer Key for Review at a Glance

1. Consciousness
2. self
3. Freud
4. unconscious
5. information processing
6. controlled
7. automatic
8. divided attention
9. behavior
10. feelings
11. visual agnosia
12. blindsight
13. adapt
14. conscious
15. unconscious
16. Global-workspace
17. circadian
18. suprachiasmatic nuclei
19. seasonal affective disorder
20. beta
21. alpha
22. sleep spindles
23. delta
24. slow-wave
25. REM
26. restoration
27. Evolutionary/circadian
28. insomnia
29. narcolepsy
30. REM-sleep behavior disorder
31. Sleep apnea
32. night terrors
33. wish fulfillment
34. latent
35. nerve impulses
36. activation-synthesis
37. problem-solving
38. cognitive-process
39. fantasy-prone
40. blood-brain
41. tolerance
42. compensatory
43. withdrawal
44. substance dependence
45. depressants
46. stimulants
47. alcohol myopia
48. stimulant
49. mescaline
50. hallucinogens
51. opiates
52. brain
53. environmental
54. norms
55. genetic
56. suggestibility
57. hypnotic susceptibility
58. Dissociation
59. consciousness
60. social cognitive
61. consistent

Answer Key for Practice Test Multiple-Choice Items

1. a
2. d
3. b
4. b
5. b
6. d
7. c
16. d
17. c
18. d
19. b
20. b
21. d
22. b

8. a	23. c
9. c	24. a
10. b	25. b
11. a	26. d
12. c	27. a
13. d	28. c
14. a	29. a
15. c	30. c

Answer Key for Practice Test True/False Questions

1. F	6. T
2. T	7. F
3. F	8. F
4. F	9. F
5. F	10. T

Answer Key for Practice Test Short-Answer Questions

1. Controlled processing involves the voluntary use of attention and conscious effort. Automatic processing occurs when we carry out routine actions or well-learned tasks with little or no conscious effort.

2. Circadian rhythms are daily biological cycles of body temperature, certain hormonal secretions, and other bodily functions. Most circadian rhythms are regulated by the brain's suprachiasmatic nuclei, which are located in the hypothalamus.

3. Insomnia is difficulty in falling asleep, staying asleep, or getting restful sleep. Narcolepsy involves extreme daytime sleepiness and sudden sleep attacks. In REM-sleep behavior disorder, the normal REM-sleep paralysis is absent. People with sleep apnea stop and restart breathing during sleep. Sleepwalking, during which the person is somewhat aware of his or her surroundings, but unresponsive to other people, is not unusual. Some sleepers, particularly children, have night terrors, which are more intense than nightmares.

4. Tolerance stems from the body's attempt to maintain homeostasis. The body will produce compensatory responses as a way of doing this. Withdrawal occurs when compensatory responses continue after the person stops using the drug.

5. According to dissociation theory, hypnosis involves a division of consciousness such that the person experiences two streams of consciousness simultaneously. Social cognitive theories suggest that hypnotic experiences result from expectations of people who are taking on the "hypnotic" role.

Answer Key for Practice Test Essay Questions

As you may have guessed, there are no right or wrong answers to the essay questions in this practice test. That does not mean, however, that all essays are equally good. To get maximum learning benefit from the essay questions, do the following:

- Review each essay a day or two after you wrote it, noting any necessary corrections and any additional support for your points that you can think of.
- Review the section in your textbook that pertains to the topic of each essay. Annotate your essay with any corrections or additional support for your points that you find in the text.
- Spend a few minutes researching the topic of each essay on the Internet. Annotate your essay further with any additional (reliable) information you find.
- Finally, reread each essay with the annotations you have added.

Chapter 7
LEARNING: THE ROLE OF EXPERIENCE

A. Learning Objectives: *These objectives are expanded from the Focus Questions found in the margins of your textbook. When you have mastered the material in this chapter, you will be able to:*

7.1   Define learning.

7.2   Define and describe habituation.

7.3   Describe the work of Pavlov in establishing the foundations of classical conditioning.

7.4   Describe how stimulus generalization, stimulus discrimination, and higher-order conditioning extend classical conditioning.

7.5   Describe how the principles of classical conditioning can be used to explain the acquisition and treatment of fears and phobias, attraction or aversion to specific stimuli, and physical symptoms with no medical cause.

7.6   Describe the work of Thorndike and Skinner in establishing the foundations of operant conditioning.

7.7   Contrast classical and operant conditioning.

7.8   Differentiate among positive reinforcement, negative reinforcement, aversive punishment, response cost, and operant extinction.

7.9   Describe the research findings regarding corporal punishment in parenting.

7.10 Describe the effects of delayed versus immediate consequences upon learning as well as on learning situations that involve reciprocal consequences.

7.11 Contrast shaping and chaining in operant conditioning.

7.12 Define and describe the various schedules of reinforcement.

7.13 Describe how the two-factor theory combines escape and avoidance conditioning with classical conditioning to explain maintenance of classically conditioned associations.

7.14 Describe how operant conditioning can be applied in educational and work settings and in specialized animal training.

7.15   Describe the five main steps in a behavioral self-regulation program.

7.16   Explain how research on conditioned taste aversions, variability of phobic stimuli, and instinctive drift supports the existence of biological preparedness.

7.17   Describe how instinctive drift illustrates biological preparedness.

7.18   Describe how research on insight and cognitive maps challenged behavioral views on learning.

7.19   Describe the role of cognition in classical and operant conditioning, and explain how Tolman illustrated latent learning.

7.20   Define observational learning, describe Bandura's modeling theory, and outline the steps in the modeling process.

7.21   Describe the application of social cognitive theory to solve global problems.

7.22   Describe how learning influences the brain, and summarize biological, psychological, and environmental factors involved in learning.

B. Chapter Overview

This chapter covers the basic processes of learning, which include habituation, classical conditioning, operant conditioning, and observational learning. Biological and cognitive aspects of learning are also addressed.

Learning is a process by which experience produces a relatively enduring change in an organism's behavior or capabilities. Research has suggested that the environment shapes behavior through both personal adaptation and species adaptation. Whereas evolution focuses on species' adaptation passed down biologically across generations, learning focuses on personal adaptation, that is, how an organism's behavior changes in response to environmental stimuli encountered during its lifetime.

The simplest type of learning process may be habituation, the decrease in response strength to a repeated stimulus. By learning not to respond to familiar stimuli, an organism may conserve resources to pay attention to more important stimuli.

Classical conditioning, in which an organism learns to associate two stimuli such that one stimulus comes to produce a response that only the other previously did, became famous through the work of Russian physiologist Ivan Pavlov with the salivary response of dogs. A stimulus that reflexively produces a response is called an unconditioned stimulus (UCS), and the response is called an unconditioned response (UCR). The stimulus repeatedly paired with the UCS that comes to produce the response is called the conditioned stimulus (CS), and the learned response to the CS is then known as the conditioned response (CR). This entire process is known as acquisition. Forward, short-delay conditioning appears to work best. In this procedure, the CS is presented first and is still present when the UCS appears. Extinction occurs when the CS is repeatedly presented without the UCS, such that the response strength diminishes significantly. For example, if a dog has been conditioned to salivate in response to a bell (CS) paired with food (UCS), but the bell is then repeatedly sounded without the food being given to the dog, the dog will stop salivating.

Occasionally, a response that has been extinguished will reappear after some time in response to the old CS, a process called spontaneous recovery. Once a CR is acquired, an organism may respond to similar stimuli in the same way, a process called stimulus generalization. Discrimination among stimuli occurs when an organism responds differently to stimuli, including those that are similar but not exactly the same as the original CS. When a neutral stimulus comes to produce a response through pairing with an already-established CS, higher-order conditioning has occurred. Many examples of this can be seen in everyday life. For example, politicians who appear in front of large American flags are using higher-order conditioning to influence the development of attitudes toward them. Classical conditioning has other applied aspects. The process can be used to influence both the acquisition and the elimination of fear. Classical conditioning processes may explain our attraction and aversion to other people and can also be associated with symptoms of allergies and other illness.

Operantly conditioned responses are emitted voluntarily rather than being elicited involuntarily as are classically conditioned responses, and they are influenced through their consequences. Thorndike's law of effect says that in a given situation, a response followed by a satisfying consequence will become more likely to occur, whereas a response followed by an annoying consequence will become less likely to occur. The term *operant behavior* was coined by B. F. Skinner to describe how an organism operates on its environment to get what it wants and to avoid what it doesn't want. Skinner's analysis of operant behavior involved studying the antecedents (A) of the behavior, the behavior emitted (B), and the consequences (C) of the behavior. In operant conditioning, the organism learns an association between the behavior and its consequences. The antecedent conditions come to signal that a certain consequence will follow if a certain behavior is emitted.

Reinforcement and punishment are the consequences that affect the likelihood of a response under the antecedent conditions. Reinforcement strengthens a response that precedes it, whereas punishment decreases the strength of a response that precedes it. Operant extinction is the weakening and eventual disappearance of a response, because it is no longer reinforced.

Primary reinforcers, such as food and water, are stimuli that satisfy biological needs. Secondary reinforcers, such as money, are conditioned reinforcers because they have become associated with primary reinforcers. For example, money can be used to buy food. Negative reinforcement is *not* the same thing as punishment. Negative reinforcement occurs when the avoidance or removal of an unpleasant stimulus results in a strengthened response. For example, we use umbrellas because they prevent us from getting wet. Punishment (often called aversive punishment) is an aversive stimulus, such as a slap or rebuke, which serves to weaken a response. In response cost, a response is weakened (punished) by the removal of an attractive stimulus. For example, taking away TV privileges or car keys is a response-cost technique that parents may use to decrease undesirable behavior in their children.

Operant conditioning can be used to shape behavior by rewarding successive approximations of the behavior. Similarly, chaining is used to condition complex behaviors. Chaining begins with the last step of the behavior chain being reinforced, and thus trained. The prior step is then reinforced by the ability to perform the next one and obtain reinforcement. This step-by-step procedure continues until the entire chain of behavior is performed and reinforced. Generalization and discrimination work with operant conditioning in much the same way as with classical conditioning. Operant generalization occurs when an operant response occurs to a new antecedent stimulus that is similar to an old one. Operant discrimination occurs when an operant response will occur to one antecedent stimulus but not to another; the behavior is then said to be under stimulus control.

Schedules of reinforcement influence much of operant behavior. On a continuous schedule, every response is reinforced, whereas only some responses are reinforced on a partial schedule. Continuous reinforcement leads to more rapid acquisition, but also to more rapid extinction of operantly conditioned behavior. Reinforcement may be administered on a fixed or a variable schedule, as well as on either a ratio or an interval schedule. Ratio schedules depend on the number of responses given, whereas interval schedules depend on the time interval since the last reinforcement. On a fixed-ratio schedule, the behavior is reinforced after a certain number of responses; for example, every sixth response is reinforced on an FR-6 schedule. On a variable-ratio schedule (e.g., VR-6), reinforcement is given after an average number of responses (e.g., sometimes after 3, sometimes after 6, sometimes after 9). On a fixed-interval schedule, the first response that occurs after a certain amount of time is reinforced—for example, after 5 minutes on FI-5. Finally, on a variable-interval schedule, the first response after a variable amount of time is reinforced—for example, at varying intervals averaging 5 minutes on a VI-5 schedule. Ratio schedules tend to produce higher rates of responding than interval schedules, and variable schedules are associated with greater resistance to extinction than fixed schedules.

Escape and avoidance responses are conditioned through negative reinforcement, when the organism escapes or avoids an aversive stimulus. The two-factor theory of avoidance learning suggests that both classical and operant conditioning are involved in avoidance responses; a fear response to an object may be acquired through classical conditioning, and the subsequent avoidance behavior is maintained through negative reinforcement.

Like classical conditioning, operant conditioning has many applications. Education, work, treatment of psychological disorders, and animal training are all areas in which operant conditioning principles have been successfully applied. Skinner's work gave rise to the field of applied behavior analysis, which combines the behavioral approach with the scientific method in an attempt to solve individual and societal problems through the use of operant conditioning techniques.

Biological and cognitive psychologists have added to our understanding of conditioned behavior. Biological psychologists remind us that an organism's evolutionary history influences behavior, placing certain biological constraints on learning. Martin Seligman's concept of preparedness suggests that animals are biologically "prewired" to learn behaviors related to their survival as a species. For example, animals develop conditioned taste aversions to learn to avoid foods and liquids that are bad for them. Similarly, animals may be prepared to fear certain stimuli. This fear then helps them to avoid or escape the stimuli, thus increasing their chances of survival and reproduction. Some responses are difficult to operantly condition because of instinctive drift, the tendency of animals to engage in instinctive behavior regardless of their training. Biology also affects animals' ability to learn through the action of brain structures such as the hypothalamus and through neurotransmitters such as dopamine.

Cognitive psychologists address the mental events that may be involved in learning. The occurrence of insight problem-solving and Tolman's research on latent learning in rats were early challenges to the strict behaviorist approach to conditioning which ignored internal cognitive processes. Cognitive models are known as S-O-R models: The initial O represents the influence of the organism's cognitive processes as an intermediate step between stimulus and response. The expectancy model, for instance, argues that in classical conditioning the CS produces an expectancy (cognition) that the UCS will occur. Cognition is also present in operant conditioning. Cognitive theorists emphasize that organisms develop an awareness, or expectancy, of the relationship between their behavior and its consequences.

Aside from classical and operant conditioning, people also learn by observing models, as emphasized in Albert Bandura's social cognitive theory (also called social learning theory). Bandura views modeling as a four-step process that includes several cognitive factors: attention, retention, reproduction, and motivation to perform the behavior. Self-efficacy represents people's belief that they have the capability to perform behaviors that will produce a desired outcome, and hence motivates them to perform the observed behavior. Research has shown that observing aggressive or prosocial models can increase children's tendency to engage in aggressive or prosocial behaviors, respectively. Modeling is often a key instructional technique in learning everyday skills, and social cognitive theory has stimulated intervention programs to address social problems worldwide.

Learning represents our ability to adapt to our environment and is highly dependent on the structure and functioning of the brain. The brain's ability to adapt and modify itself in response to experience underlies our ability to learn. No single part of the brain controls learning, although structures such as the hypothalamus, the cerebellum, and the amygdala, as well as the functioning of neurotransmitters such as dopamine, are involved in acquiring learned behaviors.

C. Chapter Outline

ADAPTING TO THE ENVIRONMENT
    Learning as Personal Adaptation
    Habituation
    In Review
CLASSICAL CONDITIONING: ASSOCIATING ONE STIMULUS WITH ANOTHER
    Pavlov's Pioneering Research
    Basic Principles
        Acquisition
        Extinction and Spontaneous Recovery
        What Do You Think? Why Did Carol's Car Phobia Persist?
        Generalization and Discrimination
        Higher-Order Conditioning
    Applications of Classical Conditioning
        Acquiring and Overcoming Fear
        What Do You Think? Was the "Little Albert" Study Ethical?
        Attraction and Aversion
        Sickness and Health
            Allergic reactions
            Anticipatory nausea and vomiting
            The immune system
    In Review
OPERANT CONDITIONING: LEARNING THROUGH CONSEQUENCES
    Thorndike's Law of Effect
    Skinner's Analysis of Operant Conditioning
        Distinguishing Operant from Classical Conditioning
    Antecedent Conditions: Identifying When to Respond
    Consequences: Determining How to Respond
        Positive Reinforcement
            Primary and secondary reinforcers
        Negative Reinforcement
        Operant Extinction
        Aversive Punishment
        Beneath the Surface: Spare the Rod . . . Spoil the Child?
        Response Cost
        Immediate, Delayed, and Reciprocal Consequences
        What Do You Think? Can You Explain the "Supermarket Tantrum"?
    Shaping and Chaining: Taking One Step at a Time
    Generalization and Discrimination
    Schedules of Reinforcement
        Fixed-Ratio Schedule

Variable-Ratio Schedule
Fixed-Interval Schedule
Variable-Interval Schedule
Reinforcement Schedules, Learning, and Extinction
Escape and Avoidance Conditioning
Applications of Operant Conditioning
Education and the Workplace
Specialized Animal Training
Modifying Problem Behaviors
Applying Psychological Science: Using Operant Principles to Modify Your Behavior
In Review

CROSSROADS OF CONDITIONING
Biological Constraints: Evolution and Preparedness
Constraints on Classical Conditioning: Learned Taste Aversions
Are We Biologically Prepared to Fear Certain Things?
Constraints on Operant Conditioning: Animals That "Won't Shape Up"
Cognition and Conditioning
Early Challenges to Behaviorism: Insight and Cognitive Maps
Cognition in Classical Conditioning
Cognition in Operant Conditioning
The role of awareness
Latent learning
Self-evaluations as reinforcers and punishers
In Review

OBSERVATIONAL LEARNING: WHEN OTHERS SHOW THE WAY
Bandura's Social Cognitive Theory
The Modeling Process and Self-Efficacy
Imitation of Aggression and Prosocial Behavior
Applications of Observational Learning
Research Close-Up: Using Social Cognitive Theory to Prevent AIDS: A National Experiment
In Review

THE ADAPTIVE BRAIN
In Review

D. Review at a Glance: *Write the term that best fits the blank to review what you learned in this chapter.*

Adapting to the Environment

(1)_____ is a process by which experience produces a relatively enduring change in an organism's behavior or capabilities. Our capacity for learning is of (2)_____ significance, as it increases our likelihood of surviving and reproducing in our environment. The environment shapes behavior in individuals through (3)_____

_____. Over time, through the process of evolution, certain behaviors in a species are likely to be selected because of their aid in survival and reproduction, a process called (4) _____ _____. There are several types of learning. One of the simplest is (5) _____, a decrease in the strength of a response to a repeated stimulus.

Classical Conditioning: Associating One Stimulus with Another

When an organism learns to associate two stimuli, one of the stimuli comes to produce a response previously produced only by the other one. This learning process is called (6) _____ _____, a phenomenon studied in dogs by (7) _____. During the period of (8) _____, a response is being learned. Initially, a stimulus known as the (9) _____ stimulus produces a response, the (10) _____ response, without learning. A second stimulus is repeatedly paired with the UCS. After several learning trials, the second stimulus is presented by itself, and the animal will then respond similarly to the second stimulus as it had originally done to the UCS. This second stimulus is then known as the (11) _____ stimulus, and the response is known as the (12) _____ response.

Classically conditioned responses can be eliminated through the use of (13) _____ procedures, during which the CS is presented repeatedly without the UCS. Sometimes extinguished responses will appear weeks, months, or even years later, a phenomenon called (14) _____ _____. Another phenomenon of classical conditioning, called (15) _____ _____, occurs when stimuli similar to the initial CS elicit a CR. Stimulus (16) _____ is the ability to distinguish between stimuli. The process of pairing a neutral stimulus with an already-established CS is known as (17) _____-_____ conditioning.

Operant Conditioning: Learning through Consequences

While Pavlov was studying classical conditioning, Edward L. Thorndike was formulating his (18) _____ _____ _____, which states that responses that are followed by satisfying consequences will become more likely to occur, whereas those responses followed by annoying consequences will become less likely to occur. B. F. Skinner studied (19) _____ conditioning, a type of learning in which behavior is influenced by its consequences. Skinner studied this conditioning experimentally by designing a special chamber called a (20) _____ _____.

Reinforcement and punishment, central features of operant conditioning, differ in this fundamental way: (21) _____ strengthens a response that precedes it, and (22) _____ weakens a response that precedes it. Skinner identified the ABCs of operant conditioning, or the (23) _____, (24) _____, and (25) _____. An antecedent condition that signifies that a particular response will now produce a consequence is called a (26) _____ stimulus.

(27)_____ reinforcement occurs when a response is strengthened by the subsequent presentation of a stimulus. There are two types of positive reinforcers. (28)_____ reinforcers are stimuli that an organism finds reinforcing because they satisfy biological needs, and (29)_____ reinforcers become reinforcers through their association with primary reinforcers. (30)_____ reinforcement occurs when a response is strengthened by the removal of an aversive stimulus. The weakening and eventual disappearance of a response, called operant (31) _____, occurs because the response is no longer being reinforced.

In the procedure called (32) _____ _____, a response is weakened by the subsequent presentation of an aversive stimulus. In (33) _____ _____, a response is weakened by the subsequent removal of an attractive stimulus. In general, reinforcement or punishment occurs immediately after a response. Sometimes people are asked to forego immediate reinforcement to wait for a better, later reinforcement. Such reinforcements are called (34)_____ consequences.

Operant conditioning can be used to create new responses and sequences of behaviors. (35)_____ is a procedure by which new behaviors or sequences of behaviors are created through reinforcements of successive approximations of the target behavior. (36)_____ creates a sequence of responses by reinforcing each response with the opportunity to perform the next behavior in the sequence. Generalization and discrimination work with operant conditioning much like they work with classical conditioning. Operant (37) _____ occurs when an operant response occurs to a new antecedent stimulus that is similar to an old one. Operant (38) _____ occurs when an operant response will occur to one antecedent stimulus but not to another; the behavior is then said to be under (39) _____ _____.

Reinforcement typically occurs on schedules of reinforcement. On a (40) _____ schedule, every response is reinforced. On (41) _____ schedules, only some responses are reinforced. On (42) _____-_____ schedules, reinforcement is given after a fixed number of responses, whereas on (43) _____-_____ schedules, reinforcement is given for the first response after a certain amount of time. On a (44) _____ _____ schedule, reinforcement is given after a variable number of responses, whereas on a (45) _____ _____ schedule, reinforcement is given for the first response after an average amount of time. (46)_____ schedules tend to produce the highest rate of response. (47)_____ schedules tend to produce the greatest resistance to extinction.

(48)_____ and avoidance responses are conditioned when the organism learns to escape or avoid an aversive stimulus. The two-factor theory of avoidance learning suggests that both (49) _____ and (50) _____ conditioning are involved in avoidance responses; a fear response to an object may be acquired through (51) _____ conditioning and the subsequent avoidance behavior is maintained through (52) _____ reinforcement.

Crossroads of Conditioning

Biological psychologists have highlighted certain biological (53) _____ on learning. Martin Seligman's concept of (54) _____ suggests that organisms may be biologically "prewired" to learn behaviors related to their survival as a species. For example, pairing a taste with the experience of illness (such as stomach illness, nausea, and vomiting) produces a (55) _____ _____ _____, and certain fear responses are easily learned, but others are not. Researchers have found that sometimes animals cannot be operantly conditioned, because they revert to behaviors that were part of their evolutionary history instead, a phenomenon called (56) _____ _____.

Cognitive psychologists address the mental events that may be involved in learning. Studies showed that chimps were able to learn by (57) _____, the sudden perception of a useful relationship. Psychologist Edward Tolman discovered that rats seem to develop a mental representation, or (58) _____ _____, of a maze. Tolman's experiments also supported the concept of (59) _____ learning, learning that occurs but is not demonstrated until there is an incentive to do so. S-O-R is an abbreviation for cognitive models, in which the O stands for the organism's (60) _____ processes and connects the stimulus and the response.

Observational Learning: When Others Show the Way

People also learn by (61) _____ others, through a process called (62) _____, which is emphasized in Albert Bandura's (63) _____-_____ theory (also called social learning theory). Bandura views modeling as a four-step process that includes several cognitive factors: attention, (64) _____, (65) _____, and motivation to perform the behavior. (66) _____-_____ represents people's belief that they have the capability to perform behaviors that will produce a desired outcome, and hence motivates them to perform the observed behavior. Research has shown that observing aggressive or prosocial models can (67) _____ children's tendency to engage in (68) _____ or (69) _____ behaviors, respectively.

The Adaptive Brain

Learning represents our ability to adapt to our (70) _____ and is highly dependent on the structure and (71) _____ of the brain. The brain's ability to (72) _____ itself in response to experience underlies our ability to learn. No single part of the brain controls learning, although structures such as the (73) _____, the cerebellum, and the amygdala, as well as the functioning of (74) _____ such as dopamine, are involved in acquiring learned behaviors.

E. Concept Cards

Truly learning a concept means integrating it into the way *you* think about things. To integrate concepts successfully, you must translate the words and examples your text or instructor provides into words and examples that are meaningful to you.

For this exercise, obtain some note cards (3" × 5" or 4" × 6") to make a deck of concept cards. On one side of each card, write the *concept* from the list below (e.g., "habituation") at the top. Read the textbook definition provided, and then write the definition *in your own words* on the concept card (e.g., for "habituation," you might write "getting used to something that keeps happening"). Simply imagine that a friend has asked you what the concept means, and write down what you would answer. Writing the definition in your own words requires you to think deeply about its meaning. When next you see your own version of the definition, it will make intuitive sense to you—no translation required.

On the second side of the card, write your own example of the concept. Again, coming up with your own example requires you to think deeply about the application of the concept, and you will more easily understand and remember the example when you study for a test. If you use an example from the text, or from class, make it your own by writing it in your own words. You can always check with your instructor that your example is indeed a good example of the concept.

CONCEPT Definition in my own words (side 1 of card)	Example of the concept in my own words, preferably drawn from my own experience (side 2 of card)

The following is a list of all the boldface concepts from your textbook with the author's definition. Write the definition in your own words, together with your own example of the concept, to create a *concept card* as described previously, or write in the space provided.

Learning: A process by which experience produces a relatively enduring change in an organism's behavior or capabilities

Habituation: A decrease in the strength of response to a repeated stimulus

Classical conditioning: A process in which an organism learns to associate two stimuli (e.g., a song and a pleasant event), such that one stimulus (the song) comes to elicit a response (feeling happy) that originally was elicited only by the other stimulus (the pleasurable event)

Unconditioned stimulus (UCS): A stimulus that elicits a reflexive or innate response (the UCR) without prior learning

Unconditioned response (UCR): A reflexive or innate response that is elicited by a stimulus (the UCS) without prior learning

Conditioned stimulus (CS): A stimulus that, through association with a UCS, comes to elicit a conditioned response similar to the original UCR

Conditioned response (CR): A response elicited by a conditioned stimulus

Extinction: A process in which the CS is presented repeatedly in the absence of the UCS, causing the CR to weaken and eventually disappear

Spontaneous recovery: The reappearance of a previously extinguished CR after a rest period and without new learning trials

Stimulus generalization: A process whereby stimuli similar to the initial CS elicit a CR

Discrimination: A process whereby a CR (such as an alarm reaction) occurs to one stimulus (a sound) but not to others

Higher-order conditioning: A process whereby a neutral stimulus becomes a CS after being paired with an already-established CS

Exposure therapies: Therapies in which a patient is exposed to a stimulus (CS) that arouses an anxiety (such as fear) without the presence of the UCS, allowing extinction to occur

Aversion therapy: Therapy that attempts to condition an aversion (a repulsion) to a stimulus that triggers unwanted behavior by pairing it with a noxious UCS

Anticipatory nausea and vomiting (ANV): A process whereby a patient becomes nauseated and may vomit anywhere from minutes to hours before a treatment session

Law of effect: A law that states that in a given situation, a response followed by a "satisfying" consequence will become more likely to occur, and a response followed by an "annoying" consequence will become less likely to occur

Operant conditioning: A type of learning in which behavior is influenced by the consequences that follow it

Skinner box: A special chamber used to study operant conditioning experimentally

Reinforcement: A process whereby a response is strengthened by an outcome that follows it

Punishment: A process whereby a response is weakened by outcomes that follow it

Discriminative stimulus: A signal that a particular response will now produce certain consequences

Positive reinforcement: A process whereby a response is strengthened by the subsequent presentation of a stimulus

Primary reinforcers: Stimuli, such as food and water, that an organism naturally finds reinforcing, because they satisfy biological needs

Secondary (conditioned) reinforcers: Stimuli that acquire reinforcing properties through their association with primary reinforcers

Negative reinforcement: A process whereby a response is strengthened by the subsequent removal (or avoidance) of a stimulus

Operant extinction: The weakening and eventual disappearance of a response, because it is no longer reinforced

Aversive punishment (also called **positive punishment** or **punishment by application**): A process whereby a response is weakened by the subsequent presentation of a stimulus

Response cost (also called **negative punishment** or **punishment by removal**): A process whereby a response is weakened by the subsequent removal of a stimulus

Shaping (also called the **method of successive approximations**): A process of reinforcing successive approximations toward a final response

Chaining: A process used to develop a sequence (chain) of responses by reinforcing each response with the opportunity to perform the next response

Operant generalization: A process whereby an operant response occurs to a new antecedent stimulus or situation that is similar to the original one

Operant discrimination: A process whereby an operant response will occur to one antecedent stimulus but not to another

Stimulus control: A situation in which discriminative stimuli influence a behavior

Continuous reinforcement: A schedule whereby every response of a particular type is reinforced

Partial (intermittent) reinforcement: A schedule whereby only some responses are reinforced

Fixed-ratio (FR) schedule: A schedule whereby reinforcement is given after a fixed number of responses

Variable-ratio (VR) schedule: A schedule whereby reinforcement is given after a variable number of correct responses, all centered around an average

Fixed-interval (FI) schedule: A schedule whereby the first correct response that occurs after a fixed time interval is reinforced

Variable-interval (VI) schedule: A schedule whereby reinforcement is given for the first response that occurs after a variable time interval

Escape conditioning: A process whereby the organism learns a response to terminate an aversive stimulus

Avoidance conditioning: A process whereby the organism learns a response to avoid an aversive stimulus

Two-factor theory of avoidance learning: Theory of how both classical and operant conditioning are involved in avoidance learning

Token economies: A system in which desirable behaviors are quickly reinforced with "tokens" (e.g., points, gold stars) that are later turned in for tangible rewards (e.g., prizes, recreation time)

Applied behavior analysis: A research field that combines a behavioral approach with the scientific method to solve individual and societal problems

Preparedness: A tendency acquired through evolution whereby animals are biologically predisposed (prewired) to learn some associations more easily than others

Conditioned taste aversion: A conditioned response in which the taste (and sometimes the sight and smell) of the food now disgusts and repulses a person

Instinctive drift: The tendency for a conditioned response to "drift back" toward instinctive behavior

Insight: The sudden perception of a useful relationship that helps to solve a problem

Cognitive map: A mental representation of the spatial layout

Latent learning: Learning that occurs but is not demonstrated until later, when there is an incentive to perform

Observational learning: Learning that occurs by observing the behavior of a model

Social cognitive theory (previously named **social learning theory**): A theory that emphasizes that people learn by observing the behavior of models and acquiring the belief that they can produce behaviors to influence events in their lives

Self-efficacy: People's belief that they have the capability to perform behaviors that will produce a desired outcome

F. What's the Difference? A Concept Card Exercise

An important skill in learning concepts is being able to differentiate among concepts that are similar or related in some way. This skill is particularly relevant for multiple-choice tests, especially if you often find yourself wavering between two answers.

Once you have created your own deck of concept cards, select them two by two, each time answering the question "What's the difference between these two concepts?" You can use the word definitions of the concepts or the examples of the concepts to enhance your mastery of the material. In each case, choose pairs of concepts to compare those that are related or similar or that sound the same or that could in some way be confused. It's much easier to spot the difference between two concepts when you are studying, with the textbook available, rather than when considering the question for the first time in a testing situation.

G. Apply What You Know

1. Classical conditioning, operant conditioning, and modeling are used a great deal in advertising. Find one advertisement that uses classical conditioning to persuade us to buy the product, one that uses operant conditioning, and one that uses modeling. Photocopy the ad (or cut it from the newspaper or magazine if it belongs to you) and attach it in the appropriate space below. Write a brief explanation of how the ad exemplifies the use of that particular model of learning.

Classical Conditioning

Explanation:

Operant Conditioning

Explanation:

# Modeling

Explanation:

2. How might you use operant conditioning to condition this cute little creature to press a lever or stand on its hind legs?

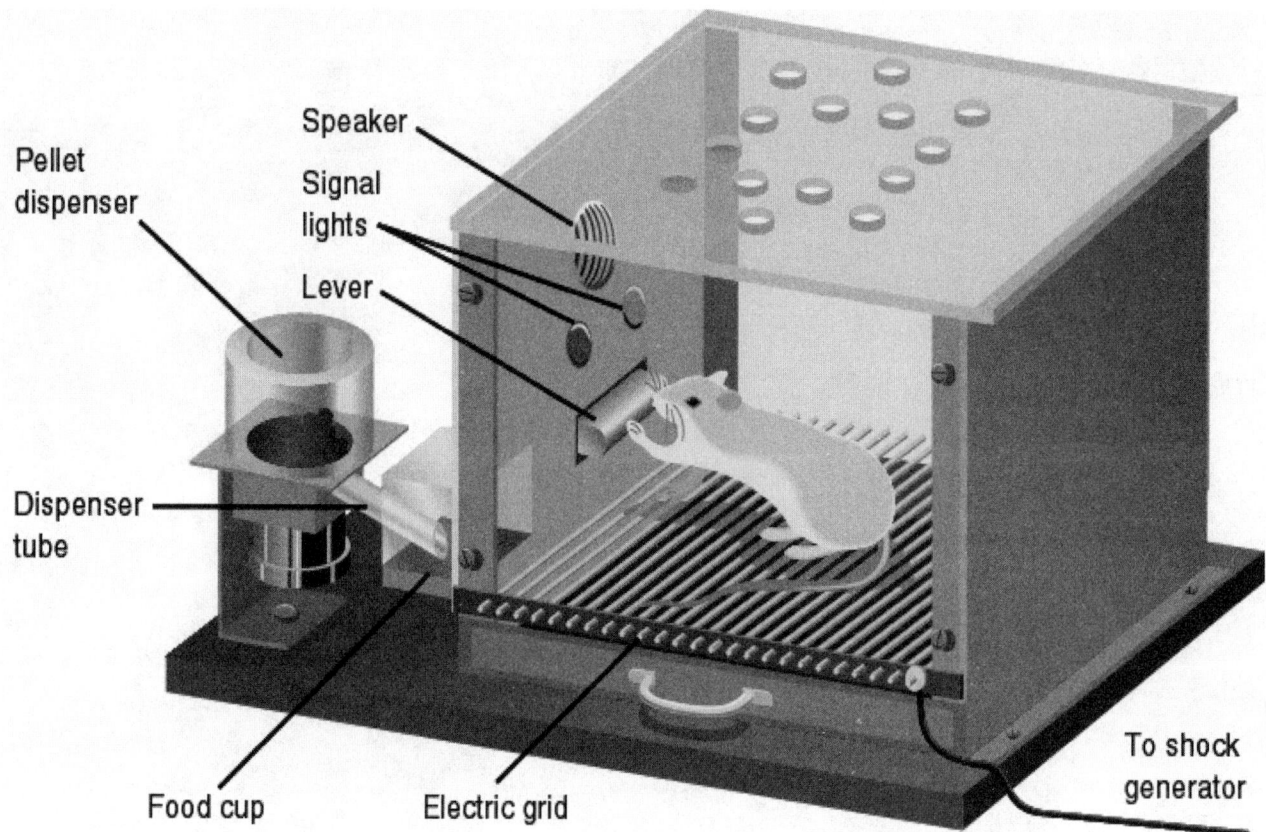

Chapter 7

H. On the Web: *As with any online research, it is important to consider how legitimate a given source is before you rely on the information it presents. Your instructor or Internet adviser may give you some specific guidelines for distinguishing which kinds of Web sites tend to be reputable.*

A. A number of individuals have made notable contributions to our understanding of learning. Search the Web for more information about some of those listed below.

Albert Bandura

Keller and Marian Breland

John Garcia

Mary Cover Jones

Wolfgang Kohler

Ivan Pavlov

B. F. Skinner

Edward L. Thorndike

John B. Watson and Rosalie Raynor

Edward Tolman

B. Take a look at the concept cards you have created for this chapter, or the key concepts listed in section E. In the space, make a list of any whose definitions or associations you are not yet confident of and any you'd like to learn more about. Try entering the terms on your list into your search engine. Make notes of any helpful information you find.

Key Concept/Information Found

C. In addition to the Skinner box, a soundproof chamber that contained a lever that an animal could press to receive food or some other stimuli, B. F. Skinner also created the "air crib," an enclosed, controlled environment for human babies. Find out about the air crib using Psychological Abstracts (available in most college libraries) as well as your search engine. (One publication you may find particularly informative is Dews, P. B. [1970]. *Festschrift for B. F. Skinner*. New York: Appleton-Century-Crofts.) What was the air crib's purpose, who used it, and what did the scientific community think of it? In view of what you have learned in this chapter about learning, do you think it was a worthwhile invention?

I. Analyze This: *Chapter 1 of your textbook begins by presenting these four basic steps in the critical thinking process:*
- *"What exactly are you asking me to believe?"*
- *"How do you know? What is the evidence?"*
- *"Are there other possible explanations?"*
- *"What is the most reasonable conclusion?"*

You might picture this as a four-step analysis to help you decide whether to accept a given theory or assertion. Now it's your turn to put your textbook to this test.

Review all of the material you can find about phobias in various sections throughout Chapter 7 of your textbook. If someone told you that the best way to cure any phobia is to force the person to experience the feared object or situation — provided it is done in a controlled environment where no ill effects will follow—would you agree? Analyze that assertion in the space provided. When you have finished, consider using this four-step analysis to evaluate other assertions you encounter.

"What exactly are you asking me to believe?"

"How do you know? What is the evidence?"

"Are there other possible explanations?"

"What is the most reasonable conclusion?"

J. Practice Test

Multiple-Choice Items: W*rite the letter corresponding to your answer in the space to the left of each item.*

_____ 1. The process by which experience produces a relatively enduring change in an organism's behavior or capabilities is called ____.
   a. learning
   b. positive reinforcement
   c. negative reinforcement
   d. shaping

_____ 2. Assume that, through a process of natural selection, a particular species of tree squirrel develops a fur coloring that allows it to blend in with its natural environment. As a result, the squirrels are more difficult to spot in the trees, are less likely to become prey for local predators, and are thus more likely to survive and reproduce than other squirrels without this coloring. This best demonstrates the process of ____.
   a. classical conditioning
   b. personal adaptation
   c. operant conditioning
   d. species adaptation

_____ 3. You have just settled down to begin studying when your roommate decides to turn on some music. At first the music distracts you, but after a short time it no longer bothers you even though it continues to play. This example most clearly demonstrates the process of ____.
   a. extinction
   b. negative reinforcement
   c. classical conditioning
   d. habituation

_____ 4. A stimulus that produces a response without learning is called a(n) ____ stimulus.
   a. conditioned
   b. reflexive
   c. unconditioned
   d. primary

_____ 5. Kim wants to teach her dog to salivate at the sound of a bell. Which of the following procedures would you recommend on the basis of your knowledge of classical conditioning?
   a. ring the bell; stop; after a minute, give the dog food
   b. give the dog food; while he is still eating, ring the bell
   c. simultaneously ring the bell and give the dog food
   d. ring the bell; and while the bell is still ringing, give the dog food

_____ 6. You are conducting an experiment in which you try to manipulate the immune response of rats by using the principles of classical conditioning. For the first several days of the experiment, you give rats artificially sweetened water

containing a drug that enhances the function of the immune system. For the next several days, you give the rats sweetened water without the drug or plain water. You find that the immune systems of the rats are boosted when they consume the sweetened water, but this does not happen with the plain water. In your experiment, the conditioned stimulus is ____.
   a. the sweetened water
   b. the drug
   c. enhanced immune system functioning in response to the drug
   d. enhanced immune system functioning in response to the sweetened water

_____ 7. A woman living in London during World War II learned to associate air-raid sirens with destruction created by bombs dropped from enemy airplanes. After moving to the United States, sirens no longer predicted such destruction, so her fear responses to sirens subsided over time. In the language of classical conditioned, the fear response has become ____.
   a. discriminated
   b. generalized
   c. extinguished
   d. spontaneously recovered

_____ 8. Tom and his father are at the toy store, where Tom cries loudly until his father buys him the train set that he wants. Tom stops crying once his father buys him the train set, thereby providing ____ for the father's behavior of buying Tom toys that he wants.
   a. negative reinforcement
   b. positive reinforcement
   c. aversive punishment
   d. response cost punishment

_____ 9. A toddler was frightened by a large dog that growled at him at the park. Now the toddler is frightened of all types of animals. The toddler's fear response to animals illustrates ____.
   a. higher-order conditioning
   b. stimulus discrimination
   c. stimulus generalization
   d. escape conditioning

_____ 10. The goal of exposure therapies is to expose a phobic person to the feared stimulus without the ____, so that the process of ____ can occur.
   a. CS; habituation
   b. CS; discrimination
   c. UCS; generalization
   d. UCS; extinction

_____ 11. Little Anna is hungry and wants a cookie but is too short to reach the table where the cookie jar is kept. She tries various things to get the jar, such as

jumping or throwing her teddy bear at the jar in hopes of knocking it off the table, but to no avail. Eventually she realizes that she can pull the tablecloth on which the jar rests and thus reach the jar. In the future, she will be likely to try this technique again because it was effective. This example best demonstrates ____.
a. Thorndike's law of effect
b. the principles of classical conditioning
c. shaping
d. partial reinforcement

_____ 12. In operant conditioning, an organism learns an association between ____.
a. punishment and negative reinforcement
b. an antecedent and a CS
c. an emitted behavior and an operant behavior
d. a behavior and a consequence

_____ 13. Joey likes to watch wrestling matches on TV, but his mother usually does not allow him to do this. However, Joey has noticed that when his mother is looking forward to going boating with her friends, she doesn't mind if he watches wrestling. As a result, Joey usually will only ask to watch wrestling if his mother has accepted a boating invitation. In this instance, the boating invitation would be considered a(n) ____.
a. conditioned stimulus
b. discriminative stimulus
c. negative reinforcer
d. consequence

_____ 14. Gina and her mother are at the supermarket, where Gina screams until her mother buys her the chocolate she wants. The mother's behavior of buying Gina chocolate to get the tantrum to stop makes it more likely that Gina will have a tantrum in the supermarket next time she wants her mother to buy her chocolate. In this situation, Gina's mother's behavior would be considered a(n) ____ of the screaming behavior.
a. negative reinforcer
b. positive reinforcer
c. aversive punishment
d. response cost

_____ 15. You are driving down the interstate rather quickly because you are late for a meeting, but you notice a police car parked on the shoulder. You quickly apply the brakes and slow down to the speed limit. In this instance, the police car represents a ____.
a. negative reinforcer
b. primary stimulus
c. discriminative stimulus
d. positive reinforcer

_____ 16. You wear a hat and long sleeves on sunny days, because you have been badly sunburned in the past, and want to avoid letting it happen again. The learning that has taken place for you is most similar to ____.
a. escape conditioning
b. a variable-ratio schedule of reinforcement
c. avoidance conditioning
d. a fixed-interval schedule of reinforcement

_____ 17. Your psychology class has two kinds of tests: four regularly scheduled major tests and surprise pop quizzes that occur at irregular intervals averaging about once every 2 weeks. The pop quizzes are administered on a(n) ____ schedule, which encourages you to study consistently throughout the semester.
a. FR
b. VR
c. FI
d. VI

_____ 18. A continuous schedule of reinforcement is actually a(n) _____ schedule.
a. FR
b. VR
c. FI
d. VI

_____ 19. Jill had a terrible headache during a blind date with a boy she found very unattractive. She excused herself and went home early because of the terrible headache. Now, whenever Jill is not enjoying a date, she complains of a headache and excuses herself. Jill's behavior of complaining of a headache best illustrates ____.
a. escape conditioning
b. avoidance conditioning
c. stimulus generalization
d. discrimination

_____ 20. B. F. Skinner's work gave rise to a field called ____, which combines a behavioral approach with the scientific method to solve individual and societal problems.
a. shaping
b. applied behavior analysis
c. chaining
d. operant conditioning

_____ 21. Alice ate curried lamb at a local restaurant, where the TV was playing Indian music and the lights were very dim. Later that night, Alice felt extremely nauseated. Research on preparedness would predict that ____.
a. Alice would develop an escape response to Indian music

b. Alice would develop an aversion to the taste of curry
c. Alice would develop an avoidance response to dim lights
d. Alice would develop an aversion to all three stimuli: curry, Indian music, and dim lights

_____ 22. When a conditioned response "drifts back" to more instinctive behavior, ____ has occurred.
a. conditioned taste aversion
b. preparedness
c. instinctive drift
d. evolution

_____ 23. Tolman demonstrated that if rats are allowed to wander through a complicated maze, they will subsequently run the maze with few errors, when a food reward is placed at the end. Their good performance demonstrates ____.
a. shaping
b. latent learning
c. delayed reinforcement
d. observational learning

_____ 24. In an experiment, rats in one group (Group 1) undergo 10 learning trials in which they receive a shock after a light comes on. Another group of rats (Group 2) undergoes the same 10 trials in which the shock is paired with the light, but they also undergo 10 additional random trials where the light is not followed by a shock. According to the expectancy model of classical conditioning, we would predict that the light will become a CS for fear for the rats ____.
a. only in Group 1
b. only in Group 2
c. in both Group1 and Group 2
d. in neither Group 1 nor Group 2

_____ 25. Eliana sees her mother put on an apron before she begins baking a cake. When her mother is out and Eliana decides to bake a cake for a friend's birthday, she puts on an apron before beginning to bake. This best illustrates the importance of ____.
a. observational learning
b. classical conditioning
c. discriminative learning
d. negative reinforcement

_____ 26. Bandura's ____ theory emphasizes that people learn from the behavior of others.
a. insight learning
b. operant conditioning

Chapter 7																																											213

       c. discriminative learning
       d. social cognitive

_____ 27. ____ represents people's belief that they have the capability to perform behaviors that will produce a desired outcome
       a. Self-efficacy
       b. Insight
       c. Preparedness
       d. Spontaneous recovery

_____ 28. Research has shown that observing aggressive models ____.
       a. can increase children's tendency to engage in aggressive behaviors
       b. does not increase children's tendency to engage in aggressive behaviors
       c. discourages children from engaging in aggressive behaviors
       d. encourages children to develop phobias

_____ 29. Studies of brain effects on learning suggest that ____.
       a. the hypothalamus is the only part of the brain that controls learning
       b. neurotransmitters are not involved in learning
       c. the cerebellum, but not the cerebral cortex, is involved in learning
       d. no single part of the brain "controls" learning

_____ 30. As we learn from our experiences, our brain ____.
       a. improves its ability to form new memories
       b. modifies itself
       c. has increasing trouble adapting to new situations
       d. is not changed

True/False Items: *Write T or F in the space provided to the left of each item.*

_____ 1. Studies of insight learning support the idea that biology constrains learning.

_____ 2. An initially neutral stimulus that through association with an unconditioned stimulus comes to produce a response initially produced only by the unconditioned stimulus is called the secondary reinforcer.

_____ 3. Extinction tends to occur after a CS has been presented repeatedly without the UCS also being present.

_____ 4. When stimuli similar to the initial CS come to produce the same response, the phenomenon is called stimulus discrimination.

_____ 5. Exposure therapies are often used to treat phobias.

_____ 6. Bandura's social cognitive theory proposes that modeling involves four steps: attention, retention, reproduction, and motivation.

_____ 7. Secondary reinforcers, such as money, become reinforcers through their association with primary reinforcers.

_____ 8. An example of negative reinforcement is spanking a child for bad behavior.

_____ 9. Interval schedules of reinforcement produce the highest rates of response.

_____ 10. Learning alters the brain.

Short-Answer Questions

1. What is habituation, and why is it important for human behavior?

2. Describe the process of the acquisition of a classically conditioned response.

3. What is the difference between shaping and chaining?

4. How do insight and cognitive maps show that cognition is important in the learning process?

5. How does a child learn prosocial behavior through observational learning?

Essay Questions

1. Suppose you wanted to design an experiment to investigate how early in life people can acquire phobias. Your hypothesis is that phobias can be acquired in infancy. How would you design your experiment, and how would you address any ethical concerns the experiment would raise?

2. To what extent do you think children's behavior is influenced by the content of TV shows and movies they see? Does this influence extend to adults as well? How do the various models of learning presented in this chapter explain such influence? What kind of TV and movie content do you think people should see if their goal is to improve their behavior?

3. Describe one of your own behaviors that you would like to change. In view of what you have learned in this chapter, devise a program for behavioral change. What models or theories of learning is your program based on, to what extent do you believe it will be successful, and why?

Answer Keys

Answer Key for Review at a Glance

1. Learning
2. adaptive
3. personal adaptation
4. species adaptation
5. habituation
6. classical conditioning
7. Pavlov
8. acquisition
9. unconditioned
10. unconditioned
11. conditioned
12. conditioned
13. extinction
14. spontaneous recovery
15. stimulus generalization
16. discrimination
17. higher-order
18. law of effect
19. operant
20. Skinner box
21. reinforcement
22. punishment
23. antecedents
24. behavior
25. consequences
26. discriminative
27. Positive
28. Primary
29. secondary
30. Negative
31. extinction
32. aversive punishment
33. response cost
34. delayed
35. Shaping
36. Chaining
37. generalization
38. discrimination
39. stimulus control
40. continuous
41. partial
42. fixed-ratio
43. fixed-interval
44. variable-ratio
45. variable-interval
46. Ratio
47. Variable
48. Escape
49. classical
50. operant
51. classical
52. negative
53. constraints
54. preparedness
55. conditioned taste aversion
56. instinctive drift
57. insight
58. cognitive map
59. latent
60. cognitive
61. observing
62. modeling
63. social cognitive
64. retention
65. reproduction
66. Self-efficacy
67. increase
68. aggressive
69. prosocial
70. environment
71. functioning
72. modify
73. hypothalamus
74. neurotransmitters

Chapter 7

Answer Key for Practice Test Multiple-Choice Items

1. a
2. d
3. d
4. c
5. d
6. a
7. c
8. d
9. c
10. d
11. a
12. d
13. b
14. a
15. c
16. c
17. d
18. a
19. a
20. b
21. b
22. c
23. b
24. a
25. a
26. d
27. a
28. a
29. d
30. b

Answer Key for Practice Test True/False Items

1. F
2. F
3. T
4. F
5. T
6. T
7. T
8. F
9. F
10. T

Answer Key for Practice Test Short-Answer Questions

1. *Habituation* refers to a decrease in the strength of a response to a stimulus that is repeated. If we paid attention to every stimulus in our environment, we would quickly become overwhelmed. Thus, through habituation, we learn to pay attention to only those stimuli that are important, and we filter out stimuli that do not provide us with important information.

2. *Acquisition* refers to the period during which a response is being learned. Initially, a stimulus called the unconditioned stimulus will elicit a response, called the unconditioned response, without learning. This is called a natural, unlearned reflex. Learning trials then occur in which a new stimulus, called a conditioned stimulus, is repeatedly paired with the unconditioned stimulus. After a number of such learning trials, the CS is presented alone, and, if the animal or human has been classically conditioned, the response that originally was elicited only by the UCS will now occur in the presence of the CS.

3. Shaping and chaining are used to condition new behaviors and complex sequences of behavior. When shaping is used, successive approximations toward the final goal are reinforced. For example, to shape a child to study 1 hour per night, you could reinforce her for studying 10 minutes a night. Next, you would reinforce her only for studying twenty minutes a night, and so on. Chaining might be used to teach a dancing bear a complex routine, for example. It involves reinforcing the last step of

the chain first and working backward. Each step then is reinforced by the opportunity to perform the next step in the chain.

4. At one time, most psychologists believed in S-R, or stimulus-response learning. That is, stimulus produced a response without any thought. Today, many psychologists believe in S-O-R models, which argue that cognition is important in behavior. German psychologist Wolfgang Köhler discovered that chimpanzees could learn to perform tasks through insight, the sudden perception of useful relationships, rather than just through the trial-and-error learning of the conditioning process. Similarly, Edward Tolman discovered that rats being trained through conditioning procedures in a maze were learning a mental representation, or cognitive map, of the maze, and were later able to use it to find food. Such findings challenged the traditional view that cognitive processes were not important in the learning process.

5. Observational learning is learning that occurs by watching the behavior of a model. The child would need to observe someone else behaving in a prosocial manner in order to learn prosocial behavior. Bandura's social cognitive theory proposes that four steps are involved in modeling: the child would need to pay attention to the model, retain the model's behavior in memory, be able to reproduce the behavior, and be motivated to do so. Observing successful models can increase the child's self-efficacy and thus motive him or her to perform the modeled prosocial behavior.

Answer Key for Practice Test Essay Questions

As you may have guessed, there are no right or wrong answers to the essay questions in this practice test. That does not mean, however, that all essays are equally good. To get maximum learning benefit from the essay questions, do the following:

- Review each essay a day or two after you wrote it, noting any necessary corrections and any additional support for your points that you can think of.
- Review the section in your textbook that pertains to the topic of each essay. Annotate your essay with any corrections or additional support for your points that you find in the text.
- Spend a few minutes researching the topic of each essay on the Internet. Annotate your essay further with any additional (reliable) information you find.
- Finally, reread each essay with the annotations you have added.

Chapter 8
MEMORY

A. Learning Objectives: *These objectives are expanded from the Focus Questions found in the margins of your textbook. When you have mastered the material in this chapter, you will be able to:*

8.1　Define memory and the processes of encoding, storage, and retrieval.

8.2　Describe sensory memory, and explain how Sperling demonstrated it.

8.3　Describe short-term and working memory.

8.4　Describe long-term memory and its limitations.

8.5　Differentiate between effortful and automatic processing.

8.6　Contrast maintenance and elaborative rehearsal.

8.7　Define schema, and explain how schemas enhance encoding.

8.8　Contrast theories of associative and neural networks, and use each to explain how memories are stored.

8.9　Differentiate between declarative memory and procedural memory.

8.10　Explain how retrieval cues assist recall,

8.11　Describe how flashbulb memories affect accuracy of memory.

8.12　Contrast and recognize examples of encoding specificity, context-dependent, state-dependent, and mood congruent recall.

8.13　Describe Ebbinghaus's research on forgetting.

8.14　Describe reasons for forgetting including encoding failure, decay theory, and interference theory.

8.15　Describe motivated forgetting, and explain why it is controversial.

8.16　Explain how schemas influence memory construction.

8.17　Describe the purpose, methods, and results of Roediger and McDermott's (1995) and Clancy, McNally, Schacter, Lenzeweger, and Pitman's (2002) studies on false memories.

8.18 Define the misinformation effect, and explain how it affects eyewitness testimony in children and adults.

8.19 Describe the research examining the recovered memory controversy.

8.20 Describe how culture affects memory.

8.21 Describe brain structures involved in memory and the process of long-term potentiation.

8.22 Describe research-based strategies for enhancing memory.

B. Chapter Overview

This chapter explores how our memories work, from the encoding and storage of memories to their retrieval; how and why we forget; the constructive process of memory; and the brain structures and activities involved with memory.

The guiding metaphor used by most cognitive psychologists today to study the mind is that the mind is an information-processing system that encodes, stores, and retrieves information. Encoding refers to getting information into the system, storage involves retaining information, and retrieval involves getting the information out of memory.

Cognitive psychologists also work with a three-stage model of memory. Sensory memory holds sensory information, including both visual memory (the iconic store) and auditory memory (the echoic store). Sensory memory has a large capacity, but information is retained only briefly. Information that we pay attention to is passed into working memory; other information is lost. Working memory, including what was previously called short-term memory, is a system that temporarily stores and processes information. It is of limited capacity (about "the magical number seven, plus or minus two" items), which can be increased by chunking, or combining individual items into larger units of meaning. Components of working memory include the phonological loop, which briefly stores mental representations of sounds; the visuospatial sketchpad, which briefly stores visual and spatial information; the episodic buffer, where information from the phonological loop, from the visuospatial sketchpad, and from long-term memory can be integrated and made conscious; and the central executive, which directs and coordinates memory activities. Long-term memory stores vast amounts of information for up to a lifetime. Research on amnesia and on the serial position effect supports the distinction between working and long-term memory.

The more effectively we encode information into long-term memory, the greater the likelihood of retrieving it. According to the levels of processing concept, the more deeply we process information, the better it will be remembered. Elaborative rehearsal involves focusing on the meaning of information, or expanding it by the use of techniques such as mnemonic devices. Compared to maintenance rehearsal, which involves simple rote repetition of material, elaborative rehearsal increases the depth of processing of information and its effective transfer into long-term memory. Prior knowledge shapes encoding through the use of schemas, which are organized patterns of thought about some aspect of the world. Mnemonists, people with superlative memories, often use basic memory principles, but experts disagree as to whether they also have exceptional ability.

One prominent theory of memory is that it can be represented by an associative network, a massive system of associated ideas and concepts. When a particular concept is active, it stimulates related items in the network, a concept known as spreading activation. Neural-network/connectionist models propose that memory may occur through the firing of synaptically connected neurons, and that it is the coordinated and distributed patterns of firing that are meaningful. Such models are also called parallel distributed processing (PDP) models. Long-term memory consists of everything we have learned in our lives. Cognitive psychologists distinguish between different aspects of long-term memory such as declarative, episodic, semantic, and procedural memories.

Memory is typically triggered via retrieval cues. The more retrieval cues we have, the more likely we are to remember information, and self-generated cues are more effective for retrieval than are cues generated by others. In general, distinctive events and those that are emotionally arousing are recalled more easily, although research has called into question the concept of "flashbulb memories" of extraordinary events. Context, state, and mood can also influence retrieval. We typically remember information better if we are in the same context and state in which the information was originally encoded, and find it easier to retrieve memories that are congruent with our current mood.

The Ebbinghaus forgetting curve shows that we rapidly lose much information, but the rate of loss levels off after a short period of time. We forget for a number of reasons. Decay theory argues that we forget things because the memory trace decays. Other theories suggest that encoding failures and interference, both proactive and retroactive, contribute to forgetting. We may also be motivated to forget undesirable experiences through repression of them. Amnesia, the most dramatic form of memory loss, takes several forms: Retrograde amnesia involves forgetting events that occurred before the onset of memory loss, whereas those suffering from anterograde amnesia cannot remember events since the onset of their memory loss. Both types of memory loss are involved in Alzheimer's disease, a progressive brain disorder characterized by dementia (impaired memory and other cognitive deficits that accompany brain degeneration). Most people cannot remember personal experiences from their earliest years of life, which is called infantile amnesia. Researchers have also studied prospective memory, which refers not to past events, but to remembering to do things in the future.

Memory is a constructive process subject to distortion. People have generalized expectancies about how things happen, called schemas, which are used to organize information and memories, and sometimes our memories are shaped to fit our schemas. Misleading postevent information can distort our recall of events (the misinformation effect), we may become confused about the source of our memories, and people sometimes even remember events that never occurred. A major controversy has emerged about the validity of children's memories. Some think that children's memories are particularly susceptible to suggestion and bias, and there is scientific controversy over "recovered memories" of childhood trauma. Culture and memory have a reciprocal relation: Culture helps to shape memories, and without memory, culture could not exist.

Scientists rely on both naturally occurring and experimentally induced lesions, as well as brain imaging, to study the biology of memory. The hippocampus and its surrounding tissue seem to play a major role in encoding and consolidating, but not storing, long-term declarative memories. The cerebral cortex plays a role in encoding by processing information from the sensory registers and also by storing semantic memories. The frontal lobes of the cortex play a central role in working memory. The amygdala seems to encode emotionally arousing and disturbing aspects of events. The cerebellum plays an important role in the formation of procedural memories. Memories in general seem to be formed biologically through physical and chemical changes in the brain's neural circuitry. Long-term potentiation, which is an increase in synaptic strength between neurons, plays a key role in memory consolidation.

To improve your memory, (1) use external aids such as lists, (2) organize and elaborate the information you want to remember, and (3) learn to take advantage of acronyms, the method of loci, and other formal memory techniques.

C. Chapter Outline

MEMORY AS INFORMATION PROCESSING
    A Three-Stage Model
        Sensory Memory
        Working/Short-Term Memory
            Memory codes
            Capacity and duration
            Putting short-term memory to work
            Components of working memory
        Long-Term Memory
    In Review
ENCODING: ENTERING INFORMATION
    Effortful and Automatic Processing
    Levels of Processing: When Deeper Is Better
    Exposure and Rehearsal
    Organization and Imagery
        Hierarchies and Chunking
        Visual Imagery
        Other Mnemonic Devices
    How Prior Knowledge Shapes Encoding

Chapter 8

      Schemas: Our Mental Organizers
      Schemas, Encoding, and Expertise
   Encoding and Exceptional Memory
   What Do You Think? Would Perfect Memory Be a Gift or a Curse?
   In Review

STORAGE: RETAINING INFORMATION
   Memory as a Network
      Associative Networks
      Neural Networks
   Types of Long-Term Memory
      Declarative and Procedural Memory
      Explicit and Implicit Memory
   In Review

RETRIEVAL: ACCESSING INFORMATION
   The Value of Multiple Cues
   The Value of Distinctiveness
   Arousal, Emotion, and Memory
   Beneath the Surface: Do We Really Remember It Like It Was Yesterday?
   The Effects of Context, State, and Mood on Memory
      Context-Dependent Memory: Returning to the Scene
      State-Dependent Memory: Arousal, Drugs, and Mood
   In Review

FORGETTING
   The Course of Forgetting
   Why Do We Forget?
      Encoding Failure
      Decay of the Memory Trace
      Interference
      Motivated Forgetting
   Forgetting to Do Things: Prospective Memory
   Amnesia
      Retrograde and Anterograde Amnesia
      Dementia and Alzheimer's Disease
      Infantile (Childhood) Amnesia
   In Review

MEMORY AS A CONSTRUCTIVE PROCESS
   Memory Distortion and Schemas
   Research Close-Up: Memory Illusions: Remembering Things That Never Occurred
   Misinformation Effects and Eyewitness Testimony
      Source Confusion
   The Child as Eyewitness
      Accuracy and Suggestibility
         Recall of traumatic events
      True Versus False Reports: Can Professionals Tell Them Apart?
   The Recovered Memory Controversy
   Culture and Memory Construction

In Review
MEMORY AND THE BRAIN
Where Are Memories Formed and Stored?
    Sensory and Working Memory
    Long-Term Memory
        Declarative memory
        Procedural memory
How Are Memories Formed?
    Synaptic Change and Memory
    Long-Term Potentiation
In Review
Applying Psychological Science: Improving Memory and Academic Learning
What Do You Think? Would Perfect Memory Be A Gift or a Curse?

D. Review at a Glance: *Write the term that best fits the blank to review what you learned in this chapter.*

Memory as Information Processing

(1)_____ refers to the processes that allow us to record and later retrieve experiences and information. Today, the mind is visualized as an information-processing system. It takes in information by translating it into a neural code that your brain processes, a process called (2) _____. The brain retains information over time through (3) _____ and pulls information out of long-term memory through (4) _____ processes.

Most cognitive psychologists suggest a three-stage model of memory. (5)_____ memory holds large amounts of incoming sensory information very briefly, including visual information in the (6)_____ store and auditory information in the (7)_____ store. Most information in sensory memory quickly fades away, but information that we pay attention to enters (8) _____ memory, which is also called (9) _____-_____ memory. The capacity of working memory is limited, but it can be increased through (10) _____, which involves combining individual items into larger units of meaning. Components of working memory include the (11) _____ loop, which briefly stores mental representations of sounds; the (12) _____ _____, which briefly stores visual and spatial information; the (13) _____ _____, where information from the phonological loop, the visuospatial sketchpad, and long-term memory can be integrated and made conscious; and the (14) _____ _____, which directs and coordinates memory activities. By rehearsing information, we can keep it in short-term memory longer. (15)_____ rehearsal involves the simple repetition of information, such as repeating a phone number in order to remember it. (16)_____ rehearsal involves focusing on the meaning of information or relating it to things we already know. Our vast library of stored information is called (17) _____-_____ memory.

Encoding: Entering Information

According to the (18) _____-_____-_____ model, the more deeply we process information, the better it will be remembered. Because of this, (19) _____ rehearsal is the best method of getting information into long-term memory. Paivio discovered that we encode information in both verbal and visual codes, which is known as his (20) _____-_____ theory. Prior knowledge also shapes encoding through the use of (21) _____, which are organized patterns of thought about some aspect of the world.

Storage: Retaining Information

After information is encoded, it is organized and stored in long-term memory. One group of theories suggests that memory is represented as a massive network of associated ideas and concepts called an (22) _____ network. In such a network, when people think about one concept, it triggers thinking about related concepts throughout the network, through the process called (23) _____ _____. The term (24) _____ refers to the activation of one concept by another. In a (25) _____ network, each concept is represented by a particular pattern of neural activity or set of nodes that becomes activated simultaneously.

There are several types of long-term memory. (26)_____ memory involves factual knowledge and consists of the following two types. Our store of factual information about the world and language is called (27) _____ memory, whereas our store of factual memory about our personal experiences is called (28) _____ memory. (29)_____ memory, or remembering "how," is reflected in skills and actions we perform. Memory retrieval can involve both conscious and unconscious processes. (30)_____ memory involves conscious memory retrieval, whereas (31)_____ memory influences our behavior without conscious awareness.

Retrieval: Accessing Information

A stimulus that activates information stored in long-term memory is called a (32) _____ cue. The more such cues we have, the more likely we are to remember information. (33)_____-_____ cues are more effective for retrieval than are cues generated by others. In general, (34) _____ events and those that are (35) _____ _____ are recalled more easily.
(36)_____ memories of extraordinary events may seem so clear that we can picture like a snapshot in time, but research suggests they may be false.

Context, state, and mood affect our ability to retrieve information. The principle that states that memory is enhanced when conditions present during retrieval match those that were present during encoding is called the (37) _____ _____ _____. Sometimes it is easier to remember information if we are in the same environment in which the information was first encoded, a phenomenon called (38)

_____-dependent memory. Similarly, our ability to retrieve information is greater when our internal state at the time of retrieval matches our original state during learning, which is called (39) _____-dependent memory. We also tend to recall information or events that are congruent with our current mood, which is known as (40) _____-_____ recall.

Forgetting

Hermann Ebbinghaus pioneered the study of (41) _____, discovering that memory declines rapidly after initial learning and then levels off. Why do we forget? One theory is that we forget things because we fail to (42) _____ them well enough. Another theory, called (43) _____ theory, suggests that, with time and disuse, the physical memory trace in the nervous system fades away. Yet another theory, (44) _____ theory, suggests that we forget because other items in long-term memory overwrite or impair our ability to retain information. (45) _____ interference occurs when material learned in the past interferes with the learning of new information. (46) _____ interference occurs when newly acquired information interferes with the ability to retrieve information stored at an earlier time. Psychodynamic theorists suggest that we may be motivated to forget particularly disturbing information through (47) _____. The most dramatic form of forgetting is (48) _____. (49) _____ amnesia refers to memory loss for events that occur after the initial onset of amnesia, whereas (50) _____ amnesia represents memory loss for events that occurred prior to the amnesia. Most of us can't remember events of our early childhood because of (51) _____ amnesia. Researchers have also studied (52) _____ memory, which refers not to past events but to remembering to do things in the future.

Memory as a Constructive Process

The use of appropriate (53) _____ helps us to organize information as we encode and retrieve it. Sometimes, though, schemas can distort information. The distortion of a memory by misleading postevent information is called the (54) _____ effect, which is sometimes also influenced by (55) _____ _____, our tendency to recall something or recognize it without being able to remember where we encountered it.

Memory and the Brain

The (56) _____ and its surrounding tissue seem to play a major role in encoding and consolidating, but not storing, long-term declarative memories. The (57) _____ _____ plays a role in encoding by processing information from the sensory registers and also by storing semantic memories. The frontal lobes of the cortex play a central role in (58) _____ memory. The (59) _____ seems to encode emotionally arousing and disturbing aspects of events. The cerebellum plays an important role in the formation of (60) _____ memories. Memories, in general, seem to be formed biologically through physical and chemical

changes in the brain's neural circuitry. (61)_____-_____
_____, which is an increase in synaptic strength between neurons, plays a key role in memory consolidation.

E. Concept Cards

Truly learning a concept means integrating it into the way *you* think about things. To integrate concepts successfully, you must translate the words and examples your text or instructor provides into words and examples that are meaningful to you.

For this exercise, obtain some note cards (3" × 5" or 4" × 6") to make a deck of concept cards. On one side of each card, write the *concept* from the list below (e.g., "encoding") at the top. Read the textbook definition provided, and then write the definition *in your own words* on the concept card (e.g., for "encoding," you might write "putting things into your memory"). Simply imagine that a friend has asked you what the concept means, and write down what you would answer. Writing the definition in your own words requires you to think deeply about its meaning. When next you see your own version of the definition, it will make intuitive sense to you—no translation required.

On the second side of the card, write your own example of the concept. Again, coming up with your own example requires you to think deeply about the application of the concept, and you will more easily understand and remember the example when you study for a test. If you use an example from the text, or from class, make it your own by writing it in your own words. You can always check with your instructor that your example is indeed a good example of the concept.

CONCEPT Definition in my own words (side 1 of card)	Example of the concept in my own words, preferably drawn from my own experience (side 2 of card)

The following is a list of all the boldface concepts from your textbook, with the author's definition. Write the definition in your own words, together with your own example of the concept, to create a *concept card* as described earlier, or write in the space provided.

Memory: The processes that allow us to record, store, and later retrieve experiences and information

Encoding: The process of getting information into the system by translating it into a neural code that your brain processes

Storage: The process of retaining information over time

Retrieval: Processes that access stored information

Sensory memory: A memory system that briefly holds incoming sensory information

Short-term memory: A memory store that temporarily holds a limited amount of information

Memory codes: Mental representations of some type of information or stimulus

Chunking: A process of combining individual items into larger units of meaning

Working memory: A limited-capacity system that temporarily stores and processes information

Long-term memory: One's vast library of relatively durable stored memories

Serial position effect: A process whereby the ability to recall an item is influenced by the item's position in a series

Levels of processing: The concept that the more deeply we process information, the better we will remember it

Maintenance rehearsal: A method of rehearsal involving simple, rote repetition

Elaborative rehearsal: A method of rehearsal that involves focusing on the meaning of information or expanding on it in some way

Dual coding theory: Theory that proposes that encoding information using both verbal and visual codes enhances memory

Method of loci: A memory aid that associates information with mental images of physical locations

Mnemonic device: A memory aid

Schema: A "mental framework"—an organized pattern of thought—about some aspect of the world

Mnemonist (or memorist): A person who displays extraordinary memory skills

Associative network: A massive network of associated ideas and concepts

Priming: The activation of one concept (or one unit of information) by another

Neural network (connectionist) models: Model of memory in which each item in memory is represented by a particular pattern or set of interconnected nodes that becomes activated simultaneously

Parallel distributed processing (PDP) models: Another term for neural network/connectionist models

Declarative memory: Memory involving factual knowledge

Episodic memory: Our store of knowledge concerning personal experiences

Semantic memory: Memory representing general factual knowledge about the world and language

Procedural (nondeclarative) memory: Memory that is reflected in skills and actions

Explicit memory: Memory that is consciously or intentionally retrieved, as when you consciously recognize or recall something

Implicit memory: A process whereby memory influences our behavior without conscious awareness

Retrieval cue: A stimulus, whether internal or external, that activates information stored in long-term memory

Autobiographical memories: Recollections of personally experienced events that make up the "story of our life"

Flashbulb memories: Recollections that seem so vivid, so clear, that we can picture them as if they were a snapshot of a moment in time

Encoding specificity principle: A principle that states that memory is enhanced when conditions present during retrieval match those that were present during encoding

Context-dependent memory: The idea that it is typically easier to remember something in the same environment in which it was originally encoded

State-dependent memory: The idea that our ability to retrieve information is greater when our internal state at the time of retrieval matches our original state during learning

Mood-congruent recall: The process whereby we tend to recall information or events that are congruent with our current mood

Decay theory: A theory that proposes that with time and disuse, the long-term physical memory trace in the nervous system fades away

Proactive interference: A process whereby material learned in the past interferes with recall of newer material

Retroactive interference: A process whereby newly acquired information interferes with the ability to recall information learned at an earlier time

Tip-of-the-tongue (TOT) state: A state in which we cannot recall something but feel that we are on the verge of remembering it

Repression: A motivational process that protects us by blocking the conscious recall of anxiety-arousing memories

Prospective memory: A process of remembering to perform an activity in the future

Retrograde amnesia: Memory loss for events that took place sometime in life before the onset of amnesia

Anterograde amnesia: Memory loss for events that occur after the initial onset of amnesia

Dementia: Impaired memory and other cognitive deficits that accompany brain degeneration and interfere with normal functioning

Alzheimer's disease (AD): A progressive brain disorder that is the most common cause of dementia among adults older than 65 years of age

Infantile amnesia (also called **childhood amnesia**): Memory loss for early experiences

Misinformation effect: The distortion of a memory by misleading postevent information

Source confusion (also called **source monitoring error**): Our tendency to recall something or recognize it as familiar but to forget where we encountered it

Memory consolidation: A hypothetical and gradual "binding" process

Long-term potentiation (LTP): An enduring increase in synaptic strength

Overlearning: Continued rehearsal past the point of initial learning, which significantly improves performance on memory tasks

F. What's the Difference? A Concept Card Exercise

An important skill in learning concepts is being able to differentiate among concepts that are similar or related in some way. This skill is particularly relevant for multiple-choice tests, especially if you often find yourself wavering between two answers.

Once you have created your own deck of concept cards, select them two by two, each time answering the question "What's the difference between these two concepts?" You can use the word definitions of the concepts or the examples of the concepts to enhance your mastery of the material. In each case, choose pairs of concepts to compare those that are related or similar or that sound the same or that could in some way be confused. It's much easier to spot the difference between two concepts when you are studying, with the textbook available, rather than when considering the question for the first time in a testing situation.

G. Apply What You Know

1. Construct two lists of 20 words. Learn one list using maintenance rehearsal techniques. Learn the other list using elaborative rehearsal techniques, such as making up a story using the words or creating mental images of the concepts the words represent in your mind. Measure your immediate recall of the words right after you've learned them by recording the number of words you can recall from each list. Then measure your recall of both lists a day later. As measured by immediate recall, do you find that you remember words from one list better than the other? If so, why? How about after one day? If so, why?

2. Suppose that you are a trial attorney and wish to use the misinformation effect to sway the testimony of an eyewitness. Describe how you could do this.

H. On the Web: *As with any online research, it is important to consider how legitimate a given source is before you rely on the information it presents. Your instructor or Internet adviser may give you some specific guidelines for distinguishing which kinds of Web sites tend to be reputable.*

A. A number of individuals have made notable contributions to our understanding of memory. Search the Web for more information about some of those listed below.

Frederick Bartlett

William Chase and Herbert Simon

Alan Collins and Elizabeth Loftus

Hermann Ebbinghaus

K. Anders Ericsson and Peter Polson

Eric Kandel

Karl Lashley

Michelle Leichtman and Stephen Ceci

Timo Mäntylä

James McConnell

Allan Paivio

Bennett Schwartz

George Sperling

Qi Wang

B. Take a look at the concept cards you have created for this chapter, or the key concepts listed in section E above. In the space below, make a list of any whose definitions or associations you are not yet confident of and any you'd like to learn more about. Try entering the terms on your list into your search engine. Make notes of any helpful information you find.

Key Concept/Information Found

C. By running "mnemonics" or "improve your memory" through your search engine, find at least five different Web sites devoted to memory improvement. In view of what you have learned in this chapter about remembering and forgetting, evaluate the information presented on these sites.

Memory Site #1: http://

Chapter 8   237

Memory Site #2: http://

Memory Site #3: http://

Memory Site #4: http://

Memory Site #5: http://

D. To learn more about false memories and the controversy over recovered memories of childhood trauma, follow these two lines of inquiry: (1) Visit the American Psychological Association Web site and look for the APA's position on recovered memories and/or a page devoted to memories of childhood abuse. (2) Visit the Web site of psychologist Elizabeth F. Loftus and read about her research on false memories. Make notes on your findings in the space below.

I. Analyze This

Chapter 1 of your textbook begins by presenting these four basic steps in the critical thinking process:
- *"What exactly are you asking me to believe?"*
- *"How do you know? What is the evidence?"*
- *"Are there other possible explanations?"*
- *"What is the most reasonable conclusion?"*

You might picture this as a four-step analysis to help you decide whether to accept a given theory or assertion. Now it's your turn to put your textbook to this test.

Review the section in Chapter 8 of your textbook under the heading "Encoding: Entering Information." If someone told you that the usual reason people cannot remember things is that they were not paying attention in the first place, would you agree? Analyze that assertion in the space below. When you have finished, consider using this four-step analysis to evaluate other assertions you encounter.

"What exactly are you asking me to believe?"

"How do you know? What is the evidence?"

"Are there other possible explanations?"

"What is the most reasonable conclusion?"

J. Practice Test

Multiple-Choice Items: *Write the letter corresponding to your answer in the space to the left of each item.*

_____ 1. In the three-stage memory model, iconic memory is part of _____ memory.
   a. sensory
   b. procedural
   c. long-term
   d. echoic

_____ 2. Both elaborative and maintenance rehearsal keep information active in _____ memory, but _____ rehearsal is more effective in transferring information to long-term memory.
   a. working; elaborative
   b. sensory; maintenance
   c. short-term; maintenance
   d. sensory; elaborative

_____ 3. According to psychologist Alan Baddeley, working memory includes _____ components.
   a. sensory, short-term, and long-term memory
   b. episodic, procedural, and semantic memory
   c. auditory, visuospatial, and central executive
   d. encoding, storage, and retrieval

_____ 4. New professor Dr. Ian Smart is faced with the unenviable task of memorizing all of his new students' names, so he decides to employ elaborative rehearsal techniques to do this. To enhance his long-term recall of student Melody Balobalo's name, Dr. Smart should _____.
   a. repeat her name over and over again
   b. associate a mental image of her with a ball bouncing up and down over a song melody
   c. divide her name into smaller chunks such as *Mel-o-dy Bal-o-bal-o*
   d. use only short-term memory

_____ 5. The process of getting information into the brain by translating it into a neural code that the brain processes is called _____.
   a. retrieval
   b. encoding
   c. recall
   d. storage

_____ 6. The capacity of short-term, or working, memory is thought to be _____ units of information.

a. an infinite number of
b. 10 ± 2
c. 7 ± 2
d. 4 to 6

_____ 7. Words at the end of a list are typically remembered better than words presented in the middle. This is known as the ____ effect, and it presumably happens because the last few words on the list remain in ____ memory.
a. serial position; sensory
b. recency; long-term
c. primacy; short-term
d. recency; short-term

_____ 8. ____ is one of the components of working memory, according to Baddeley's model.
a. The visuospatial sketchpad
b. The sensory register
c. Maintenance rehearsal
d. The neural network

_____ 9. The method of loci is a memory-enhancing technique based on ____ and is consistent with the predictions of ____ theory.
a. imagery; dual coding
b. chunking; dual coding theory
c. hierarchies; encoding specificity
d. acronyms; encoding specificity

_____ 10. If you go to see a movie in a theater, you know that the movie isn't going to start as long as the lights are on. Once the movie starts, you also know that it is considered impolite to talk during the movie and that if you need to leave, it is best to try not to disturb others. This collection of thoughts is best considered to be an example of ____.
a. overlearning
b. a schema
c. chunking
d. the amygdala's role in memory

_____ 11. If you think for a moment about the concept "school," it is likely that other concepts such as "textbooks," "teachers," and "exams" will also come to mind. The fact that these other concepts can be triggered by the concept "school" is best considered as an example of ____.
a. procedural memory
b. proactive interference
c. dual encoding
d. priming

Chapter 8   241

_____ 12. Memory researcher Dr. Brain E. Smart claims that a concept such as "dog" is triggered by the simultaneous firing of nodes 8, 47, and 123 in a network but that if node 8 is simultaneously triggered with nodes 9 and 301, an entirely different concept appears in the mind. Dr. Smart's views are most consistent with the _____ theory of memory.
   a. dual coding
   b. associative network
   c. state-dependence
   d. neural network

_____ 13. Research by Mäntylä (1986) suggests that the use of _____ cue(s) is the most effective way to improve recall memory.
   a. a single, vivid
   b. multiple, self-generated
   c. a single, self-generated
   d. multiple, expert-generated

_____ 14. According to the _____, memory is better when the conditions present during encoding match those that are present during retrieval.
   a. dual processing theory
   b. decay theory
   c. encoding specificity principle
   d. the principles of implicit memory

_____ 15. You studied for your psychology exam in your noisy dorm room and your physiological arousal was high. According to the concepts of context-dependent memory and state-dependent memory, under which of the following conditions for taking the exam would your recall be best?
   a. noisy environment, low arousal
   b. noisy environment, high arousal
   c. quiet environment, low arousal
   d. quiet environment, high arousal

_____ 16. Jim has trouble remembering to do things that he plans to do in the near future, such as mailing a letter or returning a phone call. This type of remembering is called _____ memory and the _____ is thought to play an important role in it.
   a. retroactive; cerebellum
   b. prospective; frontal lobe
   c. anterograde; amygdala
   d. retrograde; hippocampus

_____ 17. A police investigator asks an eyewitness to a crime to look through some mug shots to see if she can recognize the perpetrator. The witness then sees a police lineup of suspects, and identifies a man in the lineup as the perpetrator because he looks very familiar. Unfortunately, the man in the lineup looks

familiar not because the eyewitness saw him commit the crime but because she saw his face in the mug shot books a few hours earlier, although she has now forgotten this. This is best considered an example of _____.
   a. proactive interference
   b. retrograde amnesia
   c. source confusion
   d. memory consolidation

_____ 18. The _____ appears to be an "encoding station" for long-term declarative memory.
   a. cerebral cortex
   b. thalamus
   c. hippocampus
   d. cerebellum

_____ 19. Taneisha remembers her wedding day as if it were yesterday. She recalls how handsome Marvin looked as he stood at the altar with her and said, "I do," and how romantic it was to have the first dance together as the band played their favorite song. These happy memories form part of Taneisha's _____ memory.
   a. episodic
   b. iconic
   c. procedural
   d. semantic

_____ 20. Although Ted had last been waterskiing as a child, 15 years earlier, he was able to get up on the skis and water-ski again today without any problem, thanks to his _____ memory.
   a. declarative
   b. procedural
   c. flashbulb
   d. deep-processing

_____ 21. Making a grocery list and taking notes for a class are both examples of _____, which is encoding that is initiated intentionally and requires conscious attention.
   a. effortful processing
   b. automatic processing
   c. maintenance rehearsal
   d. state-dependent memory

_____ 22. According to the _____ concept, the more deeply we encode information, the better we will remember it.
   a. dual coding
   b. levels-of-processing
   c. maintenance rehearsal

d. chunking

_____ 23. A mnemonist is a person who _____ .
   a. cannot remember events from childhood
   b. has anterograde amnesia
   c. has a more limited working-memory capacity than average
   d. displays extraordinary memory skills

_____ 24. A massive network of associated ideas and concepts is called a(n) _____ network.
   a. associative
   b. schema
   c. neural
   d. priming

_____ 25. Caryn studied French for 4 years in high school. In college, she enrolls in a course in Italian and finds to her dismay that the French she remembers from high school interferes with her recall of newly learned Italian vocabulary and grammar. Caryn's problem is an example of _____ .
   a. retroactive interference
   b. motivated forgetting
   c. the tip-of-the-tongue phenomenon
   d. proactive interference

_____ 26. Jamie is 30 years old and has never been able to remember anything that occurred in her childhood before she started kindergarten. Jamie most likely has _____ .
   a. infantile amnesia, a perfectly normal condition
   b. anterograde amnesia, which may clear up with treatment
   c. infantile amnesia, a relatively rare condition
   d. Alzheimer's disease, which may get worse as she gets older

_____ 27. The distortion of memory by misleading postevent information is called _____ .
   a. retrograde amnesia
   b. Korsakoff's syndrome
   c. the misinformation effect
   d. priming

_____ 28. The frontal lobes of the cerebral cortex are known to play a central role in _____ .
   a. working memory
   b. implicit memory
   c. the phonological loop
   d. mood-congruent recall

_____ 29. Flashbulb memories _____.
   a. have been shown to be remarkably accurate and long lasting
   b. are the cause of the tip-of-the-tongue phenomenon
   c. are detailed, vivid recollections that seem like a snapshot of a moment in time
   d. occur for negative but not for positive events

_____ 30. An increase in synaptic strength between neurons, called _____, plays a key role in memory consolidation.
   a. long-term potentiation
   b. parallel distributed processing (PDP)
   c. dual-code processing
   d. associative networking

True/False Items: *Write T or F in the space provided to the left of each item.*

_____ 1. Combining individual items into larger units of meaning is called chunking.

_____ 2. The best technique for transferring information from short-term memory to long-term memory is maintenance rehearsal.

_____ 3. A *U*-shaped pattern that shows that recall is influenced by a word's position in a series of items is called the primacy effect.

_____ 4. According to Paivio's dual coding theory, memory is improved by encoding information using both verbal and visual cues.

_____ 5. An organized pattern of thought about some aspect of the world is called a schema.

_____ 6. Our store of knowledge concerning our own personal experiences is called declarative memory.

_____ 7. The theory of context-dependent memory is that people can best remember something in a different environment from that in which they first encoded it.

_____ 8. Proactive interference occurs when learning something new interferes with things formerly remembered.

_____ 9. Studies of the biology of memory indicate that the hippocampus plays a major role in encoding long-term declarative memories.

_____ 10. Synaptic connections seem to become stronger as a result of the stimulation involved in memory.

Chapter 8

Short-Answer Questions

1. Describe the three-component model of memory.

2. Describe the two different types of rehearsal.

3. What are associative and neural networks?

4. What are the major types of amnesia?

5. What is the misinformation effect?

Essay Questions

1. Considering what you have learned in this chapter about techniques for memorization, and the fact that to do well in this course you need to memorize a significant amount of information, explain why doing the exercises in this study guide is a better use of your time than reading your textbook over and over.

2. Parents, teachers, and other concerned adults want to be aware of whether children are being neglected or abused when in the care of others. In Chapter 8 of your text, you read about studies in which children gave false reports of events. Assuming an adult wants a child to give as truthful an account as possible of what took place in the adult's absence, how do you think the adult should question and listen to the child?

3. Describe a significant event, person, or place that you remember clearly. The memory may be from your childhood or from a more recent time. After you have written your description, seek out someone who would be in a position to corroborate this recollection. Without telling them anything about the way you remember it, ask them to describe their memory of the same event, person, or place. How do your memories compare?

Answer Keys

Answer Key for Review at a Glance

1. Memory
2. encoding
3. storage
4. retrieval
5. Sensory
6. iconic
7. echoic
8. working
9. short-term
10. chunking
11. phonological
12. visuospatial sketchpad
13. episodic buffer
14. central executive
15. Maintenance
16. Elaborative

32. retrieval
33. Self-generated
34. distinctive
35. emotionally arousing
36. Flashbulb
37. encoding specificity principle
38. context
39. state
40. mood-congruent
41. forgetting
42. encode
43. decay
44. interference
45. Proactive
46. Retroactive
47. repression

17. long-term
18. levels-of-processing
19. elaborative
20. dual-code
21. schemas
22. associative
23. spreading activation
24. priming
25. neural
26. Declarative
27. semantic
28. episodic
29. Procedural
30. Explicit
31. implicit

48. amnesia
49. Anterograde
50. retrograde
51. infantile
52. prospective
53. schemas
54. misinformation
55. source confusion
56. hippocampus
57. cerebral cortex
58. working
59. amygdala
60. procedural
61. Long-term potentiation

Answer Key for Practice Test Multiple-Choice Items

1. a
2. a
3. c
4. b
5. b
6. c
7. d
8. a
9. a
10. b
11. d
12. d
13. b
14. c
15. b
16. b
17. c
18. c
19. a
20. b
21. a
22. b
23. d
24. a
25. d
26. a
27. c
28. a
29. c
30. a

Answer Key for Practice Test True/False Items

1. T
2. F
3. F
4. T
5. T
6. F
7. F
8. F
9. T
10. T

Answer Key for Practice Test Short-Answer Questions

1. The three-component model of memory consists of sensory memory, working memory (or short-term memory), and long-term memory. Sensory memory holds

incoming sensory information just long enough for it to be recognized. Short-term/working memory holds the information that we are conscious of at any given time. Long-term memory is our vast store of more durable stored memories.

2. Maintenance rehearsal involves the simple repetition of information and is useful for retaining information in short-term memory. Elaborative rehearsal involves focusing on the meaning of information or relating it to other things we already know. Elaborative rehearsal is a better technique than maintenance rehearsal for transferring information from short-term to long-term memory.

3. An associative network is a massive network of associated ideas and concepts. In a neural network, each concept is represented by a pattern or set of nodes that becomes activated simultaneously. There is no single node for a concept in a neural network, although there is in an associative network. A neural network is a physical concept, whereas an associative network is a cognitive concept.

4. Retrograde amnesia represents memory loss for events that occurred prior to the onset of amnesia. Anterograde amnesia involves memory loss for events that occur after the initial onset of amnesia. Infantile amnesia refers to an inability to remember information from the first few years of life.

5. The misinformation effect is the distortion of memory by misleading postevent information.

Answer Key for Practice Test Essay Questions

As you may have guessed, there are no right or wrong answers to the essay questions in this practice test. That does not mean, however, that all essays are equally good. To get maximum learning benefit from the essay questions, do the following:

- Review each essay a day or two after you wrote it, noting any necessary corrections and any additional support for your points that you can think of.
- Review the section in your textbook that pertains to the topic of each essay. Annotate your essay with any corrections or additional support for your points that you find in the text.
- Spend a few minutes researching the topic of each essay on the Internet. Annotate your essay further with any additional (reliable) information you find.
- Finally, reread each essay with the annotations you have added.

Chapter 9
LANGUAGE AND THINKING

A. Learning Objectives: *These objectives are expanded from the Focus Questions found in the margins of your textbook. When you have mastered the material in this chapter, you will be able to:*

9.1 Define language.

9.2 Describe the key properties of language.

9.3 Contrast surface and deep structures of language.

9.4 Describe the hierarchy of language.

9.5 Describe the sex differences that exist in language processing.

9.6 Describe how biological factors influence language acquisition.

9.7 Describe how social learning influences language acquisition.

9.8 Contrast evidence for and against the acquisition of human language by apes.

9.9 Describe the evidence that suggests a critical period for acquiring a second language.

9.10 Describe the relationship between bilingualism and other cognitive abilities.

9.11 Explain how language influences thinking.

9.12 Define concepts and propositions, and explain their interrelation.

9.13 Recognize and contrast examples of deductive and inductive reasoning.

9.14 Recognize and describe examples of the four stages of problem solving.

9.15 Distinguish between algorithms and heuristics.

9.16 Describe the roles that uncertainty and heuristics play in decision making.

9.17 Explain why disconfirming evidence is important in making decisions.

9.18 Describe factors that inhibit and facilitate problem solving.

9.19 Describe the roles that schemas play in knowledge acquisition and expertise.

9.20 Describe the components of wisdom, and explain how wisdom and expertise differ.

9.21 Describe the major findings and importance of Shepard and Metzler's mental rotation study.

9.22 Describe research, including brain research, that supports the view that mental images are perceptual in nature.

9.23 Define metacognition; describe the two types of metacognition, and provide examples.

9.24 Describe ways to enhance metacognition based on research.

B. Chapter Overview

In this chapter, we explore what language is and how psychologists study it, and we investigate how people think, reason, solve problems, and make decisions.

Language consists of a system of symbols and rules for combining these symbols in ways that can generate an infinite number of possible messages or meanings. Scientists believe that humans have evolved an innate capacity for acquiring language.

Language is symbolic, with a rule-governed structure called grammar. The symbols of a language can be combined to generate an infinite number of messages that convey meaning, a property called generativity. Language uses sounds, written signs, or gestures to refer to objects, events, ideas, and feelings. With language, we can talk about not only the present but also the past, future, and imaginary events, a feature of language called displacement.

Language has both a surface and a deep structure. The surface structure is the way symbols are combined through rules of grammar called syntax. The deep structure refers to the underlying meaning. Semantics are the rules for connecting symbols to what they represent. Language has a hierarchical structure: Phonemes are the smallest units of sound in a language, and they combine to form morphemes, which are the smallest units of meaning. Words are a combination of morphemes; phrases, a grouping of words; and sentences, an amalgam of phrases. Discourse involves higher-level combinations of sentences.

Understanding and producing language involves both bottom-up processing, wherein individual elements are analyzed and then combined to form a unified perception, and top-down processing, whereby stimulus information is interpreted in light of existing knowledge, concepts, ideas, and expectations. Speech segmentation (knowing where words start and end in spoken language) and pragmatics (understanding language in its social context) are examples of top-down processing of language.

Language functions are distributed in many areas of the brain, but two areas are especially significant. Broca's area in the frontal lobe, near the motor cortex, is centrally involved in the production of speech, whereas Wernicke's area in the temporal lobe is centrally involved in speech comprehension. People with damage to these areas typically have aphasia or speech impairment. There is some evidence that men's language functions are typically more localized in the left hemisphere than are the language functions of women.

Speech development reflects an interplay of biological and environmental factors. All infants, regardless of culture or society, vocalize the entire range of phonemes found in the world's languages, but by age 6 months they begin to lose those phonemes not specific to their native tongue. Chomsky proposed that humans are born with a language acquisition device (LAD), or innate biological mechanism for acquiring language. Behaviorists suggest that language is developed through operant conditioning principles with rewards and punishments provided by the child's social environment. Although social learning is an important aspect of language acquisition, it cannot completely explain the development of language skills. Bruner proposed the term *language acquisition support system* (LASS) to represent factors in the social environment that facilitate the learning of a language. Most modern theorists accept that language is developed via innate mechanisms interacting with an appropriate linguistic environment. There is evidence for a sensitive period in childhood during which language is most easily learned, including sign languages, which share the deep structure of spoken languages.

Researchers have attempted to teach apes to communicate using symbols in a language-like fashion. At best, apes can communicate with symbols at the level of a very young child, but it is questionable whether they can learn syntax or generate novel ideas.

A second language is best learned and spoken most fluently when learned during the sensitive period of childhood. Bilingual children tend to perform better on a variety of cognitive tasks and on some perceptual tasks that require selective attention rather than monolingual children. In general, when people acquire a second language early in life, or learn it to a high degree of proficiency later in life, both languages use a common neural network. People who learn a second language to a moderate degree of proficiency in later life show more variability in how bilingual abilities are represented in the brain.

Benjamin Lee Whorf argued in his linguistic relativity hypothesis that language determines what we are capable of thinking. Although most modern linguists disagree with that strong assertion, researchers have found that language can influence how we think and how effectively we think in certain domains, and that vocabulary can color the way in which we encode and process information.

At the biological level, thinking involves patterns of neural activity; at the level of the mind, thinking involves a variety of mental activities. We think in propositions, or statements that express ideas; we have images that we "see", "hear," or "feel," and we mentally represent motor movements (the latter is not covered in this chapter).

Concepts are basic units of semantic memory, mental categories into which we place objects, activities, abstractions and events that share fundamental characteristics. Many concepts are defined by prototypes, the most typical and familiar members of a category, and we often categorize things by their degree of resemblance to the prototype. Prototypes may vary among people depending on their personal experience. Propositional thought involves statements using concepts, and thus how we state propositions can influence how we reason, try to solve problems, and make decisions.

We reason through both deductive (top-down) and inductive (bottom-up) reasoning. Deductive reasoning involves reasoning from general principles to a conclusion about a specific case, whereas inductive reasoning involves starting with specific facts and developing a general principle from them. Sometimes we run into stumbling blocks in reasoning. These stumbling blocks include being distracted by irrelevant information, belief bias, and the tendency to abandon logical rules in favor of one's own personal beliefs. Our emotions may interfere with logical reasoning, and how we frame, or structure, a problem affects our ability to find a solution.

To solve a problem, we must first frame it. Following that, we generate potential solutions, test the solutions, and evaluate the results. Problem-solving schemas can help us to select information and solve problems, although sometimes our schemas can hinder solving a problem when we stick to solutions that have worked in the past but are not effective for this particular situation, an obstacle called mental set.

Algorithms are formulas or procedures for solving problems that automatically generate correct solutions, whereas heuristics are general problem-solving strategies that we apply to certain classes of situations. Means-ends analysis is a heuristic that can involve generating subgoals to move from an initial state toward a desired goal state. We use the representativeness heuristic to infer how closely something or someone fits our prototype for a particular category, and therefore how likely it is to belong to that category. The availability heuristic can bias our perceptions by focusing only on what is available in our memories and disregarding information that is relevant but less available. Similar to belief bias is the confirmation bias, by which we search only for information that supports our beliefs. We tend to be overconfident in the correctness of our knowledge, beliefs, and decisions. Another obstacle to problem solving may be functional fixedness, which involves being unable to think about alternative uses for an object other than the one with which we are most familiar, a type of mental set. Creative problem solving can be aided by the use of divergent thinking and incubation.

Knowledge forms a foundation for expertise and wisdom. Acquiring knowledge is a process of building schemas—that is, mental frameworks for organizing how we think about some aspect of the world. A concept or category is a schema; a script is a schema for a sequence of events; and algorithms and heuristics are problem-solving schemas.

Experts have developed many schemas to guide problem solving in their field and, very importantly, to recognize when each schema should be applied. Schemas reside in long-term memory, which has great capacity, and can be retrieved as a coherent unit into working memory. Working memory, has limited capacity and is where problem solving takes place. Nonexperts are less able to take advantage of long-term memory in this manner. As people develop expertise, their brain functioning changes in ways that increase processing efficiency in their area of expertise.

Wisdom represents a system of knowledge about the meaning and conduct of life. According to one model, wisdom has five major components: rich factual knowledge about life; rich procedural knowledge about life, including strategies for such things as decision making and handling conflict; understanding of lifespan contexts, including a broad perspective on time; an awareness of the relativism of values and priorities; and the ability to recognize and manage uncertainty.

A mental image is a representation of a stimulus that originates inside the brain, rather than from external sensory input. Mental images of objects seem to have properties that are analogous to the properties of actual objects; for example, one can mentally "rotate" the image. Thus, one viewpoint holds that mental images are basically perceptual in nature. A second viewpoint proposes rather that mental images are based on language. Overall, brain research offers more support to the imagery-as-perception view.

Metacognition refers to our awareness and understanding of our own cognitive abilities. It includes metacomprehension, or being able to judge accurately whether we understand something, as well as metamemory, or being able to judge accurately our memory capabilities.

C. Chapter Outline

LANGUAGE
    Adaptive Functions of Language
    Properties of Language
        Language Is Symbolic and Structured
        Language Conveys Meaning
        Language is Generative and Permits Displacement
    The Structure of Language
        Surface Structure and Deep Structure
        What Do You Think? Discerning Surface and Deep Structures of Language
        The Hierarchical Structure of Language
    Understanding and Producing Language
        The Role of Bottom-Up Processing
        The Role of Top-Down Processing
        Pragmatics: The Social Context of Language
        What Do You Think? The Sleeping Policeman
        Language Functions, the Brain, and Sex Differences

Acquiring a First Language
- Biological Foundations
- Social Learning Processes
- Developmental Timetable and Sensitive Periods
- Can Animals Acquire Human Language?
  - Washoe: Early Signs of Success
  - Project Nim: Dissent from Within
  - Kanzi: Chimp versus Child
  - Is It Language?

Bilingualism
- Does Bilingualism Affect Other Cognitive Abilities?
- *Beneath the Surface: Learning a Second Language: Is Earlier Better?*
- The Bilingual Brain

Linguistic Influences on Thinking

In Review

THINKING

Thought, Brain, and Mind

Concepts and Propositions

Reasoning
- Deductive Reasoning
- Inductive Reasoning
- Stumbling Blocks in Reasoning
  - Distraction by Irrelevant Information
  - Belief Bias
  - Emotions and Framing

Problem Solving and Decision Making
- Steps in Problem Solving
  - Understanding, or Framing, the Problem
  - Generating Potential Solutions
  - Testing the Solutions
  - Evaluating Results
- The Role of Problem-Solving Schemas
  - Algorithms and Heuristics
- Uncertainty, Heuristics, and Decision Making
  - The Representativeness Heuristic
  - The Availability Heuristic
- Confirmation Bias and Overconfidence
- *Applying Psychological Science: Guidelines for Creative Problem Solving*

Knowledge, Expertise, and Wisdom
- Acquiring Knowledge: Schemas and Scripts
- The Nature of Expertise
- Expert Schemas and Memory
- What Is Wisdom?

Mental Imagery
- Mental Rotation
- Are Mental Images Pictures in the Mind?

Mental Imagery as Perception
Mental Imagery as Language
Mental Imagery and the Brain
Metacognition: Knowing Your Own Cognitive Abilities
Recognizing What You Do and Don't Know
Research Close-Up: "Why Did I Get That Wrong?": Improving College Students' Awareness of Whether They Understand Text Material
Further Advice on Improving Metacomprehension
In Review

D. Review at a Glance: *Write the term that best fits the blank to review what you learned in this chapter.*

Language

(1)_____ consists of a system of symbols and rules for combining those symbols in ways that can produce a(n) (2)_____ number of possible messages or meanings. The ability of language to represent imaginary events and objects is called (3)_____. Language has both structure and rules. The (4)_____ structure of a language consists of the way symbols are combined within a given language. The rules for such combination are called the (5)_____ of a language. The underlying meaning of the combined symbols is called (6)_____ structure. Human languages have a hierarchical structure. The smallest units of sound that are recognized as separate in a given language are called (7)_____, whereas the smallest units of meaning in a language are called (8)_____.

Understanding and producing language involves both (9)_____-_____ processing, wherein individual elements are analyzed and then combined to form a unified perception, and (10)_____-_____ processing, whereby stimulus information is interpreted in light of existing knowledge, concepts, ideas, and expectations.

Two areas of the brain are especially significant for language. Broca's area in the frontal lobe, near the motor cortex, is centrally involved in the (11)_____ of speech, whereas (12)_____ area in the temporal lobe is centrally involved in speech (13)_____.

Speech development reflects an interplay of biological and environmental factors. All infants, regardless of culture or society, vocalize the entire range of (14)_____ found in the world's languages, but by age 6 months they begin to lose sounds not specific to their native tongue. Chomsky proposed that humans are born with a (15)_____ _____ _____ (LAD), or innate biological mechanism for acquiring language. Behaviorists suggest that language is developed through (16)_____ conditioning, with rewards and punishments provided by the child's (17)_____ environment. Although social learning is an important aspect of language acquisition, it cannot completely explain the development of language skills. Bruner proposed the term (18)_____ _____ _____ _____ (LASS) to represent factors in the social environment that facilitate the learning of a language. There is evidence for a (19)_____ period in childhood during which language is most easily learned, including sign languages, which share the (20)_____ structure of spoken languages.

Researchers have attempted to teach apes to communicate using symbols in a language-like fashion. At best, apes can communicate with symbols at the level of a (21)_____ _____, but it is questionable whether they can learn (22)_____ or generate novel ideas.

A second language is best learned and spoken most fluently when learned during the sensitive period of (23)_____. Bilingual children perform better on a variety of (24)_____ tasks than monolingual children. In general, when people acquire a second language early in life, the two languages use a (25)_____ neural network.

Benjamin Lee Whorf, in his (26)_____ _____ hypothesis, argued that language determines what we are capable of thinking. Although not supporting a position as strong as Whorf's, researchers have found that language can (27)_____ how we think and that vocabulary can color the way in which we (28)_____ and process information.

Thinking

At the biological level, thinking involves patterns of (29)_____ _____. Thinking may be considered to be the "internal language of the mind." Much of our thinking occurs in terms of statements that express facts, which are called (30)_____, and in mentally manipulating (31)_____, or representations of objects that we can "see" in our minds.

The basic units of semantic memory are (32)_____, which are mental categories into which we place things that share fundamental characteristics. Many concepts are defined by (33)_____, the most typical and familiar members of a category. How we understand concepts and state propositions can influence how we reason, try to solve problems, and make decisions.

Two types of reasoning affect our abilities to make decisions and solve problems. (34)_____ reasoning involves reasoning from general principles to a conclusion about a specific case, whereas (35)_____ reasoning involves starting with specific facts and developing a general principle from them.

To solve a problem, we must first (36)_____ it. We often employ (37)_____-_____ schemas, which are step-by-step scripts for selecting information and solving certain classes of problems. Sometimes we stick to solutions that have worked in the past but are not effective for this particular situation, an obstacle called (38)_____ _____.

Formulas that automatically generate correct solutions to problems are called (39)_____. Shortcut problem-solving strategies that we often employ rather than algorithms to solve problems are called (40)_____. One type of heuristic is (41)_____-_____ _____, during which we identify differences between the desired state and our present state and make changes to reduce the differences. Often this strategy involves (42)_____ analysis, by which we form intermediate steps toward a problem solution. Another heuristic allows us to infer how closely something or someone fits our prototype for a particular class, or concept. This type of heuristic is called the (43)_____ heuristic. A heuristic that leads us to base judgments and decisions on the availability of information in memory is called the (44)_____ heuristic, and it may lead us to disregard information that is relevant but less available. Similar to belief bias is the (45)_____ bias, by which we search only for information that supports our beliefs. We tend to be (46)_____ in the correctness of our knowledge, beliefs, and decisions. Another obstacle to problem solving may be (47)_____ _____, which involves being unable to think about alternative uses for an object other than the one with which we are most familiar. Creative problem solving can be aided by the use of (48)_____ thinking and incubation.

(49)_____ forms a foundation for expertise and wisdom. Acquiring knowledge is a process of building schemas—that is, (50)_____ _____ for organizing how we think about some aspect of the world.

(51)_____ have developed many schemas to guide problem solving in their field and, very importantly, to recognize (52)_____ each schema should be applied. They are able to take advantage of (53)_____-_____ memory in a way that novices are not. As people develop expertise, their brain functioning changes in ways that increase (54)_____ _____ in their area of expertise.

Wisdom represents a system of knowledge about the (55)_____ and (56)_____ of life. According to one model, wisdom has five major components: rich (57)_____ knowledge about life; rich procedural knowledge about life, including strategies for such things as (58)_____ _____ and handling conflict; understanding of lifespan contexts, including a (59)_____ perspective on time; an awareness of the relativism of (60)_____; and the ability to recognize and manage (61)_____.

A (62)_____ _____ is a representation of a stimulus that originates inside the brain. One viewpoint holds that mental images are basically (63)_____ in nature. A second viewpoint proposes rather that mental images are based on (64)_____. Overall, brain research offers more support to the imagery-as-(65)_____ view.

(66)_____ refers to our awareness and understanding of our own cognitive abilities. It includes metacomprehension, or being able to judge accurately whether we (67) _____ something, as well as (68)_____, or being able to judge our memory capabilities accurately.

E. Concept Cards

Truly learning a concept means integrating it into the way *you* think about things. To integrate concepts successfully, you must translate the words and examples your text or instructor provides into words and examples that are meaningful to you.

For this exercise, obtain some note cards (3" × 5" or 4" × 6") to make a deck of concept cards. On one side of each card, write the *concept* from the list below (e.g., "grammar") at the top. Read the textbook definition provided, and then write the definition *in your own words* on the concept card (e.g., for "grammar," you might write "the rules of putting words together so they can mean something"). Simply imagine that a friend has asked you what the concept means, and write down what you would answer. Writing the definition in your own words requires you to think deeply about its meaning. When next you see your own version of the definition, it will make intuitive sense to you—no translation required.

On the second side of the card, write your own example of the concept. Again, coming up with your own example requires you to think deeply about the application of the concept, and you will more easily understand and remember the example when you study for a test. If you use an example from the text, or from class, make it your own by writing it in your own words. You can always check with your instructor that your example is indeed a good example of the concept.

CONCEPT Definition in my own words (side 1 of card)	Example of the concept in my own words, preferably drawn from my own experience (side 2 of card)

The following is a list of all the boldface concepts from your textbook, with the author's definition. Write the definition in your own words, together with your own example of the concept, to create a *concept card* as described earlier, or write in the space provided.

Mental representation: Images, ideas, concepts, and principles

Language: A system of symbols and rules for combining these symbols in ways that can generate an infinite number of possible messages or meanings

Psycholinguistics: The scientific field that studies psychological aspects of language

Grammar: The set of rules that dictate how symbols can be combined to create meaningful units of communication

Syntax: Rules that govern the order of words

Semantics: The meaning of words and sentences

Generativity: The capacity to generate an infinite number of messages that have novel meaning

Displacement: The capacity to communicate about events and objects that are not physically present

Surface structure: The symbols that are used in language and their order

Deep structure: The underlying meaning of the combined symbols that are used in language

Phonemes: The smallest units of sound that are recognized as separate in a given language

Morphemes: The smallest units of meaning in a language

Discourse: The combination of sentences into paragraphs, articles, books, conversations and so forth

Bottom-up processing: Processing in which individual elements of a stimulus are analyzed and then combined to form a unified perception

Top-down processing: Processing in which sensory information is interpreted in light of existing knowledge, concepts, ideas, and expectations

Speech segmentation: Perceiving where each word within a spoken sentence begins and ends

Pragmatics: Knowledge of practical aspects of using language

Aphasia: Impairment in speech comprehension and/or production

Language acquisition device (LAD): An innate biological mechanism that contains the general grammatical rules ("universal grammar") common to all languages

Language acquisition support system (LASS): Factors in the social environment that facilitate the learning of a language

Bilingualism: The use of two languages in daily life

Linguistic relativity hypothesis: The hypothesis that language not only influences but also determines what we are capable of thinking

Propositional thought: Thinking that expresses a proposition, or statement

Imaginal thought: Thinking that consists of images that we can "see," "hear," or "feel" in our mind

Motoric thought: Mental representations of motor movements

Propositions: Statements that express ideas

Concepts: Basic units of semantic memory—mental categories into which we place objects, activities, abstractions (such as "liberal" and "conservative"), and events that have essential features in common

Prototypes: The most typical and familiar members of a category, or class

Deductive reasoning: Reasoning from the "top down"—that is, from general principles to a conclusion about a specific case

Inductive reasoning: Reasoning in a "bottom-up" fashion, starting with specific facts and trying to develop a general principle

Belief bias: The tendency to abandon logical rules in favor of our own personal beliefs

Framing: The idea that the same information, problem, or options can be structured and presented in different ways

Mental set: The tendency to stick to solutions that have worked in the past

Problem-solving schemas: Mental blueprints or step-by-step scripts for selecting information and solving specialized classes of problems

Algorithms: Formulas or procedures that automatically generate correct solutions

Heuristics: General problem-solving strategies that we apply to certain classes of situations

Means-ends analysis: Identifying differences between the present situation and the desired state, or goal, and then making changes that will reduce these differences

Subgoal analysis: Formulating subgoals, or intermediate steps, toward solving a problem

Representativeness heuristic: A process of inferring how closely something or someone fits our prototype for a particular concept, or class, and therefore how likely it is to be a member of that class

Availability heuristic: A process that causes us to base judgments and decisions on the availability of information in memory

Confirmation bias: A tendency to look for evidence that will confirm what one currently believes rather than looking for evidence that could disconfirm one's beliefs

Overconfidence: The tendency to overestimate one's correctness in factual knowledge, beliefs, and decisions

Creativity: The ability to produce something that is both new and valuable

Divergent thinking: The generation of novel ideas that depart from the norm

Functional fixedness: The tendency to be so fixed in one's perception of the proper function of an object or procedure that one is blinded to new ways of using it

Incubation: A phenomenon in which the solution to a problem suddenly appears in consciousness after a problem solver has stopped thinking about it for a while

Schema: A mental framework; an organized pattern of thought about some aspect of the world

Script: A mental framework concerning a sequence of events that usually unfolds in a regular, almost standardized order

Wisdom: A system of knowledge about the meaning and conduct of life

Mental image: A representation of a stimulus that originates inside your brain rather than from external sensory input

Metacognition: Awareness and understanding of your own cognitive abilities

F. What's the Difference? A Concept Card Exercise

An important skill in learning concepts is being able to differentiate among concepts that are similar or related in some way. This skill is particularly relevant for multiple-choice tests, especially if you often find yourself wavering between two answers.

Once you have created your own deck of concept cards, select them two by two, each time answering the question "What's the difference between these two concepts?" You can use the word definitions of the concepts or the examples of the concepts to enhance your mastery of the material. In each case, choose pairs of concepts to compare those that are related or similar or that sound the same or that could in some way be confused. It's much easier to spot the difference between two concepts when you are studying, with the textbook available, rather than when onsidering the question for the first time in a testing situation.

G. Apply What You Know

1. Indicate whether each of the following statements is an example of inductive or deductive reasoning. In addition, indicate whether the reasoning is faulty. If it is faulty, cite the type of faulty reasoning it best exemplifies.

Statement	Inductive or Deductive?	Faulty? If So, How?
George is a nice guy and he has a dog. Anna, Jacob, and Betsy are also nice people and they each have a dog. Therefore, dog owners are nice people.		
Alcohol impairs driving skills. Marina has had 5 drinks in the past 2 hours. Therefore, Marina should not drive home.		

Statement	Inductive or Deductive?	Faulty? If So, How?
Great white sharks have been known to attack swimmers. Great white sharks have been known to come within a mile of New Jersey beaches. Therefore, Shawn should not swim within a mile of a New Jersey beach.		
Joel brought an umbrella with him every day last week, and it did not rain all week. Today he left his umbrella at home and it rained. Therefore, it will rain the next time Joel leaves his umbrella at home.		
All Zythmians are liars, incapable of telling the truth. I am a Zythmian.		

H. On the Web: *As with any online research, it is important to consider how legitimate a given source is before you rely on the information it presents. Your instructor or Internet adviser may give you some specific guidelines for distinguishing which kinds of Web sites tend to be reputable.*

A. A number of individuals have made notable contributions to our understanding of language and thinking. Search the Web for more information about some of those listed below.

Paul Broca

Carl Wernicke

Noam Chomsky

Chapter 9

Jerome Bruner

Allen Gardner and Beatrice Gardner

Herbert Terrace

Sue Savage-Rumbaugh

M. D. Berlitz

Bejamin Lee Whorf

B. Take a look at the concept cards you have created for this chapter, or the key concepts listed in section E. In the space provided, make a list of any whose definitions or associations you are not yet confident of and any you'd like to learn more about. Try entering the terms on your list into your search engine. Make notes of any helpful information you find.

Key Concept/Information Found

C. By typing "funny newspaper headlines" or "headline bloopers" into your search engine, find some Web sites dedicated to infelicitous headlines and other phrases whose surface-structure or deep-structure ambiguities make them hilarious. Another good search target is linguist Richard Lederer, author of books such as *Anguished*

English and *Get Thee to a Punnery* and creator of the site known as Verbivore. Choose a few of your favorites and, using the language analysis techniques described in this chapter, explain what makes them funny.

I. Analyze This: *Chapter 1 of your textbook begins by presenting these four basic steps in the critical thinking process:*
- *"What exactly are you asking me to believe?"*
- *"How do you know? What is the evidence?"*
- *"Are there other possible explanations?"*
- *"What is the most reasonable conclusion?"*

You might picture this as a four-step analysis to help you decide whether to accept a given theory or assertion. Now it's your turn to put your textbook to this test.

Review the section in Chapter 9 of your textbook under the heading "Can Animals Acquire Human Language?" There you will find a discussion of the controversy over whether apes can be taught to use human language. If someone told you that apes can indeed be taught to use human language, would you agree? Analyze that assertion in the space below. When you have finished, consider using this four-step analysis to evaluate other assertions you encounter.

"What exactly are you asking me to believe?"

"How do you know? What is the evidence?"

"Are there other possible explanations?"

"What is the most reasonable conclusion?"

J. Practice Test

Multiple-Choice Items: *Write the letter corresponding to your answer in the space to the left of each item.*

_____ 1. _____ consists of a system of symbols and rules for combining those symbols in ways that can produce an infinite number of possible messages or meanings.
   a. A proposition
   b. A schema
   c. Language
   d. Deep structure

_____ 2. The smallest units of meaning in a language are called _____.
   a. phonemes
   b. morphemes
   c. surface structures
   d. deep structures

_____ 3. An essential property of language is that it is generative. This means that _____.
   a. language consists of symbols that represent other things
   b. language has rules that govern its structure
   c. language is acquired through the language acquisition device
   d. the symbols of a language can be combined to generate an infinite number of meaningful messages

_____ 4. With language, we can talk about not only the present but also the past, the future, and imaginary events. This property of language is called _____.
   a. syntax
   b. displacement
   c. semantics
   d. pragmatics

_____ 5. Consider the statement "Last night, I shot an elephant in my pajamas." This sentence has two different interpretations (the pajamas could be worn by the person *or* they could be worn by the elephant), which means that this sentence has _____.
   a. two different deep structures and one surface structure
   b. two different surface structures and one deep structure

c. two different surface structures and two different deep structures
d. one surface structure and two tusks

_____ 6. Prior to 6 months of age, infants around the world are able to vocalize _____, but as they get older, they begin vocalizing _____.
a. only 5 to 10 phonemes; all the phonemes associated with their native language
b. only the phonemes associated with their native language; the phonemes of all languages
c. only morphemes; phonemes
d. the phonemes of all languages; only the phonemes associated with their native language

_____ 7. If all adult languages throughout the world have a common underlying deep structure, this suggests that _____.
a. deep structure is more important than surface structure
b. phonemes are more important than morphemes
c. morphemes are more important than phonemes
d. language has a biological basis

_____ 8. Many _____ are difficult to describe in words, but we often can define them using _____, which are typical and familiar members of a particular class.
a. prototypes; linotypes
b. concepts; propositions
c. concepts; prototypes
d. phonemes; morphemes

_____ 9. Speech segmentation (knowing where words start and end in spoken language) and pragmatics (understanding language in its social context) are examples of _____.
a. bottom-up processing of language
b. top-down processing of language
c. aphasia
d. phoneme sensitivity

_____ 10. Mahendra had a stroke that damaged Broca's area of his left cortex. Which of the following symptoms would you expect Mahendra to display?
a. difficulty understanding speech
b. difficulty producing speech
c. speaking so rapidly that other people can't understand what he is trying to say
d. inability to understand language in its social context

_____ 11. Chomsky's proposed language acquisition device (LAD) is _____
a. an innate biological mechanism for acquiring language
b. a factor in the social environment that facilitates the learning of a language

c. a responsive linguistic environment for developing language
d. any cognitive task that helps a child acquire language

_____ 12. Most modern theorists believe that language is developed via _____.
a. the unfolding of an innate biological process, irrespective of the environment
b. innate mechanisms interacting with an appropriate linguistic environment
c. operant conditioning with social reinforcement from the environment
d. being sensitive to a child's needs when he or she is learning to speak

_____ 13. Researchers have attempted to teach apes to communicate using symbols in a language-like fashion. What has this research suggested about apes learning to use language?
a. apes can learn to use language in the same way that humans do
b. apes can learn to use symbols to represent objects
c. apes can learn the surface structure of language, but not its deep structure
d. apes can learn syntax but not pragmatics

_____ 14. A second language is best learned and spoken most fluently _____.
a. at any age, so long as the person is immersed in the appropriate environment
b. during the sensitive period of childhood
c. after puberty, once the first language is already well established
d. between the ages of 10 and 12

_____ 15. Whorf's linguistic relativity hypothesis proposes that _____.
a. language determines what we are capable of thinking
b. language influences what we think but does not determine what we are capable of thinking
c. our thoughts are independent of the language we use to express them
d. apes have their own means of communication that is different from human language

_____ 16. _____ are mental categories into which we place objects, activities, abstractions and events that share fundamental characteristics.
a. Prototypes
b. Morphemes
c. Propositions
d. Concepts

_____ 17. In view of what you know about concept formation, to which of the following statements would a subject take longest to respond "true" or "false"
a. A rose is a flower.
b. A penguin is a bird.
c. A table is furniture.

d. A maple is a tree.

_____ 18. One morning, Ed decides to have oatmeal instead of his usual breakfast of a fruit smoothie. He performs very well on a math test that he takes later that day. He doesn't think too much about this until a few weeks later when he does very well on an English test and recalls that he had oatmeal for breakfast before this test, too. He concludes that eating oatmeal in the morning helps him to perform well on exams. This example best demonstrates the _____.
   a. use of the representativeness heuristic
   b. process of inductive reasoning
   c. use of divergent thinking
   d. process of deductive reasoning

_____ 19. You are hungry and would like something to eat. You decide to look through the pantry, where you see a box of macaroni and cheese that looks good. Without really thinking about it, you know how to do all the various steps involved in making this meal, such as filling a pot with water, boiling the water, cooking the pasta, mixing in the cheese sauce, and finding a plate on which to put the finished meal. In view of the discussion in the text, this type of specialized knowledge is best considered as an example of _____.
   a. a problem-solving schema
   b. a mentative set
   c. deductive reasoning
   d. a norm

_____ 20. You tell your friend that a man named Jack wears cowboy boots and a cowboy hat to work, and that Jack often drinks beer. If your friend says it is more likely that Jack is a professional cowboy *and* a beer drinker than that Jack is either a cowboy *or* a beer drinker, your friend is confusing _____.
   a. representativeness with availability
   b. representativeness with probability
   c. availability with confirmation bias
   d. Jack with another man

_____ 21. Shelley is attempting to solve a problem, and at this point in time, she is trying to generate as many solutions as possible and trying to incorporate new and unusual ideas into her potential solutions. Shelley is engaged in _____ thinking.
   a. convergent
   b. propositional
   c. divergent
   d. confirmatory

_____ 22. Reasoning from the top down is called _____ reasoning.
   a. deductive

b. inductive
   c. schematic
   d. propositional

_____ 23. Cases of missing or abducted children are often highly publicized in the national news. Many people have an exaggerated impression of how likely children are to be abducted. This incorrect belief is most likely due to _____.
   a. the representativeness heuristic
   b. applying an algorithm
   c. the availability heuristic
   d. the confirmation bias

_____ 24. The first step in solving a problem is to _____.
   a. test potential solutions
   b. generate potential solutions
   c. frame the problem
   d. incubate the problem

_____ 25. Tiffany couldn't remember the three-digit code to open the lock on her suitcase, so she tried every combination of three digits until she found the right one. Tiffany used _____ to solve her problem.
   a. the availability heuristic
   b. an algorithm
   c. functional fixedness
   d. belief bias

_____ 26. Means-ends analysis is a heuristic _____.
   a. for moving from an initial state toward a desired goal state
   b. for inferring how likely it is that a specific item belongs to a specific category
   c. that makes us likely to abandon logical rules in favor of our personal beliefs
   d. that is based on analyzing prototypes

_____ 27. Confirmation bias _____.
   a. leads us to search for information that supports our beliefs
   b. leads us to seek out information to disconfirm and thereby test our beliefs
   c. leads us to use algorithms rather than heuristics to solve problems
   d. involves generating subgoals to lead us to a desired goal state

_____ 28. Marissa was frustrated by her inability to solve the physics problems she had for homework today, so she went out with her friends to get a pizza. While eating the pizza, and with the physics problems far from her mind, she suddenly understood how to do the homework. This best illustrates which process in problem solving?

a. overconfidence bias, because she went out for pizza instead of doing her homework
b. divergent thinking, because she thought about the food instead of the problems
c. incubation, because the solution to the problem appeared some time after she had stopped working on it consciously
d. the availability heuristic, because the solution to the problem was available, even though she didn't realize it

_____ 29. What distinguishes experts in a field from nonexperts in solving problems in that field?
a. experts have fewer problem-solving schemas in the field, because they need fewer
b. experts solve the problems in their long-term memory rather than in their working memory
c. experts are better than nonexperts at recognizing which problem-solving schemas are applicable to different problems in their field
d. experts can rotate mental images, but non-experts cannot do so

_____ 30. Research suggests that mental images _____.
a. are perceptual in nature
b. are based on language
c. are a form of metacognition
d. are the same as a mental set

True/False Items: *Write T or F in the space provided to the left of each item.*

_____ 1. The surface structure of a language consists of the way symbols are combined within that language.

_____ 2. Phonemes are the smallest units of sound that have meaning in a given language.

_____ 3. The linguistic relativity hypothesis suggests that language determines how we think.

_____ 4. The most typical and familiar members of a category or concept are called prototypes.

_____ 5. Reasoning from general principles to a conclusion about a specific case is called inductive reasoning.

_____ 6. Using problem-solving schemas to solve problems is called a mental set.

_____ 7. The availability heuristic is involved in exaggerating the likelihood that something will occur, because it easily comes to mind.

_____ 8. Expertise represents a system of knowledge about the meaning and conduct of life.

_____ 9. Expertise and wisdom are different names for the same concept.

_____ 10. Metacognition includes being able to judge accurately whether we understand something.

Short-Answer Questions

1. What is the difference between the surface and deep structure of a language?

2. What are propositions?

3. What are algorithms and heuristics?

4. What are inductive and deductive reasoning? Give and example of each.

5. In what ways are expertise and wisdom alike and different from each other?

Essay Questions

1. Considering what you learned in this chapter about language, explain why you think it is, or is not, a valuable component of every child's education to learn a foreign language in elementary school.

2. Considering what you learned in this chapter about reasoning and problem solving, do you think it is likely that in the foreseeable future computers, and perhaps an elite class of techies who know how to program computers, will surpass humans and take over our reasoning and problem-solving functions?

3. In view of what you have learned in this chapter about knowledge, expertise, and wisdom, how would you go about acquiring wisdom?

Answer Keys

Answer Key for Review at a Glance

1. Language
2. infinite
3. displacement
4. surface
5. syntax
6. deep

35. inductive
36. frame
37. problem-solving
38. mental set
39. algorithms
40. heuristics

Chapter 9   277

7. phonemes
8. morphemes
9. bottom-up
10. top-down
11. production
12. Wernicke's
13. comprehension
14. phonemes
15. language acquisition device
16. operant
17. social
18. language acquisition support system
19. sensitive
20. deep
21. young child
22. syntax
23. childhood
24. cognitive
25. common
26. linguistic relativity
27. influence
28. encode
29. neural activity
30. propositions
31. images
32. concepts
33. prototypes
34. Deductive

41. means-end analysis
42. subgoal
43. representativeness
44. availability
45. confirmation
46. overconfident
47. functional fixedness
48. divergent
49. Knowledge
50. mental frameworks
51. Experts
52. when
53. long-term
54. processing efficiency
55. meaning
56. conduct
57. factual
58. decision making
59. broad
60. values (or priorities)
61. uncertainty
62. mental image
63. perceptual
64. language
65. perception
66. Metacognition
67. understand
68. metamemory

Answer Key for Practice Test Multiple-Choice Items

1. c
2. b
3. d
4. b
5. a
6. d
7. d
8. c
9. b
10. b
11. a
12. b
13. b
14. b
15. a

16. d
17. b
18. b
19. a
20. b
21. c
22. a
23. c
24. c
25. b
26. a
27. a
28. c
29. c
30. a

Answer Key for Practice Test True/False Items

1. T
2. F
3. T
4. T
5. F
6. F
7. T
8. F
9. F
10. T

Answer Key for Practice Test Short-Answer Questions

1. Surface structure consists of the way symbols are combined within a given language. Deep structure refers to the underlying meaning of the combined symbols.

2. Propositions are statements that express ideas. All propositions include concepts.

3. Algorithms are formulas or procedures that automatically generate correct solutions. Heuristics are general problem-solving strategies that we apply to certain classes of situations. They are mental shortcuts that may or may not provide correct solutions.

4. Inductive reasoning involves starting with specific facts and developing a general principle from them. For example, if I feel dizzy every time I drink beer, wine, or whiskey, all of which contain alcohol, I may develop the general principle that alcohol causes me to feel dizzy, via inductive reasoning. Deductive reasoning involves reasoning from a general principle to a conclusion about a specific case. For example, if I know that, as a general principle, alcohol causes me to feel dizzy, then I may decline a drink of rum, which contains alcohol, deducing that it is likely to make me feel dizzy.

5. Expertise and wisdom are alike in that both are built on a foundation of knowledge. Expertise has to do with having many relevant schemas relating to a limited area, and knowing when to apply them. Wisdom represents a system of knowledge about the meaning and conduct of life. Wisdom includes a broad perspective on time, an awareness of the relativism of values and priorities, and the ability to recognize and manage uncertainty.

Answer Key for Practice Test Essay Questions

As you may have guessed, there are no right or wrong answers to the essay questions in this practice test. That does not mean, however, that all essays are equally good. To get maximum learning benefit from the essay questions, do the following:

- Review each essay a day or two after you wrote it, noting any necessary corrections and any additional support for your points that you can think of.
- Review the section in your textbook that pertains to the topic of each essay. Annotate your essay with any corrections or additional support for your points that you find in the text.

- Spend a few minutes researching the topic of each essay on the Internet. Annotate your essay further with any additional (reliable) information you find.
- Finally, reread each essay with the annotations you have added.

Chapter 10
INTELLIGENCE

A. Learning Objectives: *These objectives are expanded from the Focus Questions found in the margins of your textbook. When you have mastered the material in this chapter, you will be able to:*

10.1 Define intelligence.

10.2 Describe how Galton and Binet differ in their approaches to measuring mental abilities.

10.3 Define IQ, and explain why today's intelligence tests no longer use the mental age concept.

10.4 Describe Wechsler's concept of intelligence and how the Wechsler scales reflect this concept.

10.5 Describe how factor analysis is used in the study of intelligence.

10.6 Describe Spearman's g factor, and cite evidence that supports it.

10.7 Describe Thurstone's primary mental abilities view of intelligence.

10.8 Differentiate between crystallized and fluid intelligence, describe their relation to types of memory, and explain how they are affected by aging.

10.9 Describe Carroll's three-stratum theory of cognitive abilities and how it originated, and relate it to other models.

10.10 Differentiate between the psychometric and cognitive processes approaches to intelligence.

10.11 Describe the three types of intelligence and the three underlying cognitive processes in Sternberg's triarchic theory.

10.12 Describe the eight abilities in Gardner's multiple intelligences theory, as well as the ability that Gardner is considering adding.

10.13 Describe the four branches of emotional intelligence, and how they are measured.

10.14 Describe the kinds of scores the Wechsler scales provide.

10.15 Describe how modern theories of intelligence have influenced recently developed tests.

10.16 Describe the controversy involving aptitude and achievement tests in relation to the measurement of intelligence.

10.17 Define the three types of test reliability.

10.18 Define validity, and describe the three kinds of test validity.

10.19 Describe how well IQ scores predict academic, job, and other life outcomes.

10.20 Describe the two meanings of standardization.

10.21 Describe the Flynn effect, and the explanations that have been suggested for it.

10.22 Describe the nature and value of dynamic testing.

10.23 Describe how intelligence is assessed in nonwestern cultures.

10.24 Describe the evidence linking neural efficiency, brain size, and high intelligence.

10.25 Describe evidence linking genetic factors to intelligence and the IQ variation they account for.

10.26 Describe how family and school environments contribute to intelligence.

10.27 Describe the effects of early intervention on disadvantaged children.

10.28 Describe how reaction range illustrates the interaction between heredity and environment.

10.29 Describe the cultural and ethnic variations in intelligence test scores.

10.30 Describe sex differences in cognitive skills, and which biological and environmental factors might be involved.

10.31 Describe how teachers' expectations and stereotyping behaviors influence academic performance.

10.32 Describe factors that allow gifted people to become eminent.

10.33 Describe causal factor differences between mild and profound mental retardation.

B. Chapter Overview

Intelligence is a concept that refers to individual differences in the ability to acquire knowledge, to think and reason effectively, and to deal adaptively with the environment. The scientific study of intelligence began with Galton's failed attempts to develop measures of nervous system efficiency that might underlie mental skills. The modern intelligence-testing movement was begun by French psychologist Alfred Binet. He assumed that mental abilities developed with age, and that the rate at which people gain mental competence, compared with their peers, is a stable individual characteristic. German psychologist William Stern developed the idea of the intelligence quotient (IQ), which was originally expressed as the ratio mental age/chronological age × 100. Psychologists no longer use the concept of mental age, but they still express an individual's intelligence score relative to the person's peer group by age, with an IQ score of 100 representing average intelligence.

Lewis Terman adapted Binet's test for use in the United States; it is now called the Stanford-Binet intelligence test. At that time, intelligence tests were administered individually, and the individual's test score was highly dependent on verbal skills. World War I stimulated the development of the Army Alpha, a test of intelligence that could be administered to groups, and also the Army Beta, a performance-based measure of intelligence. David Wechsler further extended intelligence testing with his scales for adults (Wechsler Adult Intelligence Scale, or WAIS) and children (Wechsler Intelligence Scale for Children, or WISC, and others.) The Wechsler scales measured both verbal and performance-based abilities, and revised versions of the Wechsler scales are prominent in the field of intelligence testing.

Psychologists use two major approaches in studying the nature of intelligence. The psychometric approach examines the structure of intellect and competencies involved in test performance. The cognitive processes approach studies specific thought processes underlying mental competencies.

Psychometrics is the statistical study of psychological tests, and this approach is used to map and measure the abilities underlying individual differences in intellectual performance. The statistical technique of factor analysis is used to determine the patterns of interrelationships among many specific measures of intellectual performance. By showing which measures of intelligent behavior cluster together and which are relatively independent of one another, factor analysis simplifies and reveals the structure of intelligence. Theorists may interpret the psychometric data in different ways, but factor analysis does provide an empirical basis for discussing the structure of human intellect.

On the basis of the small but consistent relationship among many measures of intelligent behavior, Charles Spearman argued for one general factor, which he called g, and which he argued underlies all mental abilities. Focusing rather on the clustering of measures of intelligence, Thurstone argued for seven distinct primary mental abilities. Cattell and Horn argued that general intelligence is of two subtypes, fluid and crystallized. Fluid intelligence consists of the ability to deal with novel problem-solving situations, whereas crystallized intelligence consists of the ability to apply existing knowledge to current problems.

John B. Carroll used factor analysis to synthesize data from more than 460 previous psychometric studies in the process of developing his three-stratum theory of cognitive abilities. The model proposes a hierarchy of three levels of mental skills—general, broad, and narrow—and relates these to earlier theories of intellectual functioning, thereby providing a detailed map of the structure of human intellect based on the psychometric approach to intelligence.

Cognitive process theories explore the specific information-processing and cognitive processes that underlie intellectual ability. Robert Sternberg, a leading proponent of the cognitive process approach, developed a triarchic theory of intelligence. Sternberg's theory addresses both the psychological processes involved in intelligent behavior and the diverse forms that intelligence can take. Metacomponents are the higher-order processes used to plan and regulate task performance, whereas performance components are the actual mental processes used to perform the task. Knowledge-acquisition components allow us to learn from our experiences, store information in memory, and combine new insights with previously acquired information. Intelligence can take three forms: analytical intelligence (academically oriented problem solving), practical intelligence (the skills needed for everyday living), and creative intelligence (mental skills for dealing with novel problems).

Other psychologists have also extended the conception of intelligence beyond mental competencies to encompass different competencies relevant to various adaptive demands. Howard Gardner, for example, has proposed a theory of multiple intelligences, including visuospatial intelligence and musical intelligence. Emotional intelligence, which combines elements of Gardner's theory, refers to the abilities to read and respond to others' emotions appropriately, to motivate oneself, and to be aware of and to control one's own emotions. Although critics protest the concept of intelligence being extended beyond its original focus on mental abilities, proponents point out that intelligent behavior can be defined very differently in various environments.

The Wechsler intelligence tests are widely used in the United States, providing a verbal IQ, a performance IQ, and a full-scale IQ for each test-taker, as well as a profile of subtest scores that can be used to identify strengths and weaknesses in intellectual functioning. More recently, tests have been developed that measure intelligence based on specific theoretical models such as fluid/crystallized intelligence or Sternberg's triarchic model. Other types of tests may be used for selection purposes—for example, achievement tests, which are designed to find out how much a person has actually learned so far in a specific area, and aptitude tests, which are intended to measure an applicant's potential for future learning and performance. Intelligence tests are thought to measure a combination of aptitude and achievement. The interpretation of test scores has raised many issues about the meaning and use of psychological testing, as tests of mental skills are used to make many important social, educational, and other decisions.

For a psychological test to be recognized by the scientific community, it must show acceptable levels of reliability, validity, and standardization. Reliability refers to consistency of measurement and includes test-retest reliability, internal consistency, and interjudge reliability. Validity refers to whether a test is measuring what it is supposed to measure and includes construct validity, content validity, and criterion-related validity. Intelligence-test scores have shown relatively high validity in predicting academic, military, and job performance. Standardization refers to controlled testing procedures and the collection of norms. Traditional procedures with standardized testing conditions involve static testing, but some newer approaches promote dynamic testing, in which the respondent is given feedback and the test includes noting how this feedback is subsequently used by the testee. Psychologists are also developing creative approaches to dealing with the special challenges that are involved in cross-cultural intelligence testing. The Flynn effect refers to the notable rise in intelligence test scores in the past century, possibly due to better living conditions, more schooling, or more complex environments.

As brain-imaging techniques continue to enhance our ability to relate intelligence to brain functioning, most neuroscientists now believe it not the absolute size of one's brain that is associated with higher intellectual functioning, but rather the brain's neural efficiency and plasticity that are important. Psychologists continue to investigate the potential for developing theories and measurement techniques based on relating intellectual functioning to activities in the brain.

Intelligence is determined by the ongoing interaction of hereditary and environmental factors. Twin studies and adoption studies provide strong evidence that genes play a significant role in intelligence, and hereditary factors may become relatively more important as people age. Shared family environment and educational experiences also affect mental skills and their influence may change over the lifespan. Apparently, heredity establishes a reaction range with upper and lower limits for intellectual potential, and environment affects the point within that range that will be reached.

Racial and gender differences have been found on IQ test scores. Asian Americans, on average, score somewhat above the White American mean on IQ tests. Hispanic Americans score, on average, roughly the same as White Americans. African Americans score, on average, 12 to 15 IQ points below the White American average. The mean differences between African Americans and White Americans have decreased over the past 25 years as greater educational and vocational opportunities for African Americans have emerged, suggesting an environmental component to group differences in intelligence.

Gender differences in cognitive abilities have also been discovered. Males tend to perform better on spatial tasks and tasks involving mathematical reasoning. Females tend to perform better on tests of perceptual speed, verbal fluency, mathematical calculation, and precise manual tasks. Both environmental and biological bases of group differences in intelligence have been suggested, but their relative contribution is a matter of debate. Stereotype threat is one potential psychological factor for both racial and sex-based performance differences.

Even intellectually gifted people show discrepancies in specific skills. Those who achieve eminence tend to have, in addition to a high IQ, high levels of interest and motivation in their chosen activities. About 3 percent to 5 percent of the U.S. population is mentally retarded, or cognitively disabled, although with educational enrichment and support, many of these individuals can learn to live independently. Cognitive disability ranges in severity and can be caused by a number of factors. Biological causes are identified in only about 25 percent of cases.

C. Chapter Outline

INTELLIGENCE IN HISTORICAL PERSPECTIVE
- Sir Francis Galton: Quantifying Mental Ability
- Alfred Binet's Mental Tests
- Binet's Legacy: An Intelligence-Testing Industry Emerges
- In Review

THE NATURE OF INTELLIGENCE
- The Psychometric Approach: The Structure of Intellect
  - Factor Analysis
  - The g Factor: Intelligence as General Mental Capacity
  - Intelligence as Specific Mental Abilities
  - Crystallized and Fluid Intelligence
  - Carroll's Three-Stratum Model: A Modern Synthesis
- Cognitive Process Approaches: The Nature of Intelligent Thinking
- Broader Conceptions of Intelligence: Beyond Mental Competencies
  - Gardner's Multiple Intelligences
  - Emotional Intelligence
- In Review

THE MEASUREMENT OF INTELLIGENCE
- Increasing the Informational Yield from Intelligence Tests
- Theory-Based Intelligence Tests
- Should We Test for Aptitude or Achievement?
- Psychometric Standards for Intelligence Tests
  - Reliability
  - Validity
    - Intelligence and Academic Performance
    - Job Performance, Income, and Longevity
  - Standardization
    - The Flynn Effect: Are We Getting Smarter?
    - Testing Conditions: Static and Dynamic Testing
- Assessing Intelligence in Non-Western Cultures
- *Beneath the Surface: Brain Size and Intelligence*
- In Review

HEREDITY, ENVIRONMENT, AND INTELLIGENCE
Applying Psychological Science: Early Childhood Interventions: A Means of Boosting Intelligence?

GROUP DIFFERENCES IN INTELLIGENCE
Ethnic Group Differences
Are the Tests Biased?
What Factors Underlie the Differences?
Sex Differences in Cognitive Abilities
Beliefs, Expectations, and Cognitive Performance
Research Close-Up: Stereotype Threat and Cognitive Performance

EXTREMES OF INTELLIGENCE
The Intellectually Gifted
What Do You Think? Are Gifted Children Maladjusted?
Mental Retardation

A CONCLUDING THOUGHT
In Review

D. Review at a Glance: *Write the term that best fits the blank to review what you learned in this chapter.*

Intelligence in Historical Perspective

Intelligence is a concept that refers to (1) _____ _____ in the ability to learn, reason, and to deal (2) _____ with the environment. In the early days of mental testing, pioneers such as Alfred (3) _____ tried to determine whether a child was performing at the correct mental level for children of that age. The result of the testing was a score called the (4) _____ age. German psychologist William Stern developed the (5) _____ _____, based on the ratio of mental age to (6) _____ _____.

In the United States, Terman adapted Binet's test to develop the (7) _____-_____ intelligence test. At that time, intelligence tests were administered (8) _____, and the individual's test score was highly dependent on (9) _____ skills. World War I stimulated two important developments: a (10) _____ test of intelligence and (11) _____-based measures of intelligence.

The Nature of Intelligence

Psychologists use two major approaches to study intelligence. The (12) _____ approach examines the structure of intellect based on IQ test performance. The statistical technique of (13) _____ _____ is used to find out which test scores cluster together and which are relatively (14) _____ of one another. Theorists do not always agree on how to (15) _____ the factors.

There is great debate about the nature of intelligence. British psychologist Charles Spearman believed that there is a general factor, known as (16) _____, in mental abilities. American psychologist L. L. Thurstone argued that there are seven distinct (17) _____ _____ abilities that underlie human mental performance. Cattell and Horn suggest two types of intelligence: (18) _____ intelligence involves the ability to apply previously acquired knowledge to solve new problems, whereas (19) _____ intelligence is used to deal with novel problem-solving situations.

John B. Carroll synthesized information from (20) _____ of previous psychometric studies to develop his model of intelligence. Carroll proposed a (21) _____ of three levels of mental skills—general, (22) _____, and narrow.

An alternative to the psychometric approach, called the (23) _____-_____ approach, studies people's thought processes in doing intellectual tasks. Sternberg's (24) _____ theory includes the processes used to plan and regulate task performance, called (25) _____, the actual mental processes used to perform the task, or (26) _____ components, and knowledge-acquisition components to encode and store information. Sternberg also proposed three forms of intelligence: (27) _____ intelligence (academically oriented problem solving), (28) _____ intelligence (the skills needed for everyday living), and (29) _____ intelligence (mental skills for dealing with novel problems).

One of the newer theories of intelligence is that it is not purely cognitive. (30) _____ _____ developed a theory of multiple intelligences. An intelligence that involves the abilities to read and respond to others' emotions appropriately, to motivate oneself, and to be aware of and to control one's own emotions, is called (31) _____ intelligence.

The Measurement of Intelligence

The (32) _____ intelligence tests are widely used in the United States, providing a (33) _____ IQ, a performance IQ, and a full-scale IQ for each test-taker, as well as (34) _____ subtests that can be used to identify strengths and weaknesses in intellectual functioning. Psychologists today distinguish between tests that measure how much someone has learned, or (35) _____ tests, and tests that measure potential for future learning and performance, or (36) _____ tests. Intelligence tests are thought to measure a combination of aptitude and achievement.

Good tests have both reliability and validity. The consistency of measurement of a test is called (37) _____. One way to measure reliability, known as (38) _____-_____ reliability, is to administer the same measure to the same group of participants on two different occasions and to correlate the scores. The consistency of measurement within the test itself is known as (39) _____ _____. Validity refers to how well a test actually measures what it is supposed to measure. (40)_____-_____ validity refers to how well a measure can predict some other criterion, like a future behavior. Intelligence test scores have shown relatively high validity in predicting (41) _____, military, and (42) _____ performance. Creating a (43) _____ environment and developing test (44) _____ define standardization, the third measurement requirement for a good test. Traditional procedures with standardized testing conditions involve static testing, but some newer approaches promote (45) _____ testing, in which the respondent is given feedback and the test includes noting how this feedback is subsequently used by the testee.

The (46)_____ effect refers to the notable rise in intelligence-test scores in the past century, possibly due to better living conditions, more schooling, or more complex environments.

As (47) _____-_____ techniques continue to enhance our ability to relate intelligence to (48) _____ _____, most neuroscientists now believe it is not the (49) _____ of one's brain that is associated with higher intellectual functioning, but rather its (50) _____ _____ and plasticity that are most important.

Heredity and Environment

Intelligence is determined by the (51) _____ of hereditary and (52) _____ factors. Twin studies and adoption studies provide strong evidence that (53) _____ play a significant role in intelligence, and hereditary factors may become relatively (54) _____ important as people age. (55)_____ family environment and (56) _____ experiences also affect mental skills, and their influence may change over the lifespan. Apparently heredity establishes a (57) _____ _____, with upper and lower limits for intellectual potential, and (58) _____ affects the point within that range that will be reached.

Group Differences in Intelligence

Asian Americans, on average, score somewhat (59) _____ the White American mean on IQ tests. (60)_____ Americans score, on average, roughly the same as White Americans. African Americans score, on average, 12 to 15 IQ points below the White American average. The mean differences between African Americans and White Americans have (61)_____ during the past 25 years as greater educational and vocational opportunities for African Americans have emerged, suggesting a(n) (62)_____ component to group differences in intelligence.

Gender differences in cognitive abilities have also been discovered. Males tend to perform better on (63) _____ tasks and tasks involving (64) _____ reasoning. Females tend to perform better on tests of perceptual speed, (65) _____ fluency, mathematical (66) _____, and precise manual tasks.

Chapter 10   289

Both environmental and biological bases of group differences in intelligence have been suggested, but their relative contribution is a matter of debate. (67)_____ threat is one potential psychological factor for both racial and sex-based performance differences.

Extremes of Intelligence

Even intellectually gifted people show (68) _____ in specific skills. Those who achieve eminence tend to have, in addition to a high IQ, high levels of interest and (69) _____ in their chosen activities. About 3 percent to 5 percent of the U.S. population is mentally retarded, or cognitively disabled, although with educational enrichment and support many of these individuals can learn to live (70)_____. Cognitive disability ranges in severity and can be caused by a number of factors. (71)_____ causes are identified in only about 25 percent of cases.

E. Concept Cards

Truly learning a concept means integrating it into the way *you* think about things. To integrate concepts successfully, you must translate the words and examples your text or instructor provides into words and examples that are meaningful to you.

For this exercise, obtain some note cards (3" × 5" or 4" × 6") to make a deck of concept cards. On one side of each card, write the *concept* from the list below (e.g., "emotional intelligence") at the top. Read the textbook definition provided, and then write the definition *in your own words* on the concept card (e.g., for "emotional intelligence," you might write "ability to tune in to your own and other people's emotions and respond appropriately"). Simply imagine that a friend has asked you what the concept means, and write down what you would answer. Writing the definition in your own words requires you to think deeply about its meaning. When next you see your own version of the definition, it will make intuitive sense to you—no translation required.

On the second side of the card, write your own example of the concept. Again, coming up with your own example requires you to think deeply about the application of the concept, and you will more easily understand and remember the example when you study for a test. If you use an example from the text, or from class, make it your own by writing it in your own words. You can always check with your instructor that your example is indeed a good example of the concept.

CONCEPT Definition in my own words (side 1 of card)	Example of the concept in my own words, preferably drawn from my own experience (side 2 of card)

The following is a list of all the boldface concepts from your textbook with the author's definition. Write the definition in your own words, together with your own example of the concept, to create a *concept card* as described earlier, or write in the space provided.

Intelligence: The ability to acquire knowledge, to think and reason effectively, and to deal adaptively with the environment

Intelligence quotient (IQ): The ratio of mental age to chronological age multiplied by 100

Psychometrics: The statistical study of psychological tests

Factor analysis: A statistical technique that reduces a large number of correlations to a smaller number of clusters, or factors, with each cluster containing variables that correlate highly with one another but less highly with variables in other clusters

***g* factor:** General intelligence

Crystallized intelligence (g_c): The ability to apply previously acquired knowledge to current problems

Fluid intelligence (g_f): The ability to deal with novel problem-solving situations for which personal experience does not provide a solution

Three-stratum theory of cognitive abilities: Theory that establishes three levels of mental skills—general, broad, and narrow—arranged in a hierarchical model

Cognitive-process theories: Theories that explore the specific information-processing and cognitive processes that underlie intellectual ability

Triarchic theory of intelligence: A theory that addresses both the psychological processes involved in intelligent behavior and the diverse forms that intelligence can take

Metacomponents: The higher-order processes used to plan and regulate task performance

Performance components: The actual mental processes used to perform a task

Knowledge-acquisition components: Processes that allow us to learn from our experiences, store information in memory, and combine new insights with previously acquired information

Emotional intelligence: A form of intelligence that involves the abilities to read others' emotions accurately, to respond to them appropriately, to motivate oneself, to be aware of one's own emotions, and to regulate and control one's own emotional responses

Achievement test: A test designed to find out how much a person has learned so far in life

Aptitude test: A test that contains novel puzzle-like problems that presumably go beyond prior learning and are thought to measure the applicant's potential for future learning and performance

Psychological test: A method for measuring individual differences related to some psychological concept, or construct, based on a sample for relevant behavior in a scientifically designed and controlled situation

Reliability: Consistency of measurement

Test-retest reliability: Reliability assessed by administering the measure to the same group of participants on two (or more) separate occasions and correlating the two (or more) sets of scores

Internal consistency: The consistency of measurement within the test itself

Interjudge reliability: The consistency of measurement when different people observe the same event or score the same test

Validity: How well a test actually measures what it is designed to measure

Construct validity: Validity based on a test successfully measuring the psychological construct it is designed to measure, as indicated by relations between test scores and other behaviors that it should be related to

Content validity: Validity based on the items on a test measuring all the knowledge or skills that are assumed to compose the construct of interest

Criterion-related validity: Validity based on the ability of test scores to correlate with meaningful criterion measures

Standardization: Both (1) the development of norms and (2) rigorously controlled testing procedures

Norms: Test scores derived from a large sample that represents particular age segments of the population

Normal distribution: A bell-shaped curve with most scores clustering around the center of the curve

Static testing: The traditional approach to testing

Dynamic testing: The standard testing followed up with an interaction in which the examiner gives the respondent guided feedback on how to improve performance and observes how the person uses the information

Outcome bias: Bias that occurs to the extent that the test underestimates a person's true intellectual ability

Predictive bias: Bias that occurs if the test successfully predicts criterion measures, such as school or job performance, for some groups but not for others

Stereotype threat: The fear or belief in the mind of members of a particular group that certain behaviors on their part would confirm a negative stereotype in the minds of others

F. What's the Difference? A Concept Card Exercise

An important skill in learning concepts is being able to differentiate among concepts that are similar or related in some way. This skill is particularly relevant for multiple-choice tests, especially if you often find yourself wavering between two answers.

Once you have created your own deck of concept cards, select them two by two, each time answering the question "What's the difference between these two concepts?" You can use the word definitions of the concepts or the examples of the concepts to enhance your mastery of the material. In each case, choose pairs of concepts to compare those that are related or similar or that sound the same or that could in some way be confused. It's much easier to spot the difference between two concepts when you are studying, with the textbook available, rather than when considering the question for the first time in a testing situation.

G. Apply What You Know

According to Robert Sternberg, intelligence can take three forms: analytic intelligence, practical intelligence, and creative intelligence. Give two examples for each form of intelligence of situations in your own life in which you or another person demonstrated each form of intelligence. Check the definition of each form of intelligence in your textbook again, after you have given the examples, to evaluate whether your examples fit the definitions.

Analytic intelligence example #1:

Analytic intelligence example #2:

Practical intelligence example #1:

Practical intelligence example #2:

Creative intelligence example #1:

Creative intelligence example #2:

H. On the Web: *As with any online research, it is important to consider how legitimate a given source is before you rely on the information it presents. Your instructor or Internet adviser may give you some specific guidelines for distinguishing which kinds of Web sites tend to be reputable.*

A. A number of individuals have made notable contributions to our understanding of intelligence. Search the Web for more information about some of those listed.

Alfred Binet

John B. Carroll

Raymond Cattell and John Horn

Francis Galton

Howard Gardner

Charles Spearman

William Stern

Robert Sternberg

Lewis Terman

L. L. Thurstone

David Wechsler

Ellen Winner

Chapter 10 297

B. Take a look at the concept cards you have created for this chapter, or the key concepts listed in section E. In the space provided, make a list of any whose definitions or associations you are not yet confident of and any you'd like to learn more about. Try entering the terms on your list into your search engine. Make notes of any helpful information you find.

Key Concept/Information Found

C. You may (or may not) be surprised at the large number of websites that offer online intelligence tests, many of them free of charge. Search for such tests using terms such as *intelligence test*, *self-discovery*, and *How smart are you?* Examine at least one of these online tests, and evaluate whether it meets the criteria for a sound psychological test.

URL of Test: http://

Reliability:

Validity:

Standardization:

I. Analyze This: *Chapter 1 of your textbook begins by presenting these four basic steps in the critical thinking process:*
- *"What exactly are you asking me to believe?"*
- *"How do you know? What is the evidence?"*
- *"Are there other possible explanations?"*
- *"What is the most reasonable conclusion?"*

You might picture this as a four-step analysis to help you decide whether to accept a given theory or assertion. Now it's your turn to put your textbook to this test.

Review the section in Chapter 10 of your textbook under the heading "Group Differences in Intelligence." There you will find a discussion of the controversy over the gap in intelligence test scores between African Americans and White Americans. If someone told you that within another 50 years this gap will disappear, would you agree? Analyze that assertion in the space below. When you have finished, consider using this four-step analysis to evaluate other assertions you encounter.

"What exactly are you asking me to believe?"

"How do you know? What is the evidence?"

"Are there other possible explanations?"

"What is the most reasonable conclusion?"

J. Practice Test

Multiple-Choice Items: *Write the letter corresponding to your answer in the space to the left of each item.*

_____ 1. Intelligence is a concept that refers to _____ in the ability to acquire knowledge, to think and reason effectively, and to deal adaptively with the environment.
   a. internal consistency
   b. individual differences

Chapter 10

       c. psychometrics
       d. factor analysis

_____ 2. Galton's early attempts to measure intelligence scientifically involved _____.
       a. measuring the shape of people's brains
       b. measuring how efficiently the nervous system processed information
       c. estimating the size of the brain
       d. cognitive tasks of increasing complexity

_____ 3. Alfred Binet introduced the concept of _____ into intelligence testing.
       a. factor analysis
       b. multiple intelligences
       c. the IQ
       d. mental age

_____ 4. Factor analysis is used in intelligence testing to _____.
       a. differentiate the verbal and performance aspects of intelligence
       b. determine which measures of intelligent behavior cluster together
       c. express an individual's intelligence score relative to the person's peer group by age
       d. develop performance-based measures of intelligence

_____ 5. Larry is taking the Wechsler Adult Intelligence Scale. His current task is to place a number of pictures that have no words into the correct order so that they tell a meaningful story. The subtest Larry is working on is part of the _____ scale of the Wechsler Adult Intelligence Scale.
       a. reliability
       b. validity
       c. verbal
       d. performance

_____ 6. As proposed by Stern, _____ was originally defined as (mental age/chronological age) × 100.
       a. aptitude
       b. achievement
       c. IQ
       d. problem-solving ability

_____ 7. The Wechsler Adult Intelligence Scale provides _____.
       a. a measure of fluid and crystallized intelligence
       b. a profile of specific strengths and weaknesses in mental functioning
       c. a score on analytic, creative, and practical intelligence
       d. scores on group intelligence factors

_____ 8. The Army Alpha test developed during World War I was groundbreaking in _____

a. using the psychometric approach to measuring intelligence
b. including verbal measures in intelligence testing
c. developing group-administered intelligence testing
d. including measures of information processing in an intelligence test

_____ 9. According to Spearman, a single type of intelligence is common to all mental abilities; this is known as _____.
a. IQ
b. verbal intelligence
c. primary mental ability
d. *g*

_____ 10. Thurstone argued that human mental performance depends on _____.
a. the *g* factor
b. primary mental abilities
c. triarchic intelligence
d. emotional intelligence

_____ 11. As one ages, it becomes more difficult to adapt to new and changed situations, but one's lifetime of accumulated experience can make up for this typical decline in _____ intelligence.
a. crystallized
b. fluid
c. emotional
d. psychometric

_____ 12. John B. Carroll synthesized data from more than 460 previous psychometric studies in the process of developing his theory of cognitive abilities, which proposes _____.
a. a hierarchy of three levels of mental skills
b. a cognitive-processes model of intelligence
c. a genetic approach to intellectual functioning
d. a triarchic theory of intelligence

_____ 13. Deepak believes that intelligent people have "faster brains" than other people, meaning that intelligent people can carry out basic mental processes and master material more quickly. Deepak's approach is most like the _____ approach.
a. multiple intelligences
b. psychometric
c. cognitive-processes
d. triarchic

_____ 14. Anna is mildly retarded. She cannot apply mental strategies to new situations. Anna's deficiency is with her _____.

a. creative intelligence
b. spatial intelligence
c. memory
d. metacognition

_____ 15. The ability to apply previously learned knowledge to current problems is called _____ intelligence.
a. crystallized
b. fluid
c. psychometric
d. deductive

_____ 16. Gardner's theory of multiple intelligences is characterized by _____.
a. including additional abilities, such as musical talents and interpersonal skills, as forms of intelligence
b. asserting that intelligence consists of several distinct mental abilities
c. asserting that there are only three different types of intelligence: linguistic, mathematical, and visuospatial
d. proposing a general g factor that is largely responsible for intelligence

_____ 17. According to Sternberg's triarchic theory, the types of intelligence that can be demanded by the environment are _____.
a. mathematical, linguistic, and visuospatial
b. musical, bodily-kinesthetic, and personal
c. crystallized and fluid
d. analytical, practical, and creative

_____ 18. Salovey & Mayer argue that "emotional intelligence" includes _____.
a. the ability to recognize the emotions of others
b. a lack of self-control
c. not examining your feelings when making decisions
d. a need for power

_____ 19. The statistical study of psychological tests is called _____.
a. psychometrics
b. standardization
c. the establishment of norms
d. the *g* factor

_____ 20. Suppose you take a psychological test, and receive a score of 82 (out of a possible 100) on it. Imagine that you take the same test again 2 days later, and this time receive a score of 46. Other people who have taken the test twice have also had similar positive and negative changes in scores. These results mean that this test has _____.
a. high internal consistency
b. low internal consistency

c. low test-retest reliability
d. high test-retest reliability

_____ 21. Intelligence-test scores have shown relatively high validity in predicting _____.
   a. overall success in life
   b. life satisfaction
   c. emotional stability
   d. academic performance

_____ 22. Researchers who accept the concept of a reaction range are most likely to view intelligence as _____.
   a. a product of the interaction between genetics and the environment
   b. the product of many separate but correlated individual mental abilities
   c. completely determined by genetic factors
   d. the result of a single underlying intelligence factor

_____ 23. The fact that the mean IQ difference between Black and White students has _____ in recent years is generally taken as evidence that this difference may be due to _____ factors.
   a. decreased; unchangeable genetic
   b. increased; unchangeable genetic
   c. remained the same; changeable environmental
   d. decreased; changeable environmental

_____ 24. A(n) _____ test is specifically intended to measure an applicant's potential for future learning and performance.
   a. achievement
   b. aptitude
   c. intelligence
   d. psychological

_____ 25. Terry was adopted as a newborn and has always lived with her adoptive family. Now, at age 30, she discovers that she has an identical twin sister. Research suggests that Terry's IQ score will most resemble that of her _____.
   a. adoptive mother
   b. adoptive brother and sister
   c. biological twin
   d. biological mother

_____ 26. In contrast to static testing, dynamic testing involves _____.
   a. controlled testing procedures
   b. the collection of norms
   c. giving the respondent feedback
   d. cross-cultural intelligence testing

_____ 27. The Flynn effect refers to _____.

a. the notable rise in intelligence test scores in the past century
b. decreased disparities among ethnic groups in mean IQ scores during the past century
c. children having more schooling during the past century
d. a slight decline in average IQ scores during the past century

_____ 28. Galton's approach to intelligence has been re-examined because _____.
a. the psychometric approach to intelligence has failed
b. the information-processing approach to intelligence has not been widely accepted
c. our ability to relate intelligence to brain functioning has increased
d. the multiple-intelligences approach has become widely accepted

_____ 29. Research suggests that higher intellectual functioning is most closely tied to
a. larger brain size
b. increased efficiency of processing in the brain
c. reduced brain plasticity
d. static and dynamic testing

_____ 30. Studies of high intelligence, or giftedness, suggest that _____.
a. being gifted is associated with psychological maladjustment
b. being gifted is associated with emotional intelligence
c. giftedness is not a sufficient condition for achieving eminence
d. gifted people have high scores on all aspects of intelligence

True/False Items: *Write T or F in the space provided to the left of each item.*

_____ 1. Psychologists currently use the formula (mental age/chronological age) × 100 to define IQ.

_____ 2. Psychometrics is the statistical study of psychological tests.

_____ 3. Factor analysis is used to simplify and reveal the structure of human intellect.

_____ 4. World War I stimulated the development of cognitive-process approaches to intelligence.

_____ 5. Carroll synthesized many psychometric studies into a three-level hierarchy of mental skills.

_____ 6. Intelligence tests are thought to measure a combination of aptitude and achievement.

_____ 7. Intelligence depends mostly on environmental factors, although heredity plays a small part.

_____ 8. Content validity refers to how highly test scores correlate with criterion measures.

_____ 9. Fluid intelligence refers to the ability to deal with novel problem-solving situations for which personal experience does not provide a solution.

_____ 10. According to Sternberg's triarchic theory of intelligence, metacomponents are used to encode and store information.

Short-Answer Questions

1. What is intelligence, and what are the major research approaches to studying intelligence?

2. What is the Flynn effect, and what explanations are proposed to explain it?

3. What does the research suggest about the effects of heredity and environment on intelligence?

4. Describe the three scientific standards for sound psychological tests.

5. What abilities make up emotional intelligence?

Essay Questions

1. Psychologists have proposed different ways of understanding and studying intelligence. What position would you take if you were an intelligence researcher? Support your answer by outlining the major areas of debate in this area and reviewing the current research evidence.

2. If you were asked to develop a program for mentally retarded people that would help them make the most of their intellectual abilities, what kind of program would you propose? Base your response on current research and theories of intelligence.

3. Taking into consideration the narrowing but still significant gap in mean intelligence test scores between White Americans and African Americans, do you support college affirmative action programs that promote the admission of African American students? Explain your position, using information about intelligence testing found in this chapter.

Answer Keys

Answer Key for Review at a Glance

1. individual differences
2. adaptively
3. Binet
4. mental
5. intelligence quotient
6. chronological age
7. Stanford-Binet
8. individually
9. verbal
10. group
11. performance

37. reliability
38. test-retest
39. internal consistency
40. Criterion-related
41. academic
42. job
43. standardized
44. norms
45. dynamic
46. Flynn
47. brain-imaging

12. psychometric
13. factor analysis
14. independent
15. interpret
16. *g*
17. primary mental
18. Crystallized
19. fluid
20. hundreds
21. hierarchy
22. broad
23. cognitive-process
24. triarchic
25. metacomponents
26. performance
27. analytical
28. practical
29. creative
30. Howard Gardner
31. emotional
32. Wechsler
33. verbal
34. performance
35. achievement
36. aptitude

48. brain functioning
49. size
50. neural efficiency
51. interaction
52. environmental
53. genes
54. more
55. Shared
56. educational
57. reaction range
58. environment
59. above
60. Hispanic
61. declined
62. environmental
63. spatial
64. mathematical
65. verbal
66. calculation
67. Stereotype
68. discrepancies
69. motivation
70. independently
71. Biological

Answer Key for Practice Test Multiple-Choice Items

1. b
2. b
3. d
4. b
5. d
6. c
7. b
8. c
9. d
10. b
11. b
12. a
13. c
14. d
15. a
16. a
17. d
18. a
19. a
20. c
21. d
22. a
23. d
24. b
25. c
26. c
27. a
28. c
29. b
30. c

Answer Key for Practice Test True/False Items

1. F	6. T
2. T	7. F
3. T	8. F
4. F	9. T
5. T	10. F

Answer Key for Practice Test Short-Answer Questions

1. Intelligence is a concept that refers to individual differences in the ability to acquire knowledge, to think and reason effectively, and to deal adaptively with the environment. Psychologists use two major approaches in studying the nature of intelligence. The psychometric approach examines the structure of intellect and competencies involved in test performance. The cognitive-process approach studies specific thought processes underlying mental competencies.

2. The Flynn effect refers to the notable rise in intelligence test scores during the past century. Proposed explanations have attributed the Flynn effect to better living conditions, more schooling, or people living in more complex environments. Genetic explanations are less likely than environmental ones because of the relatively short time span involved.

3. Intelligence is determined by interacting hereditary and environmental factors. Studies provide strong evidence that genes play a significant role in intelligence, that the environment is important, and that these factors interact. Apparently heredity establishes a reaction range with upper and lower limits for intellectual potential, and environment affects the point within that range that will be reached.

4. There are three major standards for sound psychological tests. Reliability refers to the consistency of measurement. Validity measures the extent to which a test measures what it is designed to measure. Standardization has two facets: creating a standardized environment for testing and establishing norms for comparison.

5. Emotional intelligence involves the abilities to read others' emotions accurately, to respond to them appropriately, to motivate oneself, to be aware of one's emotions, and to regulate and to control one's own emotional responses.

Answer Key for Practice Test Essay Questions

As you may have guessed, there are no right or wrong answers to the essay questions in this practice test. That does not mean, however, that all essays are equally good. To get maximum learning benefit from the essay questions, do the following:

- Review each essay a day or two after you wrote it, noting any necessary corrections and any additional support for your points that you can think of.

- Review the section in your textbook that pertains to the topic of each essay. Annotate your essay with any corrections or additional support for your points that you find in the text.
- Spend a few minutes researching the topic of each essay on the Internet. Annotate your essay further with any additional (reliable) information you find.
- Finally, reread each essay with the annotations you have added.

Chapter 11
MOTIVATION AND EMOTION

A. Learning Objectives: *These objectives are expanded from the Focus Questions found in the margins of your textbook. When you have mastered the material in this chapter, you will be able to:*

11.1 Define and differentiate between motivation and emotion.

11.2 Describe the key motivational concepts introduced by biological, cognitive, psychodynamic, and humanistic perspectives.

11.3 Describe the physiological factors that help regulate hunger, general appetite, and weight.

11.4 Describe how psychological, environmental, and cultural factors influence hunger and eating.

11.5 Describe biological and environmental factors in obesity, and how their interactions contribute to obesity among the Pima.

11.6 Describe the symptoms, health consequences, and causes of anorexia and bulimia.

11.7 Describe how sexual behaviors and attitudes have changed in recent decades.

11.8 Describe the stages of the sexual response cycle, and how hormones influence sex characteristics and sexual behavior.

11.9 Describe how psychological, cultural, and environmental factors influence sexual behavior.

11.10 Describe the findings on the effects of viewing violent pornography.

11.11 Describe the three dimensions of sexual orientation, and discuss research on the determinants of sexual orientation.

11.12 Discuss evolutionary and psychological views of affiliation, and explain why humans are social creatures.

11.13 Describe how the motives and task behaviors of high- versus low-need achievers differ.

11.14 Describe how the need for achievement develops.

11.15 Differentiate among the three main types of motivational conflict.

11.16 Describe the ways in which negative and positive emotions are adaptive.

11.17 Describe the four major components of emotions, and how they influence one another.

11.18 Describe which brain structures LeDoux believes allow simultaneous but different emotional responses to the same event.

11.19 Describe how positive and negative emotions involve different patterns of brain activation.

11.20 Describe how the assessment of emotion works in lie detection, and describe factors that affect validity.

11.21 Describe how fundamental emotional patterns are related to both facial expressions and cultural display rules.

11.22 Describe the relations among emotional arousal, task complexity, and task performance.

11.23 Compare and contrast the James-Lange and the Cannon-Bard explanations for emotional responses.

11.24 Evaluate the scientific evidence in support of the James-Lange and Cannon-Bard theories.

11.25 Describe how appraisal and arousal interact to influence emotions according to Lazarus's theory and Schachter's two-factor theory of emotion, and describe the two key experiments inspired by their theories.

11.26 Describe the factors that predict or fail to predict happiness.

11.27 Summarize research-based guidelines for increasing happiness.

B. Chapter Overview

This chapter explores motivation, including its influences on hunger and weight regulation, sex, affiliation, work and achievement, and motivational conflict. It also explores emotions, the positive or negative affects that often result when our goals are gratified, threatened, or thwarted.

Motivation is a process that influences the direction, persistence, and vigor of goal-directed behavior. Instinct theories of motivation, prominent a century ago, soon gave way to other models. The body's biological systems are balanced to ensure survival. Many behaviors may be motivated by the need to return to homeostasis, the state of internal equilibrium. Drive theory assumed that physiological disruptions to homeostasis produce drives to reduce the tension caused by the disruptions. Although homeostatic models help us understand the regulation of hunger and thirst, for example, they are less influential in explaining other behaviors.

Human beings seek to maximize pleasure and avoid pain. These universal tendencies reflect the activity of two distinct neural systems in the brain: the behavioral activation system (BAS), which is sensitive to reward, and the behavioral inhibition system (BIS), which is responsive to the potential for pain and nonreward. The BAS and BIS systems may underlie the different cognitive, physiological, and behavioral processes that are involved in pleasure-seeking and pain-avoidance behavior, and studies suggest that different neurotransmitter systems, as well as different brain regions, may be involved in the two systems.

Incentive theories focus attention on external stimuli as motivators of behavior. According to expectancy × value theory, people are motivated to behave in ways that they believe (expectancy) will lead to rewards that they value. Many cognitive theorists distinguish between extrinsic motivation, which is produced by the desire to obtain rewards and to avoid punishments, and intrinsic motivation, or performing an activity for its own sake. Psychodynamic theorists suggest that unconscious motives, thoughts, and inner tensions are an important motivator of behavior. Humanistic theorists stress the human motivation to fulfill our potential, or what humanistic theorist Abraham Maslow called self-actualization, and some people even manage to achieve a state of self-transcendence. A more recent humanistic approach, Deci and Ryan's self-determination theory, focuses on three fundamental psychological needs: needs for competence, autonomy, and relatedness. Research supports the importance of these three factors in maximizing human potential.

The body monitors its energy supplies, and this information interacts with other signals to regulate food intake. Homeostatic mechanisms are designed to prevent us from running low on energy. Some researchers believe that there is a set point around which body weight is regulated. As we eat, stomach and intestinal distention act as satiety signals, and peptides such as cholecystokinin stimulate brain receptors to decrease eating. Fat cells regulate food intake and weight over the long term by secreting leptin. Many parts of the brain also influence eating. Early studies indicated that the lateral hypothalamus seemed to be a "hunger-on" center. The ventromedial hypothalamus seemed to be a "hunger-off" center. However, modern research indicates that it is not that simple. Various neural circuits within the hypothalamus regulate food intake. Many of these pathways involve the paraventricular nucleus. Eating is also affected by psychological factors. Eating is positively reinforced by good taste and variety and is negatively reinforced by hunger reduction. Beliefs, attitudes, habits, and psychological needs also affect food intake. Studies of obesity have indicated a strong genetic component. The eating disorders anorexia nervosa, where people severely restrict their food intake, and bulimia nervosa, where people binge and then induce purging, pose serious health problems.

People engage in sex for a variety of reasons, the primary one being pleasure. The typical sexual response cycle consists of four phases: excitement, plateau, orgasm, and resolution. Secretions of gonadotropins from the pituitary glands affect the rate at which the sex organs secrete androgens and estrogens. These sex hormones have both organizational effects that direct the development of sex organs, and activational effects that stimulate sexual desire and behavior. Psychological factors, like sexual fantasy, can also trigger sexual arousal. The psychological meaning of sex depends strongly on cultural contexts and learning. Cultural norms influence which stimuli are sexually arousing and what sexual behaviors occur. Studies of pornography suggest that violent pornographic films seem to increase, at least temporarily, men's aggression toward women and may promote rape myths.

Sexual orientation may have three dimensions: self-identity, sexual attraction, and actual sexual behavior. Many researchers believe in a genetic basis for sexual orientation. Altering prenatal sex hormones can also influence sexual orientation. Studies have also suggested an environmental component. These findings, however, are correlational.

We affiliate with others to gain positive stimulation, emotional support, attention, and opportunities for social comparison. Social relationships are important contributors to life satisfaction, and can also help insulate us from stressors in our lives.

The need for achievement is influenced by both motive for success and fear of failure. Motive for success is part of the BAS system that relates to achievement, and fear of failure is a BIS function; studies support the idea that these functions are independent rather than correlated. High-need achievers (high in achievement motivation and low in fear of failure) prefer tasks of intermediate risk, rather than very easy or impossibly difficult tasks. The perceived uncertainty of the outcome is maximally motivating for high-need achievers, and they tend to outperform low-need achievers when tasks are challenging and the outcome is perceived to be uncertain.

Achievement goal theory focuses on the goals that people seek to attain in task situations, which may be mastery goals or ego goals, and may be based on a desire for success or a fear of failure. Mastery-approach goals focus on the desire to master a task and learn new knowledge or skills, whereas ego-approach goals reflect a competitive orientation that focuses on being judged favorably relative to other people. Mastery-avoidance goals reflect a fear of not performing up to one's own standards, whereas ego-avoidance goals center on avoiding being outperformed by others. Family, teachers, and significant others create a motivational climate for children by encouraging or rewarding primarily a mastery or an ego orientation, which is likely to be internalized by the child. Cultural norms also influence the nature and expression of achievement motivation.

Motivational goals may conflict with one another. Approach-approach, avoidance-avoidance, and approach-avoidance conflicts involve having to choose between two attractive alternatives, two unattractive alternatives, and attractive and unattractive aspects of the same goal, respectively.

Emotions are positive or negative affective states consisting of a pattern of cognitive, physiological, and behavioral reactions to events that have relevance to important goals or motives. Emotions have important adaptive functions. Negative emotions may help us to narrow attention and actions to deal with a threatening situation. Positive emotions may help us to form intimate relationships and to broaden our thinking and behavior so that we explore, try out new ways to achieve goals, and savor what we have. Emotions are an important form of social communication and influence how others respond to us. Our emotional states share four common features: They are triggered by internal or external responses to stimuli, they entail cognitive appraisal of these stimuli, they involve physiological responses, and they include behavioral tendencies, both expressive and instrumental. Emotion is a dynamic, ongoing process, and its four components mutually influence one another as well as the larger associative network within which they are embedded.

Internal and external stimuli trigger interpretations (cognitive appraisals) and emotional responses, which often occur with little or no awareness. Innate biological factors and learning each play a role in determining our emotional responses to different stimuli. Cross-cultural research indicates considerable agreement across cultures in the appraisals that evoke basic emotions, but also some degree of variation in more complex appraisals.

Biological factors play an important role in emotions. Subcortical structures, such as the hypothalamus, amygdala, and other limbic-system structures, are particularly involved. The ability to regulate emotion depends heavily on the prefrontal cortex. Joseph LeDoux has discovered that the thalamus sends messages along two independent neural pathways: to the cortex and to the amygdala. This dual system means that emotional responses can occur both through cortical interpretation and also via a more primitive system through the amygdala, which is likely important for survival. Left-hemisphere activation may underlie certain positive emotions, and right-hemisphere activation might influence negative ones. Such activation may also underlie subjective well-being.

The fight-or-flight arousal response is produced by the sympathetic branch of the autonomic nervous system and by hormones from the endocrine system. Some basic emotions, such as anger and fear, show characteristic autonomic processes, but there are no distinctive and universal patterns of arousal associated with different emotions. The behavioral component of emotions involves expressive behaviors, or emotional displays, and instrumental behaviors. Modern evolutionary theorists stress the adaptive value of emotional displays and suggest that some fundamental emotional patterns may be innate. Studies by Paul Ekman and his coworkers of emotional expressions have shown a wide degree of cross-cultural agreement in evaluations of expressions. The studies also show that different parts of the face provide the best clues for certain emotions, and that women are generally more accurate judges of emotional expression than men. Different cultures have different display rules for emotions, and many emotion theorists conclude that innate biological factors and cultural display rules combine to shape emotional expression across different cultures. Instrumental behaviors are directed at achieving some emotion-relevant goal. The relationship between emotional arousal and performance seems to be an inverted *U*, with performance increasing with arousal up to some optimal level, and then deteriorating with further arousal, although task complexity and need for precision also influence the relationship.

According to the James-Lange theory, which lives on as the somatic theory of emotion, bodily reactions produce perceptions of emotional states. The Cannon-Bard theory proposed that physiological arousal and the subjective experience of emotion are independent responses to an emotion-arousing stimulus. The facial-feedback hypothesis, consistent with the James-Lange theory, suggests that feedback to the brain from facial muscles produces emotions. In Schachter's two-factor theory, physiological arousal tells us how strongly we feel an emotion, and situational cues provide the information we need to cognitively label the arousal and the emotion.

Researchers studying happiness, or subjective well-being (SWB), suggest that people can be happier if they (1) develop and maintain close relationships, (2) help others, (3) seek meaning and challenge in work, (4) set and work toward meaningful personal goals, (5) make time for enjoyable activities, (6) take care of themselves physically, (7) are open to new experiences, and (8) cultivate optimism and appreciation for what they have.

C. Chapter Outline

MOTIVATION
    Perspectives on Motivation
        Evolution, Instincts, and Genes
        Homeostasis and Drives
        Approach and Avoidance Motivation: The BAS and BIS
        Cognitive Processes: Incentives and Expectancies
        Psychodynamic and Humanistic Views
            Maslow's Need Hierarchy
            Self-Determination Theory
        What Do You Think? Is Maslow's Need Hierarchy Valid?
        In Review
    Hunger and Weight Regulation
        The Physiology of Hunger
            Signals That Start and Terminate a Meal
            Signals That Regulate General Appetite and Weight
            Brain Mechanisms
        Psychological Aspects of Hunger

Chapter 11

- Environmental and Cultural Factors
- Obesity
  - Genes and Environment
  - Dieting and Weight Loss
- Eating Disorders: Anorexia and Bulimia
  - Causes of Anorexia and Bulimia
- In Review

Sexual Motivation
- Sexual Behavior: Patterns and Changes
- The Physiology of Sex
  - The Sexual Response Cycle
  - Hormonal Influences
- The Psychology of Sex
- Cultural and Environmental Influences
- Sexual Orientation
  - Prevalence of Different Sexual Orientations
  - Determinants of Sexual Orientation
- *What Do You Think? Fraternal Birth Order and Male Homosexuality*
- In Review

Social Motivation
- Why Do We Affiliate?
- In Review

Achievement Motivation
- Motive for Success and Fear of Failure
- Achievement Goal Theory
- Achievement Goal Orientations
  - Motivational Climate
- Family, Culture, and Achievement Needs
- In Review

Motivational Conflict
- In Review

EMOTION
The Nature of Emotions
- Eliciting Stimuli
- The Cognitive Component
  - Culture and Appraisal
- In Review
- The Physiological Component
  - Brain Structures and Neurotransmitters
  - Hemispheric Activation and Emotion
  - Autonomic and Hormonal Processes
- *Beneath the Surface: The Lie Detector Controversy*
- The Behavioral Component
  - Evolution and Emotional Expression
  - Facial Expression of Emotion
  - Cultural Display Rules

Instrumental Behaviors
In Review
Theories of Emotion
The James-Lange Somatic Theory
The Cannon-Bard Theory
The Role of Autonomic Feedback
The Role of Expressive Behaviors
Cognitive-Affective Theories
Research Close-Up: Cognition Arousal Relations: Two Classic Experiments
Happiness
How Happy Are People?
What Makes People Happy?
Personal Resources
Psychological Processes
Applying Psychological Science: How to Be Happy: Guidelines from Psychological Research
In Review

D. Review at a Glance: *Write the term that best fits the blank to review what you learned in this chapter.*

Motivation

Motivation is a process that influences the (1) _____, persistence, and vigor of goal-directed behavior. According to (2) _____ theory, states of internal tension motivate people to behave in ways that return them to (3) _____. The universal human tendencies to (4) _____ pleasure and avoid (5) _____ reflect the activity of two distinct neural systems in the brain: the (6) _____ _____ _____ (BAS), which is sensitive to reward, and the (7) _____ _____ _____ (BIS), which is responsive to the potential for pain or nonreward. Studies suggest that (8) _____ neurotransmitter systems as well as different (9) _____ _____ may be involved in the two systems.

According to (10) _____ × (11) _____ theory, people are motivated to behave in ways that they believe will lead to rewards that they value.
(12) _____ motivation involves external rewards to motivate behavior, whereas (13) _____ motivation involves performing an activity for its own sake.
Humanistic theorists stress the human motivation for what Abraham Maslow called (14) _____-_____. Deci and Ryan's (15) _____-_____ theory focuses on the needs for (16) _____, autonomy, and (17) _____.

The body's rate of energy (or caloric) utilization is called (18) _____. Digestive enzymes break food down into nutrients including (19) _____, a simple sugar that is the body's major source of fuel. A peptide called (20)_____ is released into the bloodstream by the small intestine as food arrives in the stomach, travels to the brain, and stimulates brain receptors. A hormone secreted by fat cells that regulates food intake over the long term is called (21) _____. Early studies of the brain proposed that a "hunger-on" center is the (22) _____ _____, whereas a proposed "hunger-off" center is the (23) _____ hypothalamus. However, later research did not support these early ideas. A cluster of neurons that are packed with receptor sites for various transmitters that stimulate or reduce appetite is called the (24) _____ nucleus. People with the eating disorder (25) _____ _____ have an intense fear of being fat and severely restrict their food intake to the point of self-starvation. People who have (26) _____ _____ are also overly concerned about being fat; they binge on food and then induce purging. A four-stage pattern of sexual response is called the (27) _____ _____ _____. The psychological meaning of sex depends strongly on (28) _____ _____ and learning. Violent pornography seems to increase men's (29) _____ toward women. (30)_____ _____ refers to one's emotional and erotic preference for partners of a particular sex. Sexual orientation may have three dimensions, namely, self-(31) _____, sexual attraction, and actual sexual behavior

We affiliate with others to enjoy positive (32) _____, emotional (33) _____, attention, and opportunities for social (34)_____. Social relationships are important contributors to life (35) _____, and can also help (36) _____ us from stressors in our lives.

(37)_____ _____ _____ represents the desire to accomplish tasks and attain standards of excellence. Motive for success is part of the (38) _____ system that relates to achievement, whereas fear of failure is a (39) _____ function; studies support the idea that these functions are (40) _____. Achievement goal theory focuses on the goals that people seek to attain in task situations, which may be (41) _____ goals or ego goals, and may be based on a desire for success or a fear of failure. (42)_____-_____goals focus on the desire to master a task and learn new knowledge or skills, whereas ego-approach goals reflect a (43) _____ orientation that focuses on being judged favorably relative to other people. Mastery-(44) _____ goals reflect a fear of not performing up to one's own standards, whereas (45) _____-avoidance goals center on avoiding being outperformed by others. Family, teachers, and significant others create a (46) _____ _____ for children by encouraging or rewarding primarily a mastery or an ego orientation, which is likely to be internalized by the child.

Motivational goals sometimes conflict with each other. An (47) _____-_____ conflict involves opposition between two attractive alternatives, an (48) _____-_____ conflict involves a choice between two undesirable alternatives, and an (49) _____-_____ conflict involves being simultaneously attracted to and repulsed by the same goal.

Emotion

(50) _____ are positive or negative affect states consisting of cognitive, physiological, and behavioral reactions to events relevant to important goals or motives. Emotions have important (51) _____ functions. Our emotional states share four common features: They are triggered by (52) _____ or (53) _____ stimuli, they result from our interpretation, or (54) _____ _____ of these stimuli, they involve physiological responses, and they include behavioral tendencies, both (55) _____ and (56) _____. Biologically speaking, the ability to regulate emotion depends heavily on the (57) _____ _____. The thalamus sends emotion-related messages independently to the cortex and the (58) _____. Basic emotions such as anger and fear show characteristic processes in the (59) _____ nervous system, but there are no universal patterns of arousal associated with different emotions.

Modern evolutionary theorists suggest that some fundamental emotional patterns may be (60) _____. Many emotion theorists conclude that innate biological factors and cultural (61) _____ _____ combine to shape emotional expression across different cultures. Performance often (62) _____ with arousal up to some optimal level, and then deteriorates with further arousal, although task (63) _____ is also important.

According to the (64) _____-_____ or (65) _____ theory of emotion, bodily reactions determine emotions, rather than the other way around. According to the (66) _____-_____ hypothesis, facial muscles involved in emotional expression send messages to the brain, which then interprets the pattern as an emotion. The (67) _____-_____ theory of emotion proposed that physiological arousal and the subjective experience of emotion are independent responses to an emotion-arousing stimulus. Schachter's (68) _____-_____ theory of emotion states that physiological arousal indicates the strength of an emotion, and situational cues facilitate cognitive labeling of the arousal and the emotion.

Psychologists use the term (69) _____ _____-_____ (SWB) to refer to happiness. Studies of factors that support high SWB suggest that people can be happier if they develop close relationships, help others, seek meaning and (70) _____ in work, have meaningful personal goals, make time for enjoyable activities, nurture their physical well-being, remain open to (71) _____ _____, and cultivate (72) _____ and count their blessings.

E. Concept Cards

Truly learning a concept means integrating it into the way *you* think about things. To integrate concepts successfully, you must translate the words and examples your text or instructor provides into words and examples that are meaningful to you.

For this exercise, obtain some note cards (3" × 5" or 4" × 6") to make a deck of concept cards. On one side of each card, write the *concept* from the list below (e.g., "homeostasis") at the top. Read the textbook definition provided, and then write the definition *in your own words* on the concept card (e.g., for "homeostasis," you might write "an internal state of balance"). Simply imagine that a friend has asked you what the concept means, and write down what you would answer. Writing the definition in your own words requires you to think deeply about its meaning. When next you see your own version of the definition, it will make intuitive sense to you—no translation required.

On the second side of the card, write your own example of the concept. Again, coming up with your own example requires you to think deeply about the application of the concept, and you will more easily understand and remember the example when you study for a test. If you use an example from the text, or from class, make it your own by writing it in your own words. You can always check with your instructor that your example is indeed a good example of the concept.

```
   CONCEPT

Definition in my own words

   (side 1 of card)
```

```
Example of the concept in my own words,
preferably drawn from my own
experience

   (side 2 of card)
```

The following is a list of all the boldface concepts from your textbook with the author's definition. Write the definition in your own words, together with your own example of the concept, to create a *concept card* as described earlier, or write in the space provided.

Motivation: A process that influences the direction, persistence, and vigor of goal-directed behavior

Instinct (fixed action pattern): An inherited characteristic, common to all members of a species that automatically produces a particular response when the organism is exposed to a particular stimulus

Homeostasis: A state of internal physiological equilibrium that the body strives to maintain

Drives: States of internal tension that motivate an organism to behave in ways that reduce this tension

Behavioral activation system (BAS): A neural system that is roused to action by signals of potential reward and positive need gratification

Behavioral inhibition system (BIS): A neural system that responds to stimuli that signal potential pain, nonreinforcement, and punishment

Incentives: Environmental stimuli that "pull" an organism toward a goal

Expectancy × value theory: A theory that proposes that goal-directed behavior is jointly determined by the strength of the person's expectation that particular behaviors will lead to a goal and by the incentive value the individual places on that goal

Extrinsic motivation: Motivation to perform an activity to obtain an external reward or avoid punishment
Intrinsic motivation: Performing an activity for its own sake

Self-actualization: Fulfilling one's human potential

Self-determination theory: A theory that focuses on three fundamental psychological needs: need for competence, for autonomy, and for relatedness

Metabolism: The body's rate of energy (or caloric) use

Set point: A biologically determined standard around which body weight (or, more accurately, fat mass) is regulated

Glucose: A simple sugar that is the body's (and especially the brain's) major source of immediately usable fuel

Cholecystokinin (CCK): A peptide (a type of hormone) that helps produce satiety

Leptin: A hormone secreted by fat cells

Paraventricular nucleus (PVN): A cluster of neurons packed with receptor sites for various transmitters that stimulate or reduce appetite

Anorexia nervosa: An eating disorder characterized by an intense fear of being fat and severely restricting food intake to the point of self-starvation

Bulimia nervosa: An eating disorder characterized by a fear of becoming fat, binge-eating, then purging the food

Sexual response cycle: The stages in sexual activity of excitement, plateau, orgasm, and resolution

Sexual dysfunction: Chronic, impaired sexual functioning that distresses a person

Sexual orientation: One's emotional and erotic preference for partners of a particular sex

Social comparison: A process of comparing our beliefs, feelings, and behaviors with those of other people

Need for achievement: A positive desire to accomplish tasks and compete successfully with standards of excellence

Achievement goal theory: A theory regarding the manner in which success is defined both by the individual and within the achievement situation itself

Mastery orientation: A definition of success that focuses upon personal improvement, giving maximum effort, and perfecting new skills

Ego orientation: A definition of success whereby one has the goal of outperforming others (hopefully, with as little effort as possible)

Motivational climate: A psychological environment that encourages or rewards either a mastery approach or an ego approach to defining success

Mastery- approach goals: A focus on the desire to master a task and learn new knowledge or skills

Ego-approach goals: A competitive orientation that focuses on being judged favorably relative to other people

Mastery-avoidance: A fear of not performing up to one's own standards

Ego-avoidance goals: A competitive orientation that centers on avoiding negative judgments by self or others

2 x 2 achievement goal theory: The theory that every person can be described in terms of an "achievement motivation profile," based on whether they are motivated by mastery- or ego-related goals, and have an approach or an avoidance orientation to achievement

Approach-approach conflict: A choice between two attractive alternatives, where selecting one means losing the other

Avoidance-avoidance conflict: A choice between two undesirable alternatives

Approach-avoidance conflict: A choice that one is simultaneously attracted to and repelled by

Emotions: Feeling (or affect) states that involve a pattern of cognitive, physiological, and behavioral reactions to events

Eliciting stimuli: Stimuli that trigger cognitive appraisals and emotional responses

Cognitive appraisals: The interpretations and meanings that we attach to sensory stimuli

Polygraph: An instrument that measures physiological responses, such as respiration, heart rate, and skin conductance (which increases in the presence of emotion because of sweat gland activity)

Expressive behavior: A person's observable emotional display

Fundamental emotional patterns: Innate emotional reactions

Cultural display rules: Norms that dictate when and how particular emotions are to be expressed

Instrumental behavior: Behavior directed at achieving some emotionally relevant goal

James-Lange theory: A theory that proposes that our bodily reactions determine the subjective emotion we experience

Cannon-Bard theory: A theory that proposes that the subjective experience of emotion and physiological arousal do not cause one another but instead are independent responses to an emotion-arousing situation

Facial feedback hypothesis: A theory that proposes that feedback from the facial muscles to the brain plays a key role in determining the nature and intensity of emotions that we experience

Two-factor theory of emotion: A theory that proposes that the intensity of physiological arousal tells us *how strongly* we are feeling something but that situational cues give us the information we need in order to label the arousal and tell ourselves *what* we are feeling

Subjective well-being (SWB): People's degree of satisfaction with various aspects of their life

Downward comparison: A process of seeing ourselves as better off than the standard of comparison

Upward comparison: A process of seeing ourselves as worse off than the standard of comparison

F. What's the Difference? A Concept Card Exercise

An important skill in learning concepts is being able to differentiate among concepts that are similar or related in some way. This skill is particularly relevant for multiple-choice tests, especially if you often find yourself wavering between two answers.

Once you have created your own deck of concept cards, select them two by two, each time answering the question "What's the difference between these two concepts?" You can use the word definitions of the concepts or the examples of the concepts to enhance your mastery of the material. In each case, choose pairs of concepts to compare those that are related or similar or that sound the same or that could in some way be confused. It's much easier to spot the difference between two concepts when you are studying, with the textbook available, rather than when considering the question for the first time in a testing situation.

G. Apply What You Know

1. Describe half a dozen of your own behaviors that support either drive theory or incentive theory. Do you see a pattern in which behaviors support which theory?

Behavior	Theory It Supports
a.	
b.	
c.	

d.

e.

f.

2. Spend 15 minutes in a location, such as a campus cafeteria, where people tend to gather and socialize in a relatively unstructured fashion. Record the emotional displays you observe people engaging in as they greet each other, carry on conversations, and say good-bye. How do your observations relate to the material you have studied in this chapter on Motivation and Emotion?

H. On the Web: *As with any online research, it is important to consider how legitimate a given source is before you rely on the information it presents. Your instructor or Internet adviser may give you some specific guidelines for distinguishing which kinds of Web sites tend to be reputable.*

A. A number of individuals have made notable contributions to our understanding of motivation and emotion. Search the Web for more information about some of those listed below.

Ray Blanchard

David M. Buss

Richard Davidson and Nathan Fox

Ed Diener and Carol Diener

Paul Ekman and Wallace Friesen

April Fallon and Paul Rozin

William James and Carl Lange

Alfred Kinsey

Joseph LeDoux

Abraham Maslow

William Masters and Virginia Johnson

David McClelland and John Atkinson

Chapter 11

Stanley Schachter

A. L. Washburn

B. Take a look at the concept cards you have created for this chapter, or the key concepts listed in section E. In the space provided, make a list of any whose definitions or associations you are not yet confident of and any you'd like to learn more about. Try entering the terms on your list into your search engine. Make notes of any helpful information you find.

Key Concept/Information Found

C. As you will see if you enter "weight loss" or "lose weight" into your search engine, there are literally millions of websites devoted to weight loss. Visit the Centers for Disease Control and Prevention (CDC) at http://www.cdc.gov and look for resources related to overweight and obesity; you will probably find them under a subhead such as "Nutrition and Physical Activity." Note what you find there. Next, explore the weight loss information available on at least three other sites. How do the CDC resources compare with resources offered by the other sites you have chosen?

CDC resources:

Weight loss site #1: http://

Weight loss site #2: http://

Weight loss site #3: http://

I. Analyze This: *Chapter 1 of your textbook begins by presenting these four basic steps in the critical thinking process:*
- *"What exactly are you asking me to believe?"*
- *"How do you know? What is the evidence?"*
- *"Are there other possible explanations?"*
- *"What is the most reasonable conclusion?"*

You might picture this as a four-step analysis to help you decide whether to accept a given theory or assertion. Now it's your turn to put your textbook to this test.

Review the section in Chapter 11 of your textbook under the heading "Sexual Orientation." There you will find a discussion of how psychologists attempt to define and describe homosexuality and bisexuality. If someone told you that 1 person in 10 of the general population is not heterosexual, would you agree? Analyze that assertion in the space following. When you have finished, consider using this four-step analysis to evaluate other assertions you encounter.

"What exactly are you asking me to believe?"

"How do you know? What is the evidence?"

Chapter 11

"Are there other possible explanations?"

"What is the most reasonable conclusion?"

J. Practice Test

Multiple-Choice Items: *Write the letter corresponding to your answer in the space to the left of each item.*

_____ 1. Homeostatic models of motivation _____.
   a. propose that self-actualization is an important motivator of human behavior
   b. help us understand the regulation of hunger and thirst
   c. underlie the expectancy × value approach to motivation
   d. explain how incentives motivate human behavior

_____ 2. Tim is just learning to play the violin and hopes to join the university orchestra next year. Although he receives little encouragement from his roommate, family, or friends, he keeps practicing because he enjoys it. Tim's continued practicing is most likely due to ____.
   a. external incentives
   b. extrinsic motivation
   c. cognitive theory
   d. intrinsic motivation

_____ 3. Marika and Phil are about to be interviewed for the same new job. They each very much want the job and believe it would substantially help their career. Marika feels very motivated and works hard to be as well prepared for the interview as she possibly can. But Phil feels less motivated and puts less effort into his preparation. The expectancy × value theory of motivation would explain this difference in motivation as being due to _____.
   a. their different expectations regarding their goal-related behaviors
   b. their different needs for self-actualization
   c. the different values they placed on the job
   d. their different internal drives

_____ 4. The behavioral activation system (BAS) _____.
   a. regulates unconscious motives, thoughts, and inner tensions
   b. is a neural system that is sensitive to the potential for punishment
   c. controls the production of leptin in the neural system

d. is a neural system that is sensitive to reward

_____ 5. People who are overweight may have difficulty losing weight by dieting for two reasons: The body responds to the food deprivation often involved in dieting by _____ the rate of basal metabolism, and, as fat mass decreases, leptin levels _____, stimulating appetite and making it harder to adhere to a diet.
   a. decreasing; increase
   b. decreasing; decrease
   c. increasing; decrease
   d. increasing; increase

_____ 6. Research on the prevalence of anorexia and bulimia has determined that these disorders are _____.
   a. most common in industrialized cultures where beauty is equated with thinness
   b. equally common in almost all cultures of the world
   c. most common in cultures that have to deal with food scarcity and famine
   d. most common in cultures where people lack personal control and freedom

_____ 7. Deci and Ryan's self-determination theory is a humanistic one that focuses on ___.
   a. maximizing pleasure and avoiding pain
   b. needs for competence, autonomy, and relatedness
   c. satisfying drives and maintaining equilibrium in the body
   d. the direction, persistence, and vigor of goal-directed behavior

_____ 8. According to Masters and Johnson, the four stages of the human sexual response cycle typically occur in this order: ____, ____, ____, and ____.
   a. plateau; excitement; orgasm; resolution
   b. plateau; excitement; resolution; orgasm
   c. excitement; orgasm; resolution; plateau
   d. excitement; plateau; orgasm; resolution

_____ 9. The fact that children in the Marquesas Islands of French Polynesia have ample opportunity to observe sexual behavior, and that parents in this society sometimes masturbate their children when the children are distressed, best demonstrates how _____ factors can impact sexual behavior.
   a. genetic
   b. personal psychological
   c. cultural
   d. biological

_____ 10. In research by Bell et al. on childhood or adolescent experiences that might predict adult sexual orientation, one consistent pattern emerged: As children, people who identify themselves as lesbian or gay _____.

a. felt that they were somehow different from their same-sex peers
b. were sexually abused by a same-sex adult
c. had domineering mothers
d. often dressed in clothing of the opposite sex

_____ 11. When we affiliate with others and compare our beliefs, feelings, and behaviors with those of the people we affiliate with, we are engaging in _____.
a. efforts to get attention
b. emotional support
c. positive stimulation
d. social comparison

_____ 12. Research suggests that social relationships _____.
a. interfere with our achievement motivation
b. minimize our opportunities for social comparison
c. maximize the effects of stressors in our lives
d. can insulate us from stressors in our lives

_____ 13. People who are high in achievement motivation and low in fear of failure prefer _____.
a. very difficult goals that others regard as almost impossible
b. extrinsic rather than intrinsic goals
c. tasks of intermediate difficulty
d. tasks where the outcome is perceived to be certain

_____ 14. Fear of failure _____.
a. is a BAS function
b. is a BIS function
c. is highly negatively correlated with motive for success
d. is highly positively correlated with motive for success

_____ 15. At this point in your review of this chapter, you are running out of time and have to decide whether to answer the rest of the practice test questions (a very undesirable alternative) or study for your biology test (another undesirable alternative). You are experiencing a(n) _____ conflict.
a. approach-approach
b. approach-avoidance
c. avoidance-avoidance
d. hopeless

_____ 16. Mary is learning a new computer program. She is excited about her increasing ability to use the program effectively and feels good about the effort she is putting into learning this new skill. According to achievement-goal theory, Mary is demonstrating _____.

a. ego-approach goals
b. ego-avoidance goals
c. mastery-approach goals
d. mastery-avoidance goals

_____ 17. Our emotional states _____.
a. are triggered by external rather than internal stimuli
b. often occur with little or no awareness
c. do not involve any cognitive processes
d. involve biological factors but not learning

_____ 18. Backpacking around Europe one summer, Harold was surprised when his hotel landlady in Italy burst into tears after Harold told her he was moving out because the shower water was too cold. Three weeks earlier he had told a landlady in Sweden the same thing, and she had reacted by saying coolly, "Well, that's up to you." The contrast between the landladies' behavior was most likely due to _____.
a. subcortical structures
b. the Schachter two-factor effect
c. the left hemisphere
d. cultural display rules

_____ 19. Emotions have important adaptive functions; for example, negative emotions may help us to _____.
a. broaden our thinking and behavior so that we explore
b. try out new ways to achieve goals
c. form intimate relationships
d. narrow attention and actions to deal with a threatening situation

_____ 20. Emotional responses can occur both through interpretation by the prefrontal cortex and through a more primitive system involving the _____, which is likely important for survival.
a. corpus callosum
b. amygdala
c. cerebellum
d. gonadotropins

_____ 21. Research involving electroencephalograms of people while they were experiencing various emotions indicated a connection between the left hemisphere and _____ emotions, and between the right hemisphere and _____ emotions.
a. positive; negative
b. strong; weaker
c. negative; positive
d. mildly positive; more strongly positive

_____ 22. According to Jeni's professor, Dr. Smart, emotional displays have significant adaptive value; she also believes that some fundamental emotional patterns may be innate. Dr. Smart is most likely a(n) _____ .
   a. humanistic psychologist
   b. psychoneuroimmunologist
   c. evolutionary theorist
   d. cognitive theorist

_____ 23. According to the research of Paul Ekman and his coworkers, _____ are generally more accurate judges of emotional facial expression than _____ are.
   a. women; men
   b. children; adults
   c. men; women
   d. women; girls

_____ 24. An early theory of emotion that survives today as the somatic theory states that bodily reactions produce our perceptions of emotional states is the _____ theory.
   a. Cannon-Bard
   b. subjective well-being
   c. need hierarchy
   d. James-Lange

_____ 25. An early theory of emotion that views physiological arousal and the subjective experience of emotion as two independent responses to an emotion-arousing stimulus is the _____ theory.
   a. Schachter
   b. social cognition
   c. Cannon-Bard
   d. positive psychology

_____ 26. The _____, which suggests that emotions are triggered by muscles in the face, is an offshoot of the James-Lange theory of emotion.
   a. facial-feedback hypothesis
   b. Cannon-Bard theory
   c. cognitive appraisal
   d. set-point theory

_____ 27. The theory of emotion that views physiological arousal as an indicator of how strong an emotion is, and situational cues as information allowing cognitive appraisal of the emotion and its intensity, is _____.
   a. now widely discredited
   b. Schachter's two-factor theory
   c. Passer's two-factor theory
   d. the James-Lange theory

_____ 28. Researchers studying subjective well-being have found that _____.
   a. having more money is positively associated with happiness
   b. most disabled people report very low levels of subjective well-being
   c. intelligence is strongly related to happiness
   d. married people are happier, on average, than single and divorced people

_____ 29. What have studies shown about the relationship between emotional arousal and performance?
   a. performance on complex tasks is enhanced by emotional arousal
   b. emotional arousal interferes with performance on simple tasks
   c. performance generally increases with arousal up to an optimal level, then deteriorates
   d. arousal interferes with performance up to a certain level and then has no effect

_____ 30. According to research on subjective well-being, which of the following contributes to happiness?
   a. needing to be taken care of by others
   b. spending time on one's own
   c. having an optimistic outlook
   d. reducing frustration by avoiding new experiences

True/False Items: *Write T or F in the space provided to the left of each item.*

_____ 1. According to drive theory, drives are produced by physiological disruptions to homeostasis.

_____ 2. Performing an activity to obtain an external reward or to avoid punishment is called intrinsic motivation.

_____ 3. The behavioral inhibition system (BIS) is a neural system that is responsive to stimuli signaling the potential for pain, punishment, and no reward.

_____ 4. Anorexia nervosa is an eating disorder in which the person severely restricts food intake and is at risk of self-starvation.

_____ 5. High-need achievers prefer extremely difficult tasks rather than tasks that are very easy or of intermediate difficulty.

_____ 6. The pattern of sexual response described by Masters and Johnson (1966) includes four stages in this order: excitement, plateau, orgasm, and resolution.

_____ 7. Deci and Ryan's self-determination theory focuses on the needs for competence, autonomy, and relatedness.

_____ 8. The need for achievement is influenced chiefly by fear of failure.

_____ 9. In the experience of emotion, cognitive appraisal is the process of appreciating and enjoying a positive emotion.

_____ 10. The somatic theory of emotion is outdated and has few adherents today.

Short-Answer Questions

1. What role may homeostasis play in motivation?

2. What are the psychological aspects of hunger?

3. How are hormones involved in sexual motivation?

4. Describe the research in which modern evolutionary theorists link emotion with adaptation.

5. What are the primary differences between the James-Lange and Cannon-Bard theories of emotion?

Essay Questions

1. Are you basically satisfied with your body? Or do you wish you were, for example, thinner, heavier, more curvaceous, or more muscular? Describe any social factors you are aware of that influence your feelings of satisfaction or dissatisfaction. How does your body compare to the average, and, if more than half of all U.S. adults are overweight or obese, what does that indicate about the meaning of "average" when it comes to weight?

2. Do you think pornography should be more strictly regulated by laws and law enforcement than it now is? If so, what standards of decency and what specific means of regulation do you advocate? Using information found in this chapter, defend your position for or against increased regulation.

3. Describe the emotional display rules in your family and any other environments in which you have spent a significant amount of time. Is there a contrast between your usual ways of displaying emotion and those of people you associate with, such as a family member, roommate, or romantic partner?

Answer Keys

Answer Key for Review at a Glance

1. direction
2. drive
3. homeostasis
4. maximize
5. pain
6. behavioral activation system
7. behavioral inhibition system
8. different
9. brain regions

37. Need for achievement
38. BAS
39. BIS
40. independent
41. mastery
42. Mastery-approach
43. competitive
44. avoidance
45. ego

Chapter 11 339

10. expectancy
11. value
12. Extrinsic
13. intrinsic
14. self-actualization
15. self-determination
16. competence
17. relatedness
18. metabolism
19. glucose
20. CCK (cholecystokinin)
21. leptin
22. lateral hypothalamus
23. ventromedial
24. paraventricular
25. anorexia nervosa
26. bulimia nervosa
27. sexual response cycle
28. cultural contexts
29. aggression
30. Sexual orientation
31. identity
32. stimulation
33. support
34. comparison
35. satisfaction
36. insulate

46. motivational climate
47. approach-approach
48. avoidance-avoidance
49. approach-avoidance
50. Emotions
51. adaptive
52. internal
53. external
54. cognitive appraisal
55. expressive
56. instrumental
57. prefrontal cortex
58. amygdala
59. autonomic
60. innate
61. display rules
62. increases
63. complexity
64. James-Lange
65. somatic
66. facial-feedback
67. Cannon-Bard
68. two-factor
69. subjective well-being
70. challenge
71. new experiences
72. optimism

Answer Key for Practice Test Multiple-Choice Items

1. b
2. d
3. a
4. d
5. b
6. a
7. b
8. d
9. c
10. a
11. d
12. d
13. c
14. b
15. c

16. c
17. b
18. d
19. d
20. b
21. a
22. c
23. a
24. d
25. c
26. a
27. b
28. d
29. c
30. c

Answer Key for Practice Test True/False Items

1. T
2. F
3. T
4. T
5. F
6. T
7. T
8. F
9. F
10. F

Answer Key for Practice Test Short-Answer Questions

1. Homeostasis is a state of internal physiological equilibrium that the body strives to maintain. Homeostatic regulation involves both unlearned and learned behaviors. According to drive theory, physiological disruptions to homeostasis produce drives, which motivate organisms to behave in ways that reduce drive.

2. From a behavioral perspective, eating is positively reinforced by good taste and negatively reinforced by hunger reduction. We have expectations that eating will be pleasurable, so cognitions about eating are important in motivation. Our beliefs, attitudes, and cultural standards about caloric intake, as well as body image, are important factors affecting eating.

3. The pituitary gland secretes hormones called gonadotropins into the bloodstream. These hormones affect the rate at which the gonads (testes in the male and ovaries in the female) secrete androgens and estrogens. These sex hormones have both organizational effects on the body by directing the development of the sex organs and activational effects by stimulating sexual desire and behavior.

4. Like Darwin, who argued that basic emotional responses help organisms avoid danger, modern evolutionary theorists stress the adaptive value of emotional expression. They have conducted cross-cultural studies that show that certain emotional expressions (e.g., rage and terror) are similar across all cultures, suggesting a universal biological basis for them. Thus they believe that a set of fundamental emotional patterns, or innate emotional reactions, are wired into the nervous system.

5. The James-Lange theory of emotion was developed more than a century ago from similar conclusions reached independently by William James and Carl Lange, who both argued that we feel an emotion because of the way our body reacts to a stimulus. This theory lives on today as the somatic theory of emotion. The Cannon-Bard theory, developed in the 1920s by Walter Cannon and his colleague L. L. Bard, is not the exact opposite of the somatic theory but instead adds a dimension of cognition. It says that physiological arousal and the cognitive, subjective experience of emotion are separate, independent responses to a stimulus.

Answer Key for Practice Test Essay Questions

As you may have guessed, there are no right or wrong answers to the essay questions in this practice test. That does not mean, however, that all essays are equally good. To get maximum learning benefit from the essay questions, do the following:

- Review each essay a day or two after you wrote it, noting any necessary corrections and any additional support for your points that you can think of.
- Review the section in your textbook that pertains to the topic of each essay. Annotate your essay with any corrections or additional support for your points that you find in the text.
- Spend a few minutes researching the topic of each essay on the Internet. Annotate your essay further with any additional (reliable) information you find.
- Finally, reread each essay with the annotations you have added.

Chapter 12
DEVELOPMENT OVER THE LIFE SPAN

A. Learning Objectives: *These objectives are expanded from the Focus Questions found in the margins of your textbook. When you have mastered the material in this chapter, you will be able to:*

12.1 Describe the broad issues that guide developmental research.

12.2 Describe prenatal development and how it can be influenced by STDs, alcohol, and other drugs.

12.3 Describe the newborn's sensory capabilities, perceptual preferences, reflexes, and learning capabilities.

12.4 Explain how nature and nurture jointly influence physical growth and motor development during infancy.

12.5 Describe the three cognitive processes and four stages of cognitive development outlined by Piaget, and describe research that supports and contradicts these ideas.

12.6 Describe how Vygotsky's zone of proximal development and information-processing approaches challenge Piaget's views.

12.7 Describe how research on violation of expectation and theory of mind challenge Piaget's views.

12.8 Describe emotional development of children including emotional expression, emotional regulation, and temperament.

12.9 Describe social development including Erikson's stages of psychosocial development.

12.10 Describe imprinting, Harlow's attachment research, and attachment in humans.

12.11 Describe how disruptions in attachment affect psychological development.

12.12 Describe the data relating day care, divorce, and remarriage to psychosocial development.

12.13 Outline parenting styles associated with the most and least positive child outcomes.

12.14 Describe how socialization shapes children's beliefs about gender.

Chapter 12

12.15 Differentiate among Kohlberg's preconventional, conventional, and postconventional stages of moral reasoning, and explain how moral reasoning is affected by culture and gender.

12.16 Describe some factors that influence adolescents' psychological reactions to puberty.

12.17 Describe how physical abilities and brain changes occur in adulthood.

12.18 Discuss the major cognitive changes that occur during adolescence.

12.19 Explain the cognitive and intellectual changes that occur in adulthood.

12.20 Discuss criticisms of the mental exercise hypothesis.

12.21 Describe how cognitive and intellectual abilities change in adulthood, and describe the characteristics of senile dementia.

12.22 Discuss adolescents' search for identity.

12.23 Explain how emotions change during adolescence.

12.24 Discuss the criteria for determining if someone has reached adulthood.

12.25 Describe the three major developmental challenges of adulthood outlined by Erikson.

12.26 Describe research findings on family structure, cohabitation and divorce, and typical changes in marital satisfaction over time.

12.27 Describe the common stages of establishing a career, and describe sex differences in career paths.

12.28 Discuss the evidence for the concept of the midlife crisis and the view that dying people experience a sequence of psychological stages.

B. Chapter Overview

This chapter traces the development of the human being from the moment of conception through the life span. It focuses in chronological order on prenatal development, infancy and childhood, and then addresses the themes of physical, cognitive, and social-emotional development throughout adolescence and the various stages of adulthood.

Developmental psychology examines biological, physical, social, and behavioral changes that occur with age. Four broad issues guide developmental research: the influence of nature and nurture, critical and sensitive periods, continuity versus discontinuity in development, and individual stability versus change over time. Developmental psychologists employ cross-sectional research designs to study cohorts at the same point in time, longitudinal designs to study the same cohort at different points in time, and sequential designs, which combine the cross-sectional and longitudinal approaches by testing several groups at one point in time and then again when they are older.

Prenatal development consists of three stages: zygote, embryo, and fetus. The 23rd pair of chromosomes in the zygote determines the child's sex. If the 23rd pair is two X chromosomes, the baby is female, and if it is one X and one Y chromosome, the baby is male. Teratogens are external agents that cause abnormal prenatal development. Some of the more common and dangerous ones are rubella; sexually transmitted diseases (STDs), including human immunodeficiency virus (HIV); alcohol; illegal drugs, such as heroin and cocaine; and nicotine.

Newborns, or neonates, have many amazing characteristics. Their visual systems are poor but develop quickly. They are able to distinguish aspects of their mother from those of other people within hours after birth, and they prefer complex and facelike patterns to simpler ones. Neonates are equipped with many reflexes to respond to specific stimuli, which help them respond to caretakers and learn other important information. Physical and motor development of newborns follows both the cephalocaudal (from head to foot) and proximodistal (from innermost to outermost) principles, and the brain develops rapidly. Although guided and constrained by genetics, physical and motor development can be powerfully affected by environmental and cultural influences that interact with biological factors.

Swiss psychologist Jean Piaget proposed that children learn about the world through schemas which are organized patterns of thought and action. New experiences are incorporated into existing schemas, a process called assimilation, or schemas are changed by new experiences, which is called accommodation. In Piaget's stage model of cognitive development, infants in the sensorimotor stage learn about the world through their sensory processes and movements. By the end of this stage, children attain a sense of object permanence. Symbolic thought begins to develop during the preoperational stage, although preoperational children do not yet understand conservation, and their thinking reflects animism and egocentrism. During the concrete operational stage, children begin to be able to perform basic mental operations on tangible objects and situations. For example, they start to understand reversibility and serial ordering. Abstract reasoning and the systematic use of hypotheses first occur during the formal operational stage. Research on Piaget's theory has found that the general cognitive abilities he proposed do occur in the same order across different cultures, but that children may acquire many cognitive skills much earlier than he suggested. Children may also perform skills that indicate they are at one stage in some ways and at another stage in other ways. Studies have found that culture influences cognitive development, and that cognitive development is more complex and variable than Piaget proposed.

Lev Vygotsky addressed the social context of cognitive development. He proposed a "zone of proximal development" in which children, when they get assistance from their parents or older peers, may do more than they might be capable of doing independently. Information-processing approaches to cognitive development focus on changes in information-search strategies, information-processing speed, attention, and response inhibition, as well as on increased memory capabilities and metacognition as children mature. Developmental psychologists use creative techniques such as violation-of-expectation experiments to make inferences about infants' understanding of basic concepts about how the world works, and "theory of mind" methods to study children's ability to understand other people's mental states.

Around 18 months of age, infants begin to develop a sense of self. As emotions become more complex with age, so does emotion regulation. Infants differ in temperament and may be categorized as easy, difficult, or slow-to-warm-up. Shyness is another facet of temperament. Erikson argued that social development occurs throughout the life span in eight major psychosocial stages, each of which involves a particular crisis in how we relate to others.

Much recent research in developmental psychology has focused on attachment, the strong emotional bond between children and their caregivers. British theorist John Bowlby hypothesized that attachment develops through a series of stages. Newborns emit indiscriminate attachment behavior; then, at about 3 months of age, discriminate attachment behavior becomes directed to familiar caregivers rather than to strangers, and by about 8 months toward specific caregivers. Mary Ainsworth's research using the "strange situation" to measure attachment and anxiety revealed different patterns of attachment, including securely attached, anxious-resistant, and anxious-avoidant infants. There is much research on the effects of early attachment styles on later behaviors. Studies of isolates and children raised in orphanages suggest that infancy is a sensitive but not a critical period during which attachment forms most easily and can facilitate subsequent development. Studies have found that children who spend time in day care do not show less attachment to their parents than children raised exclusively in the home. High-quality day care can also aid children from disadvantaged backgrounds, but the quality of family experiences is often more important in predicting children's social adjustment and academic performance.

Divorce and its effects on children are an important focus of research. The wide variation in divorces and families makes generalization difficult, but it is clear that children are challenged when their parents divorce. Different styles of parenting can influence children's development. Authoritative, authoritarian, indulgent, and neglectful parenting styles have been studied. Authoritative parents are controlling but warm, and this style is associated with the most positive childhood outcomes, whereas the children of neglectful parents, who provide neither warmth nor guidance and control, tend to fare poorest. Heredity, peer and community influences, other experiences, and their mutual interaction with parenting style all influence childhood outcomes. Through cognitive maturation and socialization, children develop gender identity and gender constancy, which influence their sense of what it means to be a girl or a boy, and they acquire sex-role stereotypes.

Kohlberg's stage model of moral development suggests that children develop morally from reasoning based on anticipated rewards and punishments, to reasoning based on social expectations and laws, to the highest level of moral reasoning based on general principles. Kohlberg's critics claim that his theory is culturally and gender biased. Moral reasoning doesn't necessarily translate into moral behavior. Skinner, for example, emphasized the direct influence of learning on moral behavior, whereas Freud proposed that children identify with their parents and develop a conscience which then regulates their moral behavior.

Many cultures mark the transition from childhood to adulthood with a rite of passage but do not recognize a years-long period of adolescence as Western industrial societies do. Adolescence begins at puberty at which time hormonal secretions stimulate the development of both primary and secondary sex characteristics.

Gradual but important changes occur in thinking, interests, social circumstances, and parental and societal expectations during adolescence. The rate of overall brain growth slows, and a process of pruning the massive number of synaptic connections developed during the explosive growth of childhood occurs, resulting in more-focused neural activity within brain regions. Changes in the prefrontal cortex and limbic system are especially pronounced, including an upsurge in activity of dopamine, a neurotransmitter involved in regulating emotional arousal, pleasure and reward, and learning.

People reach their peak of physical and perceptual functioning around their mid-20s, and after age 40 a decline in many physical capacities becomes noticeable, including reduced muscle strength and flexibility, basal metabolism, and fertility. By late adulthood, physical changes become more pronounced, but with regular exercise and good nutrition, and barring major disease, many adults remain active well into old age. Like other parts of the body, the brain declines later in adulthood. Tissue loss is normal as the brain ages, even in physically and mentally healthy older adults.

Cognitive changes during adolescence can be as dramatic as the physical ones. Adolescent thinking can become highly self-focused resulting in adolescent egocentrism. The adolescent's abstract-reasoning abilities increase substantially, and information processing becomes more efficient. Young adults are at their peak in many areas of cognitive functioning.

In later adulthood, perceptual speed, memory for new factual information, prospective memory, and recall tend to decline. Studies suggest an earlier and steadier decline in fluid intelligence, compared with crystallized intelligence, throughout adulthood. Wisdom, which includes knowledge about human nature and social relationships, strategies for making decisions and handling conflict, and an ability to manage uncertainty, appears to increase steadily from early adolescence through the mid-20s and then levels off through the mid-70s. Dementia, called senile dementia when it begins after age 65, is most common in late adulthood and may be associated with Alzheimer's disease or other causes. Although at least some degree of cognitive impairment is common in old age, studies suggest that it is not inevitable

Social-emotional development in adolescence is reflected in the pivotal crisis recognized by Erikson as identity-versus-role confusion. According to James Marcia, an individual's identity status at any time may be classified in terms of four categories; identity diffusion, foreclosure, moratorium, or identity achievement. Culture plays a major role in identity formation, incorporating elements that involve autonomy from—and interdependence with—other people. Conflict between adolescents and their parents has not been found to be as serious or as widespread as popularly believed. Peers are an important factor in adolescents' lives and can exert pressure to engage in, or to avoid, misconduct. Research by Larson et al. found early adolescence characterized by emotional ups and downs, with emotions becoming more stable but less positive in the later teen years.

The transition to adulthood is marked not only by attaining a certain age or assuming certain social roles but also by becoming a responsible, independent person, according to survey studies across the United States. Erikson proposed that the main crises of early, middle, and late adulthood are intimacy-versus-isolation, generativity-versus-stagnation, and integrity-versus-despair, respectively. Consistent with Erikson's model, many goals increase in importance as people age, and successfully resolving certain life tasks contributes to mastering others.

Freud and others viewed adult social development in terms of key life events revolving around loving and working. For many couples, marital satisfaction tends to decline in the years following the birth of children, but increases later in adulthood. Despite the stresses that accompany marriage and parenthood, studies find that married people experience greater subjective well-being than unmarried adults. Work serves important psychological and social functions, and establishing a career involves a developmental process over the life span. Overall, women experience more career gaps, and their career paths are more variable than men's.

Research on the "midlife crisis" suggests that it is largely a myth: People at all ages experience conflict, disappointments, and frustrations. Retirement can be a happy experience for those who desire it, but those who must retire due to ill health or must continue working to make ends meet are less satisfied with their "golden years." Part of being human is the fact that eventually each of us will die. Elisabeth Kübler-Ross's pioneering work emphasized several distinct stages people work through as they approach death. Although research does not support the sequence or the existence of all stages for all people, these stages nevertheless may serve as a useful framework for those contemplating their own approaching death or seeking to cope with the loss of a loved one.

C. Chapter Outline

MAJOR ISSUES AND METHODS
   In Review
PRENATAL DEVELOPMENT
   Genetics and Sex Determination
   Environmental Influences
   In Review
INFANCY AND CHILDHOOD
   The Amazing Newborn
      Sensory Capabilities and Perceptual Preferences
      Reflexes and Learning
   Physical Development
      The Young Brain
      Environmental and Cultural Influences
   Cognitive Development
      Piaget's Stage Model
         Sensorimotor Stage
         Preoperational Stage
         Concrete Operational Stage
         Formal Operational Stage
      Assessing Piaget's Theory: Stages, Ages, and Culture
      The Social Context of Cognitive Development
      Information-Processing Approaches
         Information-Search Strategies
         Processing Speed, Attention, and Response Inhibition
         Working Memory and Long-Term Memory
         Metacognition
      Understanding the Physical World
      Theory of Mind: Understanding Mental States
   Social-Emotional and Personality Development
      Early Emotions and Emotion Regulation
      Temperament
      What Do You Think? Shy Child, Shy Adult?
      Erikson's Psychosocial Theory
      Attachment
         The Attachment Process
         Types of Attachment
      Attachment Deprivation
      The Day-Care Controversy
     Applying Psychological Science: Understanding How Divorce and Remarriage Affect Children
      Styles of Parenting
      Parenting-Heredity Interactions
      Gender Identity and Socialization
   Moral Development

      Moral Thinking
      Culture, Gender, and Moral Reasoning
      Moral Behavior and Conscience
   In Review
ADOLESCENCE AND ADULTHOOD
   Physical Development
      Puberty
      The Adolescent Brain
      Physical Development in Adulthood
      The Adult Brain
   Cognitive Development
      Reasoning and Information Processing in Adolescence
      Information Processing in Adulthood
      Intellectual Changes in Adulthood
   Beneath the Surface: Aging and Mental Ability: Use it or Lose it?
      The Growth of Wisdom
      Cognitive Impairment in Old Age
   Social Development
      Adolescents' Search for Identity
      Relationships with Parents and Peers
      Emotional Changes in Adolescence
      The Transition to Adulthood
   Research Close-Up: What Does It Take to Become an Adult?
      Stages versus Critical Events in Adulthood
      Marriage and Family
      What Do You Think? Cohabitation as a "Trial Marriage"
      Establishing a Career
      Midlife Crisis: Fact or Fiction?
      Retirement and the "Golden Years"
      Death and Dying
   In Review

D. Review at a Glance: *Write the term that best fits the blank to review what you learned in this chapter.*

Major Issues and Methods

Developmental psychologists examine changes that occur as we age. A (1) _____ _____ is an age range during which certain experiences must occur for development to proceed normally. A (2) _____ period is an optimal age range for certain experiences. Developmental psychologists use (3)_____-_____ designs, which compare people of different cohorts at the same time; (4)_____ designs, which repeatedly test the same people as they grow older; and (5)_____ designs, which combine the cross-sectional and longitudinal approaches.

Prenatal Development

A fertilized egg is known as a (6) _____. From the second through the eighth week after conception, the cell mass is called a(n) (7)_____, and after that the developing organism is called a (8)_____. If the (9) _____ chromosome in the father's sperm cell is an X, the child will be genetically (10) _____. Environmental influences can affect prenatal development. (11)_____ are environmental agents that can cause abnormal development, such as (12) _____ _____ _____, which results from prenatal exposure to alcohol, especially early in the pregnancy.

Infancy and Childhood

Newborn children, or neonates, are equipped with automatic, inborn behaviors, or (13) _____, that help them to respond to specific stimuli. The genetically programmed biological process that governs our growth is called (14) _____. Physical and motor development follow both the (15) _____ principle, which reflects the tendency for development to proceed in a head-to-foot direction, and the (16) _____ principle, which states that development begins on the innermost parts of the body and proceeds toward the outermost parts. The neonate's brain develops (17) _____; one of the last areas to mature is the (18) _____ _____, which is vital to our highest-level cognitive functions. Although guided and constrained by (19) _____, physical and motor development can be powerfully affected by environmental and (20) _____ influences that interact with biological factors.

Cognitive development was studied most famously by Jean (21) _____. He argued that children organize the world in terms of (22) _____. (23)_____ is the process by which new information causes existing schemas to change, and (24) _____ is the process by which new experiences are incorporated into existing schemas. Piaget suggested that children go through four distinct cognitive stages. In the (25) _____ stage, infants understand their world through their sensory experiences and movements. During this stage, an infant comes to understand that an object continues to exist even when it cannot be directly experienced, a concept Piaget called (26) _____ _____. Children enter the (27) _____ stage around the age of two and begin to represent the world symbolically through words and mental images. Preoperational children also show (28) _____, which reflects their difficulty in viewing the world from a perspective other than their own. In the (29) _____ _____ stage, children can now perform basic mental functions involving tangible objects and situations. Finally, in the (30) _____ operational stage, individuals can think abstractly and can use the hypothetico-deductive process to solve problems. Research on Piaget's theory indicates that cognitive development is more complex and (31) _____ than Piaget proposed.

(32) _____ addressed the social context of cognitive development, arguing that there is a zone of (33) _____ _____, the difference between what children can do independently and what they can do with assistance.
(34) _____-_____ approaches to cognitive development focus on changes in information-search (35) _____, information-processing (36) _____, memory capabilities, and (37) _____ as children mature. Developmental psychologists use creative techniques such as (38) _____-_____-_____ experiments to make inferences about infants' understanding of basic concepts about how the world works, and (39) _____-_____-_____ methods to study children's ability to understand other people's mental states.

Infants differ in (40) _____ and may be categorized as easy, difficult, or (41) _____-_____-_____-_____. Theorist Erik Erikson argued that social development occurs throughout the life span in eight major (42) _____ stages, each of which involves a particular crisis in how we relate to others. (43) _____ refers to the strong emotional bond that develops between children and their primary caregivers. As an infant's attachment develops, two types of anxiety occur. (44) _____ anxiety occurs first, followed by (45) _____ anxiety. A standard procedure used to measure attachment, developed by Mary Ainsworth and colleagues, is called the (46) _____ _____. Four parenting styles have been associated with different patterns of child-rearing. Controlling but warm parents are called (47) _____, whereas controlling but cold parents are called (48) _____. Parents who have warm, caring relationships with their children, but who provide little or no rules or guidance, are called (49) _____ parents, and parents who are cold toward their children and who provide little or no rules or guidance are called (50) _____ parents.

Early in life, children develop a sense of "femaleness" or "maleness" called (51) _____ _____. As gender identity develops, children acquire beliefs about characteristics and behaviors that are appropriate for girls and those that are appropriate for boys. These beliefs are known as (52) _____-_____ _____. Kohlberg's theory of moral development suggests that children proceed from a stage of morality based on anticipated punishments or rewards, called (53) _____ moral reasoning; to conformity based on social expectations, laws, and duties, called (54) _____ moral reasoning; to the highest level of moral reasoning, (55) _____ moral reasoning, which is based on general moral principles.

Adolescence and Adulthood

Adolescence begins at (56) _____, at which time hormonal secretions stimulate the development of both primary and secondary (57) _____ characteristics. During adolescence, (58) _____ but important cognitive, emotional, and social changes occur. A major goal for adolescence is the search for one's (59) _____. The rate of overall brain growth (60) _____, and a process of (61) _____ the number of synaptic connections occurs. Changes in the prefrontal cortex and (62) _____ system are especially pronounced.

People reach their peak of physical and perceptual functioning around their mid-20s, and after age (63)_____ a decline in many physical capacities becomes noticeable, including reduced muscle strength and (64)_____, basal metabolism, and (65)_____. (66)_____ loss is normal as the brain ages, even in physically and mentally healthy older adults.

Cognitive changes during adolescence can be as dramatic as the physical ones. Adolescent thinking can become highly self-focused, resulting in adolescent (67) _____. The adolescent's (68) _____-_____ abilities increase substantially, and information processing becomes more (69) _____.

In later adulthood, perceptual (70) _____, memory for new factual information, prospective memory, and (71) _____ tend to decline. Studies suggest an earlier and steadier decline in (72) _____ intelligence, compared with crystallized intelligence, throughout adulthood. (73)_____, which includes knowledge about human nature and social relationships, strategies for making decisions and handling conflict, and an ability to manage uncertainty, appears to (74)_____ steadily from early adolescence through the mid-20s and then (75)_____ _____ through the mid-70s. Dementia is most common in late adulthood and may be associated with (76) _____ disease or other causes.

Social-emotional development in adolescence is reflected in the pivotal crisis recognized by Erikson as (77) _____-_____-_____ _____. According to James Marcia, an individual's identity status at any time may be classified in terms of four categories; identity diffusion, foreclosure, (78) _____, or identity achievement. Conflict between adolescents and their (79) _____ has not been found to be as serious or as widespread as popularly believed. (80)_____ are an important factor in adolescents' lives and can exert pressure to engage in, or to avoid, misconduct.

Erikson proposed that the main crises of early, middle, and late adulthood are intimacy-versus-(81) _____, generativity-versus-stagnation, and (82) _____-versus-despair, respectively. Freud and others viewed adult social development in terms of key life events revolving around (83) _____ and working. For many couples, marital satisfaction tends to (84) _____ in the years following the birth of children. Studies find that married people experience (85) _____ subjective well-being than unmarried adults. Work serves important (86) _____ and social functions. Overall, women experience more career (87) _____, and their career paths are more variable than men's.

Research on the "midlife crisis" suggests that it is largely (88) _____ _____. Part of being human is the fact that eventually each of us will die.

Elisabeth (89) _____-_____'s pioneering work emphasized several distinct stages people work through as they approach death.

E. Concept Cards

Truly learning a concept means integrating it into the way *you* think about things. To integrate concepts successfully, you must translate the words and examples your text or instructor provides into words and examples that are meaningful to you.

For this exercise, obtain some note cards (3" × 5" or 4" × 6") to make a deck of concept cards. On one side of each card, write the *concept* from the list following (e.g., "sensitive period") at the top. Read the textbook definition provided, and then write the definition *in your own words* on the concept card (e.g., for "sensitive period," you might write "a time when you can benefit most from a particular kind of experience.") Simply imagine that a friend has asked you what the concept means, and write down what you would answer. Writing the definition in your own words requires you to think deeply about its meaning. When next you see your own version of the definition, it will make intuitive sense to you—no translation required.

On the second side of the card, write your own example of the concept. Again, coming up with your own example requires you to think deeply about the application of the concept, and you will more easily understand and remember the example when you study for a test. If you use an example from the text, or from class, make it your own by writing it in your own words. You can always check with your instructor that your example is indeed a good example of the concept.

CONCEPT Definition in my own words (side 1 of card)	Example of the concept in my own words, preferably drawn from my own experience (side 2 of card)

The following is a list of all the boldface concepts from your textbook with the author's definition. Write the definition in your own words, together with your own example of the concept, to create a *concept card* as described previously, or write in the space provided.

Critical period: An age range during which certain experiences must occur for development to proceed normally or along a certain path

Sensitive period: An optimal age range for certain experiences

Cross-sectional design: A research design that compares people of different ages at the same point in time

Longitudinal design: A research design that repeatedly tests the same cohort as it grows older

Sequential design: A research design that combines the cross-sectional and longitudinal approaches

Zygote: Fertilized egg

Embryo: A developing human from the end of week 2 through week 8 after conception

Fetus: A developing human from week 9 after conception until birth

Teratogens: External agents that cause abnormal prenatal development

Fetal alcohol syndrome (FAS): A severe group of abnormalities that result from prenatal exposure to alcohol

Reflexes: Automatic, inborn behaviors that occur in response to specific stimuli

Maturation: The genetically programmed biological process that governs our growth

Cephalocaudal principle: A principle reflecting the tendency for development to proceed in a head-to-foot direction

Proximodistal principle: A principle reflecting the tendency for development to begin along the innermost parts of the body and continue toward the outermost parts

Schemas: Organized patterns of thought and action

Assimilation: The process by which new experiences are incorporated into existing schemas

Accommodation: The process by which new experiences cause existing schemas to change

Sensorimotor stage: The stage of cognitive development in which infants understand their world primarily through sensory experiences and physical (motor) interactions with objects

Object permanence: The understanding that an object continues to exist even when it no longer can be seen

Preoperational stage: The stage of cognitive development in which children represent the world symbolically through words and mental images but do not yet understand basic mental operations or rules

Conservation: The principle that basic properties of objects, such as their volume, mass, or quantity, stay the same (are "conserved") even though their outward appearance may change

Egocentrism: The difficulty in viewing the world from someone else's perspective

Concrete operational stage: The stage of cognitive development in which children can perform basic mental operations concerning problems that involve tangible (i.e., "concrete") objects and situations

Formal operational stage: The stage of cognitive development in which individuals are able to think logically and systematically about both concrete and abstract problems, form hypotheses, and test them in a thoughtful way

Zone of proximal development: The difference between what a child can do independently and what the child can do with assistance from adults or more advanced peers

Chapter 12　　　　　　　　　　　　　　　　　　　　　　　　　　　　　　　　　357

Theory of mind: A person's beliefs about the mind and ability to understand other people's mental states

Emotion regulation: The processes by which we evaluate and modify our emotional reactions

Temperament: A biologically based general style of reacting emotionally and behaviorally to the environment

Psychosocial stages: Stages of development, each involving a different "crisis" (i.e., conflict) over how we view ourselves in relation to other people and the world

Imprinting: A sudden, biologically primed form of attachment

Attachment: The strong emotional bond that develops between children and their primary caregivers

Stranger anxiety: Distress over contact with unfamiliar people

Separation anxiety: Distress over being separated from a primary caregiver

Strange situation: A standardized procedure for examining infant attachment

Authoritative parents: Controlling but warm parents

Authoritarian parents: Parents who exert control but do so within a cold, unresponsive, or rejecting relationship

Indulgent parents: Parents who have warm, caring relationships with their children but do not provide the guidance and discipline that help children learn responsibility and concern for others

Neglectful parents: Parents who provide neither warmth nor rules nor guidance

Gender identity: A sense of "femaleness" or "maleness" that becomes a central aspect of one's personal identity

Gender constancy: The understanding that being male or female is a permanent part of a person

Sex-typing: Treating others differently based on whether they are female or male

Preconventional moral reasoning: A stage of moral reasoning based on anticipated punishments or rewards

Conventional moral reasoning: A stage of moral reasoning based on conformity to social expectations, laws, and duties

Postconventional moral reasoning: A stage of moral reasoning involving well-thought-out, general moral principles

Adolescence: The period of development and gradual transition between childhood and adulthood

Puberty: A period of rapid maturation in which the person becomes capable of sexual reproduction

Adolescent egocentrism: A self-absorbed and distorted view of one's uniqueness and importance

Senile dementia: Dementia that begins after age 65

F. What's the Difference? A Concept Card Exercise

An important skill in learning concepts is being able to differentiate among concepts that are similar or related in some way. This skill is particularly relevant for multiple-choice tests, especially if you often find yourself wavering between two answers.

Once you have created your own deck of concept cards, select them two by two, each time answering the question "What's the difference between these two concepts?" You can use the word definitions of the concepts or the examples of the concepts to enhance your mastery of the material. In each case, choose pairs of concepts to compare those that are related or similar or that sound the same or that could in some way be confused. It's much easier to spot the difference between two concepts when you are studying, with the textbook available, rather than when considering the question for the first time in a testing situation.

G. Apply What You Know

1. Find four children who, according to their ages, should be in four different Piagetian cognitive stages. Observe their behavior, and interview them to determine what behaviors and thoughts correspond to those suggested by Piaget as appropriate for that particular stage. Determine some behaviors and thoughts that don't correspond to what Piaget believed.

Supporting   **Not Supporting**

Sensorimotor

Preoperational

Concrete Operational

Formal Operational

2. Erikson's psychosocial model provides a framework within which to better understand yourself and other people. Find out more about Erikson's theory (find a book, or search the Internet). For each of Erikson's stages following, write down the name of an individual you know who would fit into that category, plus a concise description of what Erikson's theory would lead you to believe of that person, or what behavior to expect from that person. Include yourself as a subject. Observe, interact with, or interview your subjects, as appropriate, and record your observations.

Which behaviors and thoughts were in accordance with Erikson's model, and which were not? What did you learn from your subjects, or about them or yourself, or about human development from doing this assignment? Was Erikson's model helpful? Were there other models in this chapter that were useful to you in analyzing your results?

Infancy: Birth to 18 months
Name:_____
Basic trust vs. basic mistrust

Early Childhood: 18 Months to 3 Years
Name:_____
Autonomy vs. shame and doubt

Play Age: 3 to 5 Years
Name:_____
Initiative vs. guilt

School Age: 6 to 12 Years
Name:_____
Industry vs. inferiority

Adolescence: 12 to 18 Years
   Name:_____
Identity vs. role confusion

Young adulthood: 18 to 35
   Name:_____
Intimacy vs. isolation

Middle Adulthood: 35 to 55 or 65
   Name:_____
Generativity vs. stagnation

Late Adulthood: 55 or 65 to Death
   Name:_____
Integrity vs. despair

H. On the Web: *As with any online research, it is important to consider how legitimate a given source is before you rely on the information it presents. Your instructor or Internet adviser may give you some specific guidelines for distinguishing which kinds of Web sites tend to be reputable.*

A. A number of individuals have made notable contributions to our understanding of development over the life span. Search the Web for more information about some of those listed.

Mary Ainsworth

Diana Baumrind

Chapter 12 363

John Bowlby

Erik Erikson

G. Stanley Hall

Lawrence Kohlberg

Elisabeth Kübler-Ross

Bernice Neugarten

Jean Piaget

K. Warner Schaie

Alexander Thomas and Stella Chess

Lev Vygotsky

B. Take a look at the concept cards you have created for this chapter, or the key concepts listed in section E. In the space provided, make a list of any whose definitions or associations you are not yet confident of and any you'd like to learn more about. Try entering the terms on your list into your search engine. Make notes of any helpful information you find.

Key Concept/Information Found

C. Explore several Web sites devoted to the study or promotion of child development, including

- Society for Research in Child Development
- Child Development Institute
- Foundation for Child Development
- Children's Defense Fund
- National Institute of Child Health and Human Development (of the National Institutes of Health)

Make notes on the resources you find at these sites and their usefulness for (a) psychologists and other professionals and (b) parents and other caregivers.

I. Analyze This: *Chapter 1 of your textbook begins by presenting these four basic steps in the critical thinking process:*
- *"What exactly are you asking me to believe?"*

Chapter 12

- *"How do you know? What is the evidence?"*
- *"Are there other possible explanations?"*
- *"What is the most reasonable conclusion?"*

You might picture this as a four-step analysis to help you decide whether to accept a given theory or assertion. Now it's your turn to put your textbook to this test.

Review the section in Chapter 12 of your textbook under the heading "Social-Emotional and Personality Development," paying particular attention to the subsection "Styles of Parenting." If someone told you that the authoritative style, in which parents are controlling and warm, is better than any other style of parenting, would you agree? Analyze that assertion in the space following. When you have finished, consider using this four-step analysis to evaluate other assertions you encounter.

"What exactly are you asking me to believe?"

"How do you know? What is the evidence?"

"Are there other possible explanations?"

"What is the most reasonable conclusion?"

J. Practice Test

Multiple-Choice Items: *Write the letter corresponding to your answer in the space to the left of each item.*

_____ 1. In developmental research, a(n)_____ period is an age range during which specific experiences must take place if normal development is to occur. This is in contrast to a(n)_____ period, where it is optimal although not necessarily essential for these experiences to occur.
   a. sensitive; optimal
   b. critical; receptive
   c. critical; sensitive
   d. explicit; sensitive

_____ 2. A self-esteem researcher is interested in how self-esteem varies across the life span and decides to conduct a survey comparing people of different ages to address this issue. He recruits participants to be in one of four different age groups (20 to 29, 30 to 39, 40 to 49, 50 to 59), has them complete a self-esteem survey, and then analyzes the data to see if any patterns emerge. This study would be considered an example of a ____ design.
   a. longitudinal
   b. double-blind
   c. cross-sectional
   d. sequential

_____ 3. The neonate's brain ____.
   a. is virtually completely developed at birth
   b. develops very rapidly between birth and 6 months of age
   c. develops gradually from birth to 2 years of age
   d. does not start rapid development until puberty

_____ 4. Piaget differs from the information-processing theorists regarding children's cognitive development in that Piaget's theory is based on ____ development whereas information-processing theory is based on ____ development.
   a. sensitive-period; schema
   b. schema; sensitive-period
   c. discontinuous; continuous
   d. continuous; discontinuous

_____ 5. According to ____, people go through eight major psychosocial stages in life. The stages encountered in childhood are (1) basic trust versus basic mistrust, (2) autonomy versus shame and doubt, (3) initiative versus guilt, and (4) industry versus inferiority.
   a. Erik Erikson
   b. Jean Piaget
   c. Lawrence Kohlberg
   d. Mary Ainsworth

_____ 6. ____ refers to the strong emotional bond that develops between human children and their primary caregivers. Its creation appears to be governed by a ____ period because it is most easily established during the first 2 years of a child's life.
   a. Attachment; sensitive
   b. Attachment; critical
   c. Imprinting; sensitive
   d. Imprinting; critical

_____ 7. _____ anxiety refers to how young toddlers become upset when they are apart from their primary caregivers, a stage that appears to follow _____ patterns in different cultures.
   a. Stranger; similar
   b. Separation; similar
   c. Stranger; different
   d. Separation; different

_____ 8. Nguyen is participating in an attachment experiment involving the strange situation. When his mother is present with the stranger, Nguyen explores the room and is friendly with the stranger. However, when the mother leaves, he becomes upset and starts to cry. When she returns, Nguyen happily greets her and then returns to his previous explorations. Nguyen would most likely be classified as a(n) _____ child.
   a. resistant-avoidant
   b. anxious-resistant
   c. anxious-avoidant
   d. securely attached

_____ 9. A couple with three children are considering divorce but are wondering if they should remain together for the sake of their children. Research suggests that the most important factor that they should take into consideration is _____.
   a. how old the children are
   b. how long they have been married
   c. the degree of conflict in their relationship
   d. whether adultery is involved

_____ 10. Ned is growing up in a family where his parents provide him with a great deal of warmth, and he feels that he has very close relationships with both of his parents. In terms of discipline, his parents are relatively lax and allow him to do as he pleases. Ned is somewhat immature and self-centered. Diana Baumrind would most likely classify Ned's parents as using a(n) _____ parenting style.
   a. tolerant
   b. indulgent
   c. lenient
   d. liberal

_____ 11. A father of a large family believes that certain behaviors are more appropriate for boys than for girls and tells his sons and daughters so. His wife observes that he tends to use more verbal and physical prohibition with his sons than he does with his daughters. In this family, the father's beliefs would be examples of _____, whereas the fact that he treats his children differently depending on their sex demonstrates the concept of _____.
   a. gender identities; gender constancies
   b. sex-role stereotypes; gender preferences

c. sex-role stereotypes; sex-typing
d. gender identities; sex-typing

_____ 12. Piaget was one of the first to suggest that children actively interpret information about their environments. They likely do this through the processes of _____ and _____.
a. accommodation; assimilation
b. moral development; accommodation
c. object permanence; assimilation
d. developing an anxious style of attachment; developing a zone of proximal development

_____ 13. Ray and Kira dropped out of college to get married. They are both working at low-wage jobs and are barely getting by. Their child, Kasey, spends several hours in day care Monday through Friday. Ray studied psychology in college and says that the ____ is likely to be a key determinant of Kasey's social adjustment and academic performance.
a. involvement of grandparents
b. ratio of caregivers to children at the day care center
c. consistency and punctuality of being dropped off at and picked up from day care
d. quality of their family interactions

_____ 14. People who develop a secure attachment style when they are infants tend to have better adult romantic relationships (e.g., Hazan & Shaver, 1987; Collins & Read, 1990). This is most likely because of a positive resolution of the _____ developmental conflict.
a. trust-versus-mistrust
b. generativity-versus-stagnation
c. identity-versus–role confusion
d. integrity-versus-despair

_____ 15. Vygotsky believed that cognitive development depends on_____.
a. a series of discrete stages
b. the people in a child's world and the tools the culture provides to support thinking
c. the learning of language
d. children being allowed to learn on their own without assistance

_____ 16. In Kohlberg's "Heinz's dilemma," the aspect of a person's response that indicates his or her level of moral reasoning is _____.
a. the reason the person gives for why Heinz was, or was not, right to steal the drug
b. whether the person thinks Heinz was right to steal the drug
c. whether the person thinks the druggist was right to charge so much

d. the reason the person gives for why Heinz could not raise the rest of the necessary money

_____ 17. Jill believes that you shouldn't steal because you might be caught and punished. At which stage of Kohlberg's moral reasoning is Jill functioning?
a. postconventional
b. conventional
c. preconventional
d. conservative

_____ 18. By definition, adolescence begins at _____.
a. the time a child gets his or her first job
b. puberty
c. the initial development of primary sex characteristics
d. hormonal sensitization of brain structures

_____ 19. Adolescents' overestimation of their uniqueness and their feeling of being "on stage" are part of Elkind's notion of _____.
a. adolescent egocentrism
b. intimacy versus isolation
c. the psychosocial stage theory
d. identity diffusion

_____ 20. In what way does the brain change during adolescence?
a. brain growth speeds up rapidly compared with childhood
b. pruning of synaptic connections results in more focused neural activity in the brain
c. the prefrontal cortex and the limbic system stop developing
d. brain size increases dramatically

_____ 21. According to the research, the majority of adolescents _____.
a. have stormy relationships with their parents
b. are too involved with their peers to maintain a relationship with their parents
c. maintain positive relationships with their parents
d. are influenced by their peers in negative but not in positive ways

_____ 22. Eleanor is in her eighties. She often forgets who she was talking to on the phone within a few minutes after she hangs up and is unable to understand what a Web site is when her son sits her down at a computer and tries to explain it to her. However, when her son wants to buy flooring that is sold by the square yard and he knows only the square footage of the room, Eleanor tells him to divide the square footage by 9, as she was taught in school. Eleanor's _____ is apparently still functioning well.
a. short-term memory
b. fluid memory

c. crystallized memory
d. perceptual-motor ability

_____ 23. Your grandmother is just about to celebrate her 77th birthday. According to results from studies examining information-processing changes that occur with age, which of the following cognitive skills would you expect to be easiest for your grandmother?
   a. using new information
   b. memorizing a list of items
   c. remembering familiar information
   d. processing information speedily

_____ 24. Studies indicate that most people who retire _____ very likely to become anxious, depressed, or lonely. The risks that are associated with retirement become more likely when the retirement is _____.
   a. are not; involuntary
   b. are not; voluntary
   c. are; involuntary
   d. are; voluntary

_____ 25. The popular idea of a midlife crisis in the early to mid-40s _____.
   a. has been strongly supported by subsequent research
   b. has not been supported by subsequent research
   c. has been supported by subsequent research for men but not for women
   d. has been supported by subsequent research for women but not for men

_____ 26. As people age, _____.
   a. loss of brain tissue is normal
   b. crystallized intelligence tends to decline
   c. fluid intelligence is usually maintained
   d. perceptual speed tends to increase

_____ 27. Which of the following statements is correct about wisdom as studied by psychologists?
   a. Throughout our lives, as we age we become "older but wiser".
   b. The definition of wisdom includes the ability to handle uncertainty.
   c. Wisdom is defined as the combination of fluid and crystallized intelligence.
   d. Wisdom characterizes a person in James Marcia's "moratorium" identity status.

_____ 28. According to the material reviewed in your textbook, wisdom _____.
   a. increases steadily from early adolescence through the mid-20s
   b. increases steadily from the mid-20s through the 70s
   c. levels off after adolescence
   d. is greatest after age 80

_____ 29. Which is the main crisis of late adulthood according to Erikson?
   a. intimacy versus isolation
   b. integrity versus despair
   c. generativity versus stagnation
   d. trust versus mistrust

_____ 30. Melinda has undergone a series of procedures that resulted in a diagnosis of advanced ovarian cancer. Treatments are available that may prolong her life, but her chances of surviving for more than a year are slim. Melinda is determined to follow the treatment regimen faithfully, modify her diet, and meditate daily, so that she will stay healthy enough to attend her son's graduation next year. According to Elisabeth Kübler-Ross, Melinda is experiencing the ____ stage.
   a. bargaining
   b. acceptance
   c. anger
   d. denial

True/False Items: *Write T or F in the space provided to the left of each item.*

_____ 1. A critical period is an age range during which certain experiences must occur for development to proceed normally.

_____ 2. A longitudinal design is used to compare people of different ages at the same point in time.

_____ 3. Smoking during pregnancy is an example of a teratogen.

_____ 4. Neonates prefer complex and facelike patterns to simpler ones.

_____ 5. According to Piaget, assimilation is the process by which new experiences cause existing schemas to change.

_____ 6. Kohlberg's critics claim that his theory is culturally and gender biased.

_____ 7. Wisdom represents a system of knowledge about the meaning and conduct of life.

_____ 8. Adolescence is a time of rapidly increasing growth of the brain.

_____ 9. Studies suggest an earlier decline in fluid intelligence compared with crystallized intelligence as we age.

_____ 10. Research into the relationships between adolescents and their parents has found that "storm and stress" is the rule rather than the exception.

Short-Answer Questions

1. What is object permanence?

2. What is the zone of proximal development?

3. What are the basic propositions of attachment theory?

4. What changes in cognitive development are hypothesized to take place in adolescence?

5. What intellectual changes occur in adulthood?

Essay Questions

1. Imagine that you are a participant in a longitudinal study which began when you were very young—around age 5 or 6 for example. For purposes of this essay, identify a question or phenomenon that the study is examining, and report how your development progressed with regard to the question of interest. For example, if the study examined relationships with same-sex peers, how might your peer relationships have been described when you were, respectively, 6, 8, 10, 12, 14, and 16 years old?

2. Explain what an enriched environment is and how it contributes to an infant's development. How would you recommend that low-income parents who cannot afford many toys provide an enriched environment for their infants?

3. How well do you get along with your parents? Considering what you have learned in this chapter about parenting and parent-child relationships, are there aspects of your upbringing that you think your parents could have handled better than they did? Do you think you have the ability to do a better job of parenting children in their formative years than your parents did? Explain and give specifics.

Answer Keys

Answer Key for Review at a Glance

1. critical period
2. sensitive
3. cross-sectional
4. longitudinal
5. sequential
6. zygote
7. embryo
8. fetus
9. 23rd
10. female
11. Teratogens
12. fetal alcohol syndrome
13. reflexes
14. maturation
15. cephalocaudal
16. proximodistal
17. rapidly
18. prefrontal cortex
19. genetics
20. cultural
21. Piaget
22. schemas

46. strange situation
47. authoritative
48. authoritarian
49. indulgent
50. neglectful
51. gender identity
52. sex-role stereotypes
53. preconventional
54. conventional
55. postconventional
56. puberty
57. sex
58. gradual
59. identity
60. slows
61. pruning
62. limbic
63. 40
64. flexibility
65. fertility
66. Tissue
67. egocentrism

23. Accommodation
24. assimilation
25. sensorimotor
26. object permanence
27. preoperational
28. egocentrism
29. concrete operational
30. formal
31. varied
32. Vygotsky
33. proximal development
34. Information-processing
35. strategies
36. speed
37. metacognition
38. violation-of-expectation
39. theory-of-mind
40. temperament
41. slow-to-warm-up
42. psychosocial
43. Attachment
44. Stranger
45. separation

68. information-processing
69. efficient
70. speed
71. recall
72. fluid
73. Wisdom
74. increase
75. levels off
76. Alzheimer's
77. identity-versus-role confusion
78. moratorium
79. parents
80. Peers
81. isolation
82. integrity
83. loving
84. decline
85. greater
86. psychological
87. gaps
88. a myth
89. Kubler-Ross

Answer Key for Practice Test Multiple-Choice Items

1. c
2. c
3. b
4. c
5. a
6. a
7. b
8. d
9. c
10. b
11. c
12. a
13. d
14. a
15. b
16. a
17. c
18. b
19. a
20. b
21. c
22. c
23. c
24. a
25. b
26. a
27. b
28. a
29. b
30. a

Answer Key for Practice Test True/False Items

1. T
2. F
3. T
4. T
5. F
6. T
7. T
8. F
9. T
10. F

Answer Key for Practice Test Short-Answer Questions

1. Object permanence is the belief that children develop during the sensorimotor stage of cognitive development that an object continues to exist even when it can no longer be seen.

2. Zygotsky's idea of the zone of proximal development is the difference between what a child can do independently and what he or she can do with some assistance. Thus, a child may be able to do more than someone thinks he or she can, if some help is given.

3. Attachment refers to the strong emotional bond that develops between children and their primary caregivers, and it develops in three phases. Secure attachment is associated with better developmental outcomes than is insecure attachment.

4. There are several cognitive changes that occur in adolescence. Piaget proposed that adolescents acquire formal operational thinking which is characterized by more abstract and hypothetical thought. Elkind (1978) proposed that adolescents engage in adolescent egocentrism which involves an overestimation of the uniqueness of one's feelings and experiences and a feeling of being "on stage."

5. Fluid intelligence typically begins to decline at an earlier age than crystallized intelligence according to a recent large study which provides both cross-sectional and longitudinal data. Earlier cross-sectional research suggested that fluid intelligence begins to decline in early adulthood, whereas crystallized intelligence peaks during middle adulthood and declines after that. Poorer perceptual speed, memory, vision, and hearing may contribute to the intellectual declines commonly found in late adulthood. Some findings suggest that wisdom, or knowledge about the meaning and conduct of life, rises steadily from age 13 to 25 and then remains relatively stable until about age 75. Regular physical exercise and mentally stimulating activities may help to preserve cognitive abilities as we age.

Answer Key for Practice Test Essay Questions

As you may have guessed, there are no right or wrong answers to the essay questions in this practice test. That does not mean, however, that all essays are equally good. To get maximum learning benefit from the essay questions, do the following:

- Review each essay a day or two after you wrote it, noting any necessary corrections and any additional support for your points that you can think of.
- Review the section in your textbook that pertains to the topic of each essay. Annotate your essay with any corrections or additional support for your points that you find in the text.
- Spend a few minutes researching the topic of each essay on the Internet. Annotate your essay further with any additional (reliable) information you find.
- Finally, reread each essay with the annotations you have added.

Chapter 13
PERSONALITY

A. Learning Objectives: *These objectives are expanded from the Focus Questions found in the margins of your textbook. When you have mastered the material in this chapter, you will be able to:*

13.1   Describe three characteristics of personality, and explain the usefulness of personality theories.

13.2   Discuss the three standards that determine the scientific usefulness of a personality theory.

13.3   Describe Freud's structures of personality, their operating principles, and how they interact with one another.

13.4   Describe the roles and conflicts among the id, ego, and superego, and explain the role that defense mechanisms and psychosexual development play in Freud's theory.

13.5   Describe how neo-analytic and object relations theories both depart from and build on Freudian theory.

13.6   Define object relations, and describe three adult attachment types.

13.7   Describe personal constructs and how they account for personality differences.

13.8   Describe the roles of self-consistency, congruence, threat, and conditions of worth in Rogers' self theory.

13.9   Describe how self-esteem develops, and describe the roles of self-verification and self-enhancement in motivation.

13.10 Describe research on the maintenance of self-esteem.

13.11 Describe and compare the two models of personality derived from factor analysis.

13.12 Describe the stability of personality traits across time and situation, and the factors that decrease consistency across situations.

13.13 Describe the findings of twin studies on the roles of heredity and environment in personality development.

13.14 Describe the biological factors that underlie Eysenck's extraversion-stability model and the behaviors of inhibited children and adults.

13.15 Describe the major features of social-cognitive theories and the importance of reciprocal determinism.

13.16 Describe Rotter's concepts of expectancy, reinforcement value, and locus of control.

13.17 Describe the four determinants of self-efficacy, and indicate which procedures in goal setting help enhance self-efficacy.

13.18 Summarize the procedures for successful goal setting.

13.19 Describe the five variables that constitute Mischel and Shoda's Cognitive-Affective Personality System (CAPS).

13.20 Describe how the concept of behavioral signatures helps reconcile the paradox of personality coherence and behavioral inconsistency.

13.21 Describe three ways cultures differ in influencing personality, and describe the personality and gender differences common to individualistic versus collectivistic cultures.

13.22 Describe the two characteristics that personality measures must have in order to be scientifically useful.

13.23 Describe how interviews, behavioral assessment, and remote behavioral sampling are used to measure personality variables.

13.24 Compare the rational-theoretical and empirical approaches to developing personality roles.

13.25 Describe how projective tests differ from objective tests, and describe two projective tests.

B. Chapter Overview

This chapter explores the various ways in which psychologists have attempted to define and describe personality. Personality refers to the distinctive and relatively enduring ways of thinking, feeling, and acting that characterize a person's responses to life situations. These characteristic responses distinguish people from one another, they are caused primarily by internal rather than external factors, and they have organization and structure, from which the inner personality is inferred.

Freud believed strongly that unconscious processes and psychic energy are motivators of behavior. Freud's structural theory of personality suggests that three interacting structures (id, ego, and superego) form the core of personality. The id operates according to the pleasure principle, seeking immediate gratification for its sexual and aggressive impulses. The ego, operating primarily at a conscious level, operates according to the reality principle, finding ways that the id can safely discharge its impulses. The superego is the moral arm of personality and strives to check the desires of the id. Freud believed that the interaction among all three structures of personality, along with the release of psychic energy, not only motivated behavior but also could cause anxiety unless the three structures of personality work together in harmony. The ego uses defense mechanisms, such as repression, to deal with anxiety.

Freud proposed a series of psychosexual stages through which children develop. Sexual pleasure is focused on different parts of the body during these stages (oral, anal, phallic, latency, and genital). Freud's theory has been and continues to be controversial. Freud's opposition to experimental research, and reliance on case studies and clinical observations, made his ideas difficult to evaluate scientifically. Much research fails to support the basic suppositions of Freud's theory, but some does point to the importance of the unconscious in motivating behavior. Former Freudian disciples who grew disenchanted with Freudian theory developed their own theories and, as a group, became known as the neoanalysts. These theorists suggested that social and cultural factors play a far more important role in the development of personality than Freud had believed, and argued that Freud had placed too much importance on childhood events. Another important offshoot of Freudian theory is object relations theory, which focuses on the mental representations that people form of themselves, others, and relationships. Recent research on attachment theory, derived from object relations theory, suggests that different styles of attachment are associated with adjustment and well-being.

Phenomenological-humanistic psychologists emphasize that people's behavior is a response to their immediate conscious experience of self and the environment, and that everyone has an inborn striving toward personal growth. George Kelly viewed human beings as akin to scientists in their quest to make sense of the world. His theory of personal constructs proposes that each individual perceives, categorizes, and assigns meaning to the stimuli experienced, thereby developing a unique perspective on life and associated response tendencies. Kelly's Role Construct Repertory Test ("Rep Test") is a measure designed to capture how different people construe the world on the basis of their unique and interrelated categories, and he devised fixed-role therapy as a technique for helping clients experiment with new viewpoints and behaviors.

The self is a key concept in the humanistic theory of Carl Rogers, who emphasized the importance for psychological health of consistency among our various self-concepts, as well as congruence between our self-perceptions and our experience. People strive toward self-actualization, the highest realization of human potential, unless thwarted by the environment. Inconsistency and incongruence create threat and anxiety, thus impeding self-actualization. Unconditional positive regard, or unqualified acceptance from others as well as from oneself, facilitates self-actualization. Conditional positive regard, which means that others give us approval only if we behave or think in ways that they approve of, can be detrimental. Research on the self has pointed to the importance of self-esteem, or positive self-evaluation, for healthy functioning. People are motivated to confirm their self-concept, called self-verification, as well as to regard themselves positively, called self-enhancement. Some people with low self-esteem may perceive themselves in ways that tend to verify their negative self-image.

Personality traits are relatively stable cognitive, emotional, and behavioral characteristics of people that help establish their individual identities and distinguish them from others. Trait theorists try to identify and measure the basic dimensions of personality. Factor analysis is a statistical technique often used to identify highly correlated clusters of behavior, constituting a dimension along which people may vary. Two prominent factor analytic models are Cattell's 16 personality factors theory and the 5-factor ("Big Five") model, which, not surprisingly, posit 16 and 5 basic personality factors respectively. One challenge to the trait perspective is the question of how stable or inconsistent personality is, and people differ in their tendency to tailor their behavior to what is called for by the situation, called self-monitoring. Personality traits also interact with one another in a variety of ways, and situational factors influence behavior as well.

Biological explanations for traits focus on three different causes: evolution (discussed in a previous chapter), genes, and the activity of the nervous system. A genetic basis for personality traits is suggested by a body of twin studies that show monozygotic twins to be far more alike in personality than dizygotic twins. One of the first modern theorists to suggest a biological basis for major personality traits was Hans Eysenck, who explained normal personality differences on the dimensions of Introversion/Extraversion and Stability/Instability in terms of patterns of arousal within the brain. Studies of brain activity have provided some support for Eysenck's ideas, and have indicated specifically which brain areas may be involved. Studies of temperament, which appear early in life and show some stability across the lifespan, also suggest that biologically based differences may underlie personality development.

Social-cognitive theories approach personality as an interaction between the thinking human and a social environment that provides learning experiences. According to Bandura's principle of reciprocal determinism, person factors (including personality and cognitive processes), the environment, and behavior all affect one another. Julian Rotter argued that the likelihood that we will engage in a certain behavior is governed by expectancy and how much we desire or dread the expected outcome of our behavior. *Locus of control* is a term that Rotter devised to refer to the degree to which we believe that internal or external factors control our life. Bandura has suggested that self-efficacy, or beliefs about one's ability to perform specific tasks, strongly affects how people regulate their lives. Performance experiences, observational learning, emotional arousal, and verbal persuasion all affect one's sense of self-efficacy. Goal setting is effective in improving self-efficacy if the goals are specific, behavioral, difficult but realistic, positive, oriented to both the short and long term, and time-bound.

Mischel and Shoda have described a five-variable cognitive-affective personality system (CAPS) in which the dynamic interplay among the five person factors and the responsive environment results in distinctive behavioral signatures, or characteristic patterns of individual responses to various situations. The important five factors are the person's encoding strategies, expectancies and beliefs, goals and values, affects (emotions), and self-regulatory processes and competencies. Research suggests that although individual behaviors are often inconsistent when analyzed at the level of broad traits, personality is substantially more coherent at the level of behavioral signatures, or person-by-situation interactions.

Cultures differ along dimensions such as complexity, tightness, and individualism-collectivism, all of which can affect personality development. Collectivist cultures tend to see the environment as fixed and people as having a capacity to "fit in." In contrast, individualist cultures tend to see people and their personalities as stable and the environment as malleable. People from individualist cultures tend to describe themselves in terms of personal traits, abilities, or dispositions, whereas those from collectivist cultures are more likely to describe themselves in social identity terms. Gender schemas are organized mental structures of the attributes we see as appropriate for males and females. In Western cultures, men tend to value achievement, emotional strength, and self-sufficiency, whereas women prize interpersonal skills, kindness, and helpfulness to others.

Personality assessment is accomplished through various means, including interviews, behavioral assessment, personality scales, and projective tests. In behavioral assessment, psychologists observe behaviors and tie them to elaborate coding systems. Remote behavior sampling uses pagers to assess participants' thoughts, feelings, or behaviors at random intervals. Objective personality scales, such as the NEO Personality Inventory (NEO-PI) and Minnesota Multiphasic Personality Inventory, follow the rational-theoretical and empirical approaches, respectively. The rational-theoretical approach refers to developing test items based on the theorist's conception of the personality trait to be measured, whereas the empirical approach involves choosing items based on their having been answered differently by different known groups, such as introverts and extraverts. Projective tests, such as the Rorschach inkblot test and the Thematic Apperception Test, are tests of interpretations of ambiguous stimuli. People's responses to the stimuli are thought by some psychologists to be "projections" of inner needs, feelings, and ways of viewing the world.

C. Chapter Outline

WHAT IS PERSONALITY?
    In Review
THE PSYCHODYNAMIC PERSPECTIVE
    Freud's Psychoanalytic Theory
        Psychic Energy and Mental Events
        The Structure of Personality

Conflict, Anxiety, and Defense
Psychosexual Development
Neoanalytic and Object Relations Approaches
Adult Attachment Styles
Research Close-Up: Attachment Style and Abusive Romantic Relationships
Evaluating the Psychodynamic Approach
Understanding Charles Whitman
In Review

THE PHENOMENOLOGICAL-HUMANISTIC PERSPECTIVE
George Kelly's Personal Construct Theory
Carl Rogers's Theory of the Self
The Self
The Need for Positive Regard
Fully Functioning Persons
What Do You Think? Is Self-Actualization a Useful Scientific Construct?
Research on the Self
Self-Esteem
Self-Verification and Self-Enhancement Motives
Evaluating the Phenomenological-Humanistic Approach
Understanding Charles Whitman
In Review

THE TRAIT PERSPECTIVE: MAPPING THE STRUCTURE OF PERSONALITY
Factor Analytic Approaches
Cattell's Sixteen Personality Factors
The Five Factor Model
Stability of Personality Traits over Time
Beneath the Surface: How Consistent Is Our Behavior across Situations?
Evaluating the Trait Approach
Understanding Charles Whitman
In Review

BIOLOGICAL FOUNDATIONS OF PERSONALITY
Genetics and Personality
Personality and the Nervous System
Eysenck's Extraversion-Stability Model
Temperament: Building Blocks of Personality
Evaluating the Biological Approach
Understanding Charles Whitman
In Review

BEHAVIORAL AND SOCIAL COGNITIVE THEORIES
Julian Rotter: Expectancy, Reinforcement Value, and Locus of Control
Locus of Control
Albert Bandura: Social Learning and Self-Efficacy
Self-Efficacy
Applying Psychological Science: Increasing Self-Efficacy through Systematic Goal Setting
Walter Mischel and Yuichi Shoda: The Cognitive-Affective Personality System

Chapter 13

      Encodings and Personal Constructs
      Expectancies and Beliefs
      Goals and Values
      Affects (Emotions)
      Competencies and Self-Regulatory Processes
    Reconciling Personality Coherence with Behavioral Inconsistency
    Evaluating Social Cognitive Theories
      Understanding Charles Whitman
    In Review
CULTURE, GENDER, AND PERSONALITY
    Culture Differences
    Gender Schemas
    In Review
PERSONALITY ASSESSMENT
    Interviews
    Behavioral Assessment
    Remote Behavior Sampling
    Personality Scales
    Projective Tests
    In Review

D. Review at a Glance: *Write the term that best fits the blank to review what you learned in this chapter.*

What Is Personality?

Personality refers to the relatively (1) _____ and (2) _____ ways in which a person thinks, feels, and behaves in response to life situations. The inner personality can't be observed directly, so it must be (3) _____.

The Psychodynamic Perspective

According to Freud, instinctual drives generate (4) _____ _____, which powers the mind and presses for release. Freud divided the personality into three separate but interacting structures. The (5) _____ exists totally within the unconscious mind and operates according to the (6) _____ principle. The (7) _____ operates primarily at a conscious level, testing reality and trying to satisfy the id's desires in appropriate ways, according to the (8) _____ _____. The moral arm of personality is called the (9) _____. As the personality involves a dynamic interaction between all three personality structures, anxiety may occur if they do not work in harmony. The ego may resort to (10) _____ _____, which distort reality to protect the person from experiencing anxiety. For example, in (11) _____, the ego uses some of its energy to prevent anxiety-provoking memories, feelings, and impulses from entering consciousness. Another technique the ego uses is (12) _____, by which taboo impulses are channeled into socially desirable and admirable behaviors.

Freud believed that much of adult personality structure is set during childhood. He proposed that children pass through five (13) _____ stages of development: oral, (14) _____, phallic, (15) _____, and genital. During the (16) _____ stage, boys sexually desire their mothers but fear castration by their fathers, resulting in the (17) _____ _____. Girls, similarly, desire their fathers sexually but fear their mothers' response, resulting in the (18) _____ _____. Successful resolution of these complexes leads to (19) _____ with the same-sex parent, according to Freud.

(20) _____-Freudians, who broke away from Freudian theory, developed their own ideas about personality. In his analytic theory, Carl Jung, for example, believed that all humans have a (21) _____ _____ that consists of memories accumulated throughout the entire history of the human race. These memories are represented as (22) _____, inherited tendencies to interpret experiences in certain ways. (23) _____ _____ theorists believe that early experiences with caregivers influence the images that people form of themselves and of others. Recent research suggests that different styles of (24) _____ with early caregivers are associated with adjustment and well-being.

The Phenomenological-Humanistic Perspective

Humanistic psychologists believe that humans are motivated to realize their full potential, a process called (25) _____-_____. They believe that we have a tendency to maintain our self-concept after it is established and thus have a need for an absence of conflict among self-perceptions, or (26) _____-_____, and a need for consistency between self-perceptions and experience, or (27) _____.

George Kelly viewed human beings as akin to (28) _____ in their quest to make sense of the world. His theory of (29) _____ _____ proposes that each individual develops a (30) _____ way of looking at the world. Kelly devised the (31) _____ Test to elicit an individual's personal constructs; he also developed (32) _____-_____ therapy as a technique for helping clients experiment with new viewpoints and behaviors.

Carl Rogers believed that we are born with an innate need for (33) _____ _____—that is, for acceptance, sympathy, and love from others. (34) _____ _____ _____ from parents communicates to a child that he or she is inherently worthy of love. However, when other people withhold approval unless an individual thinks or acts in a certain way, they have placed (35) _____ of worth on that individual. Rogers referred to people who had achieved self-actualization as (36) _____ _____ persons. Research on the self has shown that how positively or negatively we feel about ourselves, or our sense of

(37) _____-_____, has important implications for our lives. The proposition that people are motivated to preserve their self-concept and maintain their self-consistency and congruence is called (38) _____-_____. Processes used to gain and maintain a positive self-image are called (39) _____-_____ activities.

The Trait Perspective: Mapping the Structure of Personality

A statistical approach often used by trait theorists that identifies clusters of specific behaviors that are associated with one another so that they reflect a basic trait on which people can vary is called (40)_____ _____. One of the most popular trait theories is called the Big Five theory, which posits five major personality traits. The acronym (41) _____ can be used to remember the traits: openness, (42) _____, extraversion, (43) _____, and neuroticism. Eysenck believed that the two factors of (44) _____-_____ and (45) _____-_____ underlie normal personality. One challenge to the trait perspective questions how (46) _____ personality really is. Situational factors also influence behavior, and people differ in their tendency to tailor their behavior to what is called for by the situation, an individual difference called (47) _____-_____.

Biological Foundations of Personality

Biological approaches have suggested that evolution, (48) _____, and activity of the nervous system all play a role in the development of personality traits. A genetic basis for personality traits is suggested by a body of (49) _____ studies that show monozygotic twins to be far more alike in personality than dizygotic twins. One of the first modern theorists to suggest a biological basis for major personality traits was Hans Eysenck, who explained normal personality differences on the dimensions of (50)_____-_____ and Stability-Instability in terms of patterns of arousal within the (51)_____. Studies of (52) _____, which appear early in life and show some stability across the lifespan, also suggest that biologically based differences may underlie personality development.

Behavioral and Social-Cognitive Theories

According to Bandura's principle of (53) _____ _____, the person, the person's behavior, and the environment all influence one another in a pattern of two-way causal links. Julian Rotter believed that a sense of personal control has an important influence on our behaviors. People with an (54) _____ locus of control believe that they control their own life outcomes, whereas people with an (55) _____ locus of control believe that external factors determine their fate. Bandura also believed that people who believe that they have abilities to perform the behaviors needed to achieve desired outcomes have a high sense of (56) _____-_____.

Mischel and Shoda have described a five-variable (57) _____-_____ personality system (CAPS) in which the dynamic interplay among the five person factors and the responsive environment results in distinctive (58) _____ signatures, or characteristic patterns of individual responses to various situations. The important five factors are the person's (59) _____ strategies, expectancies and beliefs, goals and values, affects (emotions), and (60) _____-_____ processes and competencies. Research suggests that although individual behaviors are often inconsistent when analyzed at the level of broad traits, personality is substantially more coherent at the level of behavioral signatures, or (61) _____ _____ _____ interactions.

Culture, Gender and Personality

Dimensions of culture include complexity, tightness, and (62) _____-_____, all of which can affect personality. Collectivist cultures tend to see the environment as fixed and (63) _____ as malleable, whereas individualist cultures tend to see the reverse. People from individualist cultures tend to describe themselves in terms of personal traits, whereas those from (64) _____ cultures are more likely to describe themselves in social identity terms. (65) _____ _____ are organized mental structures of the attributes viewed as appropriate for males and females.

Personality Assessment

There are many techniques used to assess personality. (66) _____ are particularly valuable for the direct personal contact established between researcher and respondent. In (67) _____ _____, psychologists use an explicit coding system to code the behaviors of interest. Through (68) _____ _____ _____, researchers and clinicians collect samples of behavior from respondents as they live their daily lives. Personality scales, such as the most widely used personality inventory, the (69) _____, are developed in two major ways. In the (70) _____-_____ approach (an example of which is the NEO-PI), items are based on the theorist's conception of the personality trait to be measured. In the (71) _____ approach (an example of which is the Minnesota Multiphasic Personality Inventory, or MMPI), items are chosen because previous research has shown that the items were answered differently by groups of people known to differ in the personality characteristic of interest. Tests that assume that when a person is presented with an ambiguous stimulus, his or her interpretation of it will indicate inner feelings, anxieties, or desires, are called (72) _____ tests.

E. Concept Cards

Truly learning a concept means integrating it into the way *you* think about things. To integrate concepts successfully, you must translate the words and examples your text or instructor provides into words and examples that are meaningful to you.

For this exercise, obtain some note cards (3" × 5" or 4" × 6") to make a deck of concept cards. On one side of each card, write the *concept* from the list following (e.g., "ego") at the top. Read the textbook definition provided, and then write the definition *in your own words* on the concept card (e.g., for "ego," you might write "the conscious, practical, rational part of a person"). Simply imagine that a friend has asked you what the concept means, and write down what you would answer. Writing the definition in your own words requires you to think deeply about its meaning. When next you see your own version of the definition, it will make intuitive sense to you—no translation required.

On the second side of the card, write your own example of the concept. Again, coming up with your own example requires you to think deeply about the application of the concept, and you will more easily understand and remember the example when you study for a test. If you use an example from the text, or from class, make it your own by writing it in your own words. You can always check with your instructor that your example is indeed a good example of the concept.

CONCEPT	Example of the concept in my own words, preferably drawn from my own experience
Definition in my own words	
(side 1 of card)	(side 2 of card)

The following is a list of all the boldface concepts from your textbook with the author's definition. Write the definition in your own words, together with your own example of the concept, to create a *concept card* as described earlier, or write in the space provided.

Personality: The distinctive and relatively enduring ways of thinking, feeling, and acting that characterize a person's responses to life situations

Id: The innermost core of the personality, the only structure present at birth, and the source of all psychic energy

Pleasure principle: The principle of seeking immediate gratification or release, regardless of rational considerations and environmental realities

Ego: That part of the personality that has direct contact with reality and functions primarily at a conscious level

Reality principle: The principle of testing reality to decide when and under what conditions the id can safely discharge its impulses and satisfy its needs

Superego: The moral arm of the personality

Defense mechanisms: Unconscious mental operations that deny or distort reality

Repression: A defense mechanism whereby the ego uses some of its energy to prevent anxiety-arousing memories, feelings, and impulses from entering consciousness

Sublimation: An ego defense mechanism whereby taboo impulses are channeled into socially desirable and admirable behaviors, completely masking the sinister underlying impulses

Psychosexual stages: Stages of individual development during which the id's pleasure-seeking tendencies are focused on specific pleasure-sensitive areas of the body called erogenous zones

Fixation: A state of arrested psychosexual development in which instincts are focused on a particular psychic theme.

Regression: A psychological retreat to an earlier psychosexual stage

Oedipus complex: The conflicted situation involving love for the mother and hostility toward the father

Electra complex: The female counterpart of the Oedipus complex

Neoanalytic theorists: Psychoanalysts who disagreed with certain aspects of Freud's thinking and developed their own theories

Personal unconscious: The contents of an individual's unconscious mind based on life experiences

Collective unconscious: Memories accumulated throughout the entire history of the human race

Archetypes: Inherited tendencies to interpret experiences in certain ways

Object relations theories: Psychological theories that focus on the images or mental representations that people form of themselves and other people as a result of early experienced with caregivers

Phenomenology: A philosophical approach that emphasizes the primacy of immediate experience

Personal constructs: Cognitive categories into which individuals sort the persons and events in their lives

Role Construct Repertory (Rep) Test: A psychological test used to assess individuals' personal construct systems

Self-actualization: The highest realization of human potential

Self: An organized, consistent set of perceptions of and beliefs about oneself

Self-consistency: An absence of conflict among self-perceptions

Congruence: Consistency between self-perceptions and experience

Threat: Any experience that evokes anxiety

Need for positive regard: A need for acceptance, sympathy, and love from others

Unconditional positive regard: Unqualified acceptance and love of a person regardless of accomplishments or behavior

Need for positive self-regard: The desire to feel good about ourselves

Conditions of worth: The circumstances under which we approve or disapprove of ourselves

Fully functioning persons: Individuals who are close to achieving self-actualization

Self-esteem: How positively or negatively we feel about ourselves

Self-verification: The proposition that people are motivated to preserve their self-concept and maintain their self-consistency and congruence

Self-enhancement: A strong and pervasive tendency to gain and preserve a positive self-image

Personality traits: Relatively stable cognitive, emotional, and behavioral characteristics of people that can help establish their individual identities and distinguish them from others

Factor analysis: Analysis used to identify clusters of behaviors that are highly correlated (positively or negatively) with one another, but not with behaviors in other cultures

Self-monitoring: A process whereby people are very attentive to situational cues and adapt their behavior to what they think would be most appropriate

Temperament: Individual differences in emotional and behavioral styles that appear so early in life that they are assumed to have a biological basis

Social cognitive theories: Theories that combine the behavioral and cognitive perspectives into an approach to personality that stresses the interaction of a thinking human with a social environment that provides learning experiences

Reciprocal determinism: The idea that the person, the person's behavior, and the environment all influence one another in a pattern of two-way causal links

Internal-external locus of control: An expectancy concerning the degree of personal control we have in our lives

Self-efficacy: People's beliefs concerning their ability to perform the behaviors needed to achieve desired outcomes

Cognitive-affective personality system (CAPS): An organized system of five variables that interact continuously with one another and with the environment, generating the distinctive patterns of behavior that characterize the person

Behavior-outcome expectancies: The "if-then" links between alternative behaviors and possible outcomes

Self-reinforcement processes: Internal, self-administered rewards and punishments

Behavioral signatures: Consistent ways of responding in particular classes of situations

Gender schemas: Organized mental structures that contain our understanding of the attributes and behaviors that are appropriate and expected for males and females

Structured interviews: Interviews that contain a set of specific questions that are administered to every participant

Behavioral assessment: A technique developed by psychologists for observing behavior using an explicit coding system that contains the behavioral categories of interest

Remote behavior sampling: A psychological test in which researchers and clinicians collect self-reported samples of behavior from respondents as they live their daily lives

Rational-theoretical approach: A method of developing psychological tests in which items are based on the theorist's conception of the personality trait to be measured

NEO Personality Inventory (NEO-PI): A personality test that measures the Big Five personality traits of Openness, Conscientiousness, Extraversion, Agreeableness, and Neuroticism

Empirical approach: A method of developing psychological tests in which items are chosen not because their content seems relevant to the trait on rational grounds, but because each item has been answered differently by groups of people (for example, introverts and extraverts) known to differ in the personality characteristic of interest

Minnesota Multiphasic Personality Inventory-2 (MMPI-2): A widely used personality test developed according to the empirical approach

Projective tests: Psychological tests that present subjects with ambiguous stimuli and ask for some interpretation of them

Rorschach test: A projective personality test consisting of 10 inkblots

Thematic Apperception Test (TAT): A projective personality test consisting of a series of pictures derived from paintings, drawings, and magazine illustrations

F. What's the Difference? A Concept Card Exercise

An important skill in learning concepts is being able to differentiate among concepts that are similar or related in some way. This skill is particularly relevant for multiple-choice tests, especially if you often find yourself wavering between two answers.

Once you have created your own deck of concept cards, select them two by two, each time answering the question "What's the difference between these two concepts?" You can use the word definitions of the concepts or the examples of the concepts to enhance your mastery of the material. In each case, choose pairs of concepts to compare those that are related, or similar, or that sound the same, or that could in some way be confused. It's much easier to "spot the difference" between two concepts when you are studying, with the textbook available, rather than considering the question for the first time in a testing situation.

G. Apply What You Know

1. Chapter 13 of your textbook makes repeated reference to the tragic case of Charles Whitman. Review the sections throughout the chapter that discuss Whitman, and summarize in the space below how the various perspectives of personality theory might view Whitman and the factors that triggered his violence.

Whitman According to Trait Perspective

Whitman According to Biological Perspective

Whitman According to Psychodynamic Perspective

Whitman According to Humanistic-Phenomenological Perspective

Examine the summaries you have written above and look for patterns: Do the various perspectives seem to support or contradict each other in any noticeable ways?

2. Find a case of seemingly inexplicable behavior in current events (easily obtained from media such as documentary films, TV, newspapers, etc.) Review the sections throughout the chapter that discuss different approaches to personality, and summarize in the space below how the various perspectives of personality theory might view the seemingly inexplicable behavior under consideration.

Analysis According to Trait Perspective

Analysis According to Biological Perspective

Analysis According to Psychodynamic Perspective

Analysis According to Humanistic-Phenomenological Perspective

Examine the summaries you have written above and look for patterns: Do the various perspectives seem to support or contradict each other in any noticeable ways?

3. Review the section in your text under "Applying Psychological Science: Increasing Self-Efficacy through Systematic Goal Setting." Now think of a goal you would like to achieve within the coming week, and another that you would like to achieve within 6 months. Using the guidelines for effective goal setting that are presented there, state each goal and outline the steps you will need to accomplish in order to reach it.

Short-term goal: By this time next week, I will:

Steps I will take to reach it:

Long-term goal: Within the next six months, I will:

Steps I will take to reach it:

H. On the Web: *As with any online research, it is important to consider how legitimate a given source is before you rely on the information it presents. Your instructor or Internet adviser may give you some specific guidelines for distinguishing which kinds of Web sites tend to be reputable.*

A. A number of individuals have made notable contributions to our understanding of personality. Search the Web for more information about some of those listed.

Gordon Allport

Albert Bandura

Raymond B. Cattell

Hans Eysenck

Sigmund Freud

Carl Jung

Walter Mischel and Yoichi Shoda

Carl Rogers

Hermann Rorschach

Julian Rotter

Chapter 13 399

B. Take a look at the concept cards you have created for this chapter, or the key concepts listed in section E. In the space provided, make a list of any whose definitions or associations you are not yet confident of and any you'd like to learn more about. Try entering the terms on your list into your search engine. Make notes of any helpful information you find.

Key Concept/Information Found

C. Examine the resources for personality study offered by the Society for Personality and Social Psychology, including a page of personality psychology links found under Social Psychology Network. Another worthwhile site devoted to personality is Great Ideas in Personality. Make notes of the kinds of information and materials you find.

D. Visit a major online bookseller (or, if you prefer, let your feet do the walking through the self-help aisle of a brick-and-mortar bookstore) and make note of the books that promise to help you discover your true "personality type." To what extent do these pop psychology books support what you have learned about personality in this chapter?

I. Analyze This: *Chapter 1 of your textbook begins by presenting these four basic steps in the critical thinking process:*
- *"What exactly are you asking me to believe?"*
- *"How do you know? What is the evidence?"*
- *"Are there other possible explanations?"*
- *"What is the most reasonable conclusion?"*

You might picture this as a four-step analysis to help you decide whether to accept a given theory or assertion. Now it's your turn to put your textbook to this test.

Review the section in Chapter 13 of your textbook under the heading "Carl Rogers's Theory of the Self." There you will find a discussion of the concepts of self-consistency, the need for positive regard, and the fully functioning person. If someone told you that we all should treat everyone with unconditional positive regard, would you agree? Analyze that assertion in the space following. When you have finished, consider using this four-step analysis to evaluate other assertions you encounter.

"What exactly are you asking me to believe?"

"How do you know? What is the evidence?"

"Are there other possible explanations?"

"What is the most reasonable conclusion?"

J. Practice Test

Multiple-Choice Items: *Write the letter corresponding to your answer in the space to the left of each item.*

_____ 1. Eysenck's trait theory is based on these dimensions of personality: _____.
   a. introversion and conscientiousness
   b. stable-unstable and thoughtful-selfish
   c. psychotic-neurotic and introvert-extravert

Chapter 13   401

        d. introvert-extravert and stable-unstable

_____ 2. Which of the following is one of the Big Five personality traits?
        a. Psychoticism
        b. Agreeableness
        c. Dominance
        d. Creativity

_____ 3. The personality dimension shared by both Eysenck's theory and Big Five theory is _____.
        a. introversion-extraversion
        b. openness–close-mindedness
        c. dominance-submission
        d. psychoticism-normality

_____ 4. When confronted by potentially overwhelming or unacceptable urges, the ego may resort to _____ in order to reject or distort reality and thus reduce the anxiety that accompanies these urges.
        a. free associations
        b. id impulses
        c. archetypes
        d. defense mechanisms

_____ 5. Bob thinks that he is a good tennis player, and his results support this belief: He is better than almost all of the players in his club, and he wins most of his tennis matches. This agreement between Bob's beliefs and his actual experience would best be considered as an example of Carl Rogers's concept of _____.
        a. self-actualization
        b. congruence
        c. self-efficacy
        d. a condition of worth

_____ 6. Sarah has the belief that she is good in math, but she has just received her first D grade in her freshman calculus class. This inconsistency between Sarah's self-belief and her actual experience will most likely generate what Carl Rogers termed _____.
        a. self-actualization
        b. a condition of worth
        c. a threat
        d. a need for unconditional self-regard

_____ 7. Cindy is intellectual and imaginative and has a broad range of interests. She would most likely score highly on the Big Five measure of _____.
        a. Openness
        b. Assertiveness

c. Extraversion
d. Conscientiousness

_____ 8. Kelly's theory of personal constructs emphasizes _____.
   a. factor analysis to measure the basic dimensions of personality
   b. the collective unconscious
   c. that attachment styles can affect people's adjustment and emotional well-being
   d. that each individual perceives the world in a unique way

_____ 9. Greg doesn't think he has much of a chance of getting into his top choice for medical school. However, he still very much likes this school and desires very much to go there. On the basis of Rotter's concept of _____, we would expect Greg not to apply to this school, but Rotter's concept of _____ suggests that Greg would apply to this school.
   a. internal locus of control; external locus of control
   b. expectancy; reinforcement value
   c. self-consistency; self-efficacy
   d. reinforcement value; self-efficacy

_____ 10. Ralph tends to be rather passive. Though he is happy and content with himself, he doesn't really believe that his actions make much of a difference in the world. For instance, he doesn't vote because he assumes that most governments are run by a few powerful people and there is very little he can do to change things. Ralph would most accurately be classified as having _____.
   a. low self-esteem
   b. high self-monitoring skills
   c. an external locus of control
   d. an internal locus of control

_____ 11. Steve is an athlete who always seems to perform well under pressure. When the heat is on, he knows that he has the skills needed to succeed and tends to experience an energized excitement that allows him to play his best. According to the CAPS model of personality, Steve's belief about his skills would be classified as a(n) _____, whereas his energized excitement would be seen as a(n) _____.
   a. personal competency; affect
   b. expectation; value
   c. goals; value
   d. affect; encoding

_____ 12. When using _____ to observe personality and/or behaviors, researchers will create explicit coding systems that contain the particular behavioral categories in which they are interested.
   a. the interview method

    b. psychological tests
    c. the behavioral assessment method
    d. projective tests

_____ 13. The basic assumption underlying projective tests is that if you present someone with a(n) _____ stimulus, the interpretation for this stimulus will come from within and will reflect the person's inner needs and feelings.
    a. sexual
    b. ambiguous
    c. objective
    d. provocative

_____ 14. Differences in temperament _____.
    a. reflect people's unique way of construing the world
    b. are considered to be biologically based
    c. develop on the basis of the positive regard the child receives
    d. are not stable across the life span

_____ 15. People differ in the extent to which they can control their own behavior, a person variable referred to as _____ in Mischel and Shoda's CAPS theory of personality.
    a. self-regulatory processes
    b. encodings
    c. goals and values
    d. personal constructs

_____ 16. Studies of brain activity in relation to personality traits have indicated _____.
    a. no difference between introverts and extraverts
    b. some differences between introverts and extraverts
    c. some differences between agreeable and disagreeable individuals
    d. some differences between individualist and collectivist individuals

_____ 17. The idea that human beings, across cultures, may unconsciously share certain ideas such as the concept of "evil" is part of _____.
    a. Jung's analytic psychology
    b. Rogers's theory of the self
    c. Rotter's social cognitive theory
    d. Freud's psychosexual stages model

_____ 18. Teresa's psychology instructor is fond of telling students, "You are a thinking human, and your social environment provides you with learning experiences." Teresa's instructor is most likely oriented to the _____ perspective.
    a. psychodynamic
    b. humanistic-phenomenological
    c. social-cognitive
    d. biological

_____ 19. Neoanalytic theorists such as Alfred Adler and Carl Jung departed from traditional psychoanalytic theory in that they _____.
   a. were more pessimistic than Freud regarding human nature
   b. assumed that personality is almost entirely shaped during childhood
   c. believed childhood sexuality needed to emphasized more
   d. believed Freud did not place enough emphasis on social and cultural factors

_____ 20. Of the following, the person who is probably most fully functioning is a person who _____.
   a. is worried about his performance
   b. feels that she is free to realize her potential
   c. dislikes trying new things
   d. hates everyone

_____ 21. Of the following, the one that is an example of conditional positive regard is _____.
   a. helping another person with a problem
   b. trying to understand another person
   c. a parent showing love to a child only if the child brings home straight A's
   d. a parent showing love to a child regardless of what the child does

_____ 22. SMART is a useful acronym for _____.
   a. the five factors in the Big Five model
   b. the personality traits identified by Cattell
   c. Freud's psychosocial stages
   d. goal setting

_____ 23. How positively or negatively we feel about ourselves is called _____.
   a. self-esteem
   b. self-verification
   c. self-enhancement
   d. self-actualization

_____ 24. Attachment theory predicts that _____.
   a. attachment styles developed in adulthood are unaffected by those developed in childhood
   b. people develop a variety of different attachment styles throughout the lifespan
   c. attachment styles developed in childhood affect adult relationships
   d. attachment styles are often developed in adolescence rather than childhood

_____ 25. The personality trait that affects whether people tailor their behavior to what is called for by the situation is called _____.
   a. self-verification

Chapter 13 405

      b. self-enhancement
      c. self-actualization
      d. self-monitoring

_____ 26. Which of the following goals is most likely to be effective in improving self-efficacy?
      a. "I'm going to do my best this semester"
      b. "I'm going to study in the library from 3 to 5 p.m. each day this semester"
      c. "I'm going to raise my GPA from 2.0 to 3.8 this semester"
      d. "I'm going to remind myself that I am smart each day this semester"

_____ 27. According to Bandura's principle of reciprocal determinism, _____.
      a. behavior determines personality but not vice versa
      b. personality determines behavior but not vice versa
      c. the environment does not affect behavior
      d. the environment, person factors, and behavior all affect each other

_____ 28. Bandura has suggested that performance experiences, observational learning, emotional arousal, and verbal persuasion all affect _____.
      a. locus of control
      b. self-efficacy beliefs
      c. expectancies
      d. self-actualization

_____ 29. Consistent ways of responding to particular classes of situations are called _____.
      a. CAPS
      b. loci of control
      c. behavioral signatures
      d. personalities

_____ 30. Ambiguous stimuli, such as drawings, are a central feature of _____.
      a. projective tests
      b. CAPS
      c. MMPI-2
      d. objective tests of personality

True/False Items: *Write T or F in the space provided to the left of each item.*

_____ 1. Trait theorists try to identify and measure the basic dimensions of personality.

_____ 2. Kelly developed fixed-role therapy as a technique for helping clients experiment with new viewpoints and behaviors.

_____ 3. Freud believed that children are sexual beings.

_____ 4. Rogers believed that people are motivated for self-consistency but not for congruence.

_____ 5. Conditional positive regard communicates that a person is inherently worthy of love regardless of what he or she does.

_____ 6. Biological factors do not affect the development of personality traits.

_____ 7. Object relations theory focuses on the mental representations that people form of themselves, others, and relationships.

_____ 8. Projective tests are scored by the number of correct answers the person gives, and the correct answers are available only to psychologists qualified to administer these tests.

_____ 9. Dizygotic twins are far more alike in personality than are monozygotic twins.

_____ 10. Through remote behavior sampling, researchers and clinicians can collect samples of behavior from respondents as they live their daily lives.

Short-Answer Questions

1. What were Freud's ideas about psychic energy and mental events?

2. What did Rogers argue about positive regard?

3. What are the Big Five factors in the five-factor model of personality?

4. What is locus of control?

5. What are projective tests used for?

Essay Questions

1. How would you describe your own personality? Which of the perspectives of personality study presented in this chapter did you find useful in understanding or categorizing your personality? Do you think of your personality differently now from the way you did before you studied this chapter?

2. Consider some popular phrases related to Freud's' psychosexual stages, such as "smokers have an oral fixation" or "neatniks are anal-retentive." To what extent do you believe these characterizations are accurate, and why? What about the psychosexual stages themselves—do you recall experiencing them in your childhood, or do you observe them in children you know?

3. If you were an employer, would you consider using a personality assessment instrument (i.e., a personality test) to help you decide which applicants to hire for various jobs? Assuming your budget would cover the costs of administering virtually any of the major tests available, what kind of test would you be most likely to use, and why?

Answer Keys

Answer Key for Review at a Glance

1. enduring
2. distinctive
3. inferred

37. self-esteem
38. self-verification
39. self-enhancing

4. psychic energy
5. id
6. pleasure
7. ego
8. reality principle
9. superego
10. defense mechanisms
11. repression
12. sublimation
13. psychosexual
14. anal
15. latency
16. phallic
17. Oedipus complex
18. Electra complex
19. identification
20. Neo
21. collective unconscious
22. archetypes
23. Object relations
24. attachment
25. self-actualization
26. self-consistency
27. congruence
28. scientists
29. personal constructs
30. unique
31. Rep
32. fixed-role
33. positive regard
34. Unconditional positive regard
35. conditions
36. fully functioning
40. factor analysis
41. OCEAN
42. conscientiousness
43. agreeableness
44. introversion-extraversion
45. stability-instability
46. consistent
47. self-monitoring
48. genetics
49. twin
50. Introversion-extraversion
51. brain
52. temperament
53. reciprocal determinism
54. internal
55. external
56. self-efficacy
57. cognitive-affective
58. behavioral
59. encoding
60. self-regulatory
61. person-by-situation
62. individualism-collectivism
63. people
64. collectivist
65. Gender schemas
66. Interviews
67. behavioral assessment
68. remote behavior sampling
69. MMPI
70. rational-theoretical
71. empirical
72. projective

Answer Key for Practice Test Multiple-Choice Questions

1. d
2. b
3. a
4. d
5. b
6. c
7. a
8. d
9. b
10. c
16. b
17. a
18. c
19. d
20. b
21. c
22. d
23. a
24. c
25. d

11. a	26. b
12. c	27. d
13. b	28. b
14. b	29. c
15. a	30. a

Answer Key for Practice Test True/False Questions

1. T	6. F
2. T	7. T
3. T	8. F
4. F	9. F
5. F	10. T

Answer Key for Practice Test Short-Answer Questions

1. Freud believed that instincts created psychic energy which powers the mind and presses for direct or indirect release.

2. Rogers believed that all of us are born with a need for positive regard, a need for acceptance, sympathy, and love from others. A need for positive self-regard also develops whereby we want to feel good about ourselves. Unconditional positive regard promotes our sense of well-being and self-actualization, whereas conditions of worth impede our development.

3. The five factors can be remembered by the acronym OCEAN: Openness, Conscientiousness, Extraversion, Agreeableness, and Neuroticism.

4. Locus of control refers to our beliefs about the degree of personal control we have over what happens in our life. People with an external locus of control believe that external factors (e.g., luck, other people, environmental factors) determine their fate, whereas people with an internal locus of control believe that they have influence over what happens to them.

5. Projective tests are used to help uncover unconscious aspects of people's personalities, and consist of ambiguous stimuli to which an individual responds. Projective tests are based on the psychodynamic concept of projection, whereby people reveal their own unconscious conflicts in the perceptions they have of ambiguous stimuli.

Answer Key for Practice Test Essay Questions

As you may have guessed, there are no right or wrong answers to the essay questions in this practice test. That does not mean, however, that all essays are equally good. To get maximum learning benefit from the essay questions, do the following:

- Review each essay a day or two after you wrote it, noting any necessary corrections and any additional support for your points that you can think of.
- Review the section in your textbook that pertains to the topic of each essay. Annotate your essay with any corrections or additional support for your points that you find in the text.
- Spend a few minutes researching the topic of each essay on the Internet. Annotate your essay further with any additional (reliable) information you find.
- Finally, reread each essay with the annotations you have added.

Chapter 14
ADJUSTING TO LIFE: STRESS, COPING, AND HEALTH

A. Learning Objectives: *These objectives are expanded from the Focus Questions found in the margins of your textbook. When you have mastered the material in this chapter, you will be able to:*

14.1   Describe three models of stress, distinguishing among those that focus on stress as a stimulus, stress as a response, and stress resulting from the transaction between the organism and the environment.

14.2   Describe four types of appraisal that occur in response to a potential stressor, and explain how they correspond to primary and secondary appraisals.

14.3   Describe the three stages of Selye's General Adaptation Syndrome (GAS) and their effects on health.

14.4   Discuss evidence that stress is linked to well-being.

14.5   Describe the mechanisms through which stress can contribute to illness.

14.6   Describe the various stressors that can affect immune functioning.

14.7   Describe various ways social support can protect against stressful events.

14.8   Describe the role of stress hormones in well-being.

14.9   Describe the Type A behavior pattern and how it can contribute to coronary heart disease.

14.10 Describe how coping self-efficacy, optimism-pessimism, and spiritual beliefs affect stress outcomes.

14.11 Describe factors that create stress-resiliency in children.

14.12 Describe the three major classes of coping strategies.

14.13 Describe how trauma disclosure and emotional constraint affect well-being.

14.14 Describe how gender and cultural factors affect the tendency to use particular coping strategies.

14.15 Describe cognitive coping skills and relaxation techniques that comprise effective stress management training programs.

14.16 Describe how gate control theory explains pain perception and control, and describe how glial cells and cytokines are involved.

14.17 Describe how endorphins influence pain perception and physical well-being.

14.18 Describe how cultural factors influence pain experience and behavior.

14.19 Describe how cognitive and personality factors affect responses to pain stimuli.

14.20 Describe cognitive, informational, and behavioral strategies for pain reduction.

14.21 Describe the six stages of the transtheoretical model of behavior change and the rationale for stage-matched interventions.

14.22 Define aerobic exercise, and cite evidence that it promotes health and longevity.

14.23 Discuss exercise program dropout rates and factors that do and do not predict dropout.

14.24 Describe behavior change techniques that are used in behavioral weight control programs.

14.25 Describe the nature and effectiveness of behavior change techniques in AIDS prevention programs.

14.26 Describe the major goals and techniques in motivational interviewing.

14.27 Describe effective treatments for substance abuse problems including multimodal treatment approaches.

14.28 Describe the consequences of heavy drinking among college students.

14.29 Describe harm-reduction strategies and how they differ from abstinence-based approaches.

14.30 Describe factors that increase or decrease relapse and how relapse-prevention training addresses these factors.

B. Chapter Overview

This chapter examines the mind-body connection between psychological stress and physiological well-being, how we experience stress and how we can best cope with it. It also examines the experience of pain and pain management, and strategies to promote health and prevent illness.

Stressors are stimuli that place strong demands on us or threaten us. Stress is defined as a pattern of cognitive appraisals, physiological responses, and behavioral tendencies in response to a perceived imbalance between situational demands and the resources needed to cope with them. In other words, stress involves a perception that the demands of a situation may overwhelm our resources for meeting those demands, together with physiological and behavioral responses. Stressors can be major or minor, catastrophic or ongoing. Four aspects of the appraisal process are appraisal of demands of a situation (primary appraisal), appraisal of coping resources (secondary appraisal), judgment of the likely or potential consequences of the situation, and appraisal of the personal meaning of the situation. Early stress researcher Hans Selye posited the general adaptation syndrome (GAS), which comprises alarm, resistance, and exhaustion. The alarm stage involves immediate physiological arousal; the fight-or-flight response is triggered. During the resistance stage, the body's resources are being mobilized, and immune responses are being partially inhibited by stress hormones. If the stress persists, eventually the body reaches the exhaustion stage, with increased vulnerability to disease, collapse, and even death.

Stress has important effects on health. For example, traumatic events correlate with long-term anxiety, depression, and unhappiness. Stress can combine with other factors to influence physical illnesses such as heart disease and cancer. Physiological studies suggest a connection between stress and lowered immune system activity. Psychologists look for vulnerability factors, which increase people's susceptibility to stressful events, and protective factors, which help people cope. Social support is a strong protective factor. Physiological reactivity and the Type A behavior pattern, and particularly its hostility component, are vulnerability factors. Beliefs can be protective factors, such as coping self-efficacy, optimism, and finding spiritual meaning in stressful life events. Psychologists have also studied children who thrive in spite of the very stressful circumstances of their lives. Highly resilient children have been found to have good intellectual function, social skills, and self-efficacy and at least one caring adult in their lives who provided social support.

Methods of coping with stress can be categorized as problem-focused (dealing with the stressor directly), emotion-focused (dealing with the emotions evoked by the stressor), and social-support coping. A sense of controllability and coping efficacy seem to be particularly important, but if the stress is outside the individual's control, then emotion-focused coping and social support are generally more helpful. Research suggests that physiological health is enhanced by recognizing and disclosing negative feelings about traumatic experiences and ongoing stress. Flexibility in emotional expression and inhibition, depending on the situation, may be associated with the best outcomes. There are gender differences in coping: Men are more likely to be problem-focused (fight or flight), whereas women are more likely to be emotion-focused and to seek social support ("tend and befriend"). Cultural differences in coping styles have also been observed, with Asians and Hispanics using more emotion-focused coping, and African Americans seeking more social support, than White Americans. Stress-management training methods include cognitive coping strategies such as cognitive restructuring and self-instructional training, and relaxation techniques such as somatic relaxation and meditation.

Pain is influenced by biological, psychological, and sociocultural factors. At the biological level, free nerve endings are pain receptors. Gate control theory attributes pain to the opening and closing of "gates" in the spinal cord. Thoughts, emotions, and beliefs can influence the experience of pain via the central control mechanism in which signals from the brain are able to influence the spinal gates. The immune system is also involved in pain. Glial cells, when activated by immune challenges, may amplify pain by releasing cytokines that promote inflammation. Endorphins released by the nervous system play a major role in pain reduction. Placebos can produce expectations that reduce medical symptoms and pain. Cultural factors also influence the appraisal of painful stimuli. Negative emotional states decrease pain tolerance. Psychological techniques for pain control include (1) cognitive strategies, such as dissociative and associative techniques; (2) sensory and procedural information that increase cognitive control and support; and (3) increasing activity level to counter chronic pain.

Behavioral change is a key process in health promotion and illness prevention. The transtheoretical model identifies six stages of change: precontemplation, contemplation, preparation, action, maintenance, and termination. Exercise enhances both physical and psychological well-being. People who adhere to an exercise program for 3 to 6 months have a better chance of continuing thereafter. About a third of the American population is obese, as are 1 in 6 children and adolescents. Behavioral weight-control programs feature self-monitoring, stimulus control procedures, and strategies that encourage people to eat less but enjoy it more. Exercise also enhances weight control.

Human immunodeficiency virus (HIV) infection is spread by high-risk sexual and drug abuse behaviors. Behavioral changes have been accomplished in some, but not all, high-risk populations. Cultural factors may conflict with safer-sex practices, increasing the difficulty of reducing behaviors linked to sexually transmitted diseases. Substance abuse is often part of a larger pattern of maladjustment. Multimodal substance-abuse treatments combine techniques such as aversion training, stress-management and coping-skills training, and positive reinforcement. Motivational interviewing uses the person's own motivation to change self-defeating behaviors. Harm-reduction approaches focus on reducing the negative consequences that a behavior produces, rather than stopping the behavior itself. Relapse prevention is designed to keep occasional lapses from becoming full-blown relapses. Health psychologists have made important contributions to helping people reduce health-impairing behaviors and acquire healthier lifestyles, but many challenges remain.

C. Chapter Outline

STRESS AND WELL-BEING
    Stressors
        Measuring Stressful Life Events

The Stress Response: A Mind-Body Link
    Cognitive Appraisal
    Physiological Responses
Effects of Stress on Well-Being
    Stress and Psychological Well-Being
    What Do You Think? Do Stressful Events Cause Psychological Distress?
    Stress and Illness
    Stress and Aging
    Stress and the Immune System
In Review
Factors That Influence Stress-Health Relations
    Social Support
    Physiological Reactivity
    Type A Behavior Pattern
    Mind as Healer or Slayer
        Coping Efficacy and Control
        Optimism and Positive Attitudes
        Finding Meaning in Stressful Life Events
        Resilient Children: Superkids or Ordinary Magic?
In Review
COPING WITH STRESS
    Effectiveness of Coping Strategies
    Controllability and Coping Efficacy
    Trauma Disclosure and Emotional Release
    Bottling Up Feelings: The Hidden Costs of Emotional Constraint
    Gender, Culture, and Coping
    Research Close-Up: Hold my Hand and I'll be Fine
    Stress-Management Training
        Cognitive Coping Skills
        Relaxation Techniques
In Review
PAIN AND PAIN MANAGEMENT
    Biological Mechanisms of Pain
        Spinal and Brain Mechanisms
        The Endorphins
    Cultural and Psychological Influences on Pain
        Cultural Factors
        Meanings and Beliefs
        Personality Factors and Social Support
    Applying Psychological Science: Psychological Techniques for Controlling Pain and Suffering
    In Review
HEALTH PROMOTION AND ILLNESS PREVENTION
    How People Change: The Transtheoretical Model
    Increasing Behaviors that Enhance Health
        Exercise

Weight Control
Lifestyle Changes and Medical Recovery
Reducing Behaviors That Impair Health
Psychology and the AIDS Crisis
Combating Substance Abuse
Motivational Interviewing
Multimodal Treatment Approaches
Beneath the Surface: College-Age Drinking: Harmless Fun or Russian Roulette?
Harm-Reduction Approaches to Prevention
Relapse Prevention: Maintaining Positive Behavior Change
In Review
A Concluding Thought

D. Review at a Glance: *Write the term that best fits the blank to review what you learned in this chapter.*

Stress and Well-Being

Stimuli that place strong demands on us are called (1) _____. (2)_____ is a pattern of cognitive appraisals, physiological responses, and behavioral tendencies that occurs in response to a perceived imbalance between situational (3) _____ and the (4) _____ needed to cope with them. Lazarus suggests that when we first encounter a situation, we engage in (5) _____ appraisal, by which we perceive the situation as either benign, neutral, or threatening. Our perception of our ability to cope with a situation is called (6) _____ appraisal. Hans Selye, a pioneer in examining the body's response to stress, found three phases: alarm, (7) _____, and exhaustion, in a system he called the (8) _____ _____ syndrome.

Long-term difficulties such as (9) _____, anxiety, and unhappiness are common in people who have experienced catastrophic events. Physiological studies have found a correlation between stress and lowered (10) _____ _____ function. Factors that increase susceptibility to stress, such as physiological (11) _____, as well as the Type (12) _____ behavior pattern are called (13) _____ factors. (14)_____ factors are those that (15)_____ susceptibility to stress, such as social support. Beliefs can be protective factors, such as (16) _____, and finding (17) _____ _____ in stressful life events.

Coping with Stress

Some individuals cope better with stress than do others. The belief that we have the ability to do what is necessary to cope is called coping (18) _____-_____. (19)_____-_____ coping strategies attempt to directly deal with the problem, whereas (20) _____-_____ strategies attempt to manage the emotional aspects of the problem. A third class of coping strategies involves (21) _____ _____ _____, turning to others for assistance and emotional support in times of stress. In examining what makes children highly resilient to stress, Masten identified the presence of a caring adult who provided (22) _____ _____, among other factors, as key. Coping behaviors may vary according to (23) _____ and culture. Stress-management training includes (24) _____ coping strategies, which deal with thoughts and beliefs, and relaxation techniques such as somatic relaxation and (25) _____.

Pain and Pain Management

Pain involves a complex set of sensations and perceptions. (26) _____ _____ theory describes how the nervous system transmits pain impulses. Thoughts, emotions, and beliefs can influence the experience of pain when signals from the (27) _____ are able to influence the spinal gates. The (28) _____ system is also involved in pain through the release of (29) _____ that promote inflammation. To help us deal with pain, the brain has its own built-in analgesics called (30) _____. A phenomenon attributed to endorphins is (31) _____-_____ _____, a dramatic lack of perception of pain under extreme circumstances. Psychological pain-control strategies include dissociative and (32) _____ techniques, increasing cognitive control and support, and increasing one's (33) _____ level.

Health Promotion and Illness Prevention

A key process in health promotion and illness prevention is (34) _____ change. The (35) _____ model identifies six stages of change: precontemplation, (36) _____, preparation, (37) _____, maintenance, and (38) _____. People often quit exercise programs, but those who keep exercising for (39) _____ _____ _____ months are more likely to continue over the long term. About (40) _____ _____ of the U.S. population is obese; another third is overweight. (41) _____ weight-control programs feature self-monitoring, stimulus-control procedures, and strategies that encourage people to eat less but enjoy it more. Apart from improved eating habits, another contributor to weight control is (42) _____.

HIV infection is spread by high-risk (43) _____ and drug-abuse behaviors. According to the World Health Organization in 2004, (44) _____ made up about one half of all acquired immunodeficiency syndrome (AIDS) cases. Behavioral changes have effectively increased condom use among (45) _____ _____, but other high-risk populations continue to challenge health advocates.

Substance abuse is often part of a larger pattern of (46) _____. Multimodal substance-abuse treatments combine techniques such as aversion training, stress-management and coping skills training, and positive (47) _____. Motivational interviewing uses the person's own (48) _____ to change self-defeating behaviors. (49)_____-_____ approaches focus on reducing the negative consequences a behavior produces, not stopping the behavior itself. Relapse prevention is designed to keep occasional (50) _____ from becoming full-blown relapses. (51)_____ _____ have made important contributions to helping people reduce health-impairing behaviors and acquire healthier life styles, but many challenges remain.

E. Concept Cards

Truly learning a concept means integrating it into the way *you* think about things. To integrate concepts successfully, you must translate the words and examples your text or instructor provides into words and examples that are meaningful to you.

For this exercise, obtain some note cards (3" × 5" or 4" × 6") to make a deck of concept cards. On one side of each card, write the *concept* from the list following (e.g., "stress") at the top. Read the textbook definition provided, and then write the definition *in your own words* on the concept card (e.g., for "stress," you might write "being nervous that you can't cope with the demands made on you"). Simply imagine that a friend has asked you what the concept means, and write down what you would answer. Writing the definition in your own words requires you to think deeply about its meaning. When next you see your own version of the definition, it will make intuitive sense to you—no translation required.

On the second side of the card, write your own example of the concept. Again, coming up with your own example requires you to think deeply about the application of the concept, and you will more easily understand and remember the example when you study for a test. If you use an example from the text, or from class, make it your own by writing it in your own words. You can always check with your instructor that your example is indeed a good example of the concept.

CONCEPT	Example of the concept in my own words, preferably drawn from my own experience
Definition in my own words	
(side 1 of card)	(side 2 of card)

The following is a list of all the boldface concepts from your textbook with the author's definition. Write the definition in your own words, together with your own example of the concept, to create a *concept card* as described earlier, or write in the space provided.

Health psychology: A field of psychology that addresses factors that influence well-being and illness, as well as measures that can be taken to promote health and prevent illness

Stressors: Demanding or threatening situations

Stress: A pattern of cognitive appraisals, physiological responses, and behavioral tendencies that occurs in response to a perceived imbalance between situational demands and the resources needed to cope with them

Stress response: A response that has cognitive, physiological, and behavioral components

Primary appraisal: The interpretation of a situation as being either benign, neutral/irrelevant, or threatening in terms of its demands and its significance for one's well-being

Secondary appraisal: The interpretation of one's perceived ability to cope with a situation—that is, the resources one has available to deal with it

General adaptation syndrome (GAS): A psychological response pattern consisting of three phases: alarm, resistance, and exhaustion

Cytokines: A class of molecules released by immune cells that help produce fever and inflammation, promote healing of injured tissue, and activate and direct other immune cells

Vulnerability factors: Factors that increase people's susceptibility to stressful events

Protective factors: Environmental or personal resources that help people cope more effectively with stressful events

Type A behavior pattern: A behavior pattern characteristic of people who tend to live under great pressure and demand much of themselves and others

Coping self-efficacy: The belief that we can perform the behaviors necessary to cope successfully

Problem-focused coping: Coping strategies targeted at confronting and dealing directly with the demands of a stressful situation, or at changing the situation so that it is no longer stressful

Emotion-focused coping: Coping strategies targeted at managing the emotional responses resulting from stress

Seeking social support: Turning to others for assistance and emotional support in times of stress

Cognitive restructuring: Systematically detecting, challenging, and replacing irrational ideas

Self-instructional training: A training program in which people learn to "talk to themselves" and guide their behavior in ways that help them cope more effectively

Somatic-relaxation training: A training program that provides a means of voluntarily reducing or preventing high levels of arousal

Cognitive relaxation: A peaceful, mind-clearing state

Gate control theory: A theory that proposes that the experience of pain results from the opening and closing of "gating mechanisms" in the nervous system

Endorphins: Endogenous, or internally produced, morphines

Stress-induced analgesia: A reduction in—or absence of—perceived pain that occurs under stressful conditions

Placebos: Physiologically inert substances that have no medicinal value but are thought by the patient to be helpful

Transtheoretical model: A model that identifies six major stages in the change process

Aerobic exercise: Sustained activity, such as jogging, swimming, and bicycling, that elevates the heart rate and increases the body's need for oxygen

Motivational interviewing: A technique that leads a person to his or her own conclusions based on asking questions that focus on discrepancies between the current state of affairs and the individual's ideal self-image, desired behaviors, and desired outcomes

Multimodal treatments: Treatments that often include biological measures (e.g., the use of nicotine patches to help smokers who are trying to quit), together with psychological measures

Harm reduction: A prevention strategy that is designed not to eliminate a problem behavior but rather to reduce the harmful effects of that behavior when it occurs

Relapse prevention: An intervention that is designed to reduce the risk of relapse

Abstinence violation effect: A reaction in which a person becomes upset and self-blaming over a lapse and views it as proof that he or she will never be strong enough to resist temptation

Chapter 14

F. What's the Difference? A Concept Card Exercise

An important skill in learning concepts is being able to differentiate among concepts that are similar or related in some way. This skill is particularly relevant for multiple-choice tests, especially if you often find yourself wavering between two answers.

Once you have created your own deck of concept cards, select them two by two, each time answering the question "What's the difference between these two concepts?" You can use the word definitions of the concepts or the examples of the concepts to enhance your mastery of the material. In each case, choose pairs of concepts to compare those that are related or similar or that sound the same or that could in some way be confused. It's much easier to spot the difference between two concepts when you are studying, with the textbook available, rather than when considering the question for the first time in a testing situation.

G. Apply What You Know

1. Using the GAS model, classify some typical responses that people are likely to have to the following stressors. Notice which kinds of stressors lend themselves better to this model than others.

Stressor	**Alarm**	**Resistance**	**Exhaustion**
Being attacked by a stranger who tries to rob and sexually assault you			
Being involved in a bus accident in which others are seriously injured, but you are not			
Living for several years in extreme poverty			
Being the bride or groom in a large traditional wedding			

Stressor	Alarm	Resistance	Exhaustion
Going to an important job interview and not being offered the job			
Preparing for and getting through a week of final exams			

2. The next time you experience pain (such as a headache, heartburn, sore muscles from exercising, menstrual cramps, etc.), try implementing one or more of the psychological pain management strategies outlined in this chapter. Make notes below of the nature of the pain, the intervention(s) you tried, and how well you were able to manage the pain.

	Source of Pain	How Well Managed
Dissociative technique:		
Associative technique:		
Cognitive-control procedure:		
Social-support procedure:		
Increasing activity:		

3. How regularly do you exercise? Record your exercise for a week on the following chart. Note your reasons for exercising, any obstacles you overcame to stick with your exercise program, and any supportive factors that helped you adhere to it.

	Type and Duration of Exercise	**Obstacles; How I Overcame Them**	**Supportive Motivators**
Sunday			
Monday			
Tuesday			
Wednesday			
Thursday			
Friday			
Saturday			

H. On the Web: *As with any online research, it is important to consider how legitimate a given source is before you rely on the information it presents. Your instructor or Internet adviser may give you some specific guidelines for distinguishing which kinds of Web sites tend to be reputable.*

A. A number of individuals have made notable contributions to our understanding of stress, coping, and health. Search the Web for more information about some of those listed below.

Henry Beecher

Albert Ellis

Suzanne Kobasa

Richard Lazarus

Ann Masten and J. Douglas Coatsworth

Ronald Melzack and Patrick Wall

James Pennebaker

James Prochaska and Carlo DiClemente

Thomas Strantz and Stephen Auerbach

Shelley Taylor

John-Kar Zubieta

B. Take a look at the concept cards you have created for this chapter, or the key concepts listed in section E. In the space provided, make a list of any whose definitions or associations you are not yet confident of and any you'd like to learn more about. Try entering the terms on your list into your search engine. Make notes of any helpful information you find.

Chapter 14

Key Concept/Information Found

C. Explore the Web sites of several professional organizations related to the study of stress and health, including the following. In the space provided, make note of the resources offered by each of these organizations to professionals, students, and the general public.

- American Psychological Association Division 38 (Health Psychology), its journal (*Health Psychology*), and its newsletter (*The Health Psychologist*)

- STAR (Stress and Anxiety Research) Society

- International Stress Management Association (United Kingdom)

- American Institute of Stress

- Association for Applied and Therapeutic Humor

I. Analyze This: *Chapter 1 of your textbook begins by presenting these four basic steps in the critical thinking process:*
- *"What exactly are you asking me to believe?"*
- *"How do you know? What is the evidence?"*
- *"Are there other possible explanations?"*
- *"What is the most reasonable conclusion?"*

You might picture this as a four-step analysis to help you decide whether to accept a given theory or assertion. Now it's your turn to put your textbook to this test.

Review the sections in Chapter 14 of your textbook under the headings "Trauma Disclosure and Emotional Release" and "Bottling Up Feelings: The Hidden Costs of Emotional Constraint." There you will find a discussion of studies involving the release of negative feelings. If someone told you that people who are "out of touch" with their feelings are less healthy than other people, would you agree? Analyze that assertion in the space below. When you have finished, consider using this four-step analysis to evaluate other assertions you encounter.

"What exactly are you asking me to believe?"

"How do you know? What is the evidence?"

"Are there other possible explanations?"

"What is the most reasonable conclusion?"

J. Practice Test

Multiple-Choice Items: *Write the letter corresponding to your answer in the space to the left of each item.*

_____ 1. Janet was in New Orleans during the powerful Hurricane Katrina. Her appraisal that _____ would be correctly identified as a secondary appraisal, according to the Lazarus stress model.

a. "the hurricane is extremely threatening"
b. "the hurricane will be over soon"
c. "the hurricane may be frightening, but it will not cause much damage"
d. "I will not be able to survive this hurricane"

_____ 2. The aspect of the Type A behavior pattern that correlates most strongly with _____ is _____.
a. cancer; hostility
b. heart disease; hostility
c. heart disease; time urgency
d. allergies; perfectionism

_____ 3. Roberta is undergoing cancer treatment. When she tells her oncologist she feels depressed, he brushes aside the comment and talks about the findings on her latest magnetic resonance image. When she tells her husband she feels depressed, he says, "Look, I've got enough on my mind without having to listen to your complaining." When she tells her mother she feels depressed, her mother says, "You need to get right with God. Then God will stop punishing you." Roberta is a strong candidate for _____.
a. high resilience
b. increased activity for pain reduction
c. problem-focused coping strategies
d. seeking social support through a cancer patients' support group

_____ 4. According to research into cultural factors in coping, African American couples with marital problems were more likely to _____ than Caucasians.
a. stay married
b. seek social support
c. use problem-focused coping strategies
d. avoid coping strategies that involved confrontation

_____ 5. A physiological mechanism by which intense, chronic stress can accelerate aging is _____
a. cell death due to telomere damage
b. an increase in endorphin production
c. a decrease in levels of cortisol
d. an increase in suicidal thinking

_____ 6. The well-known "serenity prayer" ("God grant me the serenity to accept the things I cannot change, the courage to change the things I can, and the wisdom to know the difference") may help to reduce stress by _____.
a. increasing emotion-focused coping behavior
b. increasing social support
c. differentiating between stressors that are and stressors that are not amenable to problem-focused coping
d. increasing wisdom

_____ 7. Gate control theory suggests that ____.
   a. hormones control the stress response
   b. thoughts and emotions can affect the experience of pain
   c. endorphins enhance the experience of pain
   d. problem-focused coping reduces experienced stress

_____ 8. Ralph grew up with a verbally abusive mother and neglectful father. When he was 16, he was robbed and brutally beaten by an assailant who was never caught. He is working his way through community college with a sales job that pays him commissions but no salary. His older brother, with whom he has always had a positive relationship, recently got married and moved away. Ralph maintains, however, that he does not feel any negative emotions from these stressful experiences. According to Eysenck's research, Ralph is likely to be _____.
   a. a Type A person
   b. in need of training to express his negative emotions
   c. a highly resilient child
   d. in need of problem-focused coping strategies

_____ 9. The pain-free state, sometimes called "runner's high," that many people experience during sustained exercise is due to ____.
   a. naloxone
   b. glial cells
   c. gate control
   d. endorphins

_____ 10. Research has shown that excessive levels of stress can have detrimental effects on both psychological and physical health. Evolutionary theorists speculate that this may be because the physical mobilization system that was shaped by evolution to help people cope with life-threatening ____ stressors may not be adaptive for coping with the ____ stressors that characterize the modern world.
   a. physical; psychological
   b. emotional; physical
   c. psychological; emotional
   d. emotional; physical

_____ 11. Research results support a biphasic model in which acute stress ____ the immune response, and chronic stress ____ it.
   a. suppresses; enhances
   b. enhances; suppresses
   c. enhances; also enhances
   d. suppresses; also suppresses

_____ 12. According to research on cultural factors in coping, of the following groups, ____ would be most likely to avoid stressful situations involving interpersonal conflict, perhaps reflecting their culture's emphasis on interpersonal harmony.

a. Hispanics
b. African Americans
c. Asians
d. White Americans

_____ 13. Jan is about to compete in a triathlon. Though such a competition would likely inspire fear and nervousness in most people, Jan is feeling good about the race because she believes she has the skills to complete it successfully. Psychologist Albert Bandura would most likely say that Jan has high _____.
a. self-efficacy
b. self-esteem
c. self-confidence
d. self-control

_____ 14. Research on the influence of religious beliefs has suggested that they have the most positive effects in helping people to deal with _____ but can increase the stress of people dealing with _____.
a. illnesses; losses
b. losses; marital problems and abuse
c. marital problems and abuse; personal setbacks
d. marital problems and abuse; illnesses

_____ 15. Norm and Cliff have both recently been through relationship breakups. Norm decides to go to his favorite bar and talk with his friends about what's been happening. Cliff, on the other hand, decides to deal with his negative feelings through meditation. On the basis of the information provided, we would say that the coping strategy Norm uses is ___, whereas Cliff's strategy is ___.
a. seeking social support; emotion-focused coping
b. seeking social support; problem-focused coping
c. emotion-focused coping; seeking social support
d. emotion-focused coping; problem-focused coping

_____ 16. In experiments with pain control, patients sometimes report pain relief after being given a(n) _____ that is equal to the relief they report after being given an actual pain-killing drug.
a. naloxone-based drug
b. placebo
c. endorphin
d. emotion-focused coping strategy

_____ 17. Kim is very nervous during the presentation she is giving at work; her heart rate is up, and she is sweating more than usual. However, Kim's nervousness is helping her do a good job of presenting her material. As described above, Kim is operating at the _____ stage of Selye's General Adaptation Syndrome.
a. resistance

b. empathy
c. exhaustion
d. alarm

_____ 18. The first three of the six stages in the transtheoretical model of behavior change are _____.
a. primary appraisal, secondary appraisal, and action
b. contemplation, preparation, and action
c. precontemplation, contemplation, and preparation
d. precontemplation, preparation, and change

_____ 19. The last three of the six stages in the transtheoretical model of behavior change are _____.
a. action, maintenance, and termination
b. change, maintenance, and review
c. action, maintenance, and relapse
d. action, sustenance, and disengagement

_____ 20. A health-enhancing behavior that affects both psychological and physical well-being is _____.
a. cognitive restructuring
b. portion control
c. exercise
d. harm reduction

_____ 21. Women who are _____ percent overweight are more than _____ as likely to develop heart disease than are normal-weight women.
a. 30; twice
b. 20; twice
c. 10; four times
d. 30; three times

_____ 22. Charlie is overweight and has started a behavioral weight-control program. He is recording what he eats, how much, and under what circumstances. This phase of the program is called _____.
a. feedback
b. portion control
c. stimulus control
d. self-monitoring

_____ 23. A substance abuse treatment program that combines aversion training, stress-management and coping skills, and positive reinforcement would be called a(n) _____.
a. general adaptation syndrome program
b. multimodal program
c. culturally based program

d. harm-reduction program

_____ 24. Loni is seeing a counselor about her habit of using amphetamines to stay awake and study. The counselor avoids confrontation but encourages Loni herself to describe how often she uses the drug, how it affects her life, and how she might want to change her behavior to rely less on the drug. The counselor is most likely using a _____ approach.
   a. harm-reduction
   b. multimodal
   c. motivational interviewing
   d. culture-fair

_____ 25. Factors that increase people's susceptibility to stressful events are known as _____ factors.
   a. protective
   b. stress
   c. vulnerability
   d. stressor

_____ 26. The conviction that we can perform the behaviors necessary to cope with a stressor successfully is known as _____.
   a. gate control
   b. dissociation
   c. coping self-efficacy
   d. primary appraisal

_____ 27. Research indicates that _____ is an important factor that helps resilient children to thrive in spite of the stressful circumstances of their lives.
   a. caution in developing relationships
   b. a relationship with a caring adult
   c. having many siblings
   d. lack of social skills

_____ 28. Studies of stressors suggest that _____.
   a. everyone experiences stress in the same way
   b. here is little evidence that stressors have long-term effects
   c. stressors can have long-term and strong psychological impact
   d. there is little evidence that environmental factors produce stress

_____ 29. People high in _____, who tend to have intense and prolonged autonomic responses, seem more vulnerable to stress than are people low in this personality factor.
   a. extraversion
   b. sociability
   c. neuroticism
   d. social support

_____ 30. In the early 1990s, a controversy arose when condoms were distributed to high school students including those in New York City public high schools. Condom distribution is an example of a(n) ____.
   a. abstinence program
   b. motivational approach
   c. multimodal intervention
   d. harm-reduction approach

True/False Items: *Write T or F in the space provided to the left of each item.*

_____ 1. Alarm, resistance, and exhaustion are the phases of the GAS.

_____ 2. Gate control theory is a model for analyzing stress-control strategies.

_____ 3. Decreased pain tolerance is correlated with a negative emotional state.

_____ 4. The transtheoretical model uses nonjudgmental interviewing to change a self-defeating behavior through the client's own motivation.

_____ 5. Harm-reduction approaches include needle-exchange programs for intravenous drug users and condom-distribution programs for teenagers.

_____ 6. Research suggests physical health may be enhanced by talking about past traumas.

_____ 7. Appraising our ability to cope with the demands of a situation is called primary appraisal.

_____ 8. Social support is an example of a vulnerability factor.

_____ 9. Cultural factors can affect the perception of pain.

_____ 10. Studies of coping suggest that both emotion-focused coping and seeking social support are used by women more frequently than by men.

Short-Answer Questions

1. How do psychologists define (a) a stressor and (b) stress?

2. Distinguish between primary and secondary appraisal.

3. What protective factors help people cope with stress?

4. Describe the transtheoretical model of behavior change and how it works.

5. Describe some of the strategies that health psychologists use in the prevention of HIV and substance abuse.

Essay Questions

1. Describe a stressful situation that you recently encountered. Using Lazarus's model, describe how the processes of primary appraisal and secondary appraisal were involved in your experience. Were the third and fourth processes of appraisal involved as well? Which of the coping strategies outlined in this chapter did you use?

2. What do you think about the findings in Ann Masten's research on "ordinary magic" in highly resilient children that are described in Chapter 14 of your textbook? What can teachers, clergy, and other concerned adults do to increase the likelihood that a challenged child will experience this "ordinary magic" and be highly resilient?

3. Why do you think HIV/AIDS continues to be a major public health problem even though most people are well aware of the behaviors that spread the infection? Of the

illness-prevention strategies outlined in this chapter, which ones do you think are most likely to be effective in reducing the spread of HIV/AIDS, and why?

Answer Keys

Answer Key for Review at a Glance

1. stressors
2. Stress
3. demands
4. resources
5. primary
6. secondary
7. resistance
8. general adaptation
9. depression
10. immune system
11. reactivity
12. A
13. vulnerability
14. Protective
15. decrease
16. optimism
17. spiritual meaning
18. self-efficacy
19. Problem-focused
20. emotion-focused
21. seeking social support
22. social support
23. gender
24. cognitive
25. meditation
26. Gate control
27. brain
28. immune
29. cytokines
30. endorphins
31. stress-induced analgesia
32. associative
33. activity
34. behavior
35. transtheoretical
36. contemplation
37. action
38. termination
39. three to six
40. one third
41. Behavioral
42. exercise
43. sexual
44. women
45. homosexual men
46. maladjustment
47. reinforcement
48. motivation
49. Harm-reduction
50. lapses
51. Health psychologists

Answer Key for Practice Test Multiple-Choice Items

1. d
2. b
3. d
4. b
5. a
6. c
7.
16. b
17. a
18. c
19. a
20. c
21. d

Chapter 14 437

7. b
8. b
9. d
10. a
11. b
12. c
13. a
14. b
15. a

22. d
23. b
24. c
25. c
26. c
27. b
28. c
29. c
30. d

Answer Key for Practice Test True/False Items

1. T
2. F
3. T
4. F
5. T

6. T
7. F
8. F
9. T
10. T

Answer Key for Practice Test Short-Answer Questions

1. (a) A stressor is a stimulus that places strong demands on us or threatens us. (b) Stress is defined as a pattern of cognitive appraisals, physiological responses, and behavioral tendencies that occur in response to a perceived imbalance between situational demands and the resources needed to cope with them. Stress may be major or minor, event-focused or ongoing. The effects of ongoing stress are often cumulative.

2. Primary appraisal involves determining the extent to which a situation is benign, neutral, irrelevant, or threatening. Secondary appraisal involves determining one's ability to cope with the situation by examining one's coping resources. Additional appraisal steps are judging the consequences of the situation and determining the personal meaning of the situation.

3. Protective factors are environmental or personal resources that help people to cope more effectively with stressful events. These include social support, coping self-efficacy, coping skills, and optimism.

4. The transtheoretical model outlines six stages of behavior change: precontemplation, contemplation, preparation, action, maintenance, and termination (which means success—not quitting, as one might think). Notice that half the model goes by before we reach "action." However, the stages do not necessarily occur in order. Many people move forward and backward through the stages as they try to change their behavior and try repeatedly to change before they finally succeed. Still, failure at a given stage is likely if the person has not mastered previous stages.

5. Strategies for reducing high-risk sexual behavior and substance abuse include multimodal programs which combine several techniques such as aversion, stress management, and positive reinforcement; motivational interviewing which elicits the person's own motivation to change self-defeating behaviors; harm reduction which focuses on reducing the ill effects of a behavior rather than stopping the behavior; and relapse prevention which encourages the person to stick with the changed behavior even when an occasional lapse occurs.

Answer Key for Practice Test Essay Questions

As you may have guessed, there are no right or wrong answers to the essay questions in this practice test. That does not mean, however, that all essays are equally good. To get maximum learning benefit from the essay questions, do the following:

- Review each essay a day or two after you wrote it, noting any necessary corrections and any additional support for your points that you can think of.
- Review the section in your textbook that pertains to the topic of each essay. Annotate your essay with any corrections or additional support for your points that you find in the text.
- Spend a few minutes researching the topic of each essay on the Internet. Annotate your essay further with any additional (reliable) information you find.
- Finally, reread each essay with the annotations you have added.

Chapter 15
PSYCHOLOGICAL DISORDERS

A. Learning Objectives: *These objectives are expanded from the Focus Questions found in the margins of your textbook. When you have mastered the material in this chapter, you will be able to:*

15.1   Describe the demonological, behavioral, cognitive, humanistic, and sociocultural perspectives on abnormal behavior.

15.2   Describe the vulnerability-stress model of abnormal behavior and how it illustrates person-situation interactions.

15.3   Cite and define the "Three Ds" that enter into diagnoses of abnormal behavior.

15.4   Define reliability and validity as applied to diagnostic classification systems.

15.5   Describe the five axes of the *DSM-IV-TR*.

15.6   Describe the effects of psychiatric labeling on social and self perceptions.

15.7   Differentiate between competency and insanity as legal concepts, and explain how they have affected recent court cases.

15.8   Describe the four components of anxiety.

15.9   Describe characteristics of anxiety disorders including phobic disorder, generalized anxiety disorder, panic disorder, and obsessive-compulsive disorder.

15.10 Describe the four major features of posttraumatic stress disorder (PTSD).

15.11 Describe the biological factors involved in causing anxiety disorders.

15.12 Compare psychoanalytic and cognitive explanations of anxiety disorders.

15.13 Describe anxiety disorders in terms of classical conditioning, observational learning, and operant conditioning.

15.14 Describe three types of somatoform disorders and their causal factors.

15.15 Describe the three types of dissociative disorders and their causal factors.

15.16 Describe the trauma-dissociation theory of dissociative identity disorder (DID) and how critics challenge and explain DID.

15.17 Describe the four classes of symptoms that characterize depression and mania, and describe sex differences in symptom manifestation.

15.18 Cite evidence for genetic and biochemical factors in depression and mania.

15.19 Describe the cognitive triad, the depressive attributional pattern, and learned helplessness in relation to depression.

15.20 Describe how Lewinsohn's learning theory explains the downward spiral that occurs in depression.

15.21 Describe the sociocultural factors related to prevalence, manifestations, and sex differences in depression.

15.22 Describe the motives for suicide, identify the warning signs of suicide, and state four guidelines for helping a suicidal person.

15.23 Define schizophrenia, and describe the major cognitive, behavioral, emotional, and perceptual features of schizophrenia.

15.24 Describe the differences among the four major types of schizophrenic disorders.

15.25 Describe the evidence for genetic, neurological, and biochemical factors involved in causing schizophrenic disorders.

15.26 Contrast the way that psychoanalytic and cognitive theorists explain the symptoms of schizophrenia.

15.27 Describe the characteristics of antisocial personality disorder.

15.28 Compare the way that biological and behavioral theorists account for antisocial personality disorder.

15.29 Describe the Schachter-Latané study and how it supports the emotional-deficit theory of antisocial personality disorder.

15.30 Describe the major features of borderline personality disorder and the causes of the disorder.

15.31 Describe the major features and causal factors in attention deficit hyperactivity disorder (ADHD) and autistic disorders, as well as implications for adult functioning.

Chapter 15

B. Chapter Overview

Psychological disorders are so widespread that even if you never experience one in your lifetime, you will almost certainly know someone who does. Ancient humans believed that abnormal behavior is caused by supernatural forces. Up until fairly recent history, people with psychological disorders were subjected to trephination to "release" the spirit, or branded as witches. Early biological views, such as those of Greek physician Hippocrates, suggested that psychological disorders are diseases just like physical disorders. Early psychological theories focused on the use of psychoanalytic, behavioral, cognitive, and humanistic theories to explain abnormality. Today, most clinical psychologists and counselors believe in the vulnerability-stress model which suggests that we all have some susceptibility for developing a psychological disorder, given sufficient stress. Biological, psychological, and environmental and sociocultural factors all play a role in the development of psychological disorders.

Judgments about what an "abnormal" behavior is are often difficult to make, can vary from culture to culture, and can change as societies develop. A current working definition for abnormal behavior is behavior that is personally distressing, personally dysfunctional or self-defeating, and/or so culturally deviant that other people judge it to be inappropriate or maladaptive. The most widely used diagnostic system for classifying mental disorders in the United States is called the *Diagnostic and Statistical Manual of Mental Disorders, Fourth Edition, Text Revision. (DSM-IV-TR)*. *DSM-IV-TR* uses five axes (primary diagnosis, personality disorders or mental retardation, relevant medical conditions, severity of psychosocial stressors, and global assessment of functioning) to help clinicians understand disorders. The behavioral criteria in *DSM-IV-TR* are more specific than those of previous versions of the DSM, which has enhanced the reliability of diagnoses but has also made it more difficult to categorize some people. Diagnostic labeling of people can influence others' perception of and interactions with those labeled, and can also affect self-perception. Diagnostic labeling may have legal consequences too, although "insanity" is a legal and not a psychological term. Criminal "insanity" defense standards have shifted since the 1980s; defendants must now prove that they were *not* sane when they committed the crime.

In anxiety disorders, the frequency and intensity of anxiety responses are out of proportion to the situations that trigger them, and the anxiety interferes with daily life. Anxiety disorders have subjective-emotional, cognitive, physiological, and behavioral components. Phobias are strong and irrational fears of certain objects or situations. Generalized anxiety disorder is a chronic state of anxiety (called free-floating) that is not attached to specific situations or objects. Panic disorders involve sudden and unpredictable anxiety that is extremely intense. Obsessive-compulsive disorder involves repetitive and unwelcome thoughts, images, and impulses (the obsessions) and repetitive behavioral responses (the compulsions). People who have been exposed to traumatic live events may develop posttraumatic stress disorder (PTSD); symptoms include anxiety, flashbacks, avoidance of reminders of the traumatic event, and survivor guilt in cases in which others in the same situation did not survive.

Biological factors in anxiety include genetic and biochemical processes, (e.g., an overreactive autonomic system), or neurotransmitter functioning in parts of the brain that regulate emotional arousal. Psychological factors are also implicated in the development of anxiety disorders. For example, unconscious conflicts, maladaptive thought patterns and beliefs, and learning have been studied. Sociocultural factors can also play a role as indicated by the existence of various culture-bound anxiety disorders.

Somatoform disorders involve physical complaints or disabilities that suggest a medical problem but that have no known biological cause and are not produced voluntarily by the person. Somatoform disorders include hypochondriasis, pain disorder, and conversion disorder. Patients with conversion disorder present with serious neurological symptoms such as paralysis but often exhibit "la belle indifference," a strange lack of concern about their symptoms.

Dissociative disorders involve a breakdown of the normal integration of personality, resulting in significant alterations in memory or identity. These disorders include psychogenic amnesia, psychogenic fugue, and dissociative identity disorder (or DID, formerly called multiple personality disorder). According to trauma-dissociation theory, dissociative disorders develop in response to severe stress in a person's life.

Together with anxiety disorders, mood disorders are the most prevalent psychological disorders. Depression involves emotional, cognitive, motivational, and somatic (body) symptoms. Major depression may lead people to be unable to function, whereas a less intense form of depression called dysthymia has less dramatic effects on personal functioning. Bipolar disorder involves both depression and periods of mania, which is a state of excited mood and behavior. Women experience higher rates of depression, but not of bipolar disorder, than do men.

Biological factors, including genetic and neurochemical factors, play an important role in the development of mood disorders. Low levels of neurotransmitters such as serotonin, dopamine, and norepinephrine may be particularly likely to influence the development of mood disorders. Psychological factors include personality-based vulnerability often due to early traumatic losses or rejection. Cognitive processes implicated in depression include Beck's "depressive negative triad" of negative thoughts concerning the world, oneself, and the future. A typical pattern of depressive attributions is often found with depressed individuals attributing negative events to the self and positive events to outside factors. Learned helplessness theory provides another account of cognitive dysfunction associated with depression. Learning and environmental factors play an important role in the disorder with a significant loss often triggering depressive symptoms. Sociocultural factors can affect the prevalence of depressive disorders and the ways in which depression is manifested. Depression is the strongest predictor of suicide. Warning signs of suicide should be taken seriously and professional help should be sought.

Schizophrenia is a psychotic disorder that involves severe disturbances in thinking, speech, perception, emotion, and behavior. Delusions, hallucinations, and disordered speech and thinking characterize those with schizophrenia who have positive symptoms, whereas those with negative symptoms have an absence of normal reactions such as a lack of normal emotional expression or motivation. The *DSM-IV-TR* differentiates among four major types of schizophrenia: paranoid type, disorganized type, catatonic type, and undifferentiated type.

Strong evidence exists for the role of genetic factors in the development of schizophrenia. Magnetic resonance imaging studies have shown abnormalities in schizophrenic people, including brain atrophy (a loss of neurons in the cerebral cortex and the limbic system), enlarged cerebral ventricles, and physical abnormalities of the thalamus, particularly in patients who present with negative symptoms. Overactivity of the dopamine system may play a role in the development of schizophrenia, particularly in patients with positive symptoms who are often treated with antipsychotic drugs that target dopamine.

Psychological factors in schizophrenia have also been studied. Psychodynamic theorists interpret the social withdrawal that is characteristic of schizophrenia in terms of regression in the face of unbearable stress. Cognitive psychologists focus on faulty attentional mechanisms. Family dynamics, especially in families with a high level of expressed emotion (criticism, hostility, and overinvolvement) may affect the likelihood of relapse. Studies of sociocultural factors have indicated that the prevalence of schizophrenia is highest in lower-socioeconomic populations. Schizophrenia appears to be relatively "culture-free," as it occurs fairly evenly worldwide.

Personality disorders are stable, ingrained, inflexible, and maladaptive ways of thinking, feeling, and behaving. The most serious of these is antisocial personality disorder. This disorder is characterized by an egocentric and manipulative tendency toward immediate self-gratification, a lack of empathy for others, a tendency to act out impulsively, and a failure to profit from punishment. Biological studies have focused on the role of genetics, as well as physiological factors, that lead to underarousal. Psychodynamic theorists view this disorder as a failure to develop a superego, and learning theorists focus on factors such as classical conditioning and modeling as causes of antisocial personality disorder.

People with borderline personality disorder (BPD) are characterized by serious instability in their behavior, emotions, identity, and interpersonal relationships. Most frequently women, they tend to be chaotic and impulsive, often self-destructive, frequently experiencing chronic anger, loneliness, and emptiness. BPD is associated with a number of other disorders, including mood disorders, PTSD, and substance-abuse disorders. Studies have suggested there is a genetic component to BPD. Causal factors may be associated with early rejection or inconsistent parenting; thereafter, the individual's volatile behavior may evoke rejection from others, affirming their sense of worthlessness and their view of the world as malevolent. BPD also appears to be more common in unstable or rapidly changing sociocultural environments.

Children appear to be at high risk for a variety of disorders, and many childhood disorders are precursors for psychological disorders in adulthood. ADHD and autistic disorder are childhood disorders that are currently the focus of much attention. ADHD may involve inattention, hyperactivity/impulsivity, or a combination of the two. The precise causes are not known, but there seems to be some genetic component. Autistic disorder is generally a long-term disorder characterized by a lack of responsiveness to others, poor comprehension of others' emotional responses, difficulties in communication, and highly repetitive and rigid behaviors. Brain-imaging studies have found both structural and functional differences in the brains of autistic children compared with others. Current research in disorders of children continues to investigate the biological bases of both autistic disorder and ADHD.

C. Chapter Outline

HISTORICAL PERSPECTIVES ON DEVIANT BEHAVIOR
DEFINING AND CLASSIFYING PSYCHOLOGICAL DISORDERS
    What Is "Abnormal"?
    Diagnosing Psychological Disorders
    Consequences of Diagnostic Labeling
        Social and Personal Consequences
        Legal Consequences
        What Do You Think: "Do I Have That Disorder?"
    In Review
ANXIETY DISORDERS
    Phobic Disorder
    Generalized Anxiety Disorder
    Panic Disorder
    Obsessive-Compulsive Disorder
    Posttraumatic Stress Disorder
        What Do You Think: "Growth from Trauma?"
    Causal Factors in Anxiety Disorders
        Biological Factors
        Psychological Factors
            Psychodynamic Theories
            Cognitive Factors
            The Role of Learning
            Sociocultural Factors
    In Review
SOMATOFORM AND DISSOCIATIVE DISORDERS: ANXIETY INFERRED
    Somatoform Disorders
    Dissociative Disorders
        Dissociative Identity (Multiple Personality) Disorder
        What Causes DID?
    In Review
MOOD DISORDERS

Chapter 15

    Depression
    Bipolar Disorder
    Prevalence and Course of Mood Disorders
    Causal Factors in Mood Disorders
        Biological Factors
        Psychological Factors
            Personality-Based Vulnerability
            Cognitive Processes
            Learning and Environmental Factors
        Sociocultural Factors
    Applying Psychological Science: Understanding and Preventing Suicide
    In Review
SCHIZOPHRENIA
    Characteristics of Schizophrenia
    Subtypes of Schizophrenia
    Causal Factors in Schizophrenia
        Biological Factors
            Genetic Predisposition
            Brain Abnormalities
            Biochemical Factors
        Psychological Factors
        Environmental Factors
        Sociocultural Factors
    In Review
PERSONALITY DISORDERS
    Antisocial Personality Disorder
        Causal Factors
            Biological Factors
            Psychological and Environmental Factors
    Research Close-Up: Fear, Avoidance Learning, and Psychopathy
    Borderline Personality Disorder
        Causal Factors
    Beneath the Surface: How Dangerous Are People with Psychological Disorders?
    In Review
CHILDHOOD DISORDERS
    Attention Deficit/Hyperactivity Disorder
    Autistic Disorder
        Causal Factors
    In Review
    A Closing Thought

D. Review at a Glance: *Write the term that best fits the blank to review what you learned in this chapter.*

Historical Perspectives on Deviant Behavior

One of the earliest beliefs about abnormal behavior was that it was caused by supernatural forces, an idea called the (1) _____ approach. Early biological views, such as that of Hippocrates, stressed that psychological disorders have the same causes as physical diseases. Current views of abnormal behavior emphasize the (2) _____-_____ model, which proposes that everyone may be vulnerable to psychological disorders under certain stressful environmental conditions.

Defining and Classifying Psychological Disorders

What is abnormal behavior? It is frequently defined as behavior that is personally (3) _____, dysfunctional or self-defeating, and/or so culturally (4) _____ that other people judge it to be inappropriate or maladaptive. When diagnosing psychological disorders, clinicians must use criteria that are both reliable and valid. (5)_____ means that clinicians using the system should show high levels of agreement in their diagnostic decisions, whereas (6) _____ means that the diagnostic categories should capture the essential features of the various disorders. The most widely used classification system in the United States, called the (7) _____, uses five (8) _____ to guide diagnoses of psychological disorders. Diagnosis of a primary psychological disorder is recorded on Axis I, and personality disorders and mental retardation are assessed on Axis II. Relevant (9) _____ conditions, severity of psychosocial (10) _____, and global assessment of (11) _____ are all included in the evaluation. Diagnostic labeling of people may have social and also (12) _____ consequences. The "insanity defense" is a legal, not a psychological, issue, and in today's criminal cases, the burden of proof is on the (13) _____.

Anxiety Disorders

Anxiety disorders are marked by frequent and intense anxiety responses that are (14) _____ _____ _____ to the situations that trigger them, and the anxiety interferes with daily life. Strong and irrational fears of certain objects or situations are called (15) _____. Fear of public spaces is called (16) _____; excessive fear of situations in which the person might be evaluated or embarrassed is called (17) _____ phobia. Fears of dogs, snakes, spiders, airplanes and other objects are called (18) _____ phobias. When a person experiences a chronic state of "free-floating" anxiety that is not tied to any specific thing, that person's condition is diagnosed as (19) _____ _____ disorder. Sudden, unpredictable, and intense anxiety is a symptom of (20) _____ _____. Repetitive, unwelcome thoughts, images, or impulses that invade consciousness are called (21) _____, whereas repetitive behavioral responses are called (22) _____. A person who has both has (23) _____-_____ disorder. People who have been exposed to traumatic live events may experience (24) _____ _____ disorder, with symptoms including anxiety, (25) _____, avoidance of reminders of the traumatic event, and (26) _____ _____ in cases in which others in the same situation did not survive.

Biological factors in anxiety include genetic and biochemical processes (e.g., an (27) _____ autonomic system) or neurotransmitter functioning in parts of the brain that regulate emotional arousal. Psychological factors such as (28) _____ conflicts, maladaptive (29) _____ patterns and beliefs, and learning may all play a part in anxiety disorders. Sociocultural factors can also be involved, as indicated by the existence of various (30) _____-_____ anxiety disorders.

Somatoform and Dissociative Disorders: Anxiety Inferred

Somatoform disorders involve (31) _____ complaints that have no known biological cause. Patients with (32) _____ disorder present with serious neurological symptoms, such as paralysis, but often exhibit "(33) _____ _____ _____," a strange lack of concern about their symptoms. A person who complains of a variety of vague illnesses that lack a physiological basis is often found to have (34) _____. People with (35) _____ disorder experience pain that is out of proportion to their medical condition, or for which no physical problem can be found.

Dissociative disorders involve a breakdown of the normal integration of personality. In (36) _____ _____, a person responds to a stressful event with extensive but selective memory loss. (37) _____ _____ involves a loss of personal identity and the establishment of a new identity in a new location. The disorder formerly known as multiple personality disorder is called (38) _____ _____ disorder. An explanation of this disorder called (39) _____-_____ theory suggests that the development of new personalities occurs in response to severe stress, often relentless abuse during childhood.

Mood Disorders

Depression involves emotional, (40) _____, motivational, and somatic (body) symptoms. (41) _____ depression may lead people to be unable to function. A milder but more chronic form of depression called (42) _____ has less dramatic effects on personal functioning. (43) _____ disorder involves both depression and periods of mania, which is a state of (44) _____ mood and behavior. Women experience (45) _____ rates of depression, but not of bipolar disorder, than men do.

Low levels of neurotransmitters such as (46) _____, dopamine, and norepinephrine may be involved in mood disorders. (47) _____ factors, such as rejection in early childhood, have also been implicated. Cognitive processes associated with depression include Beck's "(48) _____ _____ _____" of negative thoughts concerning the world, (49) _____, and the future. A typical pattern of depressive attributions has depressed individuals attributing (50) _____ events to the self and positive events to (51) _____ factors. Learned (52) _____ theory illustrates how learning may be involved in mood disorders. Environmental factors, such as traumatic loss, may also play a role.

Sociocultural factors can affect the (53) _____ of depressive disorders and the ways in which depression is manifested. Depression is the strongest predictor of (54) _____. Warning signs should be taken seriously and (55) _____ _____ should be sought.

Schizophrenia

Schizophrenia is a psychotic disorder that involves severe disturbances in thinking, speech, (56) _____, emotion, and behavior. Schizophrenic patients sometimes have (57) _____, false beliefs that are sustained in the face of evidence to the contrary, and (58) _____, false perceptions that have a compelling sense of reality. Delusions, hallucinations, and disordered speech and thinking characterize those with schizophrenia who have (59) _____ symptoms, whereas those with (60) _____ symptoms have an absence of normal reactions, such as a lack of normal emotional expression or motivation. *The DSM-IV-TR* differentiates among four major types of schizophrenia. Delusions of persecution and grandeur are features of the (61) _____ type. Confusion, incoherence, and severe deterioration of adaptive behavior are characteristic of the (62) _____ type. The (63) _____ type involves extreme motor disturbances.

Schizophrenia is thought to have a biological basis including the influence of genetic factors. Magnetic resonance imaging studies have shown abnormalities in schizophrenic people, including (64) _____ _____ (a loss of neurons in the cerebral cortex and the limbic system), enlarged cerebral (65) _____, and physical abnormalities of the thalamus, particularly in patients who present with (66) _____ symptoms. (67) _____ psychologists focus on faulty attentional mechanisms. Environmental factors may also play a role in the development of the disorder. The prevalence of schizophrenia is (68) _____ in lower-socioeconomic populations. Schizophrenic patients are more likely to relapse after treatment if they return to a home with a high degree of (69) _____ _____.

Psychological factors in schizophrenia have also been studied. Psychodynamic theorists interpret the social withdrawal that is characteristic of schizophrenia in terms of (70) _____ in the face of unbearable stress. Cognitive psychologists focus on faulty (71) _____ mechanisms. Family dynamics, especially in families with a high level of (72) _____ and over-involvement, may affect the likelihood of relapse. Studies of sociocultural factors have indicated that the prevalence of schizophrenia is (73) _____ in lower-socioeconomic populations.

Personality Disorders

Personality disorders are characterized by stable ways of thinking, feeling, and behaving that are (74) _____. People who exhibit the most serious personality disorder, (75) _____ _____ disorder, seem to lack a conscience, are impulsive and manipulative, and don't seem to learn from (76) _____. People

Chapter 15   449

with (77) _____ _____ disorder are characterized by serious (78) _____ in their behavior, emotions, identity, and interpersonal relationships. Genetics and early rejection or (79) _____ parenting have been associated with developing BPD.

Childhood Disorders

Many childhood disorders are precursors for psychological disorders in adulthood. ADHD and (80) _____ disorder are childhood disorders that are currently the focus of much attention. (81) _____ may involve inattention, hyperactivity/impulsivity, or a combination of the two. (82) _____ children generally have trouble communicating with others from an early age and exhibit highly (83) _____ and rigid behaviors. Current research in disorders of children continues to investigate the (84) _____ bases of both autistic disorder and ADHD.

E. Concept Cards

Truly learning a concept means integrating it into the way *you* think about things. To integrate concepts successfully, you must translate the words and examples your text or instructor provides into words and examples that are meaningful to you.

For this exercise, obtain some note cards (3" × 5" or 4" × 6") to make a deck of concept cards. On one side of each card, write the *concept* from the list below (e.g., "obsessions") at the top. Read the textbook definition, provided following, and then write the definition *in your own words* on the concept card (e.g., for "obsessions," you might write "can't stop thinking about troubling thoughts"). Simply imagine that a friend has asked you what the concept means, and write down what you would answer. Writing the definition in your own words requires you to think deeply about its meaning. When next you see your own version of the definition, it will make intuitive sense to you—no translation required.

On the second side of the card, write your own example of the concept. Again, coming up with your own example requires you to think deeply about the application of the concept, and you will more easily understand and remember the example when you study for a test. If you use an example from the text, or from class, make it your own by writing it in your own words. You can always check with your instructor that your example is indeed a good example of the concept.

CONCEPT Definition in my own words (side 1 of card)	Example of the concept in my own words, preferably drawn from my own experience (side 2 of card)

The following is a list of all the boldface concepts from your textbook with the author's definition. Write the definition in your own words, together with your own example of the concept, to create a *concept card* as described earlier, or write in the space provided.

Vulnerability-stress model: A model that proposes each individual has some degree of vulnerability (ranging from very low to very high) for developing a psychological disorder, given sufficient stress

Abnormal behavior: Behavior that is personally distressing, personally dysfunctional, and/or so culturally deviant that other people judge it to be inappropriate or maladaptive

Reliability: High levels of agreement among clinical judges in their diagnostic decisions

Validity: Diagnostic categories have high validity when they accurately capture the essential features of the various disorders

Competency: A defendant's state of mind at the time of a judicial hearing

Insanity: The presumed state of mind of the defendant at the time the crime was committed

Anxiety: The state of tension and apprehension that is a natural response to perceived threat

Anxiety disorders: Disorders characterized by anxiety responses of a frequency and intensity that are out of proportion to the situation that triggers them and that interferes with daily life

Phobias: Strong and irrational fears of certain objects or situations

Agoraphobia: A fear of open or public places from which escape would be difficult

Social phobias: Excessive fear of situations in which the person might be evaluated and possibly embarrassed

Specific phobias: Phobias of particular things, such as fear of dogs, snakes, spiders, airplanes, elevators, enclosed spaces, water, injections, and germs

Generalized anxiety disorder: A chronic (ongoing) state of diffuse, or free-floating, anxiety, that is not attached to specific situations or objects

Panic disorder: Sudden, unpredictable, and intense bouts of anxiety

Obsessions: Repetitive and unwelcome thoughts, images, or impulses that invade consciousness, are often abhorrent to the person, and are very difficult to dismiss or control

Compulsions: Repetitive behavioral responses that can be resisted only with great difficulty

Posttraumatic stress disorder (PTSD): A severe anxiety disorder that can occur in people who have been exposed to traumatic life events

Neurotic anxiety: Anxiety that occurs when unacceptable impulses threaten to overwhelm the ego's defenses and explode into consciousness or action

Culture-bound disorders: Disorders that occur only in certain locales

Somatoform disorders: Disorders that involve physical complaints or disabilities that suggest a medical problem but that have no known biological cause and are not produced voluntarily by the person

Hypochondriasis: A condition in which people become unduly alarmed about any physical symptom they detect and are convinced that they have or are about to have a serious illness

Pain disorder: A condition in which people experience intense pain that either is out of proportion to whatever medical condition they might have, or for which no physical basis can be found

Conversion disorder: A somatoform disorder in which serious neurological symptoms, such as paralysis, loss of sensation, or blindness, suddenly occur

Dissociative disorders: Disorders involving a breakdown of normal personality integration resulting in significant alterations in memory or identity

Psychogenic amnesia: A condition characterized by extensive but selective memory loss in response to a stressful event

Psychogenic fugue: A profound dissociative disorder in which a person loses all sense of personal identity, gives up his or her customary life, wanders to a new faraway location, and establishes a new identity

Dissociative identity disorder (DID) (formerly called multiple personality disorder): A disorder in which two or more separate personalities coexist in the same person

Trauma-dissociation theory: A theory of dissociative identity disorder that proposes that new personalities occur in response to severe stress

Mood disorders: Emotion-based disorders which include depression and mania (excessive excitement)

Major depression: An intense depressed state that leaves the person unable to function effectively in their lives

Dysthymia: A less-intense form of depression that has less dramatic effects on personal and occupational functioning than major depression

Bipolar disorder: A condition in which depression (which is usually the dominant state) alternates with periods of mania

Mania: A state of highly excited mood and behavior that is quite the opposite of depression

Depressive cognitive triad: Negative thoughts concerning the world, oneself, and the future

Depressive attributional pattern: A pattern of attributing successes or other positive events to factors outside the self and attributing negative outcomes to personal factors

Learned helplessness theory: A theory that holds that depression occurs when people expect that bad events will occur and that there is nothing they can do to prevent them or cope with them

Suicide: The willful taking of one's own life

Schizophrenia: Severe disturbances in thinking, speech, perception, emotion, and behavior

Delusions: False beliefs that are sustained in the face of evidence that normally would be sufficient to destroy them

Hallucinations: False perceptions that have a compelling sense of reality

Paranoid schizophrenia: A subtype of schizophrenia whose most prominent features are delusions of persecution in which people believe that others mean to harm them, and delusions of grandeur in which people believe they are enormously important

Disorganized schizophrenia: A subtype of schizophrenia whose central features are confusion and incoherence together with severe deterioration of adaptive behavior, such as personal hygiene, social skills, and self-care

Catatonic schizophrenia: A subtype of schizophrenia characterized by striking motor disturbances ranging from muscular rigidity to random or repetitive movements

Undifferentiated schizophrenia: A category of schizophrenia assigned to people who exhibit some of the symptoms and thought disorders of other categories of schizophrenia but who do not meet enough of the specific criteria to be diagnosed in those categories

Positive symptoms of schizophrenia: Bizarre behaviors, such as delusions, hallucinations, and disordered speech and thinking

Negative symptoms of schizophrenia: An absence of normal reactions, such as a lack of emotional expression, loss of motivation, and an absence of speech

Dopamine hypothesis: A theory that the symptoms of schizophrenia—particularly positive symptoms—are produced by overactivity of the dopamine system in areas of the brain that regulate emotional expression, motivated behavior, and cognitive functioning

Regression: A defense mechanism in which a person retreats to an earlier and more secure (even infantile) stage of psychosocial development in the face of overwhelming anxiety

Expressed emotion: Family communication pattern that involves high levels of criticism ("All you do is sit in front of that TV"), hostility ("We're getting sick and tired of your craziness"), and overinvolvement ("You're not going unless I go with you")

Social causation hypothesis: A hypothesis that attributes the higher prevalence of schizophrenia to the higher levels of stress that low-income people experience

Social drift hypothesis: A hypothesis that proposes that as people develop schizophrenia, their personal and occupational functioning deteriorates, so that they drift down the socioeconomic ladder

Personality disorders: A disorder in which the person exhibits stable, ingrained, inflexible, and maladaptive ways of thinking, feeling, and behaving

Antisocial personality disorder: A disorder in which the person seems to lack a conscience; the person exhibits little anxiety or guilt and tends to be impulsive and unable to delay gratification of needs

Borderline personality disorder (BPD): A collection of symptoms characterized primarily by serious instability in behavior, emotion, identity, and interpersonal relationships

Splitting: The failure to integrate positive and negative aspects of another's behavior into a coherent whole

Attention deficit/hyperactivity disorder (ADHD): A disorder in which problems may take the form of inattention, hyperactivity/impulsivity, or a combination of the two

Autistic disorder: A long-term disorder characterized by extreme unresponsiveness to others, poor communication skills, and highly repetitive and rigid behavior patterns

F. What's the Difference? A Concept Card Exercise

An important skill in learning concepts is being able to differentiate among concepts that are similar or related in some way. This skill is particularly relevant for multiple-choice tests, especially if you often find yourself wavering between two answers.

Once you have created your own deck of concept cards, select them two by two, each time answering the question "What's the difference between these two concepts?" You can use the word definitions of the concepts or the examples of the concepts to enhance your mastery of the material. In each case, choose pairs of concepts to compare those that are related or similar or that sound the same or that could in some way be confused. It's much easier to spot the difference between two concepts when you are studying, with the textbook available, rather than when considering the question for the first time in a testing situation.

G. Apply What You Know

Think of at least three instances, either actual news events or fictionalized stories in movies or books, of a person with a psychological disorder engaging in criminal behavior. In the space below, describe the disorder according to what the diagnosis would most likely be, and the nature of the person's criminal behavior. Assess how typical, or realistic, the behavior is among individuals with that disorder.

News Event, Movie, Book, etc.	Type of Disorder	Criminal Behavior	How Typical or Realistic?

H. On the Web: *As with any online research, it is important to consider how legitimate a given source is before you rely on the information it presents. Your instructor or Internet adviser may give you some specific guidelines for distinguishing which kinds of Web sites tend to be reputable.*

A. A number of individuals have made notable contributions to our understanding of psychological disorders. Search the Web for more information about some of those listed below.

Aaron Beck

Eugene Bleuler

Alex B. Caldwell

Sigmund Freud

Chapter 15 459

Peter Lewinsohn

Frank Putnam

David Rosenhan

Martin Seligman

B. Take a look at the concept cards you have created for this chapter, or the key concepts listed in section E. In the space provided, make a list of any whose definitions or associations you are not yet confident of and any you'd like to learn more about. Try entering the terms on your list into your search engine. Make notes of any helpful information you find.

Key Concept/Information Found

C. Go to the Web site News of the Weird, at http://www.newsoftheweird.com, and find three cases of behaviors that you would consider abnormal. Using the criteria for what an abnormal behavior is, explain why each behavior is "abnormal."

D. Using the American Psychological Association Web site (http://www.apa.org/) as your starting point, research some gender differences in psychological disorders. For example, your textbook mentions that anxiety disorders and depression are more prevalent in women, whereas antisocial personality disorder affects predominantly men. What are the current gender statistics on these disorders? Are there differences in the *way* a disorder is experienced by men versus women? Summarize your findings, citing sources.

I. Analyze This: *Chapter 1 of your textbook begins by presenting these four basic steps in the critical thinking process:*
- *"What exactly are you asking me to believe?"*
- *"How do you know? What is the evidence?"*
- *"Are there other possible explanations?"*
- *"What is the most reasonable conclusion?"*

You might picture this as a four-step analysis to help you decide whether to accept a given theory or assertion. Now it's your turn to put your textbook to this test.

Review the sections in Chapter 15 of your textbook under the heading "Phobic Disorder." If someone told you that anyone with a phobia needs to seek professional help because the phobia is unlikely to go away by itself, would you agree? Analyze that assertion in the space provided. When you have finished, consider using this four-step analysis to evaluate other assertions you encounter.

"What exactly are you asking me to believe?"

"How do you know? What is the evidence?"

"Are there other possible explanations?"

"What is the most reasonable conclusion?"

Chapter 15

J. Practice Test

Multiple-Choice Items: *Write the letter corresponding to your answer in the space to the left of each item.*

_____ 1. A recent immigrant to the United States is having some problems and decides to see a therapist, Dr. White. After the intake interview, Dr. White makes a particular diagnosis and is discussing the case with a colleague, Dr. Broad, when Dr. Broad raises some concerns. He points out that Dr. White may need to reconsider her diagnosis because the behaviors involved are quite common, even considered normal, in the immigrant's native country. The views of Dr. Broad are most consistent with the _____ perspective on psychological disorders.
   a. sociocultural
   b. behavioral
   c. biological
   d. cognitive

_____ 2. Todd, a college student who was a well-adjusted child and teenager, was severely injured in an accident 2 years ago. Last year, his parents separated and began a bitter divorce. A month ago, his girlfriend dumped him. Last week, after failing an exam, Todd had an episode of major depression for the first time in his life. This example best illustrates _____.
   a. learned helplessness
   b. the vulnerability-stress model
   c. the demonological perspective
   d. the trauma dissociation model

_____ 3. During a psychological assessment, a client shares that she just lost her job and recently ended a long-term romantic relationship. Her therapist would record such information on Axis _____ of *DSM-IV-TR*.
   a. I, primary diagnosis
   b. II, personality/developmental disorders
   c. III, relevant physical conditions
   d. IV, severity of psychosocial stressors

_____ 4. When considering the term *insanity*, it is important to remember that _____.
   a. it is an Axis II disorder that has substantial overlap with other Axis I and II disorders
   b. although it has strong reliability, its validity has not yet been fully established
   c. it refers to a defendant's state of mind at the time of a trial, not when the crime was committed
   d. it is a legal term, not a psychological term

_____ 5. Roger is tense and anxious almost every day. Though he is frequently worried and often has the sense that something bad is about to happen, he can't relate his anxiety to any particular situation or setting. He has difficulty getting restful sleep at night and often takes antacids for his upset stomach. Roger's condition would most likely be diagnosed as _____.
   a. social phobia
   b. an environmental or situational phobia
   c. generalized anxiety disorder
   d. posttraumatic stress disorder

_____ 6. Annette is very afraid of germs and disease, so much so that she washes her hands more than 100 times a day to avoid infection. Usually she doesn't show much anxiety, but if she is in a place where she is unable to clean her hands, she can become very distressed and upset. Annette's condition would most likely be diagnosed as _____.
   a. obsessive-compulsive disorder
   b. schizophrenia paranoid type
   c. generalized anxiety
   d. a health-related phobia

_____ 7. One of the major factors in the development of dissociative identity disorder appears to be _____.
   a. very high levels of stress at the current time
   b. severe abuse as a child
   c. genetic
   d. imbalance of neurotransmitters.

_____ 8. Steve has a rather strong fear of social situations. He used to try to go to parties and other social events, but his anxiety would usually overwhelm him. When experiencing these negative emotions, he would often leave parties early, a behavior that allowed him to reduce or eliminate his anxiety. According to the principles of operant conditioning, Steve's escape behavior is being _____, and this means that he is likely to continue the escape behavior in the future.
   a. positively reinforced
   b. negatively reinforced
   c. aversively punished
   d. response-cost punished

_____ 9. The diagnosis for the condition of a person with a euphoric mood, a decreased need for sleep, and grandiose or exaggerated cognitions would most likely be _____.
   a. psychogenic fugue
   b. schizophrenia
   c. major depression
   d. mania

Chapter 15   463

_____ 10. Andy experiences a hearing impairment whenever his alcoholic father comes home. He is unconcerned that he cannot hear his father's drunken tirades. Andy most likely has _____.
   a. a conversion disorder
   b. dissociative fugue
   c. a phobia
   d. panic disorder

_____ 11. Women experience higher rates of ____, but not of ____, than do men.
   a. antisocial personality disorder; borderline personality disorder
   b. schizophrenia; anxiety disorders
   c. major depression; bipolar disorder
   d. anxiety disorders; depression

_____ 12. Jane and Marlee have both recently been accepted into a very competitive honor society. Jane has a tendency to be depressed, whereas Marlee does not. Chances are that Jane will attribute her success to _____ and that Marlee will most likely attribute her achievement to _____.
   a. external factors; external factors as well
   b. external factors; personal factors
   c. personal factors; external factors
   d. personal factors; personal factors as well

_____ 13. Which of the following is a somatoform disorder?
   a. hypochondriasis
   b. psychogenic fugue
   c. panic disorder
   d. ADHD

_____ 14. After surviving a tornado that destroyed his home and killed one of his neighbors, Dean experiences a selective memory loss for specific traumatic events that occurred during the disaster. Other than these specific memory losses, Dean's personality and subjective sense of identity are essentially unchanged. Dean most likely has _____.
   a. psychogenic fugue
   b. dissociative identity disorder
   c. schizophrenia, disorganized type
   d. psychogenic amnesia

_____ 15. Aaron's condition has been diagnosed as schizophrenia. He appears to be confused most of the time, and it is very difficult to communicate with him, because his speech is so disordered that it is often hard to understand what he means. Aaron most likely has the _____ type of schizophrenia.
   a. paranoid
   b. disorganized
   c. undifferentiated

d. catatonic

_____ 16. Many Vietnam veterans came back from the war experiencing a great deal of stress and anxiety. Psychiatrists would likely note that the stressful episodes the soldiers encountered during the war contribute to their current concerns about anxiety. The disorder that most approximates the problems of these soldiers is known as _____.
  a. posttraumatic stress disorder
  b. borderline personality disorder
  c. antisocial personality disorder
  d. panic disorder

_____ 17. A difference between positive and negative symptoms in schizophrenia is that _____.
  a. negative symptoms are more likely to respond to treatment than positive symptoms
  b. schizophrenics like positive symptoms and dislike negative symptoms
  c. positive symptoms are good and negative symptoms are bad
  d. positive symptoms are more likely to respond to treatment than negative symptoms

_____ 18. Hannah complains of numbness in her entire hand; she can't feel anything from the wrist down. Her arm has normal sensation. Hannah most likely has a(n) _____.
  a. anxiety disorder
  b. mood disorder
  c. conversion disorder
  d. hallucination

_____ 19. Which is a psychological theory of depression?
  a. learned helplessness theory
  b. the dopamine hypothesis
  c. the social drift hypothesis
  d. multiple-personality theory

_____ 20. What is Beck's "depressive negative triad"?
  a. depression, anxiety, and schizophrenia
  b. biological, psychological, and environmental factors in depression
  c. negative thoughts concerning the world, oneself, and the future
  d. negative feelings about oneself, one's family, and one's friends

_____ 21. People with multiple personalities are said to have _____.
  a. dissociative amnesia
  b. dissociative fugue
  c. dissociative identity disorder
  d. schizophrenia

_____ 22. Kelly is an intelligent, charming young professional. He got good grades in college by cheating and landed a good job by lying on his résumé and during the interview. He enjoys meeting women, impressing them by lying about his accomplishments, having sex with them, and borrowing money from them, which he does not bother to repay. Kelly feels no remorse whatsoever for his actions. We would most likely diagnose Kelly's condition as _____.
   a. paranoid schizophrenia
   b. residual schizophrenia
   c. obsessive-compulsive disorder
   d. antisocial personality disorder

_____ 23. When clinicians agree in their diagnostic decisions, _____ has been established.
   a. validity
   b. reliability
   c. DSM-IV-TR
   d. "la belle indifference"

_____ 24. Linda is 7 years old and, unlike most other second-graders, finds it impossible to sit still and pay attention in school for even a few minutes. She talks constantly and seems agitated much of the time. At recess, she plays vigorously, and at home is usually seen racing around the house. Linda most likely has _____.
   a. ADHD
   b. conversion disorder
   c. conduct disorder
   d. an internalizing disorder

_____ 25. Schizophrenic patients who are discharged from a hospital to their homes are more likely to relapse if they return to families who are _____.
   a. high in socioeconomic status
   b. low in environmental stressors
   c. high in expressed emotion
   d. low in expressed emotion

_____ 26. According to Freud, neurotic anxiety occurs when _____.
   a. the ego uses defense mechanisms
   b. unacceptable impulses threaten to overwhelm the ego's defenses
   c. a child reaches the oral stage of psychosexual development
   d. a person experiences a panic attack

_____ 27. People with borderline personality disorder are characterized by _____.
   a. unstable emotions and relationships
   b. lack of conscience
   c. delusions, hallucinations, and disordered speech
   d. a strange lack of concern about their symptoms

_____ 28. Since she was very young, Sasha has been unresponsive to others. She does not appear to understand other people's emotional responses, she communicates poorly, and she displays highly repetitive and rigid behaviors. Sasha's condition would most likely be diagnosed as ____.
   a. ADHD
   b. bipolar disorder
   c. antisocial personality disorder
   d. autistic disorder

_____ 29. Seko has schizophrenia. To treat his symptoms, he may take a drug that ____ the activity of the neurotransmitter ____ in his brain.
   a. decreases; norepinephrine
   b. decreases; dopamine
   c. increases; norepinephrine
   d. increases; dopamine

_____ 30. Low levels of ____ have been implicated in depression.
   a. social stressors
   b. serotonin
   c. superego development
   d. personality integration

True/False Items: *Write T or F in the space provided to the left of each item.*

_____ 1. According to the demonological view, psychological disorders are diseases just like physical disorders.

_____ 2. Reliability means that the diagnostic categories accurately capture the essential features of the various disorders.

_____ 3. Generalized anxiety disorder is a chronic state of anxiety (called free-floating) that is not attached to specific situations or objects.

_____ 4. A fear of riding in airplanes would be a type of specific phobia.

_____ 5. The mood disorders involve depression and mania.

_____ 6. Conversion disorder is a type of dissociative disorder.

_____ 7. In psychogenic amnesia, a person develops multiple personalities.

_____ 8. Hallucinations are false perceptions.

_____ 9. There is evidence of a biological basis for schizophrenia.

_____ 10. Autistic children have borderline personality disorder.

Short-Answer Questions

1. What does the vulnerability-stress model argue?

2. What is insanity, and how does it differ from abnormal behavior?

3. How is anxiety a learned response?

4. What are the main characteristics of schizophrenia?

5. What is autistic disorder?

Essay Questions

1. Think of some behaviors that are considered normal in the United States but that other cultures or societies would consider abnormal. Considering what you have learned in this chapter about defining and classifying psychological disorders, into what categories would you classify the "normal" behaviors you are describing?

2. Do you or anyone you know have ADHD that has been diagnosed? (If not, use this essay as a means of meeting new people.) Discuss what it is like to have the disorder, and explain why ADHD is a source of controversy among parents, teachers, school administrators, and psychological and medical professionals.

3. People who have depression are at heightened risk for suicide. Discuss how the biological, psychological, and environmental factors associated with depression might interact to increase the risk of suicide, or suicide attempts, in people with depression.

Answer Keys

Answer Key for Review at a Glance

1. demonological
2. vulnerability-stress
3. distressing
4. deviant
5. Reliability
6. validity
7. *DSM-IV-TR*
8. axes
9. medical
10. stressors
11. functioning
12. legal
13. defendant
14. out of proportion
15. phobias
16. agoraphobia
17. social
18. specific
19. generalized anxiety
20. panic disorder
21. obsessions
22. compulsions
23. obsessive-compulsive
24. posttraumatic stress
43. Bipolar
44. excited
45. higher
46. serotonin
47. Psychological
48. depressive negative triad
49. oneself
50. negative
51. outside
52. helplessness
53. prevalence
54. suicide
55. professional help
56. cognition
57. delusions
58. hallucinations
59. positive
60. negative
61. paranoid
62. disorganized
63. catatonic
64. brain atrophy
65. ventricles
66. negative

25. flashbacks
26. survivor's guilt
27. overreactive
28. unconscious
29. thought
30. culture-bound
31. physical
32. conversion
33. la belle indifference
34. hypochondriasis
35. pain
36. psychogenic amnesia
37. Psychogenic fugue
38. dissociative identity
39. trauma-dissociation
40. cognitive
41. Major
42. dysthymia
67. Cognitive
68. higher
69. expressed emotion
70. regression
71. attentional
72. hostility
73. higher
74. maladaptive
75. antisocial personality
76. punishment
77. borderline personality
78. instability
79. inconsistent
80. autistic
81. ADHD
82. Autistic
83. repetitive
84. biological

Answer Key for Practice Test Multiple-Choice Items

1. a
2. b
3. d
4. d
5. c
6. a
7. b
8. b
9. d
10. a
11. c
12. b
13. a
14. d
15. b
16. a
17. d
18. c
19. a
20. c
21. c
22. d
23. b
24. a
25. c
26. b
27. a
28. d
29. b
30. b

Answer Key for Practice Test True/False Items

1. F
2. F
3. T
4. T
5. T
6. F
7. F
8. T
9. T
10. F

Answer Key for Practice Test Short-Answer Questions

1. The vulnerability-stress model suggests that each of us has some degree of vulnerability for the development of a psychological disorder. The vulnerability may have a biological basis, such as genetics, a brain abnormality, or a hormonal factor. Personality factors, such as low self-esteem or pessimism, may also increase vulnerability. Sociocultural factors can also increase vulnerability. Vulnerability combines with a stressor or stressors to trigger the appearance of a disorder.

2. *Insanity* is a legal, rather than a psychological or psychiatric, term. It refers to the state of mind of a defendant in a criminal case, and the extent to which the person should be held legally liable for their criminal behavior. Psychologists and psychiatrists are interested in diagnosing, understanding, and treating people who behave in ways that are personally distressing, dysfunctional, and/or so culturally deviant that other people judge the behavior to be inappropriate.

3. From the behavioral perspective, anxiety disorders develop because of conditioning processes. For example, phobic reactions may occur because of associating a specific object or event (CS) with pain and trauma (UCS), producing a fear response. Phobias can also be acquired through observation (modeling). Finally, behaviors that reduce anxiety (e.g., avoidance responses) are negatively reinforced, thus maintaining the disorder through operant conditioning.

4. Schizophrenia is a psychotic disorder that involves severe disturbances in thinking, speech, perception, emotion, and behavior. It is characterized by delusions, hallucinations, disorganized speech and thought, and inappropriate or flat affect. Major types of schizophrenia include paranoid, disorganized, catatonic, and undifferentiated.

5. Autistic disorder is generally diagnosed in childhood. It is a long-term disorder characterized by a lack of responsiveness to others, poor comprehension of others' emotional responses, difficulties in communication, and highly repetitive and rigid behaviors. Brain-imaging studies have found both structural and functional differences in the brains of autistic children compared with others.

Answer Key for Practice Test Essay Questions

As you may have guessed, there are no right or wrong answers to the essay questions in this practice test. That does not mean, however, that all essays are equally good. To get maximum learning benefit from the essay questions, do the following:

- Review each essay a day or two after you wrote it, noting any necessary corrections and any additional support for your points that you can think of.
- Review the section in your textbook that pertains to the topic of each essay. Annotate your essay with any corrections or additional support for your points that you find in the text.

- Spend a few minutes researching the topic of each essay on the Internet. Annotate your essay further with any additional (reliable) information you find.
- Finally, reread each essay with the annotations you have added.

Chapter 16
TREATMENT OF PSYCHOLOGICAL DISORDERS

A. Learning Objectives: *These objectives are expanded from the Focus Questions found in the margins of your textbook. When you have mastered the material in this chapter, you will be able to:*

16.1   Explain the interaction of client, therapist and treatment in the process of therapy.

16.2   Describe the major therapeutic goal in psychoanalysis.

16.3   Describe the roles of free association, dream analysis, resistance, transference, and interpretation in psychoanalysis.

16.4   Describe how brief psychodynamic and interpersonal therapies differ from psychoanalysis, and describe research that supports their use.

16.5   Describe how the goals of humanistic therapies differ from psychodynamic therapies.

16.6   Describe the three therapist attributes Rogers found crucial to therapeutic success.

16.7   Describe the goal of Gestalt therapy.

16.8   Describe the four steps (ABCD) in Ellis's rational-emotive therapy, and explain how the model is used in therapy.

16.9   Describe which classical and operant conditioning principles are used in exposure therapy and which problems exposure is used to treat.

16.10 Compare and contrast systematic desensitization with exposure in terms of underlying principles and techniques.

16.11 Describe the limitations of aversion therapy and how its effects can be enhanced.

16.12 Describe how reinforcement and punishment are used therapeutically, and outline the efficacy of these approaches.

16.13 Describe how modeling is used in social-skills training and how self-efficacy is involved in its effectiveness.

16.14 Define eclecticism, and give two examples of new treatment approaches.

16.15 Describe the principles underlying family and marital therapy and the importance of acceptance in marital therapy.

16.16 Describe the barriers to treatment for ethnic minorities and how culturally competent therapists can overcome them.

16.17 Describe the importance of the specificity question in psychotherapy research and Eysenck's challenge of therapeutic effectiveness.

16.19 Describe the major findings of the Consumer Reports survey and on what bases Seligman's conclusions can be challenged.

16.20 Describe what meta-analyses have shown about the effectiveness of therapies.

16.21 List and describe the client variables, therapist factors, and technique variables, and describe common factors that have been shown to be important to treatment outcome.

16.22 Describe tardive dyskinesia and its causes.

16.23 Describe how antianxiety drugs achieve their effects, and indicate their effectiveness and their limitations.

16.24 Describe how antidepressant drugs work, and indicate their effectiveness and their limitations.

16.25 Describe the pros and cons of electroconvulsive therapy (ECT) and with which disorder it is effective.

16.26 Describe the rationale for deinstitutionalization, and explain why deinstitutionalization has resulted in the revolving door phenomenon.

16.27 Describe the positive and negative effects of managed care on mental health treatment.

16.28 Compare and contrast the two major approaches to prevention, and give examples of each.

B. Chapter Overview

The goal of all therapy is to help people change maladaptive thinking, feeling, and behavioral patterns. Categories of professional counselors and therapists include clinical and counseling psychologists, psychiatric social workers, marriage and family counselors, pastoral counselors, and abuse counselors. Therapeutic techniques vary widely and depend on the theories that therapists use to understand psychological disorders.

Psychoanalysis originated in Freud's psychodynamic theory, and its purpose is to help clients achieve insight, the conscious awareness of the unconscious motivations and conflicts that underlie their problems. Freudian psychoanalysts use free-association techniques and dream interpretation in therapy. Clients commonly experience resistance to dealing with painful unconscious conflicts, and transference often occurs, where the conflicts and emotions associated in dealing with others are projected onto the therapist. Psychoanalytic therapists provide interpretation to the clients in an effort to help them achieve insight into their behavior and psychodynamics. Brief psychodynamic and interpersonal therapies use basic concepts from psychoanalysis but focus more on current events and interpersonal problems than on trying to rebuild the client's personality. Conversation between therapist and client typically replaces free association, and therapy sessions are less frequent, more active, and more time-limited than in traditional psychoanalysis.

In person-centered therapy, developed by humanistic theorist Carl Rogers, the therapist's task is to provide a nurturing environment within which the client can grow and achieve his or her potential. The therapist should provide conditions of unconditional positive regard (unqualified acceptance of the person), empathy (being willing and able to view the world through the client's eyes), and genuineness (consistency between the therapist's feelings and behavior) to facilitate the client's self-actualization. Gestalt therapy, developed by Fritz Perls, is another humanistic approach that helps clients become more aware of their feelings and the way they interact with others. Gestalt therapy is often carried out in groups and typically encourages clients to conclude "unfinished business" with significant others by holding imaginary conversations with them.

Cognitive therapies focus on changing maladaptive ways of thinking about oneself and the world. Ellis's rational-emotive therapy focuses on activating events, belief systems, and the emotional and behavioral consequences of one's perceptions in the development of psychological disorders. Treatment techniques involve disputing, or challenging, erroneous beliefs in treatment. Ellis offers an ABCD model of therapy, referring to **a**ctivating event, **b**elief system, **c**onsequences, and **d**isputing erroneous beliefs. Similarly, Beck's cognitive therapy is designed to help clients point out logical errors in "automatic" thinking that underlie disturbances such as mood disorders.

Behavior therapies use basic principles of classical and operant conditioning in therapy. For example, exposure therapy is an extinction procedure using response prevention to eliminate anxiety responses. Systematic desensitization is a learning-based technique for treating anxiety disorders that uses counterconditioning. Aversion therapy is used to reduce deviant approach behaviors. Behavior modification techniques, such as the use of positive reinforcement and punishment, can also be used in therapy. The modeling of social skills can be used to help people to function more effectively in society.

Many therapists are becoming increasingly eclectic in their use of treatments, drawing on a variety of techniques from different theoretical orientations to help their clients. In part, this is based on research findings that show which approaches and techniques are more or less effective for specific problems. For example, cognitive therapy and interpersonal approaches are both highly effective for depression, as is behavior activation treatment, a behavioral technique designed to help depressed clients develop action plans that increase the amount of positive reinforcement they experience in their lives. One, some, or all of these approaches may be used in any particular case. Other integrated therapies target particular disorders such as dialectical behavior therapy (DBT) for the treatment of borderline personality disorder.

Group approaches to therapy provide clients with opportunities to interact with and learn from other people as well as to give and get support and feedback. In some cases, the family, rather than the individual, is treated because of the importance of family dynamics in the development or maintenance of some disorders. Marital therapy focuses on communication, accepting and understanding one's partner's needs, and problem-solving skills.

Cultural factors play a number of roles in the use of psychotherapy. Cultural norms can affect the likelihood of turning to professionals in time of need. A lack of access to services and a lack of skilled counselors who can provide culturally responsive forms of treatment can hinder people in getting treatment. To be culturally competent, a therapist must be able to use knowledge about the client's culture to achieve a broad understanding of the client and at the same time be attentive to how the client may differ from the cultural stereotype. Similarly, male therapists who treat female clients need to be aware of issues and social realities that women face. Cultural and gender sensitivity appear to be more important than a culture or gender match per se between therapist and client.

In evaluating psychotherapies, researchers address the specificity question: "Which types of therapies administered by which types of therapists to which types of clients having which kinds of problems produce which kinds of effects?" This question stresses the interactions among all variables in producing successful therapy. Randomized clinical trials and placebo control groups are considered critical for good research into the effectiveness of psychotherapy. An American Psychological Association task force identified several empirically supported therapies (ESTs) for treating specific disorders in the late 1990s, although critics have raised concerns about the approach. Another method currently underway is to seek empirically supported principles that predict therapeutic outcomes. Meta-analyses are used to statistically combine the results of many studies, and these indicate that therapy does have positive outcomes beyond spontaneous remission, contrary to a controversial study in 1952 that suggested otherwise. Client variables, such as openness, appear to contribute to therapy success, as do the quality of the therapist-client relationship, as well as other factors common to many therapies such as the ability to try out new behaviors. In general, different types of therapy seem to be equally efficacious, although this body of research may mask the differential effectiveness of various therapies for different disorders.

Medicine offers a range of pharmaceuticals to treat psychological disorders. Antianxiety drugs such as Valium and Xanax are widely used. Antidepressant drugs fall into three major categories: tricyclics, monoamine oxidase (MAO) inhibitors, and selective serotonin reuptake inhibitors (SSRIs). Antipsychotic drugs can reduce the need for hospitalization or increase a patient's comfort while hospitalized. Drug treatments work by affecting neurotransmission within the brain and may have undesirable side effects. Electroconvulsive therapy (ECT) is a controversial technique used for treating major depression that does not respond to other treatments. Psychosurgery, a treatment of last resort, refers to surgical procedures that remove or destroy brain tissue. Studies have shown similar alterations of brain functioning in successful treatment whether the treatment involves drug treatment or psychotherapy.

In the 1960s, a deinstitutionalization movement began in the United States, the idea being to transfer the primary focus of treatment of psychiatric disorders from the hospital to the community. Unfortunately, many patients have been released into communities that are unable to care for them, resulting in an increase in the homeless population and a "revolving door" phenomenon of repeated hospitalizations and releases. Another factor that has contributed to inadequate mental health treatment is managed care; although it has had positive effects in spurring research on the effectiveness of psychotherapies, it typically underestimates the amount of therapy needed to deal with various disorders. Preventive mental health programs use both situation-focused prevention, which is directed at reducing or preventing environmental causes of disorders, and competency-focused prevention, which is designed to increase personal resources and coping skills.

C. Chapter Outline

PSYCHOLOGICAL TREATMENTS
PSYCHODYNAMIC THERAPIES
    Psychoanalysis
        Free Association
        Dream Interpretation
        Resistance
        Transference
        Interpretation
    Brief Psychodynamic and Interpersonal Therapies
    In Review
HUMANISTIC PSYCHOTHERAPIES
    Person-Centered Therapy
    Gestalt Therapy
    In Review
COGNITIVE THERAPIES
    Ellis's Rational-Emotive Therapy
    Beck's Cognitive Therapy
BEHAVIOR THERAPIES

Exposure: An Extinction Approach
Systematic Desensitization: A Counterconditioning Approach
Aversion Therapy
Operant Conditioning Treatments
    Positive-Reinforcement Techniques
    Therapeutic Application of Punishment
    Behavioral Activation Therapy
Modeling and Social Skills Training

INTEGRATING AND COMBINING THERAPIES
In Review

GROUP, FAMILY, AND MARITAL THERAPIES
Family Therapy
Marital Therapy

CULTURAL AND GENDER ISSUES IN PSYCHOTHERAPY
Cultural Factors in Treatment Utilization
Gender Issues in Therapy
In Review

EVALUATING PSYCHOTHERAPIES
Eysenck's Great Challenge
Psychotherapy Research Methods
    Survey Research
    What Do You Think? Do Survey Results Provide an Accurate Picture of Treatment Effectiveness?
    Randomized Clinical Trials
        Empirically Supported Treatments
        The Search for Therapeutic Principles
    Meta-Analysis: A Look at the Big Picture
Factors Affecting the Outcome of Therapy
    Client Variables
    Therapist and Technique Variables
    Common Factors
In Review

BIOLOGICAL APPROACHES TO TREATMENT
Drug Therapies
    Antipsychotic Drugs
    Antianxiety Drugs
    Antidepressant Drugs
Beneath the Surface: Some Depressing Facts about Antidepressant Drugs
Electroconvulsive Therapy (ECT)
Psychosurgery
Mind, Body, and Therapeutic Interventions
Research Close-Up: Drug versus Psychological Treatments for Depression: A Randomized Clinical Trial
In Review

PSYCHOLOGICAL DISORDERS AND SOCIETY
Deinstitutionalization

Mental Health Treatment in a Managed-Care Environment
Preventive Mental Health
Applying Psychological Science: When and Where to Seek Therapy
In Review

D. Review at a Glance: *Write the term that best fits the blank to review what you learned in this chapter.*

Psychological Treatments

Psychotherapy of any kind seeks to change (1) _____ thinking, feeling, and behavior patterns. Many different therapeutic techniques are used, depending on the (2) _____ that therapists use to understand psychological disorders.

Psychodynamic Therapies

The goal of psychoanalysis is to help clients achieve (3) _____, the conscious awareness of the psychodynamics that underlie their problems. Freud asked his clients to recline on a couch and to verbally report their thoughts, a technique called (4) _____ _____. Through this technique, as well as (5) _____ _____, Freud believed that therapists could help clients understand the (6) _____ motivations of their behavior. Because it is painful to confront unconscious conflicts, clients often engage in defensive maneuvers called (7) _____ that hinder the process of therapy. Often (8) _____ occurs, where the client projects the conflicts and emotions associated in dealing with others onto the therapist. Brief psychodynamic and interpersonal therapies use basic concepts from psychoanalysis but focus more on (9) _____ events and (10) _____ problems.

Humanistic Psychotherapies

In person-centered therapy, (11) _____ _____ _____ is communicated when therapists show clients that they genuinely care about and accept them. A second vital factor in this therapy is called (12) _____, the willingness and ability of a therapist to see the world through the client's eyes. The third important therapist characteristic is (13) _____, which refers to consistency between a therapist's feelings and his or her behaviors. Another humanistic approach, (14) _____ therapy, often uses the "empty chair" technique, which allows the client to conduct unfinished business with a significant other.

Cognitive Therapies

Cognitive therapies focus on changing (15) _____ ways of (16) _____ about oneself and the world. Treatment techniques involve (17) _____ erroneous beliefs. Ellis's rational-(18) _____ therapy is embodied in his (19)

_____ model. Another approach is (20) _____ cognitive therapy, which revolves around pointing out logical errors in the client's "automatic" thinking that underlie emotional disturbance.

Behavior Therapies

Classical conditioning approaches are often used in treatment of psychological disorders. In the extinction approach called (21) _____, the feared CS is presented without the UCS while using (22) _____ _____ to prevent the response from occurring. (23) _____ _____ is a learning technique developed by Joseph Wolpe to treat anxiety disorders, particularly phobias. In this procedure, the client is first trained in relaxation techniques and is then helped to construct a (24) _____ _____ of low-anxiety to high-anxiety scenes relating to the fear. The client then practices the relaxation techniques while progressing through the stimulus hierarchy. In (25) _____ therapy, the therapist pairs a stimulus that is attractive to a person with a noxious UCS in an attempt to condition an aversion to the CS. (26) _____ _____ techniques are operant-conditioning treatments that involve trying to increase or decrease a specific behavior. In (27) _____ _____ training, clients learn new skills by observing and then imitating a model who performs a behavior.

Integrating and Combining Therapies

Today, therapists use a wide variety of techniques and approaches in treatment, which is called the (28) _____ approach. Cognitive therapy and interpersonal approaches are both highly effective for (29) _____, as is behavior (30) _____ treatment, a behavioral technique designed to help depressed clients develop action plans that increase the amount of positive (31) _____ they experience in their lives. (32) _____ behavior therapy (DBT) for the treatment of borderline personality disorder is an example of an integrated therapy targeting a specific disorder.

Group, Family, and Marital Therapies

Group therapy gives clients opportunities to (33) _____ with and (34) _____ from other people, as well as to give and get (35) _____ and feedback. Family therapy is needed when family (36) _____ are important in a psychological disorder. Marital therapy focuses on (37) _____, accepting one's partner and understanding his or her needs, and (38) _____-_____ skills.

Cultural and Gender Issues in Psychotherapy

Stanley Sue (1998) suggests that (39) _____ _____ therapists are able to use their knowledge about the client's culture to achieve a broad understanding of the client while being attentive to how the client might be different from the cultural stereotype.

Evaluating Psychotherapies

Good research designs to evaluate the effectiveness of psychotherapy involve both (40) _____ _____ trials and (41) _____ _____ groups. Researchers focus on the (42)_____ question: "Which types of therapy, administered by which types of therapists to which types of clients having which kinds of problems, produce which kinds of effects?" An American Psychological Association task force identified several (43) _____-_____ _____ (ESTs) for treating specific disorders in the late 1990s.

The statistical technique of (44) _____-_____ allows researchers to combine the results of many studies to arrive at an overall conclusion. Several factors have been found to affect the outcome of therapy. (45)_____ involves clients' willingness to invest themselves in therapy, whereas (46) _____-_____ refers to their ability to experience and understand internal states and to apply what is learned in therapy to life outside treatment. The quality of the (47) _____-_____ relationship is also important. Various therapies tend to enjoy similar success rates, suggesting that there are (48) _____ _____ shared by these therapies.

Biological Approaches to Treatment

Valium, Xanax, and BuSpar are examples of (49) _____ drugs. Antidepressant drugs fall into three major categories: (50) _____, (51) _____ _____, and (52) _____. (53)_____ drugs are used to treat schizophrenia. These drugs can produce a severe movement disorder called (54) _____ _____.
(55)_____ therapy, or ECT, is used to treat severe major depression.
(56)_____ refers to procedures to remove or destroy brain tissue in an attempt to change disordered behavior.

Psychological Disorders and Society

Concerns about the inadequacies of mental hospitals and the ability of antipsychotic drugs to "normalize" patients' behavior led to a (57) _____ movement to transfer the primary focus of treatment to the community from the hospital. Preventive mental health programs have become increasingly important. In (58)_____-_____ prevention, the focus is on reducing or eliminating the environmental causes of behavior disorders or on enhancing situational factors that help to prevent the development of disorders. (59)_____-_____ prevention programs are designed to increase personal resources and coping skills.

E. Concept Cards

Truly learning a concept means integrating it into the way *you* think about things. To integrate concepts successfully, you must translate the words and examples your text or instructor provides into words and examples that are meaningful to you.

For this exercise, obtain some note cards (3" × 5" or 4" × 6") to make a deck of concept cards. On one side of each card, write the *concept* from the list following (e.g., "eclecticism") at the top. Read the textbook definition provided, and then write the definition *in your own words* on the concept card (e.g., for "eclecticism," you might write "using all kinds of different psychotherapy methods, depending on what will help the client"). Simply imagine that a friend has asked you what the concept means, and write down what you would answer. Writing the definition in your own words requires you to think deeply about its meaning. When next you see your own version of the definition, it will make intuitive sense to you—no translation required.

On the second side of the card, write your own example of the concept. Again, coming up with your own example requires you to think deeply about the application of the concept, and you will more easily understand and remember the example when you study for a test. If you use an example from the text, or from class, make it your own by writing it in your own words. You can always check with your instructor that your example is indeed a good example of the concept.

CONCEPT Definition in my own words (side 1 of card)	Example of the concept in my own words, preferably drawn from my own experience (side 2 of card)

The following is a list of all the boldface concepts from your textbook with the author's definition. Write the definition in your own words, together with your own example of the concept, to create a *concept card* as described previously, or write in the space provided.

Insight: A person's conscious awareness of the psychodynamics that underlie his or her own problems

Free association: A technique in which clients verbally report without censorship any thoughts, feelings, or images that enter their awareness

Resistance: Defensive maneuvers that hinder the process of therapy

Transference: A process that occurs when the client responds irrationally to the analyst as if she or he were an important figure from the client's past

Interpretation: Any statement by the therapist intended to provide the client with insight into his or her behavior or dynamics

Interpersonal therapy: A therapy that focuses almost exclusively on clients' current relationships with important people in their lives

Unconditional positive regard: Unqualified acceptance and love, communicated when therapists show clients that they genuinely care about and accept them, without judgment or evaluation

Empathy: The willingness and ability to view the world through the client's eyes

Genuineness: Consistency between the way the therapist feels and the way he or she behaves

Exposure: A process of classical extinction of the anxiety response by being exposed to the feared CS in the absence of the UCS

Response prevention: A technique used with the exposure method to keep the operant avoidance response from occurring

Chapter 16

Virtual reality (VR): The use of computer technology to create highly realistic "virtual environments" that simulate actual experience so vividly that they evoke many of the same reactions that a comparable real-world environment would

Systematic desensitization: A learning-based treatment for anxiety disorders

Counterconditioning: A procedure to eliminate anxiety in which a new response that is incompatible with anxiety is conditioned to the anxiety-arousing CS

Stimulus hierarchy: Ten to 20 scenes arranged in roughly equal steps from low-anxiety scenes to high-anxiety ones

Aversion therapy: A technique whereby the therapist pairs a stimulus that is attractive to the client (the CS) with a noxious UCS in an attempt to condition an aversion to the CS

Behavior modification: Treatment techniques that apply operant conditioning procedures in an attempt to increase or decrease a specific behavior

Token economy: A system for strengthening desired behaviors through the systematic application of positive reinforcement

Social skills training: A technique whereby clients learn new skills by observing and then imitating a model who performs a socially skillful behavior

Eclecticism: A therapist's willingness to combine treatments and use whatever orientations and therapeutic techniques seem appropriate for the particular client being treated

Behavior activation treatment: A method of therapy designed to counter depression by helping clients develop action plans that increase the amount of positive reinforcement they experience in their lives

Dialectical behavior therapy (DBT): A therapy, developed by Marsha Linehan, for the treatment of borderline personality disorder

Culturally competent therapists: Therapists who can use knowledge about the client's culture to achieve a broad understanding of the client

Feminist therapy: Therapy that focuses on women's issues and strives to help women achieve greater personal freedom and self-determination

Specificity question: "Which types of therapy administered by which kinds of therapists to which kinds of clients having which kinds of problems produce which kinds of effects?"

Spontaneous remission: Symptom reduction in the absence of any treatment

Randomized clinical trial: Clients are randomly assigned to treatment or control conditions, and the treatment and control groups are compared on outcome measures

Chapter 16

Placebo control group: A control group that gets an intervention that is not expected to work

Empirically supported therapies (ESTs): Treatments that had been demonstrated in several independent studies to be efficacious for treating specific disorders

Meta-analysis: A statistical technique that allows researchers to combine the statistical results of many studies to arrive at an overall conclusion

Effect size: The percentage of clients receiving therapy who had a more favorable outcome than that of the average control client who did not receive the treatment

Dodo bird verdict: The finding of similar efficacy for widely differing therapies

Openness: Involves clients' general willingness to invest themselves in therapy and take the risks required to change themselves

Self-relatedness: Refers to a client's ability to experience and understand internal states such as thoughts and emotions, to be attuned to the processes that go on in their relationship with their therapist, and to apply what they learn in therapy to their lives outside of treatment

Common factors: Characteristics shared by these diverse forms of therapy that might contribute to their success

Tardive dyskinesia: A severe movement disorder

Psychosurgery: Surgical procedures that remove or destroy brain tissue in an attempt to change disordered behavior

Deinstitutionalization movement: A social movement dedicated to transferring the primary focus of treatment of psychological disorders from the hospital to the community

Situation-focused prevention: Efforts directed at either reducing or eliminating the environmental causes of behavior disorders or enhancing situational factors that help prevent the development of disorders

Competency-focused prevention: Activities designed to increase personal resources and coping skills

F. What's the Difference? A Concept Card Exercise

An important skill in learning concepts is being able to differentiate among concepts that are similar or related in some way. This skill is particularly relevant for multiple-choice tests, especially if you often find yourself wavering between two answers.

Once you have created your own deck of concept cards, select them two by two, each time answering the question "What's the difference between these two concepts?" You can use the word definitions of the concepts or the examples of the concepts to enhance your mastery of the material. In each case, choose pairs of concepts to compare those that are related or similar or that sound the same or that could in some way be confused. It's much easier to spot the difference between two concepts when you are studying, with the textbook available, rather than when considering the question for the first time in a testing situation.

Chapter 16

G. Apply What You Know

1. Think of three of your habitual behaviors that you would like to change. Describe each of them. Considering the forms of therapy outlined in this chapter, describe which forms of therapy would be most effective in helping you make the desired changes, and why.

Behavior 1:

Behavior 2:

Behavior 3:

2. The work of Stanley Sue and others has suggested that cultural factors can play an important role in treatment utilization and therapeutic interventions. Interview two clinical psychologists in your area to determine what cultural factors play a role in these processes in your area of the country.

Clinician 1:

Clinician 2:

H. On the Web: *As with any online research, it is important to consider how legitimate a given source is before you rely on the information it presents. Your instructor or Internet adviser may give you some specific guidelines for distinguishing which kinds of Web sites tend to be reputable.*

A. A number of individuals have made notable contributions to our understanding of the treatment of psychological disorders. Search the Web for more information about some of those listed below.

Aaron Beck

Albert Ellis

Sigmund Freud

Frederick S. (Fritz) Perls

Carl Rogers

Martin Seligman

Stanley Sue and Nolan Zane

Chapter 16

Joseph Wolpe

B. Take a look at the concept cards you have created for this chapter, or the key concepts listed in section E. In the space following, make a list of any whose definitions or associations you are not yet confident of and any you'd like to learn more about. Try entering the terms on your list into your search engine. Make notes of any helpful information you find.

Key Concept/Information Found

C. Visit the American Psychological Association's Ethics Office home page (http://www.apa.org/ethics/) and familiarize yourself with the APA Ethical Principles for Psychologists and Code of Conduct. Does this document cover any potential client-therapist situations that you had not previously thought of? Can you think of any potential client-therapist situations that it does not cover? Make note of any such issues in the space provided.

I. Analyze This:

Chapter 1 of your textbook begins by presenting these four basic steps in the critical thinking process:
- *"What exactly are you asking me to believe?"*
- *"How do you know? What is the evidence?"*
- *"Are there other possible explanations?"*
- *"What is the most reasonable conclusion?"*

You might picture this as a four-step analysis to help you decide whether to accept a given theory or assertion. Now it's your turn to put your textbook to this test.

Review the section in Chapter 16 of your textbook under the heading "Drug Therapies." There you will find a description of various classes of pharmaceuticals used to treat psychological disorders. If someone told you that the vast majority of people with psychological problems should use drug treatments, would you agree? Analyze that assertion in the space below. When you have finished, consider using this four-step analysis to evaluate other assertions you encounter.

"What exactly are you asking me to believe?"

"How do you know? What is the evidence?"

"Are there other possible explanations?"
"What is the most reasonable conclusion?"

J. Practice Test

Multiple-Choice Items: *Write the letter corresponding to your answer in the space to the left of each item.*

_____ 1. The primary therapeutic goal of _____ is to provide a nurturing environment within which the client can explore and develop his or her potential
   a. person-centered therapy
   b. cognitive therapy
   c. behavior modification
   d. brief psychodynamic therapy

Chapter 16   491

_____ 2. Susan has an anxiety disorder and has sought help from a therapist, Dr. Jonas. Dr. Jonas believes that Susan's anxiety is related to her unconscious fear of her unmet sexual impulses and that in order for Susan to get over her anxiety problem, she needs to have greater awareness of this unconscious dynamic. Dr. Jonas is most likely associated with the _____ approach to therapy and appears to be trying to produce positive changes by fostering more _____.
   a. psychodynamic; transference
   b. interpersonal; empathy
   c. psychoanalytic; insight
   d. humanistic; unconditional positive regard

_____ 3. Certain integrated therapies target a particular disorder; for example, dialectical behavior therapy focuses on the treatment of _____.
   a. clinical depression
   b. paranoid schizophrenia
   c. dissociative identity disorder
   d. borderline personality disorder

_____ 4. Josh is visiting Karen when he accidentally breaks a valuable plate. He has always considered himself clumsy, and now, he thinks, here is another instance that proves it. He begins to tell Karen how stupid he is, feels very embarrassed, and breaks out in a sweat. According to Ellis's rational-emotive ABCD model, Josh's self-criticism, feelings of embarrassment, and sweating would represent the _____.
   a. C (consequences)
   b. B (belief system)
   c. A (activating event)
   d. D (disputing of erroneous beliefs)

_____ 5. Exposure therapies operate on the assumption that _____ is the most direct way to reduce or eliminate a learned anxiety response.
   a. classical extinction
   b. positive reinforcement
   c. operant extinction
   d. response cost punishment

_____ 6. Janice has a phobia of dogs, but her new boyfriend has a Great Dane, so Janice decides to consult with a behavior therapist, Dr. Class. Dr. Class first teaches Janice a muscle relaxation technique. After she has learned this, Dr. Class helps her create a list of increasingly fearful situations involving dogs. Starting with the least feared situation, Dr. Class has Janice imagine it and then use her relaxation training to eliminate any anxiety that arises. Dr. Class is using the general technique called _____, and the list that they have created is an example of _____.

a. aversive conditioning; a punishment
b. systematic desensitization; a stimulus hierarchy
c. exposure therapy; flooding
d. behavior modification; a positive reinforcer

_____ 7. _____ is a computer technology that can create highly realistic simulations of actual experiences so vividly that they evoke many of the same reactions that a comparable real-world environment would create; this technology has been used to treat a limited number of psychological disorders.
a. Systematic desensitization
b. Psychodynamic behavior therapy
c. Virtual reality
d. Aversion therapy

_____ 8. The process in which some individuals experience complete symptom reduction in the absence of any treatment is known as _____.
a. the placebo effect
b. natural recovery
c. spontaneous remission
d. automatic adjustment

_____ 9. Dr. Steenbergen designs a study to test the effectiveness of a new treatment for anxiety disorders. After making sure that her participants are roughly similar on important demographic variables, she assigns people randomly to receive her new therapy or another therapy technique that has already been proven to be effective. Of the following statements, the one that best describes Dr. Steenbergen's study is that her study _____.
a. uses randomized clinical trials and has a placebo control group
b. uses randomized clinical trials but does not have a placebo control group
c. does not use randomized clinical trials but has a placebo control group
d. does not use randomized clinical trials and does not have a placebo control group

_____ 10. Modern meta-analyses comparing the effectiveness of various types of therapies have concluded that _____.
a. behavioral and psychodynamic therapies are the most effective
b. person-centered therapies are the most effective
c. most therapies are no more effective than receiving no treatment at all
d. no one type of therapy is the most effective overall

_____ 11. The fact that vastly different types of therapies often produce similar outcomes has led some researchers to search for what are called _____, which are similar elements shared by each of the approaches that may account for their common successes.
a. metafactors
b. joint components

c. common factors
d. shared components

_____ 12. Tricyclics, MAO inhibitors, and SSRIs are categories of drugs used to treat _____.
a. anxiety disorders
b. schizophrenia
c. depression
d. somatoform disorders

_____ 13. Bob has the belief that getting into law school is the only possible way to have a happy, fulfilling life and that if he doesn't get into law school he has no reason to live. This faulty belief would be directly attacked by the therapist in _____ therapy.
a. behavioral activation treatment
b. rational-emotive therapy
c. Gestalt treatment
d. brief psychodynamic therapy

_____ 14. _____ therapists draw on a variety of techniques from different theoretical orientations to help their clients.
a. Eclectic
b. Free-association
c. Humanistic
d. Rational-emotive

_____ 15. When clients project their anxieties, fears, or other impulses onto the therapist during psychoanalytic therapy, _____ has occurred.
a. insight
b. free association
c. transference
d. resistance

_____ 16. Which of the following is an essential component of person-centered therapy?
a. conditions of worth
b. unconditional positive regard
c. negative reinforcement
d. appropriate medication

_____ 17. In Ellis's rational-emotive therapy, the key to changing maladaptive emotions and behaviors is _____.
a. dream analysis
b. insight
c. disputing erroneous beliefs
d. dialectical behavior therapy

_____ 18. In extinction, the phobic object is _____.
   a. the UCS
   b. paired with a noxious UCS
   c. presented in the absence of the UCS
   d. the UCR

_____ 19. In aversion therapy, the behavior to be changed is _____.
   a. paired with a noxious UCS
   b. considered to be a UCS
   c. presented in the absence of the UCS
   d. negatively reinforced

_____ 20. Token economies _____.
   a. use aversion therapy procedures
   b. use extinction procedures
   c. don't work
   d. use operant-conditioning techniques to strengthen desired behaviors

_____ 21. Kim is a female Korean therapist working with both male and female clients from a variety of cultures. Which situation below would *best* ensure Kim's effectiveness with her clients?
   a. being of the same culture and gender as her clients
   b. being of either the same gender or the same culture as her clients
   c. paying little attention to her clients' culture and gender
   d. being culturally and gender sensitive with her clients

_____ 22. Eclectic therapists _____.
   a. use psychodynamic behavioral therapy exclusively
   b. believe strongly that therapists should use a single theoretical orientation
   c. use electroconvulsive therapy exclusively
   d. use a combination of different orientations and techniques

_____ 23. The question, "Which types of therapy administered by which kinds of therapists to which kinds of clients having which kinds of problems produce which kinds of effect?" is known as the _____ question.
   a. therapeutic
   b. therapist
   c. specificity
   d. clinical trial

_____ 24. A _____ allows researchers to combine the results of many studies statistically to arrive at an overall conclusion.

   a. placebo control group
   b. randomized clinical trial
   c. meta-analysis

d. correlational study

_____ 25. Which of the following factors is common in successful psychotherapy?
a. a therapist committed to a particular theoretical approach
b. an opportunity for the client to practice new behaviors
c. access to medication
d. decreased client self-efficacy

_____ 26. Empirically supported therapies _____.
a. are used as placebos in research on psychotherapy
b. have been shown by research to be effective for treating specific problems
c. refer to psychoanalysis and cognitive therapies
d. refer only to medications

_____ 27. Mahendra's therapist works with him to develop action plans that increase the amount of positive reinforcement he experiences in his life. This technique _____.
a. is called behavior activation treatment
b. is a Gestalt technique of therapy
c. was developed to treat schizophrenic clients
d. is a common feature of family therapy

_____ 28. Selective serotonin reuptake inhibitors (SSRIs) _____.
a. decrease serotonin levels
b. increase MAO levels
c. have more serious side effects than either tricyclics or MAO inhibitors
d. increase levels of serotonin in the synapse

_____ 29. Electroconvulsive therapy (ECT) is used nowadays to _____.
a. treat severely depressed people when other measures fail
b. prepare patients for psychosurgery
c. surgically remove parts of the brain
d. treat schizophrenic patients when other measures fail

_____ 30. Procedures that are used to increase people's self-efficacy are the core of _____.
a. ECT
b. competency-focused intervention
c. situation-focused intervention
d. deinstitutionalization

True/False Items: *Write T or F in the space provided to the left of each item.*

_____ 1. Resistance and transference are processes that occur during psychoanalysis.

_____ 2. Interpersonal therapy, a brief psychodynamic therapy, focuses on the client's current interpersonal problems.

_____ 3. Genuineness refers to a therapist's ability to view the world through a client's eyes.

_____ 4. In Ellis's ABCD model, the C stands for *cognitions*.

_____ 5. Systematic desensitization is a learning-based treatment for anxiety disorders.

_____ 6. Dialectical behavior therapy (DBT) is a treatment for borderline personality disorder.

_____ 7. Clinicians who are eclectic stick to one tried-and-true technique in therapy.

_____ 8. A placebo control group is used to control for client expectations of improvement.

_____ 9. A meta-analysis allows researchers to combine the results of many studies statistically to arrive at an overall conclusion.

_____ 10. The "empty chair" technique is a key feature of rational-emotive therapy.

Short-Answer Questions

1. What is free association?

2. What are the processes of person-centered therapy?

3. How is social skills training accomplished?

4. How is virtual reality being used as a therapeutic technique?

5. What is electroconvulsive therapy?

Essay Questions

1. Considering what you have learned in this chapter about treatments for psychological disorders, if you were to become a professional counselor or therapist, what therapeutic approach(es) would you be inclined to use, and why? Which kinds of disorders and/or categories of clients do you think you would be able to treat most effectively, and why?

2. Explain some reasons why couples who are having problems getting along together, but do not wish to split up, might be hesitant to seek counseling. What recent trend in the couples/marriage counseling profession might be reassuring to such couples?

3. Consider the types of preventive mental health programs described in this chapter, and describe some specific problems on your campus that they might be used to address. If you were in charge of such a program, how would you design it for maximum effectiveness? How would you assess its efficacy?

Answer Keys

Answer Key for Review at a Glance

1. maladaptive
2. theories
3. insight
4. free association
5. dream interpretation
6. unconscious
7. resistance
8. transference
9. current
10. interpersonal
11. unconditional positive regard
12. empathy
13. genuineness
14. Gestalt
15. maladaptive
16. thinking
17. disputing
18. emotive
19. ABCD
20. Beck's
21. exposure
22. response prevention
23. Systematic desensitization
24. stimulus hierarchy
25. aversion
26. Behavior modification
27. social skills
28. eclectic
29. depression
30. activation
31. reinforcement
32. Dialectical
33. interact
34. learn
35. support
36. dynamics
37. communication
38. problem-solving
39. culturally competent
40. randomized clinical
41. placebo control
42. specificity
43. empirically supported treatments
44. meta-analysis
45. Openness
46. self-relatedness
47. therapist-client
48. common factors
49. antianxiety
50. tricyclics
51. MAO inhibitors
52. SSRIs
53. Antipsychotic
54. tardive dyskinesia
55. Electroconvulsive
56. Psychosurgery
57. deinstitutionalization
58. situation-focused
59. Competency-focused

Answer Key for Practice Test Multiple-Choice Questions

1. a
2. c
3. d
4. a
5. a
6. b
7. c
8. c
9. b
10. d
11. c
12. b
13. c
14. c
15. a
16. b
17. c
18. c
19. a
20. d
21. d
22. d
23. c
24. c
25. b
26. b

Chapter 16

12. c	27. a
13. b	28. d
14. a	29. a
15. c	30. b

Answer Key for Practice Test True/False Questions

1. T	6. T
2. T	7. F
3. F	8. T
4. F	9. T
5. T	10. F

Answer Key for Practice Test Short-Answer Questions

1. Free association refers to verbal reports without any censorship of thoughts, feelings, or images that enter awareness. It was a technique pioneered by Freud.

2. Three things are important in person-centered therapy. First, the therapist should communicate unconditional positive regard. Second, the therapist should express empathy for the client's point of view. Finally, the therapist should be genuine and make sure that there is congruence between his or her feelings and his or her behaviors.

3. In social skills training, clients learn new skills by observing and then imitating a model who performs socially skillful behaviors.

4. Virtual reality involves the use of computer technology to create highly realistic environments in which behavior and emotions can be studied. Virtual reality is highly flexible, meaning that it can be used to create a number of environments in which a therapist can study a client's reactions.

5. Electroconvulsive therapy (or ECT) is a technique in which a person receives electric shock to the brain. This shock, which lasts less than a second, causes a seizure of the central nervous system. Such treatments can help people with major depression but may cause permanent memory loss in some cases.

Answer Key for Practice Test Essay Questions

As you may have guessed, there are no right or wrong answers to the essay questions in this practice test. That does not mean, however, that all essays are equally good. To get maximum learning benefit from the essay questions, do the following:

- Review each essay a day or two after you wrote it, noting any necessary corrections and any additional support for your points that you can think of.
- Review the section in your textbook that pertains to the topic of each essay. Annotate your essay with any corrections or additional support for your points that you find in the text.
- Spend a few minutes researching the topic of each essay on the Internet. Annotate your essay further with any additional (reliable) information you find.
- Finally, reread each essay with the annotations you have added.

Chapter 17
SOCIAL THINKING AND BEHAVIOR

A. Learning Objectives: *These objectives are expanded from the Focus Questions found in the margins of your textbook. When you have mastered the material in this chapter, you will be able to:*

17.1 Differentiate between personal and situational attributions, and explain how consistency, distinctiveness, and consensus affect the attributions people make.

17.2 Describe and provide examples of the fundamental attribution error and the self-serving bias, and explain how they are affected by culture.

17.3 Describe factors involved in forming impressions including the primacy effect, stereotypes, and the self-fulfilling prophecy.

17.4 Define the term attitude, and describe three factors that explain the variability of observed relations between attitudes and behaviors.

17.5 Explain the causes of cognitive dissonance and how it produces attitude change.

17.6 Citing research evidence, compare and contrast self-perception theory with dissonance theory to explain why counterattitudinal behavior leads to attitude change.

17.7 Describe how communicator, message, and audience characteristics affect the persuasion process.

17.8 Differentiate between social norms and social roles.

17.9 Explain how norms and roles guide behavior, differentiating between informational and normative social influences.

17.10 Describe situational factors that influence group conformity, and describe when minority influence will be strongest.

17.11 Describe the purpose, methods, and results of Milgram's study on obedience and the implications for society.

17.12 Describe four common compliance techniques, and explain how they work.

17.13 Describe social loafing and social compensation, and describe the causes and consequences of group polarization and groupthink.

17.14 Describe deindividuation, its main cause, and how conditions in the Stanford prison study may have fostered it.

17.15 Describe how proximity, the mere exposure effect, similarity, and beauty influence initial attraction.

17.16 Describe social exchange theory and which factors determine whether or not a relationship will be satisfying and continue.

17.17 Compare and contrast evolutionary and sociocultural explanations for sex differences in mate preference.

17.18 Describe types of love, and discuss research-based principles that may help enhance relationship quality.

17.19 Describe the psychological effects of ostracism.

17.20 Describe how implicit prejudice is measured and explain the cognitive and motivational roots of prejudice.

17.21 Describe how self-fulfilling prophecies and stereotype threat perpetuate prejudice and how equal status contact reduces prejudice.

17.22 Describe evolutionary and social learning and empathy-altruistic explanations for helping behavior.

17.23 Describe when and whom people are most likely to help and how prosocial behavior can be increased.

17.24 Describe biological, environmental, and psychological factors that contribute to aggression.

17.25 Describe catharsis and social learning views on the effects of media violence and whether or not violent video games promote aggression.

B. Chapter Overview

Attributions are judgments about the causes of behavior. One distinction we make is between personal and situational attributions. When we make a personal attribution, we believe the cause of someone's behavior is a personal characteristic of theirs. Situational attributions are made to environmental causes. According to Harold Kelley, we routinely use information on consistency, distinctiveness, and consensus in attributing behavior to personal or situational causes. A number of biases affect our judgments including the fundamental attribution error (the tendency to overestimate personal causes of other people's behavior) and the self-serving bias (our tendency to make personal attributions for our successes and situational attributions for our failures). Cultural background also influences the attributions we make; for example, people from more collectivist cultures are less likely to display a self-serving attributional bias than are those from more individualistic cultures.

Forming and maintaining impressions is another aspect of social thinking and perception. The initial information we learn about a person greatly influences our perceptions of them (primacy effect). Stereotypes and self-fulfilling prophecies can bias the way that we perceive individuals.

Attitudes are positive or negative evaluative reactions toward stimuli. Attitudes are most predictive of behavior when situational factors are weak, when subjective norms support our attitudes, and when we believe behaviors are under our control according to the theory of planned behavior. Additionally, attitudes best predict behavior when we are aware of them, and general attitudes best predict general classes of behavior, whereas specific attitudes best predict specific behaviors. Other theories, such as cognitive dissonance theory and self-perception theory, focus on how our behavior influences our attitudes. Specifically, they predict that we mold our attitudes to be consistent with how we have already behaved.

Studies of persuasion suggest three major components in the persuasive process: the communicator, the message, and the audience. Communicator credibility, largely determined by perceived expertise and trustworthiness, is a key to persuasion. Two-sided communications, which present both sides of an issue, have been found to be more persuasive than one-sided messages in many situations. Audience factors play a role in whether the central or the peripheral route to persuasion is a better technique for persuasion. When people are motivated to examine arguments critically, the central route is the better technique.

A major topic of social psychology is the study of how other people influence our behavior, or social influence. We are affected by social norms and social roles, both of which prescribe how we *should* behave. Conformity and obedience are two major topics in the area of social influence. We conform because of both informational social influence (i.e., conforming because we believe others are right) and because of normative social influence (i.e., conforming because we want others to accept us). Group size affects conformity to a certain point, and the presence of a dissenter can reduce conformity. Milgram's classic studies on obedience point to a number of situational factors that influence obedience including remoteness of victims, closeness and legitimacy of an authority figure, and diffusion of responsibility when others are seen as sharing or taking responsibility for the situation. Personal characteristics do not seem to explain obedience as well as such situational factors. Marketers use several compliance techniques to induce people to say yes when their inclination is to say no, including the norm of reciprocity, the door-in-the-face technique, the foot-in-the-door technique, and lowballing.

In groups, people may engage in social loafing, which is the tendency to expend less effort when working in a group than when working alone. Sometimes, to achieve a highly desired goal, some people may engage in social compensation—working harder in a group than alone. Under certain stressful conditions, groupthink may occur, which is the tendency for group members to suspend critical thinking in order to create a sense of group unanimity. Group polarization may take place, where discussion among a group of like-minded individuals leads a more extreme "average" opinion among group members than before their exchange of ideas. Deindividuation, resulting from the increased anonymity that sometimes accompanies being in a crowd, can fuel destructive behavior.

Attraction, liking, and loving are an important part of our social interactions. Proximity, mere exposure, similarity of attitudes, and physical attractiveness typically enhance our initial attraction toward someone. Relationships deepen as partners self-disclose and exchanges between them become more intimate and broader. Social exchange theory analyzes relationships in terms of the rewards and costs experienced by each partner. The qualities that people find most attractive in a mate vary somewhat across cultures. Many evolutionary theorists consider gender differences in mate preferences as reflecting inherited biological tendencies, but some evolutionary psychologists believe that evolution has shaped the human psyche toward seeking attachment, and that gender differences should not be overemphasized. Sociocultural theorists regard gender differences as resulting rather from socialization and gender inequities in economic opportunities. The triangular theory of love identifies passion, intimacy, and commitment as the components of various kinds of love. Partners are more likely to remain happily married when they understand each other and deal with conflicts by de-escalating their emotions and providing mutual support. Research on ostracism, where people are ignored or excluded, confirms that social rejection is experienced as painful, reduces self-esteem and feelings of control, increases vulnerability to social influence, and has been implicated as a risk factor in school shootings.

Prejudice, a negative attitude toward people based on their membership in a group, and discrimination, or treating people unfairly on the basis of the group to which they belong, remain major problems in American society. Although explicit prejudice is less commonly expressed than in previous times, implicit measures suggest that prejudice may simply be kept more hidden from oneself and from others. Categorization into in-groups and out-groups, and believing that all members of an out-group are very similar to one another (the out-group homogeneity bias) are major cognitive sources of prejudice and discrimination. Realistic conflict theory explains the motivational source of prejudice and discrimination as due to competition between groups for limited resources. Social identity theory considers prejudice and discrimination as resulting from a need to enhance our self-esteem by making sure that our in-group does well and that the out-group does poorly. Research has shown that prejudice and discrimination may become self-confirming. Stereotype threat, or the fear of being seen by others as "living up" to the stereotype they hold about one's group, may contribute to this dynamic. Equal-status contact has been used effectively to reduce prejudice. Recent research also reports some success in using educational approaches to reduce

Chapter 17 505

stereotype threat. Computer simulations have been used to reduce "shooter bias" in research with police officers and with students.

Prosocial behavior is affected by biological predispositions, learning, and by personality characteristics such as empathy. According to the empathy-altruism hypothesis, empathy produces altruism. Other factors that influence helping include simply noticing a problem, social comparison, feeling a sense of responsibility to help, and a sense of self-efficacy in dealing with the situation. The bystander effect, where the presence of multiple bystanders inhibits each person's tendency to help, has been explained in terms of social comparison and diffusion of responsibility.

Aggressive behavior is influenced by biological, environmental, and psychological factors. The hypothalamus, amygdala, and other subcortical structures seem to affect the likelihood of engaging in aggression. Recent studies have also implicated the role of the frontal lobes (site of reasoning, forethought, and impulse control) in aggressive behavior. Low levels of serotonin and high levels of testosterone have been found to correlate with aggression. Environmental stimuli that cause frustration or pain can increase aggression, as can other environmental factors such as provocation and exposure to aggressive models. Attributions of intentionality for someone's negative behavior toward us, a lack of empathy, and the inability to regulate emotions are important psychological factors influencing aggressive behavior. Studies of media violence point to a link between media and violent behavior in children, adolescents, and adults, as proposed by social learning theory. Several avenues of influence have been identified, including these: Viewers learn new aggressive behaviors through modeling, viewers believe that aggression is rewarded, and viewers become desensitized to violence and suffering. The evidence does not support Freud's concept of catharsis, the idea that performing an act of aggression discharges aggressive energy and temporarily reduces our impulse to aggress.

C. Chapter Outline

SOCIAL THINKING
    Attribution: Perceiving the Causes of Behavior
        Personal versus Situational Attributions
        Attributional Biases
        Culture and Attribution
    Forming and Maintaining Impressions
        How Important Are First Impressions?
        Seeing What We Expect to See
        Creating What We Expect to See
    Attitudes and Attitude Change
        Do Our Attitudes Influence Our Behavior?
        Does Our Behavior Influence Our Attitudes?
            Cognitive Dissonance
            Self-Perception

Persuasion
- The Communicator
- The Message
- The Audience

In Review

SOCIAL INFLUENCE

Norms, Conformity, and Obedience
- Norm Formation and Culture
- Why Do People Conform?
- Factors That Affect Conformity
- Minority Influence
- Obedience to Authority

Research Close-Up: The Dilemma of Obedience: When Conscience Confronts Malevolent Authority
- Factors That Influence Obedience
- Would People Obey Today

What Do You Think? Do Women Differ from Men in Obedience?
- Lessons Learned

Detecting and Resisting Compliance Techniques

Behavior in Groups
- Social Loafing
- Group Polarization
- Groupthink
- Deindividuation

In Review

SOCIAL RELATIONS

Attraction: Liking and Loving Others
- Initial Attraction: Proximity, Mere Exposure, and Similarity
- Spellbound by Beauty
  - Facial Attractiveness: Is "Average" Beautiful?
  - Affiliating with Beautiful People
- As Attraction Deepens: Close Relationships
- Sociocultural and Evolutionary Views
- Love

Applying Psychological Science: Making Close Relationships Work: Lessons from Psychological Research
- Ostracism: Rejection Hurts

Prejudice: Bias against Others
- Explicit and Implicit Prejudice
- Cognitive Roots of Prejudice
  - Categorization and "Us-Them" Thinking
  - Stereotypes and Attributional Distortions
- Motivational Roots of Prejudice
  - Competition and Conflict
  - Enhancing Self-Esteem
- How Prejudice Confirms Itself

Chapter 17

    Reducing Prejudice
        An Educational Approach to Reducing Stereotype Threat
        Promoting Equal Status Contact to Reduce Prejudice
        Using Simulations to Reduce "Shooter Bias"
Prosocial Behavior: Helping Others
    Why Do People Help?
        Evolution and Prosocial Behavior
        Social Learning and Cultural Influences
        Empathy and Altruism
    What Do You Think: Does Pure Altruism Really Exist?
    When Do People Help?
    Whom Do People Help?
    Increasing Prosocial Behavior
Aggression: Harming Others
    Biological Factors in Aggression
    Environmental Stimuli and Learning
    Psychological Factors in Aggression
    Media (and Video Game) Violence: Catharsis versus Social Learning
Beneath the Surface: Do Violent Video Games Promote Aggression?
In Review
A Final Word

D. Review at a Glance: *Write the term that best fits the blank to review what you learned in this chapter.*

Social Thinking

Social psychologists study the process of (1) _____, by which we make judgments about the causes of our own and other's behaviors. One major distinction made by social psychologist Fritz Heider was between attributions to internal individual characteristics, called (2)_____ attributions, and attributions to environmental causes of behavior, called (3)_____ attributions. According to Harold Kelley we routinely use information on consistency, (4) _____ and consensus in attributing behavior to personal or situational causes. A number of biases affect our judgments, including the (5) _____ _____ _____ (the tendency to overestimate personal causes of other people's behavior) and the self-serving bias (our tendency to make (6) _____ attributions for our successes and (7) _____ attributions for our failures). Cultural background also influences the attributions we make, for example, people from more (8) _____ cultures are less likely to display a self-serving attributional bias than those from more (9) _____ cultures.

As social beings, we constantly form impressions of others. The tendency to attach more importance to the initial information we learn about a person is called the (10) _____ effect. Generalized beliefs about a group or category of people are called (11) _____. When people's erroneous expectations about a person or group of people lead them to act toward others in a way that brings about the expected behavior, a (12) _____-_____ _____ has occurred.

Attitudes are positive or negative (13) _____ reactions toward stimuli. Attitudes are most predictive of behavior when situational factors are (14) _____, when subjective norms (15) _____ our attitudes, and when we believe behaviors are under (16) _____ control, according to the theory of planned behavior. Additionally, attitudes best predict behavior when we are (17) _____ of them, and (18) _____ attitudes best predict general classes of behavior, whereas specific attitudes best predict (19) _____ behaviors. Other theories, such as cognitive (20) _____ theory and self-perception theory, focus on how our (21) _____ influences our attitudes. Specifically, they predict that we mold our attitudes to be (22) _____ with how we have already behaved.

Studies of persuasion suggest three major components in the persuasive process: the communicator, the (23) _____, and the audience. Communicator credibility, largely determined by perceived (24) _____ and (25) _____, is a key to persuasion. Two-sided communications, which present both sides of an issue, have been found to be (26) _____ persuasive than one-sided messages in many situations. Audience factors play a role in whether the central or the (27) _____ route to persuasion is a better technique for persuasion. When people are motivated to examine arguments critically, the (28) _____ route is the better technique.

Social Influence

A major topic of social psychology is the study of how other people influence our behavior, or (29) _____ _____. We are affected by social norms and social (30) _____, both of which prescribe how we *should* behave. Conformity and obedience are two major topics in the area of social influence. We conform because of both (31) _____ social influence (i.e., conforming because we believe others are right) and because of (32) _____ social influence (i.e., conforming because we want others to accept us). Group (33) _____ affects conformity to a certain point, and the presence of a (34) _____ can reduce conformity. Milgram's classic studies on (35) _____ point to a number of (36) _____ factors that influence obedience, including remoteness of victims, closeness and legitimacy of an (37) _____ figure, and diffusion of (38) _____ when others are seen as sharing or taking responsibility for the situation. (39)_____ characteristics do not seem to explain obedience as well as such situational factors. Marketers use several compliance techniques to induce people to say yes when their inclination is to say no, including the norm of (40) _____, the (41) _____-in-the-face technique, the (42) _____-in-the-door technique, and lowballing.

In groups, people may engage in (43) _____ _____, which is the tendency to expend less effort when working in a group than when working alone.

Sometimes, to achieve a highly desired goal, some people may engage in social (44) _____, working harder in a group than alone. Under certain stressful conditions, (45) _____ may occur, which is the tendency for group members to suspend (46) _____ _____ in order to create a sense of group unanimity. Group (47) _____ may take place, where discussion among a group of like-minded individuals leads a more (48) _____ "average" opinion among group members than before their exchange of ideas. Deindividuation, resulting from the increased (49) _____ that sometimes accompanies being in a crowd, can fuel destructive behavior.

Social Relations

Attraction, liking, and loving are an important part of our social interactions. Proximity, mere (50) _____, (51) _____ of attitudes, and physical (52) _____ typically enhance our initial attraction toward someone. Relationships deepen as partners (53) _____-_____ and exchanges between them become more intimate and broader. Social (54) _____ theory analyzes relationships in terms of the rewards and costs experienced by each partner. The qualities that people find most attractive in a mate vary somewhat across (55) _____. Many (56) _____ theorists consider gender differences in mate preferences as reflecting inherited (57) _____ tendencies, but some evolutionary psychologists believe that evolution has shaped the human psyche toward seeking (58) _____, and that gender differences should not be overemphasized. Sociocultural theorists regard gender differences as resulting rather from (59) _____ and gender inequities in economic opportunities. The triangular theory of love identifies passion, (60) _____, and commitment as the components of various kinds of love. Partners are more likely to remain happily married when they understand each other and deal with conflicts by (61) _____ their emotions and providing mutual support. Research on ostracism, where people are ignored or excluded, confirms that social rejection is experienced as (62)_____, reduces self-(63)_____ and feelings of control, increases vulnerability to social influence, and has been implicated as a risk factor in school shootings.

(64)_____, a negative attitude toward people based on their membership in a group, and (65) _____, or treating people unfairly on the basis of the (66) _____ to which they belong, remain major problems in American society. Although explicit prejudice is less commonly expressed than in previous times, (67) _____ measures suggest that prejudice may simply be kept more (68) _____ from oneself and from others. Categorization into in-groups and (69) _____-_____, and believing that all members of an out-group are very similar to one another (the out-group (70) _____ bias) are major cognitive sources of prejudice and discrimination. Realistic conflict theory explains the motivational source of prejudice and discrimination as due to (71) _____ between groups for (72) _____ resources. Social identity theory considers prejudice and discrimination as resulting from a need to enhance our (73)

_____-_____ by making sure that our in-group does well and that the out-group does poorly. Research has shown that prejudice and discrimination may become (74) _____-_____. Stereotype (75) _____, or the fear of being seen by others as "living up" to the stereotype they hold about one's group, may contribute to this dynamic. (76) _____-_____ contact has been used effectively to reduce prejudice. Recent research also reports some success in using (77) _____ approaches to reduce stereotype threat. Computer simulations have been used to reduce "(78) _____ bias" in research with police officers and with students.

Prosocial behavior is affected by biological predispositions, (79) _____, and by personality characteristics such as (80) _____. According to the empathy-altruism hypothesis, (81) _____ produces (82) _____. Other factors that influence helping include simply noticing a problem, social (83) _____, feeling a sense of responsibility to help, and a sense of (84) _____-_____ in dealing with the situation. The (85) _____ effect, where the presence of multiple bystanders inhibits each person's tendency to help, has been explained in terms of social comparison and (86) _____ of responsibility.

Aggressive behavior is influenced by biological, environmental, and psychological factors. The (87) _____, amygdala, and other subcortical structures seem to affect the likelihood of engaging in aggression. Recent studies have also implicated the role of the (88) _____ lobes (site of reasoning, forethought, and impulse control) in aggressive behavior. Low levels of (89) _____ and (90) _____ levels of testosterone have been found to correlate with aggression. Environmental stimuli that cause frustration or pain can increase aggression, as can other environmental factors such as provocation and exposure to aggressive (91) _____. Attributions of (92) _____ for someone's negative behavior toward us, a lack of empathy, and the inability to (93) _____ emotions are important psychological factors influencing aggressive behavior. Studies of media violence point to a link between media and violent behavior in children, adolescents, and adults, as proposed by (94) _____ _____ theory. Several avenues of influence have been identified, including these: Viewers learn new aggressive behaviors through (95) _____, viewers believe that aggression is (96) _____, and viewers become (97) _____ to violence and suffering. The evidence does not support Freud's concept of (98) _____, the idea that performing an act of aggression discharges aggressive energy and temporarily (99) _____ our impulse to aggress.

E. Concept Cards

Truly learning a concept means integrating it into the way *you* think about things. To integrate concepts successfully, you must translate the words and examples your text or instructor provides into words and examples that are meaningful to you.

For this exercise, obtain some note cards (3" × 5" or 4" × 6") to make a deck of concept cards. On one side of each card, write the *concept* from the list following (e.g., "attributions") at the top. Read the textbook definition provided, and then write the definition *in your own words* on the concept card (e.g., for "attributions," you might write "our opinions about why a person did something"). Simply imagine that a friend has asked you what the concept means, and write down what you would answer. Writing the definition in your own words requires you to think deeply about its meaning. When next you see your own version of the definition, it will make intuitive sense to you—no translation required.

On the second side of the card, write your own example of the concept. Again, coming up with your own example requires you to think deeply about the application of the concept, and you will more easily understand and remember the example when you study for a test. If you use an example from the text, or from class, make it your own by writing it in your own words. You can always check with your instructor that your example is indeed a good example of the concept.

CONCEPT	Example of the concept in my own words, preferably drawn from my own experience
Definition in my own words	
(side 1 of card)	(side 2 of card)

The following is a list of all the boldface concepts from your textbook with the author's definition. Write the definition in your own words, together with your own example of the concept, to create a *concept card* as described earlier, or write in the space provided.

Attributions: Judgments about the causes of our own and other people's behavior and outcomes

Fundamental attribution error: Our tendency to underestimate the impact of the situation and overestimate the role of personal factors when explaining other people's behavior

Self-serving bias: The tendency to make personal attributions for successes and situational attributions for failures

Primacy effect: Our tendency to attach more importance to the initial information that we learn about a person

Stereotype: A generalized belief about a group or category of people

Self-fulfilling prophecy: A process whereby people's erroneous expectations lead them to act toward others in a way that brings about the expected behaviors thereby confirming their original impressions

Attitude: A positive or negative evaluative reaction toward a stimulus

Theory of planned behavior: A theory proposing that our intention to engage in a behavior is strongest when we have a positive attitude toward that behavior, when subjective norms (our perceptions of what other people think we should do) support our attitudes, and when we believe that the behavior is under our control

Theory of cognitive dissonance: A theory proposing that people strive for consistency in their cognitions

Self-perception theory: A theory proposing that we make inferences about our own attitudes in much the same way as we make inferences about others people's attitudes: by observing how we behave

Communicator credibility: How believable we perceive the communicator to be

Central route to persuasion: Persuasion that occurs when people think carefully about the message and are influenced because they find the arguments compelling

Peripheral route to persuasion: Persuasion that occurs when people do not scrutinize the message but are influenced mostly by other factors

Social norms: Shared expectations about how people should think, feel, and behave

Social role: A set of norms that characterizes how people, in a given social position, ought to behave

Informational social influence: Conformity to the opinions or behavior of other people, because we believe they have accurate knowledge and what they are doing is "right"

Normative social influence: Conformity to the opinions or behavior of other people in order to obtain the rewards that come from being accepted by them while avoiding their rejection

Norm of reciprocity: The expectation that when others treat us well, we should respond in kind

Door-in-the-face technique: A persuasive technique whereby the persuader makes a large request, expecting you to reject it (you "slam the door" in the persuader's face), and then presents a smaller request

Foot-in-the-door technique: A persuasive technique whereby the persuader gets you to comply with a small request first (getting the "foot in the door") and later presents a larger request

Lowballing: A persuasive technique whereby the persuader gets you to commit to some action and then—before you actually perform the behavior—he or she increases the "cost" of that same behavior

Social loafing: The tendency for people to expend less individual effort when working in a group than when working alone

Social compensation: The phenomenon of working harder in a group than alone to compensate for other members' lower output

Group polarization: A process whereby, after a group of like-minded people discuss an issue, the "average" opinion of group members tends to become more extreme

Groupthink: The tendency of group members to suspend critical thinking, because they are striving to seek agreement

Deindividuation: A loss of individuality that leads to disinhibited behavior

Mere exposure effect: The phenomenon whereby repeated exposure to a stimulus typically increases our liking for it

Matching effect: The phenomenon whereby we are most likely to have a partner whose level of physical attractiveness is similar to our own

Social exchange theory: A theory that proposes that the course of a relationship is governed by rewards and costs that the partners experience

Attachment: A deep bond between two individuals

Passionate love: Intense emotion, arousal, and yearning for the partner

Companionate love: Affection and deep caring about the partner's well-being

Triangular theory of love: A theory proposing that love involves three major components: passion, intimacy, and commitment

Prejudice: A negative attitude toward people based on their membership in a group

Discrimination: Overt behavior that involves treating people unfairly on the basis of the group to which they belong

Explicit prejudice: Prejudice that people express publicly

Implicit prejudice: Prejudice that is hidden from public view

Realistic conflict theory: A theory proposing that competition for limited resources fosters prejudice

Social identity theory: A theory proposing that prejudice stems from a need to enhance our self-esteem

Stereotype threat: A concept proposing that stereotypes create self-consciousness among stereotyped group members, and a fear that they will "live up" to other people's stereotypes

Equal status contact: A situation in which people (1) engage in sustained close contact, (2) have equal status, (3) work to achieve a common goal that requires cooperation, and (4) are supported by broader social norms; it is proposed that prejudice will be reduced under these conditions

Kin selection: A theory proposing that organisms are most likely to help others with whom they share the most genes, namely, their offspring and genetic relatives

Empathy-altruism hypothesis: A hypothesis stating that altruism is produced by empathy—the ability to puts oneself in the place of another and to share what that person is experiencing

Chapter 17

Bystander effect: The phenomenon whereby the presence of multiple bystanders inhibits each person's tendency to help, largely due to social comparison or diffusion of responsibility

Catharsis: The concept that performing an act of aggression discharges aggressive energy and temporarily reduces our impulse to aggress

F. What's the Difference? A Concept Card Exercise

An important skill in learning concepts is being able to differentiate among concepts that are similar or related in some way. This skill is particularly relevant for multiple-choice tests, especially if you often find yourself wavering between two answers.

Once you have created your own deck of concept cards, select them two by two, each time answering the question "What's the difference between these two concepts?" You can use the word definitions of the concepts or the examples of the concepts to enhance your mastery of the material. In each case, choose pairs of concepts to compare those that are related or similar or that sound the same or that could in some way be confused. It's much easier to spot the difference between two concepts when you are studying, with the textbook available, rather than when considering the question for the first time in a testing situation.

G. Apply What You Know

1. Choose three television commercials. Describe each commercial and how communicator, message, and audience factors play roles in the persuasive process of the ad. Record your findings on the chart below.

Commercial	Communicator	Message	Audience

2. Describe how you would design a study to examine whether the primacy or recency effect was more important in the forming of impressions.

3. Watch three children's cartoons, and record the number of aggressive acts that you see in each program. Make sure that you operationally define each category. What aggressive acts occur most often? Did the results surprise you? Why or why not?

Cartoon	Physical Aggression (Definition:)	Verbal Aggression (Definition:)

Chapter 17

H. On the Web: *As with any online research, it is important to consider how legitimate a given source is before you rely on the information it presents. Your instructor or Internet adviser may give you some specific guidelines for distinguishing which kinds of Web sites tend to be reputable.*

A. A number of individuals have made notable contributions to our understanding of social thinking and behavior. Search the Web for more information about some of those listed.

Albert Bandura

C. Daniel Batson

Leon Festinger

Sigmund Freud

Anthony Greenwald

David Grossman

Harold Kelley

Richard LaPiere

Bibb Latané and John Darley

Stanley Milgram

Max Ringelmann

Muzafer Sherif

Robert Sternberg

Claude Steele

Elaine Walster

Robert Zajonc

Philip Zimbardo

B. Take a look at the concept cards you have created for this chapter, or the key concepts listed in section E. In the space provided, make a list of any whose definitions or associations you are not yet confident of and any you'd like to learn more about. Try entering the terms on your list into your search engine. Make notes of any helpful information you find.

Chapter 17

Key Concept/Information Found

C. Conflicts between ethnic groups in various parts of the world (e.g., the Balkans, the Middle East, Northern Ireland) have been sources of international concern for many years. Choose a long-standing ethnic conflict, and search online for information about its causes and effects, focusing on the prejudices and discrimination that occur on both sides. Summarize your findings in the space provided, citing your sources.

D. Using the American Psychological Association Web site as your starting point, examine the table of contents of a recent issue in the *Journal of Personality and Social Psychology,* and make note of the proportion of social psychology-related articles versus those on personality topics. Next, navigate to the APA home page for Divisions. You will see that the APA does not have a social psychology division but instead links social psychology issues to a variety of different APA divisions. Make note of these various divisions and their importance to the study of social psychology.

I. Analyze This: *Chapter 1 of your textbook begins by presenting these four basic steps in the critical thinking process:*
- *"What exactly are you asking me to believe?"*
- *"How do you know? What is the evidence?"*
- *"Are there other possible explanations?"*
- *"What is the most reasonable conclusion?"*

You might picture this as a four-step analysis to help you decide whether to accept a given theory or assertion. Now it's your turn to put your textbook to this test.

Review the section in Chapter 17 of your textbook under the heading "Behavior in Groups." There you will find discussions of various behaviors that tend to occur when people collaborate in groups. If someone told you that whenever possible, it is better to accomplish goals and make decisions individually than to participate in a group, would you agree? Analyze that assertion in the space provided. When you have finished, consider using this four-step analysis to evaluate other assertions you encounter.

"What exactly are you asking me to believe?"

"How do you know? What is the evidence?"

"Are there other possible explanations?"

"What is the most reasonable conclusion?"

J. Practice Test

Multiple-Choice Items: W*rite the letter corresponding to your answer in the space to the left of each item.*

_____ 1. The fact that Japanese individuals typically sit farther apart when conversing than Americans do, and that Greeks are more likely than Britons to touch during a social interaction, are *best* considered as examples of _____.
   a. groupthink

b. stereotype threat
c. social norms
d. informational social influence

_____ 2. Suppose you were designing an obedience study, and wanted to reduce or lower the obedience rates found by Milgram. Of the following tactics, the one *most* likely decrease participants' obedience would be to _____.
   a. have an authority figure who is perceived to be legitimate
   b. have the participants feel fully responsible for the victim's welfare
   c. place the victims in a separate room where the participant can't see them
   d. have your participants all be women

_____ 3. The fact that guards in the Stanford Prison study did not use their actual names, did not know that they were being observed, and wore reflective sunglasses that prevented direct eye contact all suggest that _____ may have played a key role in producing the results obtained in this experiment.
   a. the self-fulfilling prophecy
   b. social exchange theory
   c. perceived legitimacy of the authority figures
   d. deindividuation

_____ 4. The belief that one's individual performance within a group is *not* being monitored and having a task goal that is not very meaningful or valuable to a person are two factors that are *most* likely to increase the chance of _____.
   a. groupthink
   b. social loafing
   c. minority influence
   d. group polarization

_____ 5. A group of public officials is meeting to decide what to do about a budget shortage. The principle of group polarization would predict that this group of people would be *most* likely to reach a highly conservative decision if _____.
   a. the group has a relatively small number of people in it (four or five)
   b. the group members believe that their individual performance within the group is being monitored
   c. the group members are generally conservative to begin with
   d. the group has an authority figure who is perceived to be legitimate

_____ 6. In a group that is considering assassinating the president of a foreign country, some group members ensure that information that would cast doubt on the wisdom of the idea does not reach the group. This *best* illustrates the groupthink process of _____.
   a. direct pressure
   b. the illusion of unanimity
   c. self-censorship
   d. mind guarding

_____ 7. Don went to three different dances this past week. Prior to this, he had a slightly negative attitude toward dancing, but after observing his behavior he starts to conclude that he must in fact enjoy it, or otherwise he wouldn't have attended so many dances. This change in Don's attitude is *most* consistent with the predictions of _____.
   a. social identity theory
   b. cognitive dissonance theory
   c. the theory of planned behavior
   d. self-perception theory

_____ 8. Alison is at a workshop where a presenter is attempting to persuade people to make a rather risky but potentially profitable financial investment. After carefully considering the presenter's arguments, Alison finds this person's idea sound and compelling and decides to invest. This example *best* demonstrates the _____.
   a. peripheral route to persuasion
   b. norm of reciprocity
   c. central route to persuasion
   d. door-in-the-face technique

_____ 9. A phone solicitor calls and asks if you would be interested in volunteering to work on a local political campaign. The job involves working 20 hours per week, you must work on both Saturday and Sunday for the next 6 months, and you would receive no financial compensation. After you politely refuse this request, the solicitor asks if you would be willing to work one evening a month on the campaign. This example *best* demonstrates the persuasion strategy known as _____.
   a. the foot-in-the-door technique
   b. the door-in-the-face technique
   c. the norm of reciprocity
   d. lowballing

_____ 10. A person on campus walks up to you and asks if you would be willing to wear a ribbon to show support for her cause. Though the ribbon is a bit unattractive, it is small so you agree to wear it. After you agree to this request, the solicitor then asks you if you would be willing to make a donation of $15. This example best demonstrates the persuasion technique called _____.
   a. the foot-in-the-door
   b. the door-in-the-face
   c. the norm of reciprocity
   d. lowballing

_____ 11. Juan is in the process of forming an opinion about someone he has just met when a friend who is taking a psychology class tells him to avoid making snap judgments and to consider the evidence carefully. The net result of this advice

is that Juan feels more accountable for his opinions. The advice of Juan's friend should *most* likely decrease the _____.
a. recency effect
b. primacy effect
c. fundamental attribution error
d. self-serving bias

_____ 12. A person with implicit prejudicial feelings against gays and lesbians would most likely have the *slowest* reaction times to which of the following word pairs presented using the implicit association test? _____.
a. gay-wrong
b. straight-right
c. lesbian-bad
d. gay-good

_____ 13. A mother risks her own life by rushing into a burning building to save her son. According to the _____, she is *most* likely performing this altruistic behavior because _____.
a. norm of social responsibility; she feels she should help when others treat her kindly
b. concept of reciprocal altruism; she feels she should contribute to the welfare of society
c. norm of reciprocity; it increases the likelihood of receiving help in return
d. principle of kin selection; she shares genes with her child

_____ 14. In his study of murderers, Adrian Raine (1998) found that impulsive murderers had _____ than murderers who had committed their crimes as a planned predatory act.
a. lower frontal lobe activity
b. greater frontal lobe activity
c. less subcortical activity
d. more subcortical activity

_____ 15. Realistic conflict theory argues that _____.
a. we use the out-group homogeneity bias to classify out-groups
b. prejudice is due to illusory correlations
c. prejudice and discrimination exist because groups of people are competing for the same things
d. prejudice and discrimination are due to repressed frustrations that people have

_____ 16. The likelihood that person A will be attracted to person B is enhanced by all of the following *except* _____.
a. similarity of attitudes between persons A and B
b. physical attractiveness of person B
c. absence of person B, which makes the heart grow fonder

d. mere exposure to each other

_____ 17. Sternberg's triangular theory of love proposes _____.
   a. that love progresses through separate, consecutive phases of passion, intimacy, and commitment
   b. that love will become more passionate if a third party gets involved, forming a love triangle
   c. passion, intimacy, and commitment as ingredients of love
   d. that love requires equal amounts of passion, intimacy, and commitment to exist

_____ 18. Professor Love believes that his married friends chose each other on the basis of gender inequities in economic opportunity and socialization that promotes mating with a member of one's own social class. The professor is most likely taking the _____ view of mate selection.
   a. cognitive
   b. evolutionary
   c. sociocultural
   d. situational attribution

_____ 19. Shared expectations about how people should think, feel, and behave are called _____.
   a. social norms
   b. informational social influences
   c. normative social influences
   d. self-perceptions

_____ 20. Going along with a group's opinion because we believe the group is "right" is called _____.
   a. social norming
   b. informational social influence
   c. normative social influence
   d. a self-perception

_____ 21. Studies of the effect of group size on conformity suggest that _____.
   a. group size has no effect on conformity
   b. a group of 20 produces more conformity that a group of 5
   c. the larger the group, the more likely there is to be just one dissenter
   d. increasing group size up to about five people increases conformity

_____ 22. Studies of personal characteristics in obedience have found that _____.
   a. more intelligent people are less likely to be obedient
   b. more religious people are more likely to be obedient
   c. women are less likely than men to be obedient
   d. gender is not related to obedience rates

_____ 23. A generalized belief about a group of category of people is called a(n) _____.
   a. stereotype
   b. self-perception
   c. self-schema
   d. self-fulfilling prophecy

_____ 24. According to research on factors contributing to marital satisfaction, which of the following newly wed couples is most likely to remain happily married?
   a. Darren and Diana, who habitually criticize and find fault with each other
   b. David and Dee, who rarely argue
   c. Doug and Darla, who argue often but de-escalate their conflicts with humor and mutual support
   d. Don and Donna, who avoid arguments by stonewalling

_____ 25. According to _____ theory, prejudice stems from a need to enhance our self-esteem.
   a. realistic conflict theory
   b. social identity
   c. norm of reciprocity
   d. attribution

_____ 26. On an icy day, an automobile accident occurs at an intersection. Gene, who did not see or hear the crash, is asked what he thought caused it. He says it was probably because one of the drivers was drunk. Gene is most likely subject to the _____.
   a. fundamental attribution error
   b. self-serving bias
   c. primacy effect
   d. recency effect

_____ 27. People are most likely to help those who share their genes, a principle called _____.
   a. the norm of reciprocity effect
   b. kin selection
   c. social loafing
   d. the empathy-altruism hypothesis

_____ 28. The idea that we help others, because it helps us to reduce our own personal distress, is called _____.
   a. the norm of reciprocity effect
   b. kin selection
   c. the negative state relief model
   d. the empathy-altruism hypothesis

_____ 29. Atypically low levels of _____ appear to play a role in impulsive aggression.
   a. exposure to aggressive models

b. serotonin
   c. blood alcohol
   d. testosterone

_____ 30. Studies of the effects of media violence on viewers' behavior have found that _____.
   a. viewers learn new aggressive behaviors through modeling
   b. studies generally support Freud's idea of catharsis
   c. viewers learn that aggression is rarely rewarded
   d. fears that viewers will become desensitized to violence are unfounded

True/False Items: *Write T or F in the space provided to the left of each item.*

_____ 1. The fundamental attribution error refers to our tendency to underestimate personal causes of other people's behavior.

_____ 2. Normative social influence occurs when people conform because they want to be accepted by others.

_____ 3. The presence of a dissenter tends to increase conformity.

_____ 4. Personal characteristics have been found to be more important than situational characteristics in obedient behavior.

_____ 5. Social loafing is more likely to occur when people believe that individual performance is not being monitored.

_____ 6. A relationship that lacks passion, intimacy, and commitment is not a love relationship by Sternberg's definition.

_____ 7. According to social exchange theory, we evaluate personal relationships by the benefits and costs that they entail.

_____ 8. The peripheral route to persuasion occurs when people carefully scrutinize the content of a message.

_____ 9. Ostracism increases vulnerability to social influence.

_____ 10. We are more likely to help people who are similar to us than those we perceive as different.

Short-Answer Questions

1. What is the difference between social loafing and social compensation?

2. Why do influence processes produce conformity?

3. What does cognitive dissonance theory argue?

4. What are the cognitive roots of prejudice?

5. What does social exchange theory argue?

Essay Questions

1. Think of a time when you were persuaded to comply with a behavior you initially did not wish to engage in. Considering what you have learned in this chapter about persuasion, compliance, and obedience, describe the situation and the technique(s) that were used to win you over. How did you feel about the experience, in retrospect, and why?

2. Almost certainly you love, or have loved, someone—whether it be a romantic partner, a family member, a close friend, or a spiritual higher power. Describe your love. Would you classify it as companionate or passionate? To what degree is it mutual? To what degree does it involve intimacy and commitment? Is this love a source of positive feelings (i.e., rewards) for you; does it also entail costs?

3. Describe a situation in which a stranger or acquaintance chose to help you when he or she could have ignored your plight. Considering what you have learned in this chapter about prosocial behavior, what do you think their reasons were for choosing to help? Do you think you would have done the same if the circumstances had been reversed? Why or why not?

Answer Keys

Answer Key for Review at a Glance

1. attribution
2. personal
3. situational
4. distinctiveness
5. fundamental attribution error
6. personal
7. situational
8. collectivist
9. individualistic
10. primacy
11. stereotypes
12. self-fulfilling prophecy
13. evaluative
14. weak
15. support
16. our
17. aware
18. general
19. specific
20. dissonance
21. behavior
22. consistent
23. message
24. expertise
25. trustworthiness
26. more
27. peripheral
28. central
29. social influence
30. roles
31. informational
32. normative
33. size
51. similarity
52. attractiveness
53. self-disclose
54. exchange
55. cultures
56. evolutionary
57. biological
58. attachment
59. socialization
60. intimacy
61. de-escalating
62. painful
63. esteem
64. Prejudice
65. discrimination
66. group
67. implicit
68. hidden
69. out-groups
70. homogeneity
71. competition
72. limited
73. self-esteem
74. self-confirming
75. threat
76. Equal-status
77. educational
78. shooter
79. learning
80. empathy
81. empathy
82. altruism
83. comparison

Chapter 17

34. dissenter
35. obedience
36. situational
37. authority
38. responsibility
39. Personal
40. reciprocity
41. door
42. foot
43. social loafing
44. compensation
45. groupthink
46. critical thinking
47. polarization
48. extreme
49. anonymity
50. exposure

84. self-efficacy
85. bystander
86. diffusion
87. hypothalamus
88. frontal
89. serotonin
90. high
91. models
92. intentionality
93. regulate
94. social learning
95. modeling
96. rewarded
97. desensitized
98. catharsis
99. reduces

Answer Key for Practice Test Multiple-Choice Items

1. c
2. b
3. d
4. b
5. c
6. d
7. d
8. c
9. b
10. a
11. b
12. d
13. d
14. a
15. c
16. c
17. c
18. c
19. a
20. b
21. d
22. d
23. a
24. c
25. b
26. a
27. b
28. c
29. b
30. a

Answer Key for Practice Test True/False Questions

1. F
2. T
3. F
4. F
5. T
6. T
7. T
8. F
9. T
10. T

Answer Key for Practice Test Short-Answer Questions

1. Social loafing is the tendency for people to expend less effort when working in groups than when working alone. Social compensation is the tendency for people sometimes, in order to achieve a desired goal, to expend *more* effort in a group than when working alone, to compensate for other members' lower output.

2. People conform because of both informational and normative social influence. When people conform because they believe others are right, informational social influence has occurred. When people conform because they want to be accepted by others, normative social influence has occurred.

3. Cognitive dissonance theory argues that people strive for consistency in their cognitions. When two or more cognitions contradict one another, people are motivated to change them so that they are consistent. Thus, when one has the cognition of having behaved in a manner that is inconsistent with one's attitude, cognitive dissonance motivates changing one's attitude to conform with the behavior, which cannot be changed after the fact. In this way, a person is motivated to justify his or her behavior, and hence attitudes may be shaped by one's behavior.

4. People tend to categorize the world into "in-groups," groups to which we feel we belong, and "out-groups," groups to which we don't feel that we belong. We tend to believe that the members of a given out-group are quite similar to one another, which is called the out-group homogeneity bias. Stereotypes are formed through this process. We tend to place exceptions to the stereotype in a special subcategory (the "exceptions"), so that we may maintain the stereotype.

5. Social exchange theory proposes that the course of a relationship is governed by the rewards and costs that the partners experience. If they find that the rewards outweigh the costs, the relationship will continue.

Answer Key for Practice Test Essay Questions

As you may have guessed, there are no right or wrong answers to the essay questions in this practice test. That does not mean, however, that all essays are equally good. To get maximum learning benefit from the essay questions, do the following:

- Review each essay a day or two after you wrote it, noting any necessary corrections and any additional support for your points that you can think of.
- Review the section in your textbook that pertains to the topic of each essay. Annotate your essay with any corrections or additional support for your points that you find in the text.
- Spend a few minutes researching the topic of each essay on the Internet. Annotate your essay further with any additional (reliable) information you find.
- Finally, reread each essay with the annotations you have added.